Richard C. Harrier is Associate Professor of English at New York University, where he teaches Shakespeare and Tudor literature. He received the B.A. degree from Muhlenburg College and the M.A. and Ph.D. degrees from Harvard University. Professor Harrier's articles and reviews have appeared in *Review of English Studies, Seventeenth-Century News, Notes and Queries, Journal of English and Germanic Philology,* and the *Shakespeare Quarterly,* and his study "Troilus Divided" was included in *Studies in the English Renaissance Drama,* edited by Bennett, Cargill and Hall. An authority on the manuscripts and poetry of Sir Thomas Wyatt, Professor Harrier has been awarded a Folger Library study grant and a research grant from The American' Philosophical Society.

JACOBEAN DRAMA
An Anthology
Volume I

EVERY MAN IN HIS HUMOUR	*by Jonson*
THE MALCONTENT	*by Marston*
THE WHITE DEVIL	*by Webster*
BUSSY D'AMBOIS	*by Chapman*

EDITED

WITH AN INTRODUCTION, NOTES, AND VARIANTS

BY

RICHARD C. HARRIER

The Norton Library

W · W · NORTON & COMPANY · INC ·
NEW YORK

To

Constance Smith Harrier

COPYRIGHT © 1963 BY DOUBLEDAY & COMPANY, INC.

FIRST PUBLISHED IN THE NORTON LIBRARY 1968 BY ARRANGEMENT
WITH DOUBLEDAY & COMPANY, INC.

W. W. Norton & Company, Inc. is also the publisher of *The Norton Anthology of English Literature,* edited by M. H. Abrams, Robert M. Adams, David Daiches, E. Talbot Donaldson, George H. Ford, Samuel Holt Monk, and Hallett Smith; *The American Tradition in Literature,* edited by Sculley Bradley, Richmond Croom Beatty, and E. Hudson Long; *World Masterpieces,* edited by Maynard Mack, Kenneth Douglas, Howard E. Hugo, Bernard M. W. Knox, John C. McGalliard, P. M. Pasinetti, and René Wellek; *The Norton Reader,* edited by Arthur M. Eastman, Caesar R. Blake, Hubert M. English, Jr., Alan B. Howes, Robert T. Lenaghan, Leo F. McNamara, and James Rosier; and the NORTON CRITICAL EDITIONS, in hardcover and paperbound: authoritative texts, together with the leading critical interpretations, of major works of British, American, and Continental literature.

Printed in the United States of America

1 2 3 4 5 6 7 8 9 0

CONTENTS

INTRODUCTION

The four plays in this volume exemplify the close relation of satire and tragedy notable towards the end of Elizabeth's reign and the beginning of James I's.

Ben Jonson's *Every Man in His Humour* was performed in its first version at the Curtain, September 1598, by the Lord Chamberlain's Men. Shakespeare was in the cast and may have played old Kno'well, who then had the name Lorenzo di Pazzi Senior. The Italian setting of this earlier version was a stalking horse under whose belly Jonson shot at English affectation. Jonson's fame was immediately almost as great as his genius merited, but his critical spirit was one that could not charm an audience for long. Devoted to his vision of the truth and its perfect embodiment in art, Jonson came inevitably to give *Every Man in His Humour* the superior English form presented in this volume. When he revised the play about 1612, he had already illuminated English scenes in *Epicoene* (1609) and *The Alchemist* (1610), but his uniquely moving *Volpone* (1607) was set in Venice. He was at the peak of his artistry and working towards an unprecedented gesture, that of collecting his plays for serious reading, then and forever. The collection appeared in 1616 as his *Works*, including for the first time the revised *Every Man in His Humour*, with its prologue manifesto.

If one reads history as simple chronology, Jonson may share with George Chapman the distinction of having brought to the English stage the comedy of humours. But he need share with no one the honor of having defined and explored its art, giving to English drama and fiction an inexhaustible heritage. For the significance of the term "humour" the student will find more light in Jonson's plays than in the manuals of Elizabethan medicine.[1] But it is necessary to work within the context of Elizabethan English, in which the heart could and did think, and the fluids of the body were one with the moods of the spirit.

There is no single or simple type of humour character. Some, like Volpone, seem to be completely possessed by an abstract drive which affords them a rich artistry. Others, like Mosca, Face, or Brain-Worm, have the artistry, but with a large degree of self-awareness and malicious gaiety. Many are would-be humourists who never achieve the completeness of manner and gesture they so much desire. They remain awkward mimics, some naive and some hypocritical. But every man has his humour, including those figures who seem to merge into the familiar movements of everyday reality. The differences in kind and degree, however, allow Jonson an arrangement of contrasts and opposites which propel the action to a resolving conflict. The structure of human fantasy finally breaks against the laws of reality.

As the Prologue to *Every Man in His Humour* reveals, Jonson's humour was that of the lonely realist. He thought of his fellow dramatists, even Shakespeare, as indulging the time's appetite for romantic egoism. He alone represented men as they were and could be, using the theatre as a way back to good sense and health. In this role Jonson clashed with another scourger of the time's abuses, John Marston. Their dispute was vigorous but brief, being more a competition of like minds than a struggle of spirits opposed. The provocation may have been the figure of Chrisoganus in Marston's revision of the old play *Histriomastix*. Chrisoganus spoke Marston's peculiar brand of fustian in his role of corrector, but Jonson reacted as if he had seen himself in a comic mirror. The language of Clove in *Every Man Out of His Humour* was studded with phrases from Marston's satires and the orations of Chrisoganus himself. Marston then went Jon-

---

[1] See Herford and Simpson, IX, 391–395. Full notation for all works referred to in brief form will be found at the end of this volume.

son one better with the cuckolding of Brabant Senior in *Jack Drum's Entertainment. Cynthia's Revels,* Jonson's continuation, provoked the image of Lampatho Doria in Marston's *What You Will.* Thomas Dekker also entered the arena when he saw himself as Anaides in *Cynthia's Revels* next to Marston as Hedon. In the figure of Horace in his *Poetaster,* Jonson administered an emetic to Crispinus-Marston and put Demetrius-Dekker to silence as well. Almost simultaneously, Marston and Dekker countered with *Satiromastix,* burlesquing the humourous poet who assumed the titles of Crites and Quintus Horatius Flaccus. Then the quarrel, which had been a commercial success and artistic failure, was over. In 1604 Marston dedicated *The Malcontent* to his accomplished friend Ben Jonson, and in 1605 he joined Jonson and Chapman in writing *Eastward Ho!* Another public gesture was Marston's laudatory poem printed in the 1605 quarto of Jonson's *Sejanus.*

To some extent the stage quarrel had consumed energies frustrated by the authorities. In June 1599 the Archbishop of Canterbury called in all available copies of satires and epigrams, burned them, and forbade any future publication of their like. Among them was Marston's *Scourge of Villainy,* the most foul-jawed laceration of the times. But the London scene merited no less. The migration of gentlemen to the town meant rural decay and urban vice. The country was drained of its wealth to indulge those who could spend it at court or in the city. The monopolies granted to the queen's favorites were so notoriously abused that she revoked them all. This gesture was called her Golden Speech and for the moment she was again Diana, the fairy queen and savior of her people. But the threat of civil war could not be ignored so long as the old queen refused to name an heir. Then the Earl of Essex bungled into treason, surrendered and was executed. When two years later Elizabeth died, the worst was awaited, but the maneuvering of her ministers brought James to the throne and prevented civil bloodshed. As Dekker expressed it in *The Wonderful Year,* a miracle had occurred. Even the plague which had laid siege to London abated. But again the rejoicing was brief. James brought with him a horde of Scots who combined rapacity with grotesque manners. Knighthoods were sold by the dozen to furnish the king with luxuries unthinkable in the court of Elizabeth, notably the masques which exalted the art of Inigo Jones over Jonson's. And most disquieting was the national division in religion, the extremes of Puritan and Roman Catholic, which made reasonable discussion and gradual reform increasingly impossible.

Writers like Ben Jonson or John Donne, a more private commentator in his satires, could be involved in history and still grow in art. But that was not Marston's case. Especially in *The Malcontent*, his best piece, he writes with a personal disgust so strong that a comic dissolution of reality was necessary to escape nervous disorder. Not surprisingly, he left his *Insatiate Countess* unfinished in 1608, entered the Church of England, and disappeared into oblivion. In fact, his gravestone in the choir of Temple Church bears only the words *Oblivioni Sacrum*.

Just when *The Malcontent* was written and first produced is not certain, but 1604 is the most probable date. Its Induction, by John Webster, is the unique record of a longer and deeper struggle than any personal enmities could occasion. This struggle was between the boy players of Blackfriars and St. Paul's and their adult rivals of the Globe, the Red Bull, the Fortune and other "popular" theatres. Shakespeare turns this situation to dramatic advantage in *Hamlet* (II. ii), when the players come to Elsinore because they have lost their audience in the city to their *decimo sexto* rivals. The immediate issue behind Webster's Induction was apparently a performance by the children of *The Spanish Tragedy*, which the King's Men claimed as their own. In retaliation Shakespeare's group was performing Marston's Blackfriars play. Marston had a share in the Blackfriars profits, but we do not know of any more personal enmity caused by this mutual thievery.

Webster's Induction to *The Malcontent* suggests his uneasy relation with the audiences of theatres like the Globe; and in his address "To the Reader" heading the 1612 quarto of *The White Devil*, he records a strikingly poignant experience of the artist. The occasion was the first performance of *The White Devil*, most probably in February 1612 at the Red Bull Theatre. The physical discomfort of the open structure on a dark winter day was not the worst of the situation. Rather, it was the failure of the audience to respond that made the day a black or bleak one. But such a disappointing reception could have been predicted, for the Red Bull was notorious for its crude spectacles of romantic wonders bolstered with a piety to the taste of the lower middle classes.[2] No doubt Shakespeare's Globe attracted many persons capable of rising to Webster's artistry, although a whole theatre full of the judicious could not be expected even there.

The White Devil is one of the two plays in this volume drawing freely on history. How freely may be judged from the following facts. The White Devil was in history Vittoria Accoramboni, born at Gubbio in 1557. Her parents were aristocratic but impoverished. At sixteen Vittoria was married to Francesco Peretti (Webster's Camillo), nephew of Cardinal Montalto (Monticelso). Paulo Giordano Orsini, Duke of Bracciano (Brachiano), was born in 1537 and married Isabella Medici in 1558. He fathered three children, including an heir Virginio, before his encounter with the White Devil. Bracciano's later marriage with Vittoria was made possible by the murder of Isabella but for another reason: she was discovered to have taken a lover, another of the Orsini. In 1581 Bracciano, having met and fallen in love with Vittoria, had Francesco Peretti murdered in a musket ambush. Secretly marrying Vittoria—the first of three ceremonies—he lived with her until forced to separate by Pope Gregory XIII. The murder of Peretti was investigated, and for a while Vittoria was prisoner in Castle San Angelo in Rome. During the next four years the couple held off the Pope and the law, part of the time living together openly after a second marriage. When Pope Gregory died in April 1585, Bracciano married Vittoria

[2] See the work of G. F. Reynolds and Alfred Harbage's study of *Shakespeare and the Rival Traditions*.

still once more, this time publicly; but they were stunned by the announcement of the new Pope's identity—Cardinal Montalto. Montalto took the name Sixtus V, not Paul IV, as the play has it.

Fleeing, Vittoria and Bracciano went to Venice, then Padua. But travel was hard on Bracciano, for he was very corpulent and in bad health; so they settled at Salò on Lake Garda, where he died in November of 1585. Vittoria soon followed him. She was murdered in Padua by a band of cutthroats headed by Lodovico Orsini, chiefly to protect the rights of young Virginio against Vittoria's claim.

No single source can be found for Webster's dramatic version of the story. Possibly it was a lost Italian account behind a surviving copy of a Fugger newsletter.[3] All that has been discovered so far indicates that Webster used his plot sources as he did his verbal borrowings, with an almost perverse individuality.

Born some five years before both Shakespeare and Marlowe, George Chapman made a belated and grandiloquent appearance in English letters with *The Shadow of Night* (1594). He broke in as a dramatist with the Admiral's Men at the Rose, offering two successful comedies, *The Blind Beggar of Alexandria* (1596) and *An Humourous Day's Mirth* (1597). Chapman's true genius, however, lay in heroic platonism, and he is justly remembered as the translator of Homer and the author of *Bussy D'Ambois*.

This fascinating tragedy was probably written in 1604, and was performed by the boys of St. Paul's, as the quarto of 1607 tells us. But that is not the version offered here, for Chapman thoroughly revised the play before his death; and the impending close of the theatres induced the company to put it into print in 1641.

If Chapman used any single source for his original version it is not known, since none of the contemporary chronicles in English or French offers the material dramatized. It would

[3] MS 8959 in the Nationalbibliothek, Vienna. See Brown's edition, pp. xxvi ff.

be surprising indeed if any account were found characterizing Bussy in any way similar to Chapman's Achillean spirit. In this instance, the reader is more likely to give Chapman's hero his imaginative interest if he knows something about the historical man. He was born Louis de Clermont d'Amboise, Sieur de Bussy, in 1549. The religious wars of his time were thoroughly congenial to his fighting spirit, and when he was not wounded he was winning fame. During the Massacre of St. Bartholomew, August 1572, he murdered a Huguenot relative with whom he had been disputing at law. Although he was in the service of Henri III, that monarch heartily detested him; and in 1575 he joined the retinue of Monsieur, the heir apparent. Monsieur made him governor of Anjou, where he met Françoise de Maridort, a widow who had married Charles de Chambes, Comte de Monsoreau (Montsurry). Bussy courted the comtesse until he won a promise of an assignation. Being boastful by nature, Bussy gloated over the conquest in a letter to Monsieur, who happened to give the letter to the King. Henri III seized the occasion to eliminate Bussy by showing the letter to Monsoreau. Returning to La Coutanciere, his château, Monsoreau forced his wife at pistol point to invite Bussy to a tryst. On August 15, 1579, he kept the appointment, unarmed and with a friend. Monsoreau was waiting with a band of hired assassins. When the news of Bussy's death reached the Monsieur he was in London, courting Queen Elizabeth. His stoical reaction immediately gave rise to rumors that he had known of the plan to trap Bussy, which is not unlikely. Aside from the intrepidity of spirit, there is little of the historical Bussy in Chapman's complete man.

In his essay on four Elizabethan dramatists, Webster, Tourneur, Middleton and Chapman, T. S. Eliot remarks that Chapman was potentially the greatest artist of the group. His style is the furthest from realism, but therefore closer to the internal consistency of true dramatic art. The reader will find *Bussy D'Ambois* the greatest challenge in this volume, and in meeting that challenge he will come closer to the art of all Tudor and Stuart drama.

The texts of the plays are in the spelling of the quartos and Jonson's first folio, with the exception of *i, j, u* and *v*, which are used in the modern fashion. The purpose of this editorial policy is to take the student forcibly back into the language of the period in which the works were written. Since the modernization of Shakespeare's texts became fashionable, many editions of Tudor and Stuart plays have been produced in modern spelling. The result has been a loss of comprehension, despite the proliferation of glosses and notes. Modernized texts encourage the ignoring of glosses and eliminate the rich context of verbal association which illuminated the originals.

Some consistent alteration has been made in order to focus the student's eye on the language of the play. Titles and names of characters have been regularized or modernized. Abbreviations have been silently expanded. Stage directions are placed and phrased for the most part in modern style; but I have made no attempt to locate any scene since the dramatists did not concern themselves with the matter. Punctuation has sometimes been altered for sense without notation in the variants, but the seventeenth century uses of the period and colon have been preserved wherever possible. Capitals have been added, but no capital has been removed from a word meant to be set off within the line. Wherever the apostrophe occurs it has been kept but placed where a modern writer would place it.

Occasional changes in spelling and emendations are recorded in the variants. In addition, a considerable number of variants from the earlier version of *Every Man in His Humour* are presented, and a complete set of verbal variants for the earlier version of *Bussy D'Ambois*. Both sets offer material for critical study, and the variants for *Bussy D'Ambois* are not entirely duplicated elsewhere in print. The author is grateful for the generosity of the Houghton Library of Harvard University, Cambridge, Mass., in allowing him to edit from their copies of the plays, and for the generosity of the Pierpont Morgan Library, New York City, in allowing him to print variants from their copy of the first quarto of *Bussy D'Ambois*.

A table of events in which the careers of Jonson, Marston,

Webster and Chapman are outlined against the major events of the age follows. Since Shakespeare's career is most frequently described, it is represented here at only a few major points. The authorities for dating are Alfred Harbage, C. S. Lewis and Douglas Bush.

A NOTE ON FOOTNOTES

There are three sets of footnotes for the text in this edition, all numbered by scenes:

(a) footnotes, or glosses to difficult or obscure words, indicated in the text by a superscript number, as, for example, [1,2,3,] etc. are to be found on the bottom of the page in which the relevant text appears;

(b) variants, or alternate manuscript versions, designated in the text by a superscript number in *brackets*, as, for example, [1],[2],[3], etc. are to be found in the back of the book;

(c) explanatory notes, or more extended commentary, designated by a superscript number in *parentheses* in the text, as, for example, [(1),(2),(3),] etc. are to be found also in the back of the book.

CHRONOLOGY

1558 Elizabeth I accedes to the throne.
Robert Greene born.

1559 George Chapman born in Hitchin, Hertfordshire.
Matthew Parker becomes Archbishop of Canterbury.
Mirror for Magistrates published.
Jasper Heywood's translation of Seneca's *Troas* published.
Gammer Gurton's Needle probably written for performance
at Christ's College, Cambridge.

1560 Jasper Heywood's translation of Seneca's *Thyestes* published.
Geneva Bible published.

1561 *Gorboduc* acted at Christmas in the great Hall of the Inner
Temple before Queen Elizabeth.
Jasper Heywood's translation of Seneca's *Hercules Furens*
published.
Francis Bacon born.
Sir Thomas Hoby translates Castiglione's *Book of the
Courtier.*

1562 Civil War in France; Elizabeth makes a secret treaty with
the Huguenots.
Arthur Brooke publishes *Romeus and Juliet.*
Lope de Vega born.

1563 John Foxe publishes *Acts and Monuments* (*Book of
Martyrs*).
The Thirty-nine Articles define the national church.
Plague in London.

1564 Shakespeare, Christopher Marlowe, and Galileo born.
John Calvin, Michelangelo, and Vesalius die.
Flemish Protestant refugees come to England.

1566 George Gascoigne's *Supposes* probably acted at Christmas
in Gray's Inn.
John Studley's translation of Seneca's *Agamemnon* and
Medea published.
Gismonde of Salerne acted before the queen.
James (later James I) born.

1567 Revolt in the Netherlands.
1568 Mary Queen of Scots flees to England.
1569 Rebellion of Norfolk and northern earls crushed.
1570 Pope Pius V excommunicates Elizabeth.
1571 Battle of Lepanto.
1572 Ben Jonson born in or near London.
     John Donne born.
     Massacre of St. Bartholomew.
     Statute against vagabonds including actors without patrons.
1576 John Marston born at Wardington, Oxfordshire.
     The Theatre is built in London.
     Blackfriars Theatre opened.
1577 Curtain Theatre built.
     Robert Burton born.
     Francis Drake begins his voyage around the world.
1578 John Lyly publishes *Euphues.*
1579 John Fletcher born.
     Stephen Gosson attacks plays in *The School of Abuse.*
     Spenser publishes *The Shepherd's Calendar.*
     Sir Thomas North's translation of Plutarch's *Lives* published.
     Negotiations opened for marriage of Elizabeth to Alençon,
          Duke of Anjou.
1580 Thomas Middleton born. Approximate date of John Web-
          ster's birth.
1581 Seneca's *Ten Tragedies* published.
     Alençon (Monsieur) in England, courting Elizabeth.
1582 Plague in London.
1583 Philip Massinger born.
     The Queen's Players formed.
     John Whitgift becomes Archbishop of Canterbury.
1584 Francis Beaumont born.
     John Lyly's *Campaspe* and *Sapho and Phao* played before
          the queen by the boys of the Royal Chapel and St. Paul's.
     George Peele's *Arraignment of Paris* acted before the queen
          by the Chapel children.
     William of Orange assassinated.
1585 Cardinal Montalto becomes Sixtus V.
     Expedition to the Netherlands under the Earl of Leicester.
     Ronsard dies.
1586 John Ford born.

Probable date for performance of Thomas Kyd's *Spanish Tragedy* (if not earlier).

Sir Philip Sidney dies from wounds at the Battle of Zutphen.

Trial of Mary Queen of Scots.

1587　Marlowe's *Tamburlaine* Part I acted.

Greene's *Alphonsus King of Aragon* acted.

Holinshed's *Chronicles* (2nd ed.) published.

Mary Queen of Scots executed.

Pope Sixtus V proclaims crusade against England.

1588　Defeat of the Armada.

Marlowe's *Tamburlaine* Part II acted.

John Lyly's *Galathea* and *Endimion* acted before the queen at Greenwich.

The Misfortunes of Arthur acted before the queen, with dumb shows by Francis Bacon.

1589　Marlowe's *Jew of Malta* acted.

1590　John Lyly's *Midas* acted.

Sidney's *Arcadia* (I, II, part of III) published.

Spenser's *Faerie Queene* (I–III) published.

Approximate date of Shakespeare's Henry VI plays, through 1592.

1591　Robert Greene's *Orlando Furioso* acted.

Sidney's *Astrophel and Stella* (bad text) published.

Spenser's *Complaints, Daphnaida* published.

English forces aid Henri IV in France.

1592　Robert Greene dies, having attacked Shakespeare as an "upstart crow" in his *Groatsworth of Wit*.

Plague in London.

Montaigne dies.

1593　Theatres closed by plague.

Marlowe slain by Ingram Frizer at Deptford.

Shakespeare publishes *Venus and Adonis*.

Sidney's *Arcadia* (I–V) published.

Henri IV is converted to Catholicism.

1594　George Chapman publishes *Shadow of Night*.

Shakespeare publishes *The Rape of Lucrece*.

Thomas Kyd dies.

1595　Shakespeare's *Midsummer Night's Dream* and *Richard II* probably acted; Shakespeare paid as Chamberlain's man, with Richard Burbage and Will Kempe.

Sidney's *Defence of Poesy* published.

Spenser's *Colin Clout, Amoretti,* and *Epithalamion* published.

1596   Chapman's *Blind Beggar of Alexandria* acted by Admiral's Men.

George Peele dies.

Spenser's *Faerie Queene* (I–VI) published, also *Four Hymns* and *Prothalamion.*

1597   Chapman's *An Humourous Day's Mirth* acted by Admiral's Men.

Lost play *The Isle of Dogs* by Jonson and Thomas Nashe acted; Jonson imprisoned, and theatres closed.

Shakespeare's *Henry IV* probably acted.

1598   Jonson's *Every Man in His Humour* acted.

Chapman's *Achilles' Shield, Iliad* (I–VII) published.

Marston's *Metamorphosis of Pygmalion's Image* published with *Certain Satires,* also his *Scourge of Villainy.*

Sidney's *Arcadia, Lady of May, Certain Sonnets,* and *Astrophel* published.

Francis Meres, in *Palladis Tamia,* commends Shakespeare, Jonson, and Chapman.

Jonson kills Gabriel Spencer in a duel.

1599   Globe Theatre opened.

Jonson's *Every Man Out of His Humour* acted at the Globe.

Marston's *Antonio and Mellida* (Part I) probably acted, also his revision of *Histriomastix.*

Shakespeare's *Henry V* acted.

Thomas Dekker's *Shoemaker's Holiday* acted.

Spenser dies.

Elizabeth sends Essex to Ireland; he returns and is imprisoned.

The Archbishop of Canterbury publicly burns satires and pamphlets.

1600   The Fortune Theatre built.

Every Man Out of His Humour published; *Cynthia's Revels* acted.

1601   Jonson's *Poetaster* acted; *Every Man in His Humour* published.

Marston's *What You Will* probably acted.

Dekker and Marston's *Satiromastix* acted at the Globe.

Essex attempts revolt, is executed.

1602   Chapman's *Gentleman Usher* and *May Day* probably acted.

1603   Elizabeth dies; James I accedes. Plague.

       Jonson's *Sejanus* acted at the Globe by the new King's Men.

       Marston's *Dutch Courtesan* probably acted.

       Shakespeare's *Hamlet* (first quarto) published.

       John Florio's translation of Montaigne's *Essays* published.

1604   Marston's *Malcontent* acted.

       Chapman's *Bussy D'Ambois* probably acted.

       Jonson's *Entertainment at Highgate* performed.

       Hamlet (second quarto) published.

       Hampton Court Conference.

       Bancroft becomes Archbishop of Canterbury.

1605   Jonson, Chapman, and Marston collaborate on *Eastward Ho!;* all three are imprisoned.

       Marston's *The Fawne* probably acted.

       Jonson's *Masque of Blackness* performed at Whitehall.

       Bacon's *Advancement of Learning* published.

       Gunpowder plot.

1606   Jonson's *Volpone* acted at the Globe, Cambridge and Oxford.

       Marston's *Sophonisba* published.

       John Lyly dies.

1607   Jonson's *Theobald's Entertainment* performed.

1608   Chapman's Charles *Duke of Byron* acted.

       John Fletcher's *Faithful Shepherdess* acted.

       Jonson's *Masque of Beauty* probably performed.

       Marston is imprisoned in Newgate for offensive play at Blackfriars.

1609   Jonson's *Epicoene* acted; also his *Masque of Queens* performed.

       Beaumont and Fletcher's *Philaster* acted.

       John Marston enters the Church.

1610   Jonson's *The Alchemist* acted.

       Chapman's *Revenge of Bussy D'Ambois* probably acted.

       Cyril Tourneur's *Atheist's Tragedy* probably acted.

1611   Jonson's *Catiline* acted; also his masques, *Oberon* and *Love Freed from Ignorance and Folly.*

       Beaumont and Fletcher's *King and No King* and *Maid's Tragedy* acted.

       Shakespeare's *The Tempest* acted.

       Abbot becomes Archbishop of Canterbury.

Parliament dissolved.

The King James Bible is published.

1612   John Webster's *The White Devil* acted.

Jonson quarrels with Inigo Jones, accompanies the son of Sir Walter Raleigh to France as tutor.

Thomas Shelton's translation of *Don Quixote* (I) published.

Prince Henry dies.

Lancashire witches hanged.

1613   Jonson returns to England.

Chapman's *Tragedy of Chabot* probably acted.

Marston's *Insatiate Countess* printed.

The Globe burns down at a performance of *Henry VIII.*

Princess Elizabeth is married to the Elector Palatine.

Webster publishes *A Monumental Column,* with other elegies for Prince Henry by Chapman, Heywood, Tourneur, Donne, Herbert, Campion *et al.*

Sir Thomas Overbury dies in the Tower.

1614   Webster's *Duchess of Malfi* probably acted.

Jonson's *Bartholomew Fair* acted.

Sir Thomas Overbury's *Characters* published.

1615   Jonson's masque *Mercury Vindicated* performed.

Trial of Sir Thomas Overbury's murderers.

1616   Shakespeare and Francis Beaumont die.

Jonson's *The Devil is an Ass* and his masque *The Golden Age Restored* are performed.

Chapman publishes *The Whole Works of Homer* and *The Divine Poem of Musaeus*

Jonson's *Works* are published, including the revised *Every Man in His Humour;* he receives a royal pension.

1617   Jonson's masque *Vision of Delight* performed.

1618   Jonson travels to Scotland, converses with Drummond of Hawthornden; Jonson's masque *Pleasure Reconciled to Virtue* performed.

Chapman publishes his translation of Hesiod.

Sir Walter Raleigh is executed.

The Thirty Years War begins in Germany.

1619   Jonson made M.A. of Oxford, meets with the Tribe of Ben in the Apollo Room, Devil's Head Tavern.

John Fletcher's *Humourous Lieutenant* acted.

Nathan Field dies.

Ten Shakespeare quartos are printed in a collection.

Queen Anne dies.

1620 Webster's *The Devil's Law Case* probably acted.

Thomas Shelton's translation of *Don Quixote* (II) published.

1621 Jonson's masques, *News from the New World discovered in the Moon* and *Metamorphosed Gypsies* performed.

Robert Burton's *Anatomy of Melancholy* published (revised editions 1624, 1628, 1632, 1638, 1651).

1622 Jonson's *Masque of Augurs* performed.

Thomas Middleton and William Rowley's *The Changeling* acted.

1623 The Shakespeare First Folio is published.

Webster publishes *Monuments of Honour* (Lord Mayor's pageant).

Jonson's manuscripts are destroyed by fire; his masque *Time Vindicated* performed.

Philip Massinger's *The Bondman* acted.

Prince Charles and the Duke of Buckingham go to Madrid.

1624 Jonson's masques, *Neptune's Triumph* and *Pan's Anniversary* performed.

Middleton's *A Game at Chess* acted.

Marriage between Prince Charles and Henrietta Maria arranged.

1625 James I dies; Charles I accedes and marries.

Jonson's masque of *The Fortunate Isles* acted.

Massinger's *New Way to Pay Old Debts* acted.

John Fletcher dies.

Plague in London.

1626 Jonson's *Staple of News* acted.

Massinger's *The Roman Actor* acted.

James Shirley's *The Wedding* acted.

Cyril Tourneur and William Rowley die.

Francis Bacon and Lancelot Andrewes die.

1627 William Davenant's *The Cruel Brother* acted.

Thomas Middleton dies.

1628 Jonson suffers a paralytic stroke, succeeds Middleton as City Chronologer.

John Ford's *The Lover's Melancholy* acted.

Richard Brome's *The City Wit* acted.

1629 Jonson pensioned by Charles I, his *New Inn* acted.

Brome's *The Northern Lass* acted.

1630   Arthur Wilson's *Inconstant Lady* probably acted.

1631   Massinger's *Believe as You List* acted.

James Shirley's *The Traitor* acted.

John Donne dies and John Dryden is born.

1632   The Shakespeare Second Folio is published.

John Lyly's *Six Court Comedies* are published.

Jonson's *Magnetic Lady* is acted.

William Prynne's *Histriomastix* published (dated 1633).

Thomas Dekker dies.

1633   Marston's *Tragedies and Comedies* are published.

Ford's *'Tis Pity She's A Whore, The Broken Heart,* and *Love's Sacrifice* are published.

Shirley's *Bird in a Cage, Young Admiral,* and *The Gamester* are acted.

William Laud becomes Archbishop of Canterbury.

1634   George Chapman and John Marston die.

Richard Brome and Thomas Heywood's *The Late Lancashire Witches* acted.

Milton's *Masque* (*Comus*) performed.

William Prynne is pilloried and imprisoned until 1637.

1635   Jonson's son dies.

Thomas Cartwright's *The Ordinary* acted.

Shirley's *The Lady of Pleasure* acted.

Davenant's *News from Plymouth, Temple of Love* and *The Platonic Lover* acted.

1636   Cartwright's *The Royal Slave* acted.

Davenant's *Triumphs of the Prince D'Amour* acted.

Massinger's *Bashful Lover* acted.

1637   Ben Jonson dies.

Milton's *Masque* (*Comus*) published.

John Suckling's *Aglaura* acted.

1638   John Webster dies.

Ford's *The Lady's Trial* acted, *The Fancies Chaste and Noble* published.

Jonsonius Virbius published (33 memorial poems).

Davenant is pensioned as assumed Poet Laureate.

1639   Davenant's *Spanish Lovers* acted.

Shirley's *The Politician* acted.

War with Scotland.

1640   Jonson's *Works* (II) published (later plays, masques, verse and prose).

Philip Massinger and Robert Burton die.

Francis Beaumont's *Poems* published.

The Long Parliament impeaches Strafford and Laud.

1641 Brome's *The Jovial Crew* acted.

Shirley's *The Cardinal* acted.

Thomas Heywood dies and William Wycherley is born.

Laud is imprisoned and Strafford executed.

Princess Mary is married to William of Orange.

1642 Shirley's *The Sisters* acted.

Abraham Cowley's *The Guardian* acted.

King Charles leaves London for Oxford, raises his standard.

The theatres are closed on September 2nd.

EVERY MAN IN HIS HUMOUR

BY

BEN JONSON

Euery

MAN IN

HIS

HVMOVR.

A Comœdie.

Acted in the yeere 15 9 8. By the then
Lord Chamberlaine his
Seruants.

The Author B. I.

IUVEN.

Haud tamen inaideds vati, quem pulpita pascunt.

LONDON,

Printed by VVILLIAM STANSBY.

M. DC. XVI.

TO THE MOST LEARNED,
AND MY HONOR'D FRIEND,
M*r*. *Cambden,* [*Clarentiaux.*]

SIR,

There are, no doubt, a supercilious race in the world, who will esteeme all office, done you in this kind, an injurie; so solemne a vice it is with them to use the authoritie of their ignorance, to the crying downe of Poetry, or the Professors: But, my gratitude must not leave to correct their error; since I am none of those, that can suffer the benefits confer'd upon my youth, to perish with my age. It is a fraile memorie, that remembers but present things: And, had the favour of the times so conspir'd with my disposition, as it could have brought forth other, or better, you had had the same proportion, & number of the fruits, the first. Now, I pray you, to accept this, such, wherein neither the confession of my manners shall make you blush; nor of my studies, repent you to have beene the instructer: And, for the profession of my thanke-fulnesse, I am sure, it will, with good men, find either praise, or excuse.

Your true lover,
Ben. Jonson.

The Persons of the Play.

KNO'WELL, *An old Gentle-man.*

EDWARD KNO'WELL, *His Sonne.*

BRAYNE-WORME, *The Fathers man.*

MASTER STEPHEN, *A countrey Gull.*

DOWNE-RIGHT, *A plaine Squier.*

WELL-BRED, *His halfe Brother.*

JUSTICE CLEMENT, *An old merry Magistrat.*

ROGER FORMALL, *His Clarke.*

KITELY, *A merchant.*

DAME KITELY, *His Wife.*

MISTRESS BRIDGET, *His Sister.*

MASTER MATTHEW, *The towne-gull.*

CASH, *Kitelies Man.*

COB, *A Water-bearer.*

TIB, *His Wife.*

CAPTAIN BOBADILL, *A Paules-Man.*

[Servants]

THE SCENE
LONDON.

This Comoedie was first
Acted, in the yeere
1598.
By the then L. Chamberlayne
his Servants.
The principall Comoedians were.

WILL. SHAKESPEARE.	RIC. BURBADGE.
AUG. PHILIPS.	JOH. HEMINGS.
HEN. CONDEL.	THO. POPE.
WILL. SLYE.	CHR. BEESTON.
WILL. KEMPE.	JOH. DUKE.

With the allowance of the Master of REVELLS.

EVERY MAN IN HIS HUMOUR.

Though neede make many *Poets,* and some such
As art, and nature have not betterd much;
Yet ours, for want, hath not so lov'd the stage,
As he dare serve th'ill customes of the age :
Or purchase your delight at such a rate,   5
As, for it, he himselfe must justly hate.
To make a child, now swadled, to proceede
Man, and then shoote up, in one beard, and weede,[1]
Past threescore yeeres : or, with three rustie swords,
And[(1)] helpe of some few foot-and-halfe-foote words,   10
Fight over *Yorke,* and *Lancasters* long jarres :
And in the tyring-house[2] bring wounds, to scarres.[(1)]
He rather prayes, you will be pleas'd to see
One such, today, as other playes should be.
Where neither *Chorus* wafts you ore the seas;[(2)]   15
Nor creaking throne comes downe, the boyes to
                    please;[(3)]
Nor nimble squibbe is seene, to make afear'd[(4)]
The gentlewomen; nor roul'd bullet heard[(5)]
To say, it thunders; nor tempestuous drumme   20
Rumbles, to tell you when the storme doth come;
But deedes, and language, such as men doe use :
And persons, such as *Comoedie* would chuse,
When she would shew an Image of the times,
And sport with humane follies, not with crimes.   25
Except, we make 'hem such by loving still

---

[1] *weede* : garment.   [2] *tyring-house* : dressing room.

Our popular errors, when we know th'are ill.
I meane such errors, as you'll all confesse
By laughing at them, they deserve no lesse :
Which when you heartily doe, there's hope left, then,
You, that have so grac'd monsters,[6] may like men.   5

ACT I. SCENE I.

[*Enter*] KNO'WELL [*and*] BRAYNE-WORME.   10
[KNO'WELL.] A goodly day toward! and a fresh morning!
                     Brayne-Worme,
  Call up your yong master : bid him rise, sir.
  Tell him, I have some businesse to employ him.
BRAYNE-WORME. I will sir, presently.   15
KNO'WELL.   But heare you, sirah,
  If he be'at his booke, disturbe him not.
BRAYNE-WORME.   Well sir.
                               [*Exit.*]
KNO'WELL. How happie, yet, should I esteeme my selfe   20
  Could I (by any practise[1]) weane the boy
  From one vaine course of studie, he affects.
  He is a scholler, if a man may trust
  The liberall voice of fame, in her report
  Of good accompt, in both our *universities*, [1], (1)   25
  Either of which hath favour'd him with graces :[2]
  But their indulgence, must not spring in me
  A fond[2] opinion, that he cannot erre.
  My selfe was once a student; and, indeed,
  Fed with the selfe-same humour, he is now,   30
  Dreaming on nought but idle *poetrie*,
  That[3] fruitlesse, and unprofitable art,
  Good unto none, but least to the professors,
  Which, then, I thought the mistresse of all knowl-
                     edge :[3]   35

ACT I. SCENE I.
[1] *practise :* device.   [2] *fond :* foolish.

8

But since, time, and the truth have wak'd my judge-
ment,
And reason taught me better to distinguish,
The vaine, from th'usefull learnings.

[*Enter* STEPHEN.]   5

Cossin⁽²⁾ Stephen!
What newes with you, that you are here so early?

STEPHEN. Nothing, but eene come to see how you doe,
uncle.

KNO'WELL. That's kindly done, you are wel-come, cousse.   10

STEPHEN. I, I know that sir, I would not ha' come else.
How doe my cousin Edward, uncle?

KNO'WELL. O, well cousse, goe in and see : I doubt he
be scarse stirring yet.

STEPHEN. Uncle, afore I goe in, can you tell me, an'³   15
he have ere a booke⁽³⁾ of the sciences of hawking,
and hunting? I would faine borrow it.

KNO'WELL. Why, I hope you will not a hawking now,
will you?

STEPHEN. No wusse⁴; but I'll practise against next yeere   20
uncle : I have bought me a hawke, and a hood, and
bells, and all; I lacke nothing but a booke to keepe
it by.

KNO'WELL. O, most ridiculous.

STEPHEN. Nay, looke you now, you are angrie, uncle :   25
why you know, an' a man have not skill in the hawking, and hunting-languages now a dayes, I'll not give
a rush for him. They are more studied then the
Greeke, or the *Latine.* He is for no gallants companie without 'hem. And by gads lid⁵ I scorne it, I,   30
so I doe, to be a consort for every *hum-drum,* hang
'hem scroyles,⁶ there's nothing in 'hem, i' the world.
What doe you talke on it? Because I dwell at
Hogsden,⁽⁴⁾ I shall keepe companie with none but

---

³ *an'* : if. *And* can also mean *if.*   as *Slid* below.

⁴ *wusse* : surely.   ⁶ *scroyles* : scabby-faced rogues.

⁵ *gads lid* : God's eyelid. Same

9

the archers of *Finsburie?* or the citizens, that come a
ducking to *Islington*⁽⁵⁾ ponds? A fine jest ifaith! Slid
a gentleman mun⁷ show himselfe like a gentleman.
Uncle, I pray you be not angrie, I know what I have
to doe, I trow, I am no novice.   5
KNO'WELL. You are a prodigall absurd cocks-combe :[4]
                           Goe to.
Nay never looke at me, it's I that speake.
Tak't as you will sir, I'll not flatter you.
Ha' you not yet found meanes enow, to wast   10
That, which your friends have left you, but you must
Goe cast away your money on a kite,⁸
And know not how to keepe it, when you ha' done?
O it's comely! this will make you a gentleman!
Well cosen, well! I see you are eene past hope   15
Of all reclaime. I, so, now you are told on it,
You looke another way.
STEPHEN.   What would you ha' me doe?
KNO'WELL. What would I have you doe? I'll tell you
                           kinsman,   20
Learne to be wise, and practise how to thrive,
That would I have you doe : and not to spend
Your coyne on every bable,⁹ that you phansie,
Or every foolish braine, that humors you.
I would not have you to invade each place,   25
Nor thrust your selfe on all societies,
Till mens affections, or your owne desert,
Should worthily invite you to your ranke.
He, that is so respectlesse in his courses,
Oft sells his reputation, at cheape market.   30
Nor would I, you should melt away your selfe
In flashing braverie,¹⁰ least¹¹ while you affect
To make a blaze of gentrie to the world,
A little puffe of scorne extinguish it,

---

⁷ *mun :* must.   ⁹ *bable :* bauble.
⁸ *kite :* hawk; bird of prey. Cf.¹⁰ *braverie :* ostentation.
    Kitely.   ¹¹ *least :* lest.

And you be left, like an unsavourie snuffe,[12]
Whose propertie is onely to offend.
I'ld ha' you sober, and containe your selfe;
Not, that your sayle be bigger then your boat :
But moderate your expences now (at first)   5
As you may keepe the same proportion still.[13]
Nor, stand so much on your gentilitie,
Which[5] is an aërie, and meere borrow'd thing,
From dead mens dust, and bones : and none of yours
Except you make, or hold it. Who comes here?[5]   10

Act I. Scene ii.[(1)]

[*Enter*] SERVANT.   15

[SERVANT.] Save you, gentlemen.

STEPHEN. Nay, we do' not stand much on our gentilitie,
friend; yet, you are wel-come, and I assure you, mine
uncle here is a man of a thousand a yeare, *Middlesex*
land : hee has but one sonne in all the world, I am   20
his next heire (at the common law) master Stephen,
as simple as I stand here, if my cossen die (as there's
hope he will) I have a prettie living o' mine owne
too, beside, hard-by here.

SERVANT. In good time, sir.   25

STEPHEN. In good time, sir? why! and in very good time,
sir. You doe not flout, friend, doe you?

SERVANT. Not I, sir.

STEPHEN. Not you, sir? you were not best, sir; an' you
should, here bee them can perceive it, and that   30
quickly to : goe to. And they can give it againe
soundly to, and neede be.

SERVANT. Why, sir, let this satisfie you : good faith, I
had no such intent.

STEPHEN. Sir, an' I thought you had, I would talke with   35
you, and that presently.

---

[12] *snuffe :* candle-end.   [13] *still :* always.

SERVANT. Good master Stephen, so you may, sir, at your
  pleasure.

STEPHEN. And so I would sir, good my saucie companion! an' you were out o' mine uncles ground, I can
  tell you; though I doe not stand upon my gentilitie   5
  neither in't.

KNO'WELL. Cossen! cossen! will this nere be left?

STEPHEN. Whorson base fellow! a mechanicall serving-
  man! By this cudgell, and't were not for shame, I
  would—   10

KNO'WELL. What would you doe, you peremptorie[1] gull?
  If you can not be quiet, get you hence.
  You see, the honest man demeanes himselfe
  Modestly to'ards you, giving no replie
  To your unseason'd, quarrelling, rude fashion :   15
  And, still you huffe it, with a kind of cariage,
  As voide of wit,[2] as of humanitie.
  Goe, get you in; fore heaven, I am asham'd
  Thou hast a kinsmans interest in me. [*Exit* STEPHEN.]

SERVANT. I pray you, sir. Is this master Kno'well's   20
  house?

KNO'WELL. Yes, marie,[3] is it sir.

SERVANT. I should enquire for a gentleman, here, one
  master Edward Kno'well : doe you know any such,
  sir, I pray you?   25

KNO'WELL. I should forget my selfe else, sir.

SERVANT. Are you the gentleman? crie you mercie sir :
  I was requir'd by a gentleman i' the citie, as I rode
  out at this end o' the towne, to deliver you this letter,
  sir.   30

KNO'WELL. To me, sir! What doe you meane? pray you
  remember your court'sie.[4] (*To his most selected
  friend, master* EDWARD KNO'WELL.) What might the

ACT I. SCENE II.

[1] *peremptorie :* complete; over-
  bearing fool.

[2] *wit :* intelligence.

[3] *marie :* by Mary; surely.

[4] *court'sie :* the expected doffing
  of the hat.

gentlemans name be, sir, that sent it? nay, pray you
be cover'd.

SERVANT. One master Well-bred, sir.

KNO'WELL. Master Well-bred! A yong gentleman? is he
not?   5

SERVANT. The same sir, master Kitely married his sister :
the rich merchant i' the old *Jewrie.*

KNO'WELL. You say very true. Brayne-worme,

[*Enter* BRAYNE-WORME.]

BRAYNE-WORME. Sir.   10

KNO'WELL. Make this honest friend drinke here : pray
you goe in. [*Exeunt* BRAYNE-WORME *and* SERVANT.]
This letter is directed to my sonne :
Yet, I am Edward Kno'well too, and may
With the safe conscience of good manners, use   15
The fellowes error to my satisfaction.
Well, I will breake it ope (old men are curious)
Be it but for the stiles sake, and the phrase,
To see, if both do answere my sonnes praises,
Who is, almost, growne the idolater[1]   20
Of this yong Well-Bred : what have we here? what's
this?[1]

> The letter.

*Why, Ned, I beseech thee; hast thou for-sworne
all thy friends i' the old* Jewrie?[2] *or dost thou*   25
thinke us all Jewes *that inhabit there, yet? If thou*
dost, come over, and but see our fripperie : change
an olde shirt,[3] *for a whole smocke,[5] with us. Doe*
not conceive that antipathy betweene us, and Hogs-
den; as was betweene Jewes, *and hogs-flesh. Leave*   30
thy vigilant father, alone, to number over his greene
apricots, evening, and morning, o' the north-west
wall: An' I had beene his sonne, I had sav'd him the
labor, long since; if, taking in all the yong wenches,
that passe by, at the back-dore, and codd'ling[6] every 35
kernell of the fruit for 'hem, would ha' serv'd. But,

---

[5] *smocke :* wench.   [6] *codd'ling :* stewing.

*pr'y thee, come over to me, quickly, this morning: I
have such a present for thee (our* Turkie *com-
panie*⁽⁴⁾ *never sent the like to the* Grand-Signior.)
One is a Rimer sir, o' your owne batch,⁽⁵⁾ *your owne
levin*[7]*; but doth think himselfe* Poet-major, *o' the*   5
*towne: willing to be showne, and worthy to be
seene. The other—I will not venter his description
with you, till you come, because I would ha' you
make hether with an appetite. If the worst of 'hem
be not worthy your jorney, draw your bill of charges,*   10
*as unconscionable, as any Guild-hall verdict will give
it you, and you shall be allow'd your* viaticum.[8]

From the Wind-Mill.⁽⁶⁾

From[2] the *Burdello,* it might come as well;
The *Spittle:* or *Pict-hatch.*⁽⁷⁾ Is this the man,[2]   15
My sonne hath sung so, for the happiest wit,
The choysest braine, the times hath sent us forth?
I know not what he may be, in the arts;
Nor what in schooles: but surely, for his manners,
I judge him a prophane, and dissolute wretch: 20
Worse, by possession of such great good guifts,
Being the master of so loose a spirit.
Why, what unhallow'd ruffian would have writ,
In such a scurrilous manner, to a friend!
Why should he thinke, I tell my Apri-cotes?   25
Or play th'*Hesperian* Dragon, with my fruit,
To watch it? Well, my sonne, I'had thought
Y' had had more judgement, t'have made election
Of your companions, then t'have tane on trust,
Such petulant, geering gamsters, that can spare   30
No argument, or subject from their jest.
But I perceive, affection makes a foole
Of any man, too much the father. Brayne-Worme,

[*Enter* BRAYNE-WORME.]

BRAYNE-WORME. Sir.   35
KNO'WELL. Is the fellow gone that brought this letter?

---

[7] *levin:* leaven; flavor; sort.   [8] *viaticum:* travel expenses.

14

BRAYNE-WORME. Yes, sir, a pretie while since.
KNO'WELL. And, where's your yong master?
BRAYNE-WORME. In his chamber sir.
KNO'WELL. He spake not with the fellow! did he?
BRAYNE-WORME. No sir, he saw him not.   5
KNO'WELL. Take you this letter, and deliver it my sonne,
     But with no notice, that I have open'd it, on your
     life.
BRAYNE-WORME. O lord, sir, that were a jest, indeed!
                                              [*Exit.*]   10
KNO'WELL. I am resolv'd, I will not stop his journey;
     Nor practise any violent meane, to stay
     The unbridled course of youth in him : for that,
     Restrain'd, growes more impatient, and, in-kind,
     Like to the eager, but the generous[9] grey-hound;   15
     Who ne're so little from his game with-held,
     Turnes head, and leapes up at his holders throat.
     There[3] is a way of winning, more by love,
     And urging of the modestie, then feare :
     Force workes on servile natures, not the free.   20
     He, that's compell'd to goodnesse, may be good;
     But 'tis but for that fit[10] : where others drawne
     By softnesse, and example, get a habit.
     Then, if they stray, but warne 'hem : and, the same
     They should for vertu'have done, they'll doe for   25
                         shame.[3]   [*Exit.*]

                    ACT I. SCENE III.
                                                                 30
[*Enter*] EDWARD KNO'WELL [*and*] BRAYNE-WORME.
[E. KNO'WELL.] Did he open it, sayest thou?
BRAYNE-WORME. Yes, o' my word sir, and read the
     contents.
E. KNO'WELL. That scarse contents me. What counte-   35

[9] *generous :* bred to high spirit.   [10] *fit :* period of time.

nance (pr'y thee) made he, i' the reading of it? was
he angrie, or pleas'd?

BRAYNE-WORME. Nay sir, I saw him not reade it, nor
open it, I assure your worship.

E. KNO'WELL. No? how know'st thou, then, that he did   5
either?

BRAYNE-WORME. Marie sir, because he charg'd me, on
my life, to tell nobodie, that he open'd it : which,
unlesse hee had done, hee would never feare to have
it reveal'd.   10

E. KNO'WELL. That's true : well I thanke thee, Brayne-
Worme.[1]

[*Enter* STEPHEN.]

STEPHEN. O, Brayne-Worme, did'st thou not see a fellow here in a what-sha'-call-him doublet! he brought   15
mine uncle a letter e'en now.

BRAYNE-WORME. Yes, master Stephen, what of him?

STEPHEN. O, I ha' such a minde to beate him—Where
is hee? canst thou tell?

BRAYNE-WORME. Faith, he is not of that mind : he is   20
gone, master Stephen.

STEPHEN. Gone? which way? when went he? how long
since?

BRAYNE-WORME. He is rid hence. He tooke horse, at the
streete dore.   25

STEPHEN. And, I staid i' the fields! horson *scander-*
bag(1) rogue! ô that I had but a horse to fetch him
backe againe.

BRAYNE-WORME. Why, you may ha' my masters geld-
ing, to save your longing, sir.   30

STEPHEN. But, I ha' no bootes, that's the spight on't.

BRAYNE-WORME. Why, a fine wispe of hay, rould hard,
master Stephen.

STEPHEN. No faith, it's no boote[1] to follow him, now :

ACT I. SCENE III.
[1] *boote :* profit.

let him eene goe, and hang. 'Pray thee, helpe to
trusse[2] me, a little. He dos so vexe me—

BRAYNE-WORME. You'll be worse vex'd, when you are
truss'd, master Stephen. Best, keepe unbrac'd; and
walke your selfe, till you be cold : your choller may   5
foundre you else.

STEPHEN. By my faith, and so I will, now thou tell'st
me on't : How dost thou like my legge, Brayne-
Worme?

BRAYNE-WORME. A very good leg! master Stephen! but   10
the woollen stocking do's not commend it so well.

STEPHEN. Foh, the stockings be good inough, now summer is comming on, for the dust : Ile have a paire
of silke, again' winter, that I goe to dwell i' the towne.
I think my legge would shew in a silke-hose.   15

BRAYNE-WORME. Beleeve me, master Stephen, rarely
well.

STEPHEN. In sadnesse,[3] I thinke it would : I have a reasonable good legge.

BRAYNE-WORME. You have an excellent good legge, mas-   20
ter Stephen, but I cannot stay, to praise it longer
now, and I am very sorie for't.

STEPHEN. Another time will serve, Brayne-Worme.
Grammercie for this.   [Exit BRAYNE-WORME.]

E. KNO'WELL. Ha, ha, ha!   25

        KNO'WELL laughes having read the letter.

STEPHEN. Slid, I hope, he laughes not at me, and he
doe—

E. KNO'WELL. Here was a letter, indeede, to be inter-
cepted by a mans father, and doe him good with   30
him! Hee cannot but thinke most vertuously, both of
me, and the sender, sure; that make the carefull
Costar'-monger[2] of him in our familiar Epistles.[3] Well, if he read this with patience, Ile be
gelt,[2] and troll ballads for Master John Trun-   35
dle,[4] yonder, the rest of my mortalitie. It is true,

---

[2] trusse : to tie clothing laces.   [3] sadnesse : seriousness.

and likely, my father may have as much patience
as another man; for he takes much physicke : and,
oft taking physicke makes a man very patient. But
would your packet, master Well-Bred, had arriv'd at
him, in such a minute of his patience; then, we had   5
knowne the end of it, which now is doubtfull, and
threatens—What! my wise cossen! Nay, then, Ile furnish our feast with one gull more to 'ard the messe.[4]
He writes to me of a brace, and here's one, that's
three : O, for a fourth; Fortune, if ever thou'lt use   10
thine eyes, I intreate thee—

STEPHEN. O, now I see, who hee laught at. He laught
at some-body in that letter. By this good light, and
he had laught at me—

E. KNO'WELL. How now, coussen Stephen, melan-   15
choly?[3],(5)

STEPHEN. Yes,[4] a little. I thought, you had laught at
me, cossen.

E. KNO'WELL. Why, what an' I had cousse, what would
you ha' done?   20

STEPHEN. By this light, I would ha' told mine uncle.

E. KNO'WELL. Nay, if you wold ha' told your uncle, I
did laugh at you, cousse.

STEPHEN. Did you, indeede?

E. KNO'WELL. Yes, indeede.   25

STEPHEN. Why, then—

E. KNO'WELL. What then?

STEPHEN. I am satisfied, it is sufficient.[4]

E. KNO'WELL. Why, bee so gentle cousse. And, I pray
you let me intreate a courtesie of you. I am sent for,   30
this morning, by a friend i' the old *Jewrie* to come
to him; It's but crossing over the fields to *More-gate* :
Will you beare me companie? I protest, it is not to
draw you into bond or any plot against the state,
cousse.   35

---

[4] *messe* : a group of four at a
banquet.

STEPHEN. Sir, that's all one, and 't were; you shall command me, twise so farre as *More-gate* to doe you good, in such a matter. Doe you thinke I would leave you? I protest—

E. KNO'WELL. No, no, you shall not protest, cousse.　　5

STEPHEN. By my fackins,[5] but I will, by your leave; Ile protest more to my friend, then Ile speake off, at this time.

E. KNO'WELL. You speake very well, cousse.

STEPHEN. Nay, not so neither, you shall pardon me : but　　10 I speake, to serve my turne.

E. KNO'WELL. Your[5] turne, couss? Doe you know, what you say? A gentleman of your sort, parts,[6] carriage, and estimation, to talke o' your turne i' this companie, and to me, alone, like a tankard-bearer, at　　15 a conduit! Fie. A wight,[7] that (hetherto) his every step hath left the stampe of a great foot behind him, as every word the savour of a strong spirit! and he! this man! so grac'd, guilded, or (to use a more fit *metaphore*) so tin-foild by nature, as not ten house-　　20 wives pewter (again' a good time) shew's more bright to the world then he! and he (as I said last, so I say againe, and still shall say it) this man! to conceale such reall ornaments as these, and shaddow their glorie, as a Millaners wife do's here wrought stom-　　25 acher, with a smokie lawne,[8] or a black cypresse? O couss! It cannot be answer'd, goe not about it. Drakes old ship,[6] at *Detford,* may sooner circle the world againe. Come, wrong not the qualitie of your desert, with looking downeward, couz; but hold up your　　30 head, so : and let the *Idea* of what you are, be pourtray'd i' your face, that men may reade i' your physnomie, (*Here, within this place, is to be seene the true, rare, and accomplish'd monster, or miracle*

---

[5] *fackins* : faith.　　　　　　　　[7] *wight* : being.
[6] *parts* : talents.　　　　　　　　[8] *lawne* : dark linen or crepe.

of nature, which is all one.) What thinke you of this,
couss?[5]

STEPHEN. Why, I doe thinke of it; and I will be more
prowd, and melancholy, and gentleman-like, then I
have beene : I'le ensure you.   5

E. KNO'WELL. Why, that's resolute master Stephen!
[*Aside.*] Now if I can but hold him up to his height,
as it is happily begunne, it will doe well for a
suburbe-humor : we may hap have a match with the
citie, and play him for fortie pound. Come, couss.   10

STEPHEN. I'le follow you.

E. KNO'WELL. Follow me? you must goe before.[9]

STEPHEN. Nay, an' I must, I will. Pray you, shew me,
good cousin.   [*Exeunt.*]

                                                               15

ACT I. SCENE IV.

[*Enter*] MASTER MATTHEW.

[MATTHEW.] I thinke, this to be the house : what,   20
hough?

[*Enter* COB.]

COB. Who's there? O, master Matthew! gi' your worship
good morrow.

MATTHEW. What! Cob! how do'st thou, good Cob? do'st   25
thou inhabite here, Cob?

COB. I, sir, I and my linage ha'kept a poore house, here,
in our dayes.

MATTHEW. Thy linage, *Monsieur* Cob, what linage?
what linage?   30

COB. Why, sir, an ancient linage, and a princely. Mine
ance'trie came from a Kings belly, no worse man :
and yet no man neither (by your worships leave, I
did lie in that) but *Herring* the King of fish (from
his belly, I proceed) one o' the Monarchs o' the world,   35
I assure you. The first red herring, that was broil'd

---

[9] Servants preceded masters.

in Adam, and Eve's kitchin, doe I fetch my pedigree
from, by the Harrots[1] bookes. His Cob, was my
great-great-mighty-great Grand father.

MATTHEW. Why mightie? why mightie? I pray thee.

COB. O, it was a mightie while agoe, sir, and a mightie   5
great Cob.

MATTHEW. How know'st thou that?

COB. How know I? why, I smell his ghost, ever and anon.

MATTHEW. Smell a ghost? ô unsavoury jest! and the
ghost of a herring Cob!   10

COB. I sir, with favour of your worships nose, Master
Matthew, why not the ghost of a herring-cob, as well
as the ghost of rasher-bacon?

MATTHEW. Roger Bacon,(1), thou wouldst say?

COB. I say rasher-bacon. They were both broyl'd o' the   15
coles? and a man may smell broyld-meate, I hope?
you are a scholler, upsolve me that, now.

MATTHEW. O raw ignorance! Cob, canst thou shew me
of a gentleman, one Captayne Bobadill, where his
lodging is?   20

COB. O, my guest, sir! you meane.

MATTHEW. Thy guest! Alas! ha, ha.

COB. Why doe you laugh, sir? Doe you not meane Captayne Bobadill?

MATTHEW. Cob, 'pray thee, advise thy selfe well : doe   25
not wrong the gentleman, and thy selfe too. I dare
bee sworne, hee scornes thy house : hee! He lodge in
such a base, obscure place, as thy house! Tut, I know
his disposition so well, he would not lye in thy bed,
if tho'uldst gi'it him.   30

COB. I will not give it him, though, sir. Masse, I thought
somewhat was in't, we could not get him to bed, all
night! Well, sir, though he lye not o' my bed, he lies
o' my bench : an't please you to goe up, sir, you shall
find him with two cushions under his head, and his   35

ACT I. SCENE IV.
1 *Harrots* : Herald's.

cloke wrapt about him, as though he had neither wun
nor lost, and yet (I warrant) he ne're cast[2] better in
his life, then he has done, to night.

MATTHEW. Why? was he drunke?

COB. Drunke, sir? you heare not me say so. Perhaps, hee   5
swallow'd a taverne-token,[3, (2)] or some such device,
sir : I have nothing to doe withall. I deale with water,
and not with wine. Gi'me my tankard there, hough.
God b'w'you, sir. It's sixe a clocke : I should ha' carried two turnes, by this. What hough? my stopple[4]?   10
come.

[Enter TIB *with tankard.]*

MATTHEW. Lye in a water-bearers house! A gentleman
of his havings! Well, I'le tell him my mind.

COB. What Tib, shew this gentleman up to the Cap-   15
tayne.   *[Exit* MATTHEW *with* TIB.]
O, an' my house were the *Brasen-head*[(3)] now!
faith, it would eene speake, *Mo fooles yet.* You should
ha' some now would take this Master Matthew to be
a gentleman, at the least. His father's an honest man,   20
a worshipfull[(4)] fish-monger, and so forth; and now
dos he creepe, and wriggle into acquaintance with
all the brave gallants about the towne, such as my
guest is : (ô, my guest is a fine man) and they flout
him invincibly. Hee useth[5] every day to a Merchants   25
house (where I serve water) one master Kitely's, i'
the *old Jewry;* and here's the jest, he is in love with
my masters sister, (mistris Bridget) and calls her
mistris : and there hee will sit you a whole after-
noone some-times, reading o' these same abominable,   30
vile, (a poxe on 'hem, I cannot abide them) rascally
verses, *poyetrie, poyetrie,* and speaking of *enterludes,*
'twill make a man burst to heare him. And the

[2] *cast :* vomited his drink.
[3] *swallow'd a taverne-token :*
   got very drunk; *pun on* "small
   coin" and "inn sign and all."

[4] *stopple :* stopper for the
   tankard.
[5] *useth :* usually goes.

wenches, they doe so geere, and ti-he at him—well,
should they do so much to me, Ild for-sweare them
all, by the foot of Pharaoh. There's an oath? How
many water-bearers shall you heare sweare such an
oath? ô, I have a guest (he teaches me) he dos   5
sweare the legiblest, of any man christned : By St.
George, the foot of Pharaoh, the body of me, as I am
gentleman, and a souldier : such daintie oathes! and
withall, he dos take this same filthy roguish *tabacco,*
the finest, and cleanliest! it would doe a man good   10
to see the fume come forth at's tonnells[6]! Well, he
owes mee fortie shillings (my wife lent him out of her
purse, by sixe-pence a time) besides his lodging : I
would had it. I shall ha'it, he saies, the next *Action.*[7]
Helter skelter, hang sorrow, care'll kill a cat, up-tailes 15
all, and a louse for the hang-man.   [*Exit.*]

Act I. Scene v.

20

BOBADILL *is discovered*[1] *lying on his bench.*
[BOBADILL.] Hostesse, hostesse.
              [*Enter* TIB.]
TIB. What say you, sir?
BOBADILL. A cup o' thy small beere, sweet hostesse.   25
TIB. Sir, there's a gentleman, below, would speake with
  you.
BOBADILL. A gentleman! 'ods so,[2] I am not within.
TIB. My husband told him you were, sir.
BOBADILL. What a plague—what meant he?   30
MATTHEW. Captaine Bobadill?
BOBADILL. Who's there? (take away the bason, good
  hostesse) come up, sir.
TIB. He would desire you to come up, sir.
              [*Enter* MATTHEW.]   35
You come into a cleanly house, here.

---

[6] *tonnells :* nostrils.   [7] *Action :* legal session.

MATTHEW. 'Save you, sir. 'Save you, Captayne.

BOBADILL. Gentle master Matthew! Is it you, sir? Please
you sit downe.

MATTHEW. Thanke you, good Captaine, you may see, I
am some-what audacious.   5

BOBADILL. Not so, sir. I was requested to supper, last
night, by a sort[1] of gallants, where you were wish'd
for, and drunke to, I assure you.

MATTHEW. Vouchsafe me, by whom, good Captaine.

BOBADILL. Mary, by yong Well-Bred, and others : Why,   10
hostesse, a stoole here, for this gentleman.

MATTHEW. No haste, sir, 'tis very well.

BOBADILL. Body of me! It was so late ere we parted
last night, I can scarse open my eyes, yet; I was but
new risen, as you came : how passes the day abroad,   15
sir? you can tell.

MATTHEW. Faith, some halfe houre to seven : now trust
mee, you have an exceeding fine lodging here, very
neat, and private!

BOBADILL. I, sir : sit downe, I pray you. Master Matthew 20
(in any case) possesse no gentlemen of our acquaintance, with notice of my lodging.

MATTHEW. Who? I sir? no.

BOBADILL. Not that I need to care who know it, for the
Cabbin is convenient, but in regard I would not be   25
too popular, and generally visited, as some are.

MATTHEW. True, Captaine, I conceive you.

BOBADILL. For, doe you see, sir, by the heart of valour,
in me, (except it be to some peculiar and choice
spirits, to whom I am extraordinarily ingag'd, as your 30
selfe, or so) I could not extend thus farre.

MATTHEW. O Lord, sir, I resolve so.[2]

BOBADILL. I confesse, I love a cleanely and quiet privacy,
above all the tumult, and roare of fortune. What new
booke ha' you there? What! *Goe by, Hieronymo!*[3]   35

ACT I. SCENE V.
[1] *sort :* group.   [2] *resolve so :* believe it certainly.

24

MATTHEW. I, did you ever see it acted? is't not well pend?

BOBADILL. Well pend? I would faine see all the *Poets,* of these times, pen such another play as that was! they'll prate and swagger, and keepe a stir of arte and devices, when (as I am a gentleman) reade'hem, they are the most shallow, pittifull, barren fellowes, that live upon the face of the earth, againe!

MATTHEW. Indeed, here are a number of fine speeches in this booke! *O eyes,*[4] *no eyes, but fountaynes fraught with teares!* There's a conceit[3]! fountaines fraught with teares! *O life, no life, but lively forme of death!* Another! *O world, no world, but masse of publique wrongs!* A third! *Confus'd and fil'd with murder, and misdeeds!* A fourth! O, the *Muses!*[4] Is't not excellent? Is't not simply the best that ever you heard, Captayne? Ha? How doe you like it?

BOBADILL. 'Tis good.

MATTHEW. *To*[5] *thee, the purest object to my sense,*
The most refined essence heaven covers,
Send I these lines, wherein I doe commence
The happy state of turtle-billing lovers.
If they prove rough, un-polish't, harsh, and rude,
 Haste made the wast. Thus, mildly, I conclude.[5]
   BOBADILL *is making him ready all this while.*

BOBADILL. Nay, proceed, proceed. Where's this?

MATTHEW. This, sir? a toy o' mine owne, in my nonage : the infancy of my *Muses!* But, when will you come and see my studie? good faith, I can shew you some very good things, I have done of late—That boot becomes your legge, passing well, Captayne, methinkes!

BOBADILL. So, so, It's the fashion, gentlemen now use.

MATTHEW. Troth, Captayne, an' now you speake o' the fashion, master Well-Bred's elder brother, and I, are fall'n out exceedingly : this other day, I hapned to en-

---

[3] *conceit :* metaphor.

ter into some discourse of a hanger,[4] which I assure
you, both for fashion, and worke-man-ship, was most
peremptory-beautifull,[1] and gentlemanlike! Yet,
he condemn'd, and cry'd it downe, for the most
pyed,[5] and ridiculous that ever he saw. . 5

BOBADILL. Squire Downe-Right? the halfe-brother? was't
not?

MATTHEW. I sir, he.

BOBADILL. Hang him, rooke,[6] he! why, he has no more
judgement then a malt-horse.[7] By St. George, I won- 10
der you'ld loose a thought upon such an animal:
the most peremptory absurd clowne[8] of *christendome*,[2] this day, he is holden.[9, (6)] I protest to
you, as I am a gentleman, and a souldier, I ne're
chang'd wordes, with his like. By his discourse, he 15
should eate nothing but hay. He was borne for the
manger, pannier,[10] or pack-saddle! He ha's not so
much as a good phrase in his belly, but all old iron,
and rustie proverbes! a good commoditie for some
smith, to make hob-nailes of. 20

MATTHEW. I, and he thinks to carry it away with his
man-hood still, where he comes. He brags he will gi'
me the *bastinado*, as I heare.

BOBADILL. How! He the *bastinado*! how came he by that
word, trow? 25

MATTHEW. Nay, indeed, he said cudgell me; I term'd
it so, for my more grace.

BOBADILL. That may bee : For I was sure, it was none
of his word. But, when? when said he so?

MATTHEW. Faith, yesterday, they say : a young gallant, 30
a friend of mine told me so.

BOBADILL. By[3] the foot of Pharaoh, and't were my

[4] *hanger :* strap supporting a sword.
[5] *pyed :* tasteless, gaudily colored.
[6] *rooke :* fool.

[7] *malt-horse:* huge, shaggy horse.
[8] *clowne :* peasant, fool.
[9] *holden :* held; considered.
[10] *pannier :* large basket.

case now, I should send him a *chartel*,[11] presently.
The *bastinado* a most proper, and sufficient *depend-*
ance,[12] warranted by the great Caranza.[(7)] Come
hither. You shall *chartel* him. I'll shew you a trick,
or two, you shall kill him with, at pleasure : the first   5
stoccata,[13] if you will, by this ayre.[3]

MATTHEW. Indeed, you have absolute knowledge i' the
mysterie,[14] I have heard, sir.

BOBADILL. Of whom? Of whom ha' you heard it, I beseech you?   10

MATTHEW. Troth, I have heard it spoken of divers, that
you have very rare, and un-in-one-breath-utter-able
skill, sir.

BOBADILL. By heaven, no, not I; no skill i' the earth :
some small rudiments i' the science, as to know my   15
time, distance, or so. I have profest it more for noblemen, and gentlemens use, then mine owne practise,
I assure you. Hostesse, accommodate[(8)] us with another bed-staffe[15] here, quickly: [*Enter* TIB.] Lend
us another bed-staffe. [*Exit* TIB.] The woman do's   20
not understand the wordes of *Action*. Looke you, sir.
Exalt not your point above this state, at any hand,
and let your poynard[16] maintayne your defence,
thus: [*Re-enter* TIB.] (give it the gentleman, and
leave us) so, sir. [*Exit* TIB.] Come on: O, twine your   25
body more about, that you may fall to a more sweet
comely gentleman-like guard. So, indifferent.[17] Hollow your body more sir, thus. Now, stand fast o' your
left leg, note your distance, keepe your due proportion of time—Oh, you disorder your point, most ir-   30
regularly!

MATTHEW. How is the bearing of it, now, sir?

11 *chartel* : challenge.
12 *dependance* : ground for a duel.
13 *stoccata* : thrust.
14 *mysterie* : technical skill; trade.

15 *bed-staffe* : stick for beating and smoothing a bed.
16 *poynard* : dagger.
17 *indifferent* : pretty good.

BOBADILL. O, out of measure ill! A well-experienc'd
hand would passe upon you, at pleasure.

MATTHEW. How meane you, sir, passe[18] upon me?

BOBADILL. Why, thus sir (make a thrust at me) come
in, upon the answere, controll your point, and make   5
a full carreere,[19] at the body. The best-practis'd gallants of the time, name it the *passada*(9) : a most
desperate thrust, beleeve it!

MATTHEW. Well, come, sir.

BOBADILL. Why, you doe not manage your weapon with   10
any facilitie, or grace to invite mee : I have no spirit
to play with you. Your dearth of judgement renders
you tedious.

MATTHEW. But one *venue*,[20] sir.

BOBADILL. *Venue!* Fie. Most grosse denomination, as   15
ever I heard. O, the *stoccata*,(10) while you live, sir.
Note that. Come, put on your cloke, and we'ell goe
to some private place, where you are acquainted,
some taverne, or so—and have a bit—Ile send for one
of these Fencers, and hee shall breath you, by my   20
direction; and, then, I will teach you your tricke. You
shall kill him with it, at the first, if you please. Why,
I will learne you, by the true judgement of the eye,
hand, and foot, to controll any enemies point i' the
world. Should your adversarie confront you with a   25
pistoll, 'twere nothing, by this hand, you should, by
the same rule, controll his bullet, in a line : except it
were hayle-shot, and spred. What money ha' you
about you, Master Matthew?

MATTHEW. Faith, I ha' not past a two shillings, or so.   30

BOBADILL. 'Tis somewhat with the least : but, come. We
will have a bunch of redish, and salt, to tast our
wine;[4] and a pipe of *tabacco*, to close the orifice
of the stomach :(11) and then, wee'll call upon yong

---

[18] *passe* : may mean "condemn" or "impose on," as
well as "thrust."

[19] *carreere* : lunge.

[20] *venue* : thrust (French and
out of fashion).

Well-Bred.[4] Perhaps wee shall meet the Coridon,[21] his brother, there: and put him to the
question.   [*Exeunt.*]

Act II. Scene i.   5

[*Enter*] KITELY, CASH, [*and*] DOWNE-RIGHT.
[KITELY.] Thomas,[1] Come hither.
  There lyes a note, within upon my deske,
  Here, take my key: It is no matter, neither.   10
  Where is the Boy?
CASH.   Within, sir, i' the ware-house.
KITELY. Let him tell over, straight, that *Spanish* gold,
  And weight it, with th' pieces of eight.[1] Doe you
  See the delivery of those silver stuffes,   15
  To Master Lucar. Tell him, if he will,
  He shall ha' the grogran's,[2] at the rate I told him,
  And I will meet him, on the *Exchange,* anon.
CASH. Good, sir.   [*Exit.*]
KITELY. Doe you see that fellow, brother Downe-Right?   20
DOWNE-RIGHT. I, what of him?[1]
KITELY. He is a jewell, brother.
  I tooke him of a child, up, at my dore,[2]
  And christned him, gave him mine owne name,
                                         Thomas,   25
  Since bred him at the Hospitall;[1] where proving
  A toward impe, I call'd him home, and taught him
  So much, as I have made him my Cashier,
  And giv'n him, who had none, a surname, Cash:[2]
  And find him, in his place so full of faith,   30
  That, I durst trust my life into his hands.
DOWNE-RIGHT. So, would not I in any bastards,
                                         brother,[3]

---

[21] *Coridon:* Country lad.
  Act II. Scene i.
[1] *pieces of eight:* Spanish silver   [2] *grogran's:* gummed fabric of
    peso.   silk, mohair and wool.

As, it is like, he is : although I knew
My selfe his father. But you said yo' had some-
　　　　　what[3]
To tell me, gentle brother, what is't? what is't?
KITELY. Faith, I am very loath, to utter it,　　　　　5
As fearing, it may hurt your patience :
But, that I know, your judgement is of strength,
Against the neerenesse of affection[3]—
DOWNE-RIGHT. What needs this circumstance? pray you
be direct.　　　　　10
KITELY. I will not say, how much I doe ascribe
Unto your friendship; nor, in what regard
I hold your love : but, let my past behaviour,
And usage of your sister, but confirme
How well I'ave beene affected to your—　　　　　15
DOWNE-RIGHT. You are too tedious, come to the matter,
the matter.
KITELY. Then (without further ceremonie) thus.
My brother Well-Bred, sir, (I know not how)
Of late, is much declin'd in what he was,　　　　　20
And greatly alter'd in his disposition.
When he came first to lodge here in my house,
Ne're trust me, if I were not proud of him :
Me thought he bare himselfe in such a fashion,
So full of man, and sweetnesse in his carriage,　　　　　25
And (what was chiefe) it shew'd not borrowed in
　　　　　him,
But all he did, became him as his owne,
And seem'd as perfect, proper, and possest
As breath, with life, or colour, with the bloud.　　　　　30
But, now, his course is so irregular,
So loose, affected, and depriv'd of grace,
And he himselfe withall so farre falne off
From that first place, as scarse no note remaines,
To tell mens judgements where he lately stood.　　　　　35
Hee's growne a stranger to all due respect,

---

[3] *affection* : passion.

Forgetfull of his friends, and not content
To stale himselfe in all societies,
He makes my house here common, as a *Mart*,
A *Theater*, a publike receptacle
For giddie humour, and diseased riot;   5
And here (as in a taverne, or a stewes[4])
He, and his wild associates, spend their houres,
In repetition of lascivious jests,
Sweare, leape,[5] drinke, dance, and revell night by
                              night,   10
Controll my servants : and indeed what not?

DOWNE-RIGHT.[4] 'Sdeynes,[6] I know not what I should
say to him, i' the whole world! He values me, at a
crackt three-farthings,[(2)] for ought I see : It will
never out o' the flesh that's bred i' the bone! I have   15
told him inough, one would thinke, if that would
serve : But, counsell to him, is as good, as a shoulder
of mutton to a sicke horse. Well! he knowes what to
trust to, for George. Let him spend, and spend, and
domineere, till his heart ake; an' hee thinke to bee   20
reliev'd by me, when he is got into one o' your citie
pounds, the Counters,[7, (3)] he has the wrong sow
by the eare, ifaith : and claps his dish[8] at the wrong
mans dore. I'le lay my hand o' my halfe-peny, e're I
part with't, to fetch him out, I'le assure him.[4]   25

KITELY. Nay, good brother, let it not trouble you, thus.

DOWNE-RIGHT. 'Sdeath, he mads me, I could eate my
very spur-lethers, for anger! But, why are you so
tame? Why doe you not speake to him, and tell him
how he disquiets your house?   30

KITELY. O, there are divers reasons to disswade,
                              brother.[(4)]
But, would your selfe vouchsafe to travaile in it,
(Though, but with plaine, and easie circumstance)

---

[4] *stewes* : brothel.   [6] *'Sdeynes* : by God's dignity.
[5] *leape* : act riotously; perhaps   [7] *Counters* : Debtor's prison.
    "fornicate."   [8] *dish* : beggar's bowl.

31

It would, both come much better to his sense,
And savour lesse of stomack,[9] or of passion.
You are his elder brother, and that title
Both gives, and warrants you authoritie;
Which (by your presence seconded) must breed   5
A kinde of dutie in him, and regard :
Whereas, if I should intimate the least,
It would but adde contempt, to his neglect,
Heape worse on ill, make up a pile of hatred
That, in the rearing, would come tottring downe,   10
And, in the ruine, burie all our love.
Nay, more then this, brother, if I should speake
He would be readie from his heate of humour,[5]
And over-flowing of the vapour, in him,[6]
To blow[10] the eares of his familiars,   15
With the false breath, of telling, what disgraces,
And low disparadgments, I had put upon him.
Whilst they, sir, to relieve him, in the fable,
Make their loose comments, upon every word,
Gesture, or looke, I use; mocke me all over,[7]   20
From my flat cap,[5] unto my shining shooes :[7]
And, out of their impetuous rioting phant'sies,
Beget some slander, that shall dwell with me.
And what would that be, think you? mary, this.
They would give out (because my wife is faire,   25
My selfe but lately married, and my sister
Here sojourning a virgin in my house)
That I were jealous! nay, as sure as death,
That they would say. And how that I had quar-
                                            rell'd[6]   30
My brother purposely, thereby to finde
An apt pretext, to banish them my house.
DOWNE-RIGHT. Masse perhaps so: They'are like inough
    to doe it.
KITELY. Brother, they would, beleeve it : so should I   35
    (Like one of these penurious quack-salvers)

---

[9] *stomack :* resentment.   [10] *blow :* inflate; incite.

But set the bills[11] up, to mine owne disgrace,
And trie experiments upon my selfe :
Lend scorne and envie, oportunitie,
To stab my reputation, and good name—

5

Act II. Scene ii.

[Enter] MATTHEW *[and]* BOBADILL.
[MATTHEW.] I will speake to him—   10
BOBADILL. Speake to him? away, by the foot of Pharaoh,
   you shall not, you shall not doe him that grace. The
   time of day, to you, Gentleman o' the house.[1] Is
   Master Well-Bred stirring?
DOWNE-RIGHT. How then? what should he doe?[1]   15
BOBADILL. Gentleman of the house, it is[2] to you : is he
   within, sir?
KITELY. He came not to his lodging to night[(1)] sir, I
   assure you.
DOWNE-RIGHT. Why, doe you heare? you.   20
BOBADILL. The gentleman-citizen hath satisfied mee, Ile
   talke to no scavenger.
                    [Exeunt BOBADILL *and* MATTHEW.]
DOWNE-RIGHT. How, scavenger? stay sir, stay?
KITELY. Nay, brother Downe-Right.   25
DOWNE-RIGHT. 'Heart! stand you away, and you love me.
KITELY. You shall not follow him now, I pray you,
   brother, Good faith you shall not : I will over-rule
   you.
DOWNE-RIGHT. Ha? scavenger? well, goe to, I say little :   30
   but, by this good day (god forgive me I should
   sweare) if I put it up so, say, I am the rankest
   cow,[2] that ever pist. 'Sdeynes, and I swallow this,
   Ile ne're draw my sword in the sight of *Fleet-street*

11 *bills :* advertisements.   does he mean?
   Act II. Scene ii.   2 *it is :* my question is.
1 *what should he doe? :* what

33

againe, while I live; Ile sit in a barne, with Madge-
howlet,[3] and catch mice first. Scavenger? 'Heart, and
Ile goe neere to fill that huge tumbrell-slop[4] of yours,
with somewhat, and I have good lucke : your *Gara-*
gantua[(2)] breech cannot carry it away so.   5

KITELY. Oh doe not fret your selfe thus, never thinke
on't.

DOWNE-RIGHT. These are my brothers consorts, these!
these are his *Cam'rades,* his walking mates! hee's a
gallant, a *Cavaliero* too, right hang-man cut[5]! Let me   10
not live, and I could not finde in my heart to swinge
the whole ging of'hem, one after another, and begin
with him first. I am griev'd, it should be said he is
my brother, and take these courses. Wel, as he
brewes, so he shall drinke, for George, againe. Yet,   15
he shall heare on't, and that tightly[6] too, and I live,
Ifaith.

KITELY. But, brother, let your reprehension (then)
Runne in an easie current, not ore-high
Carried with rashnesse, or devouring choller[7];   20
But rather use the soft perswading way,
Whose powers will worke more gently, and compose
Th'imperfect thoughts you labour to reclaime :
More winning, then enforcing the consent.

DOWNE-RIGHT. I, I, let me alone for that, I warrant you.   25
                                              Bell rings.

KITELY. How now? oh, the bell rings to breakfast.
Brother, I pray you goe in, and beare my wife
Companie, till I come; Ile but give order
For some dispatch of businesse, to my servants—   30
                                    [*Exit* DOWNE-RIGHT.]

[3] *Madge-howlet :* a barn owl.
[4] *trumbrell-slop :* bell-like
trousers.

[5] *cut :* style; character.
[6] *tightly :* vigorously; smartly.
[7] *choller :* wrath.

34

ACT II. SCENE III.

[*Enter*] COB.   5

[KITELY.] What, Cob? our maides will have you by the
           back (Ifaith)
  For coming so late this morning.

COB. (*He passes by with his tankard.*) Perhaps so, sir,
  take heed some body have not them by the belly, for   10
  walking so late in the evening.

KITELY. Well, yet my troubled spirit's somewhat eas'd,
  Though not repos'd in that securitie,
  As I could wish : But, I must be content.
  How e're I set a face on't to the world,   15
  Would I had lost this finger, at a venter,
  So Well-Bred had ne're lodg'd within my house.
  Why't cannot be, where there is such resort
  Of wanton gallants, and yong revellers,
  That any woman should be honest[1] long.   20
  Is't like, that factious beautie will preserve
  The publike weale of chastitie, un-shaken,
  When such strong motives muster, and make head
  Against her single peace? no, no. Beware,
  When mutuall appetite doth meet to treat,   25
  And spirits of one kinde, and qualitie,
  Come once to parlee, in the pride of bloud : (1)
  It is no slow conspiracie, that followes.[1]
  Well (to be plaine) if I but thought, the time
  Had answer'd their affections : all the world   30
  Should not perswade me, but I were a cuckold.
  Mary, I hope, they ha'not got that start :
  For oportunitie hath balkt 'hem yet,
  And shall doe still, while I have eyes, and eares
  To attend the impositions of my heart.   35

ACT II. SCENE III.
[1] *honest :* chaste.

35

My presence shall be as an iron barre,
'Twixt the conspiring motions of desire :
Yea, every looke, or glance, mine eye ejects,
Shall checke occasion, as one doth his slave,
When he forgets the limits of prescription.   5

[*Enter* DAME KITELY.]

DAME KITELY. Sister Bridget, pray you fetch downe the
rose-water[2] above in the closet. Sweet heart, will
you come in, to breakefast?

KITELY. [*Aside.*] An' shee have over-heard me now?   10

DAME KITELY. I pray thee (good Musse[2]) we stay for
you.

KITELY. By heaven I would not for a thousand angells.[3]

DAME KITELY. What aile you sweet heart? are you not   15
well? speake good Musse.

KITELY. Troth my head akes extremely, on a sudden.

DAME KITELY. Oh, the lord! [*Putting her hand on his
forehead.*]

KITELY. How now? what?   20

DAME KITELY. Alas, how it burnes? Musse, keepe you
warme, good truth it is this new disease! there's a
number are troubled withall! for loves sake, sweet
heart, come in, out of the aire.

KITELY. How simple, and how subtill are her answeres?   25
A new disease,[4] and many troubled with it!
Why, true : shee heard me, all the world to nothing.

DAME KITELY. I pray thee, good sweet heart, come in;
the aire will doe you harme,[5] in troth.[2]

KITELY. The aire! shee has me i' the wind! sweet heart! 30
Ile come to you presently : 't will away, I hope.

DAME KITELY. Pray heaven it doe.   [*Exit.*]

KITELY. A new disease? I know not, new, or old,
But it may well be call'd poore mortalls plague :
For, like a pestilence, it doth infect   35
The houses[6] of the braine. First it begins

---

[2] *Musse* : Mouse.

Solely to worke upon the phantasie,
Filling her seat with such pestiferous aire,
As soone corrupts the judgement; and from thence
Sends like contagion to the memorie :
Still each to other giving the infection.   5
Which, as a subtle vapor, spreads it selfe,
Confusedly, through every sensive part,
Till not a thought, or motion, in the mind,
Be free from the blacke poyson of suspect.[3]
Ah, but what miserie' is it, to know this?   10
Or, knowing it, to want the mindes erection,[4, 3]
In such extremes? Well, I will once more strive,
(In spight of this black cloud) my selfe to be,
And shake the feaver off, that thus shakes me. [*Exit.*]
                                                                 15

Act II. Scene iv.

[*Enter*] brayne-worme
[*Disguised as a maimed soldier.*]   20
[brayne-worme.] S'Lid, I cannot choose but laugh, to
see my selfe trans-lated thus, from a poore creature
to a creator; for now must I create an intolerable sort
of lyes, or my present profession looses the grace :
and yet the lye to a man of my coat, is as ominous a   25
fruit, as the *Fico*.[1, 1] O sir, it holds for good politie
ever, to have that outwardly in vilest estimation, that
inwardly is most deare to us. So much, for my borrowed shape. Well, the troth is, my old master intends to follow my yong, drie foot,[2] over *More-fields*,   30
to *London,* this morning : now I, knowing, of this
hunting-match, or rather conspiracie, and to insinu-
ate with my yong master (for so must we that are

---

[3] *suspect :* suspicion.
[4] *erection :* power of reason over
error.

Act II. Scene iv.
[1] *Fico :* Fig; obscene insult.
[2] By the scent.

blew-waiters,[3] and men of hope and service doe, or
perhaps wee may weare motley[4] at the yeeres end,
and who weares motley, you know) have got me
afore, in this disguise, determining here to lye in
ambuscado, and intercept him, in the mid-way. If I 5
can but get his cloke, his purse, his hat, nay, any
thing, to cut him off, that is, to stay his journey, *Veni,
vidi, vici*,[5] I may say with Captayne Caesar,[(2)] I
am made for ever, ifaith. Well, now must I practice
to get the true garb of one of these *lance-knights*,[6, (3)] 10
my arme here, and my—yong master! and his cousin,
Master Stephen, as I am true counterfeit man of
warre, and so souldier![1]   [*He retires.*]
         [*Enter* EDWARD KNO'WELL *and* STEPHEN.]
E. KNO'WELL. So sir, and how then, couss?   15
STEPHEN. 'Sfoot, I have lost my purse, I thinke.
E. KNO'WELL. How? lost your purse? where? when had
    you it?
STEPHEN. I cannot tell, stay.
BRAYNE-WORME. [*Aside.*] 'Slid, I am afeard, they will 20
    know mee, would I could get by them.
E. KNO'WELL. What? ha' you it?
STEPHEN. No, I thinke I was bewitcht, I—
E. KNO'WELL. Nay, doe not weepe the losse, hang it, let
    it goe.   25
STEPHEN. Oh, it's here : no, and it had beene lost, I had
    not car'd, but for a jet[(4)] ring mistris Mary sent me.
E. KNO'WELL. A jet ring? oh, the *poesie*,[7] the *poesie?*
STEPHEN. Fine, ifaith! *Though fancie sleep, my love is
    deepe.* Meaning that though I did not fancie her, yet 30
    shee loved me dearely.
E. KNO'WELL. Most excellent!
STEPHEN. And then, I sent her another, and my *poesie*

---

[3] *blew-waiters* : servants.
[4] *motley* : fool's garment.
[5] *Veni, vidi, vici* : I came, I saw,
    I conquered.

[6] *lance-knights* : mercenary
    soldiers.
[7] *poesie* : rimed sentiment
    inscribed.

was : *The deeper, the sweeter, Ile be judg'd by St. Peter.*

E. KNO'WELL. How, by St. Peter? I doe not conceive that!

STEPHEN. Mary, St. Peter, to make up the meeter.

E. KNO'WELL. Well, there the Saint was your good pa-   5
tron, hee help't you at your need : thanke him, thanke
him.

BRAYNE-WORME. (*He is come back.*) I cannot take leave
on 'hem, so : I will venture, come what will. Gentlemen, please you change a few crownes, for a very   10
excellent good blade, here? I am a poore gentleman, a
souldier, one that (in the better state of my fortunes)
scorn'd so meane a refuge, but now it is the humour
of necessitie, to have it so. You seeme to be gentlemen, well affected to martiall men, else I should   15
rather die with silence, then live with shame [5] : how
ever, vouchsafe to remember, it is my want speakes,
not my selfe. This condition agrees not with my
spirit—

E. KNO'WELL. Where hast thou serv'd?   20

BRAYNE-WORME. May it please you, sir, in all the late
warres of *Bohemia, Hungaria, Dalmatia, Poland,*
where not, sir? I have beene a poore servitor, by sea
and land, any time this fourteene yeeres, and follow'd
the fortunes of the best Commanders in *christendome.*   25
I was twice shot at the taking of *Alepo,* once at the
reliefe of *Vienna;* I have beene at *Marseilles, Naples,*
and the *Adriatique* gulfe, [2], [6] a gentleman-slave
in the galleys, thrice, where I was most dangerously
shot in the head, through both the thighs, and yet,   30
being thus maym'd, I am void of maintenance, nothing left me but my scarres, the noted markes of my
resolution.

STEPHEN. How will you sell this rapier, friend?

BRAYNE-WORME. Generous sir, I referre it to your owne   35
judgement; you are a gentleman, give me what you
please.

STEPHEN. True, I am a gentleman, I know that friend :

but what though? I pray you say, what would you
aske?

BRAYNE-WORME. I assure you, the blade may become
the side, or thigh of the best prince, in *Europe*.

E. KNO'WELL. I, with a velvet scabberd, I thinke. 5

STEPHEN. Nay, and't be mine, it shall have a velvet scabberd, Couss, that's flat : I'de not weare it as 'tis, and
you would give me an angell.

BRAYNE-WORME. At your worships pleasure, sir; nay, 'tis
a most pure *Toledo*. 10

STEPHEN. I had rather it were a *Spaniard!* but tell me,
what shall I give you for it? An' it had a silver hilt—

E. KNO'WELL. Come, come, you shall not buy it; hold,
there's a shilling fellow,[3] take thy rapier.

STEPHEN.[4] Why, but I will buy it now, because you 15
say so, and there's another shilling, fellow. I scorne
to be outbidden. What, shall I walke with a cudgell,
like *Higgin-Bottom?*[7] and may have a rapier, for
money?

E. KNO'WELL. You may buy one in the citie. 20

STEPHEN. Tut, Ile buy this i' the field, so I will, I have a
mind to't, because 'tis a field rapier.[4] Tell me your
lowest price.

E. KNO'WELL. You shall not buy it, I say.

STEPHEN. By this money, but I will, though I give more 25
then 'tis worth.

E. KNO'WELL. Come away, you are a foole.

STEPHEN. Friend, I am a foole, that's granted : but Ile
have it, for that words sake. Follow me, for your
money. 30

BRAYNE-WORME. At your service, sir.   [*Exeunt.*]

ACT II. SCENE V.

35

[*Enter*] KNO'WELL.

[KNO'WELL.][1] I cannot loose the thought, yet, of this
letter,

Sent to my sonne : nor leave t'admire[1] the change
Of manners, and the breeding of our youth,
Within the kingdome, since my selfe was one.
When I was yong, he liv'd not in the stewes,
Durst have conceiv'd a scorne, and utter'd it,   5
On a grey head; age was authoritie
Against a buffon[2] : and a man had, then,
A certaine reverence pai'd unto his yeeres,
That had none due unto his life.[1] So much
The sanctitie of some prevail'd, for others.   10
But,[2] now, we all are fall'n; youth, from their
          feare :
And age, from that, which bred it, good example.
Nay, would our selves were not the first, even parents,
That did destroy the hopes, in our owne children :   15
Or they not learn'd our vices, in their cradles,
And suck'd in our ill customes, with their milke.
Ere all their teeth be borne, or they can speake,
We make their palats cunning! The first wordes,
We forme their tongues with, are licentious jests!   20
Can it call, whore? crie, bastard? ô, then, kisse it,
A wittie childe! Can't sweare? The fathers dearling!
Give it two plums. Nay, rather then't shall learne
No bawdie song, the mother'her selfe will teach it!
But, this is in the infancie; the dayes   25
Of the long coate : when it puts on the breeches,
It will put off all this. I, it is like :
When it is gone into the bone alreadie.
No, no : This die goes deeper then the coate,
Or shirt, or skin. It staines, unto the liver,[3]   30
And heart,[4] in some. And, rather, then it should
          not,
Note, what we fathers doe! Looke, how we live!
What mistresses we keepe! at what expense,
In our sonnes eyes! where they may handle our gifts,   35

Act II. Scene v.
[1] t'admire : wonder at.   [2] buffon : buffoon.

Heare our lascivious courtships, see our dalliance,
Tast of the same provoking meates, with us, (2)
To ruine of our states! Nay, when our owne
Portion³ is fled, to prey on their remainder,
We call them into fellowship of vice!   5
Baite 'hem with the yong chamber-maid, to seale!⁴
And teach 'hem all bad wayes, to buy affliction!
This is one path! but there are millions more,
In which we spoile our owne, with leading them.
Well, I thanke heaven, I never yet was he,   10
That travail'd with my sonne, before sixteene,
To shew him, the *Venetian cortezans.*
Nor read the grammar of cheating, I had made
To my sharpe boy, at twelve : repeating still
The rule, *Get money;* still, *Get money, Boy;*   15
No matter, by what meanes; Money will doe
More, Boy, then my Lords letter. Neither have I
Drest snailes, or mushromes curiously before him,
Perfum'd my sauces, and taught him to make 'hem;
Preceding still, with my grey gluttonie,   20
At all the ordinaries⁵ : and only fear'd⁶
His palate should degenerate, not his manners.
These are the trade of fathers, now! how ever
My sonne, I hope, hath met within my threshold,
None of these houshold precedents;(5) which are   25
                              strong,
And swift, to rape youth, to their precipice.
But, let the house at home be nere so cleane-
Swept, or kept sweet from filth; nay, dust, and cob-
                              webs :   30
If he will live, abroad, with his companions,
In dung, and leystalls⁷; it is worth a feare.
Nor is the danger of conversing lesse,
Then all that I have mention'd of example.[1]

³ *Portion :* Inherited capital.
⁴ *to seale :* to sign away their
property.

⁵ *ordinaries :* taverns.
⁶ *fear'd :* afraid.
⁷ *leystalls :* dung heaps.

42

[*Enter* BRAYNE-WORME.]

BRAYNE-WORME. [*Aside.*] My master? nay, faith have
at you : I am flesht[8] now, I have sped so well. Worshipfull sir, I beseech you, respect the estate of a
poore souldier; I am asham'd of this base course of   5
life (god's my comfort) but extremitie provokes me
to't, what remedie?

KNO'WELL. I have not for you, now.

BRAYNE-WORME. By the faith I beare unto truth, gentleman, it is no ordinarie custome in me, but only to   10
preserve manhood. I protest to you, a man I have
beene, a man I may be, by your sweet bountie.

KNO'WELL. 'Pray thee, good friend, be satisfied.

BRAYNE-WORME. Good sir, by that hand, you may doe
the part of a kind gentleman, in lending a poore soul-   15
dier the price of two cannes of beere (a matter of
small value) (6) the king of heaven shall pay you,
and I shall rest thankfull : sweet worship—

KNO'WELL. Nay, and you be so importunate—

BRAYNE-WORME. (*He weepes.*) Oh, tender sir, need will   20
have his course : I was not made to this vile use!
well, the edge of the enemie could not have abated
mee so much : It's hard when a man hath serv'd in
his Princes cause, and be thus—Honorable worship,
let me derive a small piece of silver from you, it shall   25
not bee given in the course of time,[9] by this good
ground, I was faine to pawne my rapier last night for
a poore supper, I had suck'd the hilts long before, I
am a pagan else : sweet honor.

KNO'WELL. Beleeve me, I am taken with some wonder,   30
To thinke a fellow of thy outward presence
Should (in the frame, and fashion of his mind)
Be so degenerate, and sordid-base!
Art thou a man? and sham'st thou not to beg?
To practise such a servile kind of life?   35

---

[8] *flesht :* aroused by success.   [9] *shall not . . . time :* shall be
repaid.

Why, were thy education ne're so meane,
Having thy limbs, a thousand fairer courses
Offer themselves, to thy election.
Either the warres might still supply thy wants,
Or service of some vertuous gentleman,   5
Or honest labour : nay, what can I name,
But would become thee better then to beg?
But men of thy condition feed on sloth,
As doth the beetle, on the dung shee breeds in,
Not caring how the mettall[7] of your minds   10
Is eaten with the rust of idlenesse.
Now, afore me, what e're he be, that should
Relieve a person of thy qualitie,
While thou insist's in this loose desperate course,
I would esteeme the sinne, not thine, but his.   15

BRAYNE-WORME. Faith sir, I would gladly finde some
   other course, if so—

KNO'WELL. I, you'ld gladly finde it, but you will not
   seeke it.

BRAYNE-WORME. Alas sir, where should a man seeke? in   20
   the warres, there's no ascent by desert in these dayes,
   but—and for service, would it were as soone purchast,
   as wisht for (the ayre's my comfort[10]) I know, what
   I would say—

KNO'WELL. What's thy name?   25

BRAYNE-WORME. Please you, Fitz-Sword,[2] sir.

KNO'WELL. Fitz-Sword?
   Say, that a man should entertayne thee now,
   Would'st thou be honest, humble, just, and true?

BRAYNE-WORME. Sir, by the place, and honor of a   30
   souldier—

KNO'WELL. Nay, nay, I like not those affected othes;
   Speake plainely man : what think'st thou of my
                                       wordes?

BRAYNE-WORME. Nothing, sir, but wish my fortunes   35
   were as happy, as my service should be honest.

---

[10] *comfort :* witness.

KNO'WELL. Well, follow me, Ile prove[11] thee, if thy
    deedes
Will carry a proportion to thy words.
BRAYNE-WORME. Yes sir, straight, Ile but garter my hose.
                              [*Exit* KNO'WELL.]   5
                                        O that
my belly were hoopt now, for I am readie to burst
with laughing! never was bottle, or bag-pipe fuller.[3]
S'lid, was there ever seene a foxe in yeeres to betray
himselfe thus? now shall I be possest of all his coun-   10
sells : and by that conduit,[12] my yong master. Well,
hee is resolv'd to prove my honestie; faith, and I am
resolv'd to prove his patience : oh I shall abuse him
intollerably. This small piece of service, will bring
him cleane out of love with the souldier, for ever.   15
He[4] will never come within the signe of it, the
sight of a cassock,[13] or a musket-rest[(8)] againe.[4]
Hee will hate the musters at Mile-end[(9)] for it, to
his dying day. It's no matter, let the world thinke me
a bad counterfeit, if I cannot give him the slip,[14] at   20
an instant : why, this is better then to have staid his
journey! well, Ile follow him : oh, how I long to bee
imployed.   [*Exit.*]

                                                    25

Act III. Scene i.

[*Enter*] MATTHEW, WELL-BRED, [*and*] BOBADILL.
[MATTHEW.] Yes faith, sir, we were at your lodging to
seeke you, too.   30
WELL-BRED. Oh, I came not there to night.
BOBADILL. Your brother delivered us as much.
WELL-BRED. Who? my brother Downe-Right?
BOBADILL. He. Master Well-Bred, I know not in what
kind you hold me, but let me say to you this : as sure   35

---

11 *prove :* test.   13 *cassock :* soldier's cloak.
12 *conduit :* guide.   14 *slip : Pun on* counterfeit coin.

as honor, I esteeme it so much out of the sunne-shine
of reputation, to through the least beame of reguard,
upon such a—

WELL-BRED. Sir, I must heare no ill wordes of my
brother.   5

BOBADILL. I, protest to you, as I have a thing to be sav'd
about me, I never saw any gentleman-like part—

WELL-BRED. Good Captayne, *faces about,* to some other
discourse.

BOBADILL. With your leave, sir, and there were no more   10
men living upon the face of the earth, I should not
fancie him, by St. George.

MATTHEW. Troth, nor I, he is of a rusticall cut, I know
not how : he doth not carry himselfe like a gentleman
of fashion—   15

WELL-BRED. Oh, Master Matthew, that's a grace peculiar but to a few; *quos aequus amavit Jupiter.* [1]

MATTHEW. I understand you sir.

WELL-BRED. No question, you doe, or you doe not, sir.
      Yong KNO'WELL *enters* [*with* STEPHEN].   20
Ned Kno'well! by my soule welcome; how doest thou
sweet spirit, my *Genius*[1]? S'lid I shall love Apollo,
and the mad *Thespian* girles[2] the better, while I live,
for this; my dear *furie :* now, I see there's some love
in thee! Sirra, these bee the two I writ to thee of (nay,   25
what a drowsie humour is this now? why doest thou
not speake?) [2]

E. KNO'WELL. Oh, you are a fine gallant, you sent me a
rare letter!

WELL-BRED. Why, was't not rare?   30

E. KNO'WELL. Yes, Ile bee sworne, I was ne're guiltie of
reading the like; match it in all Plinie, or Symmachus[3] epistles,[1] and Ile have my judgement
burn'd in the eare for a rogue : make much of thy
vaine, for it is inimitable. But I marle[3] what camell   35

ACT III. SCENE I.   [3] *marle :* marvel.
[1] *Genius :* Attendant spirit.   [2] *Thespian girles :* Muses.

46

it was, that had the carriage of it? for doubtlesse, he
was no ordinarie beast, that brought it!

WELL-BRED. Why?

E. KNO'WELL. Why, saiest thou? why doest thou thinke
that any reasonable creature, especially in the morn-   5
ing (the sober time of the day too) could have mis-
tane my father for me?

WELL-BRED. S'lid, you jest, I hope?

E. KNO'WELL. Indeed, the best use wee can turne it too,
is to make a jest on't, now : but Ile assure you, my   10
father had the full view o' your flourishing stile,[2]
some houre before I saw it.

WELL-BRED. What a dull slave was this? But, sirrah,
what said hee to it, Ifaith?

E. KNO'WELL. Nay, I know not what he said : but I have   15
a shrewd gesse what hee thought.

WELL-BRED. What? what?

E. KNO'WELL. Mary, that thou art some strange dissolute
yong fellow,[3] and I a graine or two better, for
keeping thee companie.   20

WELL-BRED. Tut, that thought is like the moone in her
last quarter, 'twill change shortly : but, sirrha, I pray
thee be acquainted with my two hang-by's,[4] here;
thou wilt take exceeding pleasure in 'hem if thou
hear'st 'hem once goe : my wind-instruments. Ile   25
wind 'hem up—but what strange piece of silence is
this? the signe of the dumbe man⁴?

E. KNO'WELL. Oh sir, a kinsman of mine, one that may
make your musique the fuller, and he please, he has
his humour, sir.   30

WELL-BRED. Oh, what ist? what ist?

E. KNO'WELL. Nay, Ile neither doe your judgement, nor
his folly that wrong, as to prepare your apprehension : Ile leave him to the mercy o' your search, if
you can take him, so.   35

---

⁴ *dumbe man :* sign-board of an
inn.

WELL-BRED. (*To* MASTER STEPHEN.) Well, Captaine
Bobadill, Master Matthew, pray you know this gentleman here, he is a friend of mine, and one that will
deserve your affection. I know not your name sir, but
I shall be glad of any occasion, to render me more   5
familiar to you.

STEPHEN. My name is Master Stephen, sir, I am this
gentlemans owne cousin, sir, his father is mine unckle,
sir, I am somewhat melancholy, but you shall command me, sir, in whatsoever is incident to a gentle-   10
man.

BOBADILL. (*To* KNO'WELL.) Sir, I must tell you this, I
am no generall man,[5] but for Master Well-Bred's sake
(you may embrace it, at what height of favour you
please) I doe communicate with you : and conceive   15
you, to bee a gentleman of some parts, I love few
wordes.

E. KNO'WELL.[5] And I fewer, sir. I have scarce inow,
to thanke you.[5]

MATTHEW. (*To* MASTER STEPHEN.) But are you indeed,   20
sir? so given to it?

STEPHEN. I, truely, sir, I am mightily given to melancholy.

MATTHEW. Oh, it's your only fine humour, sir, your true
melancholy, breeds your perfect fine wit, sir : I am   25
melancholy my selfe divers times, sir, and then doe I
no more but take pen, and paper presently, and overflow you halfe a score, or a dozen of sonnets, at a
sitting.

(E. KNO'WELL. Sure, he utters[6] them then, by the   30
grosse.) [4]

STEPHEN. Truely sir, and I love such things, out of
measure.

E. KNO'WELL. I faith,[5] better then in measure, Ile
under-take.   35

---

[5] *general man :* familiar with   [6] *utters : Pun on* sells, *or* circu-
many.   lates.

MATTHEW. Why, I pray you, sir, make use of my studie,
it's at your service.

STEPHEN. I thanke you sir, I shall bee bold, I warrant
you; have you a stoole there, to be melancholy' upon?

MATTHEW. That I have, sir, and some papers there of   5
mine owne doing, at idle houres, that you'le say
there's some sparkes of wit in 'hem, when you see
them.

WELL-BRED. [*Aside.*] Would the sparkes would kindle
once, and become a fire amongst 'hem, I might see   10
selfe-love burn't for her heresie.

STEPHEN. Cousin, is it well? am I melancholy inough?

E. KNO'WELL. Oh I, excellent!

WELL-BRED. Captaine Bobadill: why muse you so?

E. KNO'WELL. He is melancholy, too.   15

BOBADILL. Faith, sir, I was thinking of a most honorable
piece of service, was perform'd to morrow, being St.
Markes day: shall bee some ten yeeres, now?

E. KNO'WELL. In what place, Captaine?

BOBADILL. Why, at the beleag'ring of *Strigonium*,(6)   20
where, in lesse then two houres, seven hundred resolute gentlemen, as any were in *Europe*, lost their lives
upon the breach. Ile tell you, gentlemen, it was the
first, but the best league, that ever I beheld, with
these eies, except the taking in of—what doe you call   25
it,[6] last yeere, by the *Genowayes*, but that (of all
other) was the most fatall, and dangerous exploit,
that ever I was rang'd in, since I first bore armes before the face of the enemie, as I am a gentleman, &
souldier.   30

STEPHEN. 'So, I had as liefe, as an angell, I could sweare
as well as that gentleman!

E. KNO'WELL. Then, you were a servitor, at both it
seemes! at *Strigonium*? and what doe you call't?[7]

BOBADILL. Oh lord, sir? by St. George, I was the first   35
man, that entred the breach: and, had I not effected
it with resolution, I had beene slaine, if I had had a
million of lives.

E. KNO'WELL. 'Twas pittie, you had not ten; a cats, and
your owne, ifaith. But, was it possible?

(MATTHEW. 'Pray you, marke this discourse, sir.

STEPHEN. So, I doe.)

BOBADILL. I assure you (upon my reputation) 'tis true,   5
and your selfe shall confesse.

E. KNO'WELL. [*Aside.*] You must bring me to the racke,
first.

BOBADILL. Observe me judicially, sweet sir, they had
planted mee three demi-culverings,(7) just in the   10
mouth of the breach; now, sir (as we were to give
on7) their master gunner (a man of no meane skill,
and marke, you must thinke) confronts me with his
linstock,8 readie to give fire; I spying his intendment,
discharg'd my petrionel9 in his bosome, and with   15
these single armes, my poore rapier, ranne violently,
upon the *Moores*, that guarded the ordinance, and
put 'hem pell-mell to the sword.

WELL-BRED. To the sword? to the rapier, Captaine?

E. KNO'WELL. Oh, it was a good figure observ'd, sir! but   20
did you all this, Captaine, without hurting your blade?

BOBADILL. Without any impeach,10 o' the earth : you
shall perceive sir. It is the most fortunate weapon,
that ever rid on poore gentlemans thigh : shal I tell
you, sir? you talke of *Morglay*,(8) *Excalibur, Durin-*   25
dana, or so? tut, I lend no credit to that is fabled of
'hem, I know the vertue of mine owne, and therefore
I dare, the boldlier, maintaine it.

STEPHEN. I mar'le whether it be a *Toledo*, or no?

BOBADILL. A most perfect *Toledo*, I assure you, sir.   30

STEPHEN. I have a countriman of his, here.

MATTHEW. Pray you, let's see, sir : yes faith, it is!

BOBADILL. This a *Toledo?* pish.

STEPHEN. Why doe you pish, Captaine?

BOBADILL. A *Fleming*, by heaven, Ile buy them for a   35

---

7 *give on* : attack.   9 *petrionel* : large pistol.
8 *linstock* : igniting stick.   10 *impeach* : injury.

guilder,[9] a piece, an' I would have a thousand of them.

E. KNO'WELL. How say you, cousin? I told you thus much?

WELL-BRED. Where bought you it, Master Stephen? 5

STEPHEN. Of a scurvie rogue souldier (a hundred of lice goe with him) he swore it was a *Toledo.*

BOBADILL. A poore provant[11] rapier, no better.

MATTHEW. Masse, I thinke it be, indeed! now I looke on't, better. 10

E. KNO'WELL. Nay, the longer you looke on't, the worse. Put it up, put it up.

STEPHEN. Well, I will put it up, but by—(I ha' forgot the Captaynes oath, I thought to ha' sworne by it) an' ere I meet him— 15

WELL-BRED. O, it is past helpe now, sir, you must have patience.

STEPHEN. Horson connie-catching[12] raskall! I could eate the very hilts for anger!

E. KNO'WELL. A signe of good digestion! you have an 20
ostrich stomack, cousin.

STEPHEN. A stomack? would I had him here, you should see, an' I had a stomack.

WELL-BRED. It's better as 'tis: come, gentlemen, shall we goe? 25

Act III. Scene ii.

[Enter] BRAYNE-WORME.

[E. KNO'WELL.] A miracle, cousin, looke here! looke 30
here!

STEPHEN. Oh, gods lid, by your leave, doe you know me, sir?

BRAYNE-WORME. I sir, I know you, by sight. 35

---

[11] *provant :* Government issue   [12] *connie-catching :* swindling.
(inferior).

51

STEPHEN. You sold me a rapier, did you not?

BRAYNE-WORME. Yes, marie, did I sir.

STEPHEN. You said, it was a *Toledo,* ha?

BRAYNE-WORME. True, I did so.

STEPHEN. But, it is none? 5

BRAYNE-WORME. No sir, I confesse it, it is none.

STEPHEN. Doe you confesse it? gentlemen, beare witnesse, he has confest it. By gods will, and you had not
confest it—

E. KNO'WELL. Oh cousin, forbeare, forbeare. 10

STEPHEN. Nay, I have done, cousin.

WELL-BRED. Why you have done like a gentleman, he
ha's confest it, what would you more?

STEPHEN. Yet, by his leave, he is a raskall, under his
favour, doe you see? 15

E. KNO'WELL. I, by his leave, he is, and under favour :
a prettie piece of civilitie! [*Aside.*] Sirra, how doest
thou like him?

WELL-BRED. Oh, it's a most pretious foole, make much
on him : I can compare him to nothing more happily, 20
then a drumme[1]; for every one may play upon
him.

E. KNO'WELL.[2] No, no, a childes whistle were farre
the fitter.[2]

BRAYNE-WORME. Sir, shall I intreat a word with you? 25

E. KNO'WELL. With me, sir? you have not another
Toledo to sell, ha' you?

BRAYNE-WORME. You are conceipted,[1] sir, your name
is Master Kno'well, as I take it?

E. KNO'WELL. You are i' the right; you meane not to 30
proceede in the catechisme, doe you?

BRAYNE-WORME. No sir, I am none of that coat.[2]

E. KNO'WELL. Of as bare a coat, though? well, say sir.

BRAYNE-WORME. Faith sir, I am but servant to the drum
extraordinarie, and indeed (this smokie varnish being 35

ACT III. SCENE II.

[1] *conceipted :* witty.   [2] *that coat :* the clergy.

washt off, and three or four patches remov'd) I appeare your worships in reversion,[3] after the decease
of your good father, Brayne-Worme.

E. KNO'WELL. Brayne-Worme! S'light, what breath of a
conjurer, hath blowne thee hither in this shape?   5

BRAYNE-WORME. The breath o' your letter, sir, this morning : the same that blew you to the Wind-Mill, and
your father after you.

E. KNO'WELL. My father?

BRAYNE-WORME. Nay, never start, 'tis true, he has fol-   10
low'd you over the field's by the foot, as you would
doe a hare i' the snow.

E. KNO'WELL. Sirra, Well-Bred, what shall we doe, sirra?
my father is come over, after me.

WELL-BRED. Thy father? where is he?   15

BRAYNE-WORME. At Justice Clements house here, in
Colman-street,[(1)] where he but staies my returne;
and then—

WELL-BRED. Who's this? Brayne-Worme?

BRAYNE-WORME. The same, sir.   20

WELL-BRED. Why how, i' the name of wit, com'st thou
trans-muted, thus?

BRAYNE-WORME. Faith, a devise, a devise : nay, for the
love of reason, gentlemen, and avoiding the danger,
stand not here, withdraw, and Ile tell you all.   25

WELL-BRED. But, art thou sure, he will stay thy returne?

BRAYNE-WORME. Doe I live, sir? what a question is that?

WELL-BRED. Wee'le prorogue[4] his expectation then, a little : Brayne-Worme, thou shalt goe with us. Come on,
gentlemen, nay, I pray thee, sweet Ned, droope not :   30
'heart, and our wits be so wretchedly dull, that one
old plodding braine can out-strip us all, would we
were eene prest,[5] to make porters of; and serve out
the remnant of our daies, in *Thames*-street, or at

---

[3] *in reversion :* by inheritance.   [5] *prest :* forced into service.
[4] *prorogue :* delay (*legal term*).

Custome-house key, in a civill warre, against the car-
men.(2)

BRAYNE-WORME. Amen, Amen, Amen, say I. [*Exeunt*.]

5

ACT III. SCENE III.

[*Enter*] KITELY [*and*] CASH.

[KITELY.] What saies he, Thomas? Did you speake with
him? 10

CASH. He will expect you, sir, within this halfe houre.

KITELY. Has he the money readie, can you tell?

CASH. Yes, sir, the money was brought in, last night.

KITELY. O,(1) that's well : fetch me my cloke, my
cloke. 15

Stay, let me see, an houre, to goe and come;
I, that will be the least : and then 'twill be
An houre, before I can dispatch with him;
Or very neere : well, I will say two houres.
Two houres? ha? things, never dreamt of yet, 20
May be contriv'd, I, and effected too,
In two houres absence : well, I will not goe.
Two houres; no, fleering oportunitie,
I will not give your subtilitie that scope.
Who will not judge him worthie to be rob'd, 25
That sets his doores wide open to a thiefe,
And shewes the fellon, where his treasure lies?
Againe, what earthie spirit but will attempt
To taste the fruit of beauties golden tree,
When leaden sleepe seales up the Dragons eyes? 30
I will not goe. Businesse, goe by, for once.
No[1] beautie, no; you are of too good caract,¹
To be left so, without a guard, or open!
Your lustre too'll enflame, at any distance,
Draw courtship to you, as a jet doth strawes,(2) 35

ACT III. SCENE III.
¹ *caract :* carat; value.

54

Put motion in a stone, strike fire from ice,
Nay, make a porter leape[3] you, with his burden!
You must be then kept up, close, and well-watch'd,
For, give you oportunitie, no quick-sand
Devoures, or swallowes swifter! He that lends   5
His wife (if shee be faire) or time, or place;
Compells her to be false. I will not goe.
The dangers are to many. And, then, the dressing
Is a most mayne attractive! Our great heads,
Within the citie, never were in safetie,   10
Since our wives wore these little caps[4] : Ile change
                    'hem,
Ile change 'hem, streight, in mine. Mine shall no more
Weare three-pild akornes, to make my hornes ake.[4]
Nor, will I goe. I am resolv'd for that.   15
Carry' in my cloke againe. Yet, stay. Yet, doe too.
I will deferre going, on all occasions.[1]

CASH. Sir. Snare, your scrivener, will be there with
    th'bonds.
KITELY. That's true! foole on me! I had cleane forgot it, 20
    I must goe. What's a clocke?
CASH.   *Exchange* time,[5] sir.
KITELY. 'Heart, then will Well-Bred presently be here,
                    too,
With one, or other of his loose consorts.   25
I am a knave, if I know what to say,
What course to take, or which way to resolve.
My braine (me thinkes) is like an houre-glasse,
Wherein, my' imaginations runne, like sands,
Filling up time; but then are turn'd, and turn'd :   30
So, that I know not what to stay upon,
And lesse, to put in act. It shall be so.
Nay, I dare build upon his secrecie,
He knowes not to deceive me. Thomas?
CASH.   Sir.   35
KITELY. Yet now, I have bethought me, too, I will not.
    Thomas, is Cob within?
CASH.   I thinke he be, sir.

KITELY. But hee'll prate too, there's no speech of him.
No, there were no man o' the earth to Thomas,
If I durst trust him; there is all the doubt.
But, should he have a chinke in him, I were gone,
Lost i' my fame for ever : talke for th'Exchange.   5
The manner he hath stood with, till this present,
Doth promise no such change! what should I feare
                                    then?
Well, come what will, Ile tempt my fortune, once.
Thomas—you may deceive me, but, I hope—   10
Your love, to me, is more—
CASH.   Sir, if a servants
Duetie, with faith, may be call'd love, you are
More then in hope, you are possess'd of it.
KITELY. I thanke you, heartily, Thomas; Gi' me your   15
                                    hand :
With all my heart, good Thomas. I have, Thomas,
A secret to impart, unto you—but
When once you have it, I must seale your lips up :
(So farre, I tell you, Thomas.)   20
CASH.   Sir, for that—
KITELY. Nay, heare me, out. Thinke, I esteeme you,
                                    Thomas,
When, I will let you in, thus, to my private.[2]
It is a thing sits, neerer, to my crest,[3]   25
Then thou art ware of, Thomas. If thou should'st
Reveale it, but—
CASH.   How? I reveale it?
KITELY.   Nay,
I doe not thinke thou would'st; but if thou should'st : 30
'Twere a great weakenesse.
CASH.   A great trecherie.
Give it no other name.
KITELY.   Thou wilt not do't, then?
CASH. Sir, if I doe, mankind disclaime me, ever.   35

---

[2] *private :* personal matters.   [3] *crest :* family honor; forehead
                                             (*suggesting horns*).

KITELY. [*Aside.*] He will not sweare, he has some
                reservation,
  Some conceal'd purpose, and close meaning, sure :
  Else (being urg'd so much) how should he choose,
  But lend an oath to all this protestation?   5
  H'is no precision,[4] that I am certaine of.
  Nor rigid *Roman*-catholike. Hee'll play,
  At *Fayles*, and *Tick-tack*,[5] I have heard him sweare.
  What should I thinke of it? urge him againe,
  And by some other way? I will doe so.   10
  Well, Thomas, thou hast sworne not to disclose;
  Yes, you did sweare?
CASH.   Not yet, sir, but I will,
  Please you—
KITELY.   No, Thomas, I dare take thy word.   15
  But; if thou wilt sweare, doe, as thou think'st good;
  I am resolv'd without it; at thy pleasure.
CASH. By my soules safetie then, sir, I protest.
  My tongue shall ne're take knowledge of a word,
  Deliver'd me in nature of your trust.   20
KITELY. It's too much, these ceremonies need not,
  I know thy faith to be as firme as rock.
  Thomas, come hither, neere : we cannot be
  Too private, in this businesse. So it is,
  (Now, he ha's sworne, I dare the safelier venter)   25
  I have of late, by divers observations—
  (But, whether his oath can bind him, yea, or no;
  Being not taken lawfully? ha? say?
  I will aske counsell, ere I doe proceed :)
  Thomas, it will be now too long to stay,   30
  Ile spie some fitter time soone, or to morrow.
CASH. Sir, at your pleasure?
KITELY.   I will thinke. And, Thomas,
  I pray you search the bookes 'gainst my returne,
  For the receipts 'twixt me, and Traps.   35

[4] *precision :* Puritan.   [5] *Fayles, Tick-tack :* Back-
                                    gammon games.

CASH.   I will, sir.

KITELY. And, heare you, if your mistris brother, Well-
                  Bred,
Chance to bring hither any gentlemen,
Ere I come backe; let one straight bring me word.   5

CASH. Very well, sir.

KITELY.   To the Exchange; doe you heare?
Or here in *Colman*-street, to Justice Clements.
Forget it not, nor be not out of the way.

CASH. I will not, sir.   10

KITELY.   I pray you have a care on't.
Or whether he come, or no, if any other,
Stranger, or else, faile not to send me word.

CASH. I shall not, sir.

KITELY.   Be't your speciall businesse   15
Now, to remember it.

CASH.   Sir. I warrant you.

KITELY. But, Thomas, this is not the secret, Thomas,
I told you of.

CASH.   No, sir. I doe suppose it.   20

KITELY. Beleeve me, it is not.

CASH.   Sir. I doe beleeve you.

KITELY. By heaven, it is not, that's enough. But, Thomas,
I would not, you should utter it, doe you see?
To any creature living, yet, I care not.   25
Well, I must hence. Thomas, conceive thus much.
It was a tryall of you, when I meant
So deepe a secret to you, I meane not this,
But that I have to tell you, this is nothing, this.
But, Thomas, keepe this from my wife, I charge you,   30
Lock'd up in silence, mid-night, buried here.
No greater hell, then to be slave to feare.   [*Exit.*]

CASH. Lock'd up in silence, mid-night, buried here.
Whence should this floud of passion (trow) take
                  head? ha?   35
Best, dreame no longer of this running humour,
For feare I sinke! the violence of the streame
Alreadie hath transported me so farre,

58

That I can feele no ground at all! but soft,
Oh, 'tis our water-bearer : somewhat ha's crost him,
    now.

Act III. Scene iv.

[Enter] cob.

[cob.] Fasting dayes? what tell you me of fasting
dayes?[1] S'lid, would they were all on a light fire
for me : They say, the whole world shall bee consum'd with fire one day, but would I had these
ember-weekes, and villanous fridayes burnt, in the
meane time, and then—

cash. Why, how now Cob, what moves thee to this
choller? ha?

cob. Collar, master Thomas? I scorne your collar, I sir,
I am none o' your cart-horse, though I carry, and
draw water. An' you offer to ride me, with your collar,
or halter either, I may hap shew you a jades trick,
sir.

cash. O, you'll slip your head out of the collar? why,
goodman Cob, you mistake me.

cob. Nay, I have my rewme,[1, (2)] & I can be angrie as
well as another, sir.

cash. Thy rewme, Cob? thy humour, thy humour? thou
mistak'st.

cob. Humour? mack,[2] I thinke it be so, indeed : what
is that humour? some rare thing, I warrant.

cash. Mary, Ile tell thee, Cob : It is a gentleman-like
monster, bred, in the speciall gallantrie of our
time,[1] by affectation; and fed by folly.

cob. How? must it be fed?

cash. Oh I, humour is nothing, if it bee not fed. Didst

thou never heare that? it's a common phrase, *Feed
my humour.*

COB. Ile none on it : Humour, avaunt, I know you not,
be gone. Let who will make hungrie meales for your
monster-ship, it shall not bee I. Feed you, quoth he? 5
S'lid, I ha' much adoe, to feed my selfe; especially,
on these leane rascally dayes, too; and't had beene
any other day, but a fasting-day (a plague on them
all for mee) by this light, one might have done the
common-wealth good service, and have drown'd them 10
all i' the floud, two or three hundred thousand yeeres
agoe. O, I doe stomack³ them hugely! I have a maw
now, and't were for Sir Bevis his horse, against 'hem.

CASH. I pray thee, good Cob, what makes thee so out
of love with fasting-dayes? 15

COB. Mary that, which will make any man out of love
with 'hem, I thinke : their bad conditions, and you
will needs know. First, they are of a *Flemmish*(3)
breed, I am sure on't, for they raven up more butter,(3) then all the dayes of the weeke, beside; next, 20
they stinke of fish, and leeke-porridge miserably :
thirdly, they'le keepe a man devoutly hungrie, all day,
and at night send him supperlesse to bed.

CASH. Indeed, these are faults, Cob.

COB. (*He pulls out a red herring.*) Nay, and this were 25
all, 'twere something, but they are the only knowne
enemies, to my generation. A fasting-day, no sooner
comes, but my lineage goes to racke, poore cobs they
smoke for it, they are made martyrs o' the gridiron,
they melt in passion : and your maides too know this, 30
and yet would have me turne Hannibal,⁴ and eate
my owne fish, and bloud : My princely couz, fear
nothing; I have not the hart to devoure you, & I
might be made as rich as King Cophetua.(4) O, that
I had roome for my teares, I could weepe salt-water 35

---

³ *stomack* : resent; suffer hunger   ⁴ *Hannibal* : for "cannibal."
for.

enough, now, to preserve the lives of ten thousand of
my kin. But, I may curse none but these filthie
Almanacks, for an't were not for them, these dayes of
persecution would ne're be knowne. Ile bee hang'd,
an' some Fish-mongers sonne doe not make of   5
'hem[2]; and puts in more fasting-dayes then he
should doe, because hee would utter[5] his fathers
dryed stock-fish, and stinking conger.(5)

CASH. S'light, peace, thou'lt bee beaten like a stock-fish,
else : here is Master Matthew. Now must I looke out   10
for a messenger to my master.   [*Exeunt.*]

ACT III. SCENE V.

15

[*Enter*] WELL-BRED, E. KNO'WELL, BRAYNE-WORME,
    BOBADILL, MATTHEW, [*and*] STEPHEN.

[WELL-BRED.] Beshrew me, but it was an absolute good
jest, and exceedingly well carried!

E. KNO'WELL. I, and our ignorance maintain'd it as well,   20
did it not?

WELL-BRED. Yes faith, but was't possible thou should'st
not know him? I forgive Master Stephen, for he is
stupiditie it selfe!

E. KNO'WELL. 'Fore god, not I, and I might have been   25
joyn'd patten[1] with one of the seven wise masters,(1)
for knowing him. He had so writhen[2] himselfe, into
the habit of one of your poore *Infanterie,* your
decay'd, ruinous, worme-eaten gentlemen of the
round[3] : such as have vowed to sit on the skirts of the   30
citie, let your Provost, and his halfe-dozen of halber-
diers doe what they can; and have translated begging
out of the old hackney pace, to a fine easie amble,

---

[5] *utter :* sell.
    ACT III. SCENE V.
[1] *joyn'd patten :* made official
    by letter patent.

[2] *writhen :* distorted.
[3] *gentlemen of the round :*
    sentries.

and made it runne as smooth, of the tongue, as a
shove-groat shilling.[2] Into the likenesse of one of
these *Reformado's*[3] had he moulded himselfe so
perfectly, observing every tricke of their action, as
varying the accent, swearing with an *emphasis*, in-   5
deed all, with so speciall, and exquisite a grace, that
(hadst thou seene him) thou would'st have sworne,
he might have beene Serjeant-*Major*,[4] if not Lieu-
tenant-*Coronell* to the regiment.

WELL-BRED. Why, Brayne-Worme, who would have   10
thought thou hadst beene such an artificer?[1]

E. KNO'WELL. An artificer![2] An architect! except a
man had studied begging all his life-time, and beene
a weaver of language, from his infancie, for the
clothing of it! I never saw his rivall.   15

WELL-BRED. Where got'st thou this coat, I mar'le?

BRAYNE-WORME. Of a *Hounds-ditch* man,[5] sir. One
of the devil's neere kinsmen, a broker.

WELL-BRED. That cannot be, if the proverbe hold; for,
a craftie knave needs no broker.   20

BRAYNE-WORME. True sir, but I did need a broker, *Ergo*.

WELL-BRED. (Well put off) no craftie knave, you'll say.

E. KNO'WELL. Tut, he ha's more of these shifts.[6]

BRAYNE-WORME. And yet where I have one, the broker
ha's ten, sir.   25

[*Enter* CASH.]

CASH. Francis, Martin, ne're a one to be found, now?
what a spite's this?

WELL-BRED. How now, Thomas? is my brother Kitely,
within?   30

CASH. No sir, my master went forth eene now : but master Downe-Right is within. Cob, what Cob? is he gone
too?

WELL-BRED. Whither went your master? Thomas, canst
thou tell?   35

CASH. I know not, to Justice Clements, I thinke, sir. Cob.

[*Exit.*]

E. KNO'WELL. Justice Clement, what's he?

62

WELL-BRED. Why, doest thou not know him? he is a citie-magistrate, a Justice here, and excellent good Lawyer, and a great scholler : but the onely mad, merrie, old fellow in *Europe!* I shew'd him you, the other day. 5

E. KNO'WELL. Oh, is that he? I remember him now. Good faith, and he ha's a very strange presence, mee thinkes; it shewes as if hee stood out of the ranke, from other men : I have heard many of his jests i' *universitie.* They say, he will commit a man, for tak- 10 ing the wall, of his horse.

WELL-BRED. I, or wearing his cloke of one shoulder, or serving of god : any thing indeed, if it come in the way of his humour.

[*Enter* CASH.] 15

CASH. (CASH *goes in and out calling.*) Gasper, Martin, Cob : 'heart, where should they be, trow?

BOBADILL. Master Kitely's man, 'pray thee vouchsafe us the lighting of this match.

CASH. Fire on your match, no time but now to vouch- 20 safe? Francis. Cob. [*Exit.*]

BOBADILL. Bodie of me! here's the remainder of seven pound, since yesterday was seven-night. 'Tis your right *Trinidado*[4]! did you never take any, master Stephen? 25

STEPHEN. No truely, sir; but I'le learne to take it now, since you commend it, so.

BOBADILL. Sir, beleeve mee (upon my relation) for what I tell you, the world shal not reprove. I have been in the *Indies* (where this herb growes) where neither 30 my selfe, nor a dozen gentlemen more (of my knowl- edge) have received the tast of any other nutriment, in the world, for the space of one and twentie weekes, but the fume of this simple onely. Therefore, it can- not be, but 'tis most divine! Further, take it in the 35 nature, in the true kind so, it makes an *antidote,* that

---

[4] *Trinidado :* a tobacco.

(had you taken the most deadly poysonous plant in all *Italy*), it should expell it, and clarifie you, with as much ease, as I speake. And, for your greene wound, your *Balsamum*, and your St. John's *woort*[5] are all mere gulleries, and trash to it, especially your *Trini-* 5 *dado*: your *Nicotian*[7] is good too. I could say what I know of the vertue of it, for the expulsion of rhewmes,[8] raw humours, crudities, obstructions, with a thousand of this kind; but I professe my selfe no *quack-salver*. Only, thus much, by Hercules, I doe 10 hold it, and will affirme it (before any Prince in *Europe*) to be the most soveraigne, and precious weede, that ever the earth tendred to the use of man.

E. KNO'WELL. This speech would ha' done decently in a *tabacco*-traders mouth![9]   15

[*Enter* CASH *and* COB.]

CASH. At Justice Clements, hee is: in the middle of *Colman*-street.

COB. O, oh?

BOBADILL. Where's the match I gave thee? Master   20 Kitelies man?

CASH. Would his match, and he, and pipe, and all were at Sancto Domingo! I had forgot it.   [*Exit.*]

COB. By gods mee, I marle, what pleasure, or felicitie they have in taking this roguish *tabacco!* it's good for   25 nothing, but to choke a man, and fill him full of smoke, and embers: there were foure dyed out of one house, last weeke, with taking of it, and two more the bell went for, yester-night; one of them (they say) will ne're scape it; he voided a bushell of soot   30 yester-day, upward, and downeward. By the stocks, an' there were no wiser men then I, I'ld have it pres- ent whipping, man, or woman, that should but deale with a *tabacco*-pipe; why, it will stifle them all in the

---

[5] *woort*: weed; herb.

end, as many as use it; it's little better then ratsbane, or rosaker.[6]

   BOBADILL *beates him with a cudgell.*

ALL. Oh, good Captayne, hold, hold.

BOBADILL. You base cullion,[10] you.   5

   [*Enter* CASH.]

CASH. Sir, here's your match : come, thou must needs be
talking, too, tho'art well inough serv'd.

COB. Nay, he will not meddle with his match, I warrant
you : well it shall be a deare beating, and I live. 10

BOBADILL. Doe you prate? Doe you murmure?

E. KNO'WELL. Nay, good Captayne, will you regard the
humour of a foole? away, knave.

WELL-BRED. Thomas, get him away.

   [*Exeunt* CASH *and* COB.] 15

BOBADILL. A horson filthie slave, a dung-worme, an ex-
crement! Body o' Caesar, but that I scorne to let forth
so meane a spirit, I'ld ha' stab'd him, to the earth.

WELL-BRED. Mary, the law forbid, sir.

BOBADILL. By Pharoahs foot, I would have done it. 20

STEPHEN. Oh, he sweares admirably! (by Pharoahs
foot) (body of Caesar) I shall never doe it, sure
(upon mine honor, and by Saint George) no, I ha'
not the right grace.

MATTHEW. Master Stephen, will you any? By this aire, 25
the most divine *tabacco*, that ever I drunke[7]!

STEPHEN. None, I thanke you, sir. O, this gentleman do's
it, rarely too! but nothing like the other. By this aire,
as I am a gentleman : by—

   [*Exeunt* BOBADILL *and* MATTHEW.] 30

BRAYNE-WORME. Master, glance, glance! Master Well-
Bred!

   MASTER STEPHEN *is practising, to the post.*[11]

STEPHEN. As I have somewhat to be saved, I protest—

---

[6] *rosaker :* Arsenic   [7] *drunke :* smoked.
(like ratsbane).

WELL-BRED. [*Aside.*] You are a foole: It needes no
    affidavit.

E. KNO'WELL. Cousin, will you any *tabacco*?

STEPHEN. I sir! upon my reputation—

E. KNO'WELL. How now, cousin!   5

STEPHEN. I protest, as I am a gentleman, but no souldier,
    indeed—

WELL-BRED. No, Master Stephen? as I remember your
    name is entred in the artillerie garden?[12]

STEPHEN. I sir, that's true: Cousin, may I swear, as I   10
    am a souldier, by that?

E. KNO'WELL. Oh yes, that you may. It's all you have
    for your money.

STEPHEN. Then, as I am a gentleman, and a souldier, it
    is divine *tabacco!*   15

WELL-BRED. But soft, where's Master Matthew? gone?

BRAYNE-WORME. No, sir, they went in here.

WELL-BRED. O, let's follow them: master Matthew is
    gone to salute his mistris, in verse. Wee shall ha' the
    happinesse, to heare some of his poetrie, now. Hee   20
    never comes unfurnish'd. Brayne-Worme?

STEPHEN. Brayne-Worme? Where? Is this Brayne-
    Worme?

E. KNO'WELL. I, cousin, no wordes of it, upon your
    gentilitie.   25

STEPHEN. Not I, body of me, by this aire, St. George,
    and the foot of Pharoah.

WELL-BRED. Rare! your cousins discourse is simply
    drawn out with oathes.

E. KNO'WELL. 'Tis larded with 'hem. A kind of french   30
    dressing,[13] if you love it.   [*Exeunt.*]

ACT III. SCENE VI.

                                                                35

[*Enter*] KITELY [*and*] COB.

[KITELY.] Ha? how many are there, sayest thou?

COB. Mary sir, your brother, master Well-Bred—

KITELY. Tut, beside him : what strangers are there, man?

COB. Strangers? let me see, one, two; masse I know not
well, there are so many.

KITELY. How? so many?

COB. I, there's some five, or sixe of them, at the most.   5

KITELY. A swarme, a swarme,
Spight of the devill, how they sting my head[1]
With forked stings, thus wide, and large! But,
Cob,[2]

How long hast thou beene comming hither, Cob?   10

COB. A little while, sir.

KITELY. Did'st thou come running?

COB. No, sir.

KITELY. Nay, then I am familiar with thy haste!
Bane to my fortunes : what meant I to marry?   15
I, that before was rankt in such content,
My mind at rest too, in so soft a peace,
Being free master of mine owne free thoughts,
And now become a slave? What? never sigh,
Be of good cheere, man : for thou art a cuckold,   20
'Tis done, 'tis done! nay, when such flowing store,
Plentie it selfe, falls in my wives lap,
The *Cornu-copiae*[1] will be mine, I know. But, Cob,
What entertaynement had they? I am sure
My sister, and my wife, would bid them welcome! ha?   25

COB. Like inough, sir, yet, I heard not a word of it.

KITELY. No : their lips were seal'd with kisses, and the
voyce
Drown'd in a floud of joy, at their arrivall,
Had lost her motion, state, and facultie.   30
Cob, which of them was't, that first kist my wife?
(My sister, I should say) my wife, alas,
I feare not her : ha? who was it, say'st thou?

COB. By my troth, sir, will you have the truth of it?

Act III. Scene vi.
1 *Cornu-copiae :* Horn of
Plenty.

KITELY. Oh I, good Cob : I pray thee, heartily.

COB. Then, I am a vagabond, and fitter for *Bride-well*,[1] then your worships companie, if I saw any bodie to be kist, unlesse they would have kist the post, in the middle of the ware-house; for there I left them all, at their *tabacco*, with a poxe. 5

KITELY. How? were they not gone in, then, e're thou cam'st?

COB. Oh no sir.

KITELY. Spite of the devill! what[2] doe I stay here, then? Cob, follow me. [*Exit.*] 10

COB. Nay, soft and faire, I have egges on the spit;[3] I cannot goe yet, sir. Now am I for some five and fiftie reasons hammering, hammering revenge : oh, for three or foure gallons of vineger, to sharpen my wits. 15 Revenge : vineger revenge : vineger, and mustard revenge[3] : nay, and hee had not lyen in my house, 't would never have griev'd me, but being my guest, one, that Ile be sworne, my wife ha's lent him her smock off her back, while his one shirt ha's beene at 20 washing; pawn'd her neckerchers for cleane bands[4] for him; sold almost all my platters, to buy him *tabacco;* and he to turne monster of ingratitude, and strike his lawfull host! well, I hope to raise up an host of furie for't : here comes Justice Clement. 25

ACT III. SCENE VII.

[*Enter*] CLEMENT, KNO'WELL, [*and*] FORMALL.

[CLEMENT.] What's master Kitely gone? Roger? 30

FORMALL. I, sir.

CLEMENT. 'Hart of me! what made him leave us so abruptly! How now, sirra? what make you here? what would you have, ha?

COB. And't please your worship, I am a poore neighbour 35 of your worships—

CLEMENT. A poore neighbour of mine? why, speake poore neighbour.

68

COB. I dwell, sir, at the signe of the water-tankerd, hard
by the Greene Lattice[1, (1)] : I have paid scot, and
lot[2] there, any time this eighteene yeeres.

CLEMENT. To the Greene Lattice?

COB. No, sir, to the parish : mary, I have seldome scap't   5
scot-free, at the Lattice.

CLEMENT. O, well! what businesse ha's my poore neighbour with me?

COB. And't like your worship, I am come, to crave the
peace of your worship.   10

CLEMENT. Of mee knave? peace of mee, knave? did I
e're hurt thee? or threaten thee? or wrong thee? ha?

COB. No, sir, but your worships warrant, for one that
ha's wrong'd me, sir : his armes are at too much
libertie, I would faine have them bound to a treatie   15
of peace, an' my credit could compasse it, with your
worship.

CLEMENT. Thou goest farre inough about for't, I am
sure.

KNO'WELL. Why, doest thou goe in danger of thy life   20
for him? friend?

COB. No, sir; but I goe in danger of my death, every
houre, by his meanes : an' I die, within a twelve-
moneth and a day,[(2)] I may sweare, by the law of
the land, that he kill'd me.   25

CLEMENT. How? how knave? sweare he kill'd thee? and
by the law? what pretence? what colour hast thou
for that?

COB. Mary, and't please your worship, both black, and
blew; colour inough, I warrant you. I have it here,   30
to shew your worship.

CLEMENT. What is he, that gave you this, sirra?

COB. A gentleman,[1] and a souldier, he saies he is,
o'the citie here.[1]

ACT III. SCENE VII.
[1] *Greene Lattice :* a tavern.   [2] *lot :* parish taxes.

CLEMENT. A souldier o' the citie? What call you him?

COB. Captayne Bobadill.

CLEMENT. Bobadill? And why did he bob, and beate
you, sirrah? How began the quarrell betwixt you :
ha? speake truely knave, I advise you. 5

COB. Mary, indeed, and please your worship, onely because I spake against their vagrant *tabacco,* as I came
by 'hem, when they were taking on't, for nothing else.

CLEMENT. Ha? you speake against *tabacco?* Formall, his
name. 10

FORMALL. What's your name, sirra?

COB. Oliver, sir, Oliver Cob, sir.

CLEMENT. Tell Oliver Cob, he shall goe to the jayle,
Formall.

FORMALL. Oliver Cob, my master, Justice Clement, 15
saies, you shall goe to the jayle.

COB. O, I beseech your worship, for gods sake, deare
master Justice.

CLEMENT. Nay, gods pretious : and such drunkards,
and tankards, as you are, come to dispute of *tabacco* 20
once; I have done! away with him.

COB. O, good master Justice, sweet old gentleman.

KNO'WELL. Sweet Oliver,(3) would I could doe thee
any good : Justice Clement, let me intreat you, sir.

CLEMENT. What? a thred-bare rascall! a begger! a slave 25
that never drunke out of better then pisse-pot met-
tle(4) in his life! and he to deprave, and abuse the
vertue of an herbe, so generally receiv'd in the courts
of princes, the chambers of nobles, the bowers of
sweet ladies, the cabbins of souldiers! Roger, away 30
with him, by gods pretious—I say, goe too.

COB. Deare master Justice; Let mee bee beaten againe,
I have deserv'd it : but not the prison, I beseech you.

KNO'WELL. Alas, poore Oliver!

CLEMENT. Roger, make him a warrant (hee shall not 35
goe) I but feare³ the knave.

---

³ *feare :* frighten.

FORMALL.[2] Doe not stinke, sweet Oliver, you shall
not goe, my master will give you a warrant.[2]

COB. O, the Lord maintayne his worship, his worthy
worship.

CLEMENT. Away, dispatch him. 5

[*Exeunt* FORMALL *and* COB.]
How now, master
Kno'well! In dumps? In dumps? Come, this becomes
not.

KNO'WELL. Sir, would I could not feele my cares—[3] 10

CLEMENT. Your cares are nothing! they are like my cap,
soone put on, and as soone put off. What? your sonne
is old inough, to governe himselfe : let him runne his
course, it's the onely way to make him a stay'd man.
If he were an unthrift, a ruffian, a drunkard, or a 15
licentious liver, then you had reason; you had reason
to take care : but, being none of these, mirth's my
witnesse, an' I had twise so many cares, as you have,
I'ld drowne them all in a cup of sacke.(5) Come,
come, let's trie it : I muse, your parcell of a souldier 20
returnes not all this while. [*Exeunt.*]

Act IV. Scene i.
25
[*Enter*] DOWNE-RIGHT [*and*] DAME KITELY.

[DOWNE-RIGHT.] Well sister, I tell you true : and you'll
finde it so, in the end.

DAME KITELY. Alas brother, what would you have mee
to doe? I cannot helpe it : you see, my brother brings 30
'hem in, here, they are his friends.

DOWNE-RIGHT. His friends? his fiends. S'lud,(1) they doe
nothing but hant him, up and downe, like a sort of
unluckie sprites, and tempt him to all manner of villanie, that can be thought of. Well, by this light, a 35
little thing would make me play the devill with some
of 'hem; and't were not more for your husbands sake,
then any thing else, I'ld make the house too hot for

71

the best on 'hem : they should say, and sweare, hell
were broken loose, e're they went hence. But, by gods
will, 'tis no bodies fault, but yours : for, an' you had
done, as you might have done, they should have
beene perboyl'd,[1] and bak'd too, every mothers   5
sonne, e're they should ha' come in, e're a one of
'hem.

DAME KITELY. God's my life! did you ever heare the
like? what a strange man is this! Could I keepe out
all them, thinke you? I should put my selfe, against   10
halfe a dozen men? should I? Good faith, you'ld mad
the patient'st body in the world, to heare you talke
so, without any sense, or reason!

                                                        15

Act IV. Scene ii.

[*Enter*] MISTRESS BRIDGET [*and*] MASTER MATTHEW,
    [*followed by*] WELL-BRED, STEPHEN, E. KNO'WELL,
            BOBADILL, [*and*] BRAYNE-WORME.   20
[BRIDGET.] Servant[(1)] (in troth) you are too prodigall
    Of your wits treasure, thus to powre it forth,
    Upon so meane a subject, as my worth?
MATTHEW. You say well, mistris; and I meane, as well.
DOWNE-RIGHT. Hoy-day, here is stuffe!   25
WELL-BRED. O, now stand close : pray heaven, shee can
    get him to reade : He should doe it, of his owne natu-
    rall impudencie.
BRIDGET. Servant, what is this same, I pray you?
MATTHEW. Mary, an *Elegie,* an *Elegie,* an odde toy—   30
DOWNE-RIGHT. To mock an ape withall. O, I could sow
    up his mouth, now.
DAME KITELY. Sister, I pray you let's heare it.
DOWNE-RIGHT. Are you rime-given, too?
MATTHEW. Mistris, Ile reade it, if you please.   35

ACT IV. SCENE I.
[1] *perboyl'd :* thoroughly boiled.

BRIDGET. Pray you doe, servant.

DOWN-RIGHT. O, here's no fopperie! Death, I can endure
the stocks, better.   [*Exit.*]

E. KNO'WELL. What ayles thy brother? can he not hold
his water, at reading of a ballad?   5

WELL-BRED. O, no : a rime to him, is worse then cheese,
or a bag-pipe. But, marke, you loose the protestation.

MATTHEW. Faith, I did it in an humour; I know not
how it is : but, please you come neere, sir. This gentleman ha's judgement, hee knowes how to censure   10
of a—(2)pray you sir, you can judge.

STEPHEN. Not I, sir : upon my reputation, and, by the
foot of Pharoah.

WELL-BRED. O, chide your cossen, for swearing.

E. KNO'WELL. Not I, so long as he do's not forsweare   15
himselfe.

BOBADILL. Master° Matthew, you abuse the expectation
of your deare mistris, and her faire sister : Fie, while
you live, avoid this prolixitie.

MATTHEW. I shall, sir : well, *Incipere dulce.*¹   20

E. KNO'WELL. How! *Insipere dulce?* a sweet thing to be
a foole, indeed.

WELL-BRED. What, doe you take *Incipere,*[1] in that
sense?

E. KNO'WELL. You doe not? you? This was your villanie,   25
to gull him with a *motte.*²

WELL-BRED. O, the Benchers³ phrase : *pauca verba,*
*pauca verba.*⁴

MATTHEW. *Rare*(3) *creature, let me speake without*
offence,   30
Would god my rude wordes had the influence,
To rule my thoughts, as thy faire lookes doe mine,
Then should'st thou be his prisoner, who is thine.(3)

Act IV. Scene ii.
¹ *Incipere dulce :* To begin is
sweet.
² *motte :* word.

³ *Benchers' :* Benchloafer's;
lawyers.
⁴ *pauca verba :* few words.

E. KNO'WELL. This is in *Hero and Leander?*

WELL-BRED. O, I! peace, we shall have more of this.

MATTHEW. *Be not unkinde, and faire, mishapen stuffe*
Is of behaviour boysterous, and rough:

WELL-BRED. How like you that, sir?　　　　　　　5

　　　MASTER STEPHEN *answeres with shaking his head.*

E. KNO'WELL. S'light, he shakes his head like a bottle,
to feele and there be any braine in it!

MATTHEW. But observe the *catastrophe*, now,
And I in dutie will exceede all other,　　　　　10
As you in beautie doe excell loves mother.

E. KNO'WELL. Well, Ile have him free of[5] the wit-
brokers, for hee utters nothing, but stolne remnants.

WELL-BRED. O, forgive it him.[2]

E. KNO'WELL. A filching rogue? hang him. And, from　15
the dead? it's worse then sacrilege.

WELL-BRED. Sister, what ha' you here? verses? pray
you, lets see. Who made these verses? they are excellent good!

MATTHEW. O, master Well-Bred, 'tis your disposition to　20
say so, sir. They were good i' the morning, I made
'hem, *extempore*, this morning.

WELL-BRED. How? *extempore?*

MATTHEW. I, would I might bee hang'd else; aske Captayne Bobadill. He saw me write them, at the—(poxe　25
on it) the Starre, yonder.

BRAYNE-WORME. Can he find, in his heart, to curse the
starres, so?

E. KNO'WELL. Faith, his are even with him: they ha'
curst him ynough alreadie.　　　　　　　　　30

STEPHEN. Cosen, how doe you like this gentlemans
verses?

E. KNO'WELL. O, admirable! the best that ever I heard,
cousse!　　　　　　　　　　　[*Enter* DOWNE-RIGHT.]

STEPHEN. Body o' Caesar! they are admirable!　　　35
The best, that ever I heard, as I am a souldier.

[5] *free of :* a full member of.

DOWNE-RIGHT. I am vext, I can hold ne're a bone of mee
still! Heart, I thinke, they meane to build, and breed
here!

WELL-BRED. Sister, you have a simple servant, here, that
crownes your beautie, with such *encomions*,[6] and de-   5
vises : you may see, what it is to be the mistris of a
wit! that can make your perfections so transparent,
that every bleare eye may looke through them, and
see him drown'd over head, and eares, in the deepe
well of desire. Sister Kitely, I marvaile, you get you   10
not a servant, that can rime, and doe tricks,[(4)] too.

DOWNE-RIGHT. Oh monster! impudence it selfe! tricks?[(4)]

DAME KITELY. Tricks, brother? what tricks?[(4)]

BRIDGET. Nay, speake, I pray you, what tricks?[(4)]

DAME KITELY. I, never spare any body here : but say,   15
what tricks?

BRIDGET. Passion of my heart! doe tricks?

WELL-BRED. S'light, here's a trick vyed and revyed[7]!
why, you munkies, you? what a catter-waling doe
you keepe? ha's hee not given you rimes, and verses,   20
and tricks?

DOWNE-RIGHT. O, the fiend!

WELL-BRED. Nay, you, lampe of virginitie, that take it
in snuffe[(5)] so! come, and cherish this tame *poeti-
call furie,* in your servant, you'll be begg'd else,   25
shortly, for a concealement[(6)] : goe to, reward his
muse. You cannot give him lesse then a shilling, in
conscience, for the booke, he had it out of, cost him
a teston,[8] at least. How now, gallants? Master Matthew? Captayne? What? all sonnes of silence? no   30
spirit?

DOWNE-RIGHT. Come, you might practise your ruffian-
tricks somewhere else, and not here, I wusse : this is
no taverne, nor drinking-schole, to vent your exploits
in.   35

[6] *encomions :* songs of praise.   [8] *teston :* sixpence.
[7] *revyed :* bet made and raised.

WELL-BRED. How now! whose cow ha's calv'd?

DOWNE-RIGHT. Mary, that ha's mine, sir. Nay, Boy,
never looke askance at me, for the matter; Ile tell you
of it, I, sir, you, and your companions,[7] mend your
selves, when I ha' done?   5

WELL-BRED. My companions?

DOWNE-RIGHT. Yes sir, your companions, so I say, I am
not afraid of you, nor them neither : your hang-byes
here. You must have your Poets, and your potlings,
your *soldado's,* and *foolado's,* to follow you up and   10
downe the citie, and here they must come to domineere, and swagger. Sirrha, you, ballad-singer, and
slops,[9] your fellow there, get you out; get you home :
or (by this steele) Ile cut off your eares, and that,
presently.   15

WELL-BRED. S'light, stay, let's see what he dare doe : cut
off his eares? cut a whetstone.[8] You are an asse,
doe you see? touch any man here, and by this hand,
Ile runne my rapier to the hilts in you.

DOWNE-RIGHT. Yea, that would I faine see, boy.   20

*They all draw, and they of the house make out to
part them.*

DAME KITELY. O Jesu! murder. Thomas, Gaspar!

BRIDGET. Helpe, help, Thomas.

[*Enter* CASH *and some servants.*]   25

E. KNO'WELL. Gentlemen, forbeare, I pray you.

BOBADILL. Well, sirrah, you, Holofernes[10, (9)] : by my
hand, I will pinck your flesh, full of holes, with my
rapier for this; I will, by this good heaven : Nay, let
him come, let him come, gentlemen, by the body of   30
Saint George, Ile not kill him.

They offer to fight againe, and are parted.

CASH. Hold, hold, good gentlemen.

DOWNE-RIGHT. You whorson, bragging coystrill![11, (10)]

---

[9] *slops :* big britches; fancy
pants (Bobadill).

[10] *Holofernes :* tyrant.

[11] *coystrill :* knave.

Act IV. Scene iii.

[*Enter*] KITELY.   5

[KITELY.] (*To them.*) Why, how now? what's the mat-
    ter? what's the stirre here?
    Whence springs the quarrell? Thomas! where is he?
    Put up your weapons, and put off this rage.
    My wife and sister, they are cause of this,   10
    What, Thomas? where is this knave?
CASH. Here, sir.
WELL-BRED. Come, let's goe : this is one of my brothers
    ancient humours, this.
STEPHEN. I am glad, no body was hurt by his ancient   15
    humour.
          [*Exeunt* WELL-BRED, STEPHEN, E. KNO'WELL,
             MATTHEW, BOBADILL, *and* BRAYNE-WORME.]
KITELY. Why, how now, brother, who enforst this
    brawle?   20
DOWNE-RIGHT. A sort of lewd rake-hells, that care
    neither for god, nor the devill! And, they must come
    here to reade ballads, and rogery, and trash! Ile
    marre the knot of 'hem ere I sleepe, perhaps : espe-
    cially Bob, there : he that's all manner of shapes! and   25
    Songs, and sonnets,[1] his fellow.
BRIDGET. Brother, indeed, you are too violent,
    To sudden, in your humour : and, you know
    My brother Well-Breds temper will not beare
    Anie reproofe, chiefly in such a presence,   30
    Where every slight disgrace, he should receive,
    Might wound him in opinion, and respect.
DOWNE-RIGHT. Respect? what talke you of respect 'mong
              such,
    As ha' nor sparke of manhood, nor good manners?   35
    'Sdeynes I am asham'd, to heare you! respect? [*Exit.*]
BRIDGET. Yes, there was one a civill gentleman,
    And very worthily demean'd himselfe!

KITELY. O, that was some love of yours, sister!

BRIDGET. A love of mine? I would it were no worse,
brother!

You'lld pay my portion sooner, then you thinke for.

DAME KITELY. Indeed, he seem'd to be a gentleman of   5
an exeeding faire disposition, and of verie excellent
good parts!   [*Exeunt* DAME KITELY *and* BRIDGET.]

KITELY. Her love, by heaven! my wifes minion[1]!
Faire disposition? excellent good parts?
Death, these phrases are intollerable!   10
Good parts? how should shee know his parts?
His parts? Well, well, well, well, well, well!
It is too plaine, too cleere : Thomas, come hither.
What, are they gone?

CASH.   I, sir, they went in.   15
My mistris, and your sister—

KITELY. Are any of the gallants within?

CASH. No, sir, they are all gone.

KITELY. Art thou sure of it?

CASH. I can assure you, sir.   20

KITELY. What gentleman was that they prais'd so,
Thomas?

CASH. One, they call him master Kno'well, a handsome
yong gentleman, sir.

KITELY. I, I thought so : my mind gave me as much.   25
Ile die, but they have hid him i' the house,
Somewhere; Ile goe and search : goe with me,
Thomas.

Be true to me, and thou shalt find me a master.[2]

[*Exeunt.*]   30

ACT IV. SCENE III.

[1] *minion* : darling; paramour.

78

Act IV. Scene iv.

[*Enter*] cob.   5

[cob.] What Tib, Tib, I say.

tib. [*Within.*] How now, what cuckold is that knocks so
 hard? [*Enter* tib.] O, husband, ist you? what's the
 newes?

cob. Nay, you have stonn'd me, Ifaith! you ha' giv'n me   10
 a knock o' the forehead, will stick by me! cuckold?
 'Slid, cuckold?

tib. Away, you foole, did I know it was you, that
 knockt? Come, come, you may call me as bad, when
 you list.   15

cob. May I? Tib, you are a whore.

tib. You lye in your throte, husband.

cob. How, the lye? and in my throte too? doe you long
 to bee stab'd, ha?

tib. Why, you are no souldier, I hope?   20

cob. O, must you be stab'd by a souldier? Masse, that's
 true! when was Bobadill here? your Captayne? that
 rogue, that foist,[1] that fencing *Burgullian?*[(1)] Ile
 tickle him, ifaith.

tib. Why, what's the matter? trow!   25

cob. O, he has basted me, rarely, sumptiously! but I
 have it here in black and white; for his black, and
 blew : shall pay him. O, the Justice! the honestest old
 brave *Troian* in *London!*[(2)] I doe honour the very
 flea of his dog. A plague on him though, he put me   30
 once in a villanous filthy feare; mary, it vanisht away,
 like the smoke of *tabacco;* but I was smok't soundly
 first. I thanke the devill, and his good angell, my
 guest. Well, wife, or Tib (which you will) get you in,
 and lock the doore, I charge you, let no body in to   35

Act IV. Scene iv.
[1] *foist :* pickpocket.

you; wife, no body in, to you : those are my wordes.
Not Captayne Bob himselfe, nor the fiend, in his likenesse; you are a woman; you have flesh and bloud
enough in you, to be tempted : therefore, keepe the
doore, shut, upon all commers.   5

TIB. I warrant you, there shall no body enter here, without my consent.

COB. Nor, with your consent, sweet Tib, and so I leave
you.

TIB. It's more, then you know, whether you leave me so.   10

COB. How?

TIB. Why, sweet.

COB. Tut, sweet, or sowre, thou art a flowre,
Keepe close thy dore, I aske no more.   [*Exeunt.*]
                                                                          15

ACT IV. SCENE V.

[*Enter*] E. KNO'WELL, WELL-BRED, STEPHEN,
                [*and*] BRAYNE-WORME.   20

[E. KNO'WELL.] Well Brayne-Worme, performe this businesse, happily, and thou makest a purchase of my
love, for-ever.

WELL-BRED. Ifaith, now let thy spirits use their best
faculties. but, at any hand, remember the message, to   25
my brother : for, there's no other meanes, to start
him.[1]

BRAYNE-WORME. I warrant you, sir, feare nothing : I
have a nimble soule ha's wakt all forces of my phan-
t'sie, by this time, and put 'hem in true motion. What   30
you have possest mee withall, Ile discharge it amply,
sir. Make it no question.

WELL-BRED. Forth, and prosper, Brayne-Worme.
                                  [*Exit* BRAYNE-WORME.]
                                                    Faith,   35

ACT IV. SCENE V.
[1] One *starts* a hare in hunting.

Ned, how dost thou approve of my abilities in this
devise?

E. KNO'WELL. Troth, well, howsoever : but, it will come
excellent, if it take.

WELL-BRED. Take, man? why, it cannot but choose but   5
take, if the circumstances miscarrie not : but, tell me,
ingenuously, dost thou affect my sister Bridget, as
thou pretend'st?[1]

E. KNO'WELL. Friend, am I worth beliefe?

WELL-BRED. Come, doe not protest. In faith, shee is a   10
maid of good ornament, and much modestie : and,
except I conceiv'd very worthily of her, thou shouldest
not have her.

E. KNO'WELL. Nay, that I am afraid will bee a question
yet, whether I shall have her, or no?   15

WELL-BRED. Slid, thou shalt have her; by this light,
thou shalt.

E. KNO'WELL. Nay, doe not sweare.

WELL-BRED. By this hand, thou shalt have her : Ile goe
fetch her, presently. Point, but where to meet, and as   20
I am an honest man, I'll bring her.

E. KNO'WELL. Hold, hold, be temperate.

WELL-BRED. Why, by—what shall I sweare by? thou
shalt have her, as I am—

E. KNO'WELL. 'Pray thee, be at peace, I am satisfied :   25
and doe beleeve, thou wilt omit no offered occasion,
to make my desires compleat.

WELL-BRED. Thou shalt see, and know, I will not.

                                        [*Exeunt.*]

                                                        30

Act IV. Scene vi.

          [*Enter*] FORMALL [*and*] KNO'WELL.

[FORMALL.] Was your man a souldier, sir?   35

KNO'WELL. I, a knave, I tooke him begging o' the way,
This morning, as I came over *More*-fields!

          [*Enter* BRAYNE-WORME.]

                        81

O, here he is! yo' have made faire speed, beleeve me :
Where, i' the name of sloth, could you be thus—

BRAYNE-WORME. Mary, peace be my comfort, where I
thought I should have had little comfort of your wor-
ships service.   5

KNO'WELL. How so?

BRAYNE-WORME. O, sir! your comming to the citie, your
entertainment of me, and your sending me to watch
—indeed, all the circumstances either of your charge,
or my imployment, are as open to your sonne, as to   10
your selfe!

KNO'WELL. How should that be! unlesse that villaine,
Brayne-Worme,
Have told him of the letter, and discover'd
All that I strictly charg'd him to conceale? 'tis so!   15

BRAYNE-WORME. I am, partly, o' the faith, 'tis so indeed.

KNO'WELL. But, how should he know thee to be my
man?

BRAYNE-WORME. Nay, sir, I cannot tell; unlesse it bee
by the black art! Is not your sonne a scholler, sir?   20

KNO'WELL. Yes, but I hope his soule is not allied
Unto such hellish practise : if it were,
I had just cause to weepe my part in him,
And curse the time of his creation.
But, where didst thou find them, Fitz-Sword?   25

BRAYNE-WORME. You should rather aske, where they
found me, sir, for, Ile bee sworne I was going along
in the street, thinking nothing, when (of a suddain)
a voice calls, Master Kno'well's man; another cries,
souldier : and thus, halfe a dosen of 'hem, till they   30
had cal'd me within a house where I no sooner came,
but they seem'd[1] men, and out flue al their rapiers
at my bosome, with some three or foure score oathes
to accompanie 'hem, & al to tel me, I was but a dead
man, if I did not confesse where you were, and how   35
I was imployed, and about what; which, when they
could not get out of me (as I protest, they must ha'
dissected, and made an *Anatomie*[2] o' me, first, and

so I told 'hem) they lockt mee up into a roome i' the
top of a high house, whence, by great miracle (having a light heart) I slid downe, by a bottom[1] of
pack-thred, into the street, and so scapt. But, sir, thus
much I can assure you, for I heard it, while I was   5
lockt up, there were a great many rich merchants,
and brave citizens wives with 'hem at a feast, and
your sonne, Master Edward, with-drew with one of
'hem, and has pointed to meet her anon, at one Cobs
house, a water-bearer, that dwells by the wall. Now,   10
there, your worship shall be sure to take him, for
there he preyes, and faile he will not.

KNO'WELL. Nor, will I faile, to breake his match, I doubt
   not.

Goe thou, along with Justice Clement's man,   15
And stay there for me. At one Cobs house, sai'st thou?

BRAYNE-WORME. I sir, there you shall have him.

      [*Exit* KNO'WELL.]
      Yes? Invisible?

Much wench, or much sonne! 'Slight, when hee has   20
staid there, three or four houres, travelling with the
expectation of wonders, and at length be deliver'd
of aire : ô, the sport, that I should then take, to looke
on him, if I durst! But, now, I meane to appeare no
more afore him in this shape. I have another trick, to   25
act, yet. O, that I were so happy, as to light on a
nupson,[2] now, of[3] this Justices novice. Sir, I make
you stay somewhat long.

FORMALL. Not a whit, sir. 'Pray you, what doe you
  meane? sir?   30

BRAYNE-WORME. I was putting up some papers—

FORMALL. You ha' beene lately in the warres, sir, it
  seemes.

BRAYNE-WORME. Mary have I, sir; to my losse : and
  expence of all, almost—   35

Act IV. Scene vi.   [2] *nupson :* simpleton.
[1] *bottom :* ball.   [3] *of :* in the person of.

FORMALL. Troth sir, I would be glad to bestow a pottle
of wine o' you, if it please you to accept it—

BRAYNE-WORME. O, sir—

FORMALL. But, to heare the manner of your services,
and your devices in the warres, they say they be very   5
strange, and not like those a man reades in the
Romane histories, or sees, at *Mile-end*.

BRAYNE-WORME. No, I assure you, sir, why, at any time
when it please you, I shall be readie to discourse to
you, all I know : and more too, somewhat.   10

FORMALL. No better time, then now, sir; wee'll goe to
the Wind-Mill : there we shall have a cup of neate
grist, wee call it. I pray you, sir, let mee request you,
to the Wind-Mill.

BRAYNE-WORME. Ile follow you, sir, [*Aside.*] and make   15
grist o' you, if I have good lucke.   [*Exeunt.*]

Act IV. Scene vii.

20

[*Enter*] MATTHEW, E. KNO'WELL, BOBADILL,
[*and*] STEPHEN.

[MATTHEW.] Sir, did your eyes ever tast the like clowne
of him, where we were today, Master Well-Bred's
halfe brother? I thinke, the whole earth cannot shew   25
his paralell, by this day-light.

E. KNO'WELL. We were now speaking of him : Captayne
Bobadill tells me, he is fall'n foule o'you, too.

MATTHEW. O, I, sir, he threatned me, with the bastinado.   30

BOBADILL. I, but I thinke, I taught you prevention, this
morning, for that—You shall kill him, beyond question : if you be so generously[1] minded.

MATTHEW. Indeed, it is a most excellent trick!

BOBADILL. (*He practises at a post.*) O, you doe not give   35

ACT IV. SCENE VII.
[1] *generously :* nobly; heroically.

spirit enough, to your motion, you are too tardie, too
heavie! ô, it must be done like lightning, hay?[1]

MATTHEW. Rare Captaine!

BOBADILL. Tut, 'tis nothing, and't be not done in a—
punto[2]!   5

E. KNO'WELL. Captaine, did you ever prove your selfe,
upon any of our masters of defence, here?

MATTHEW. O, good sir! yes, I hope, he has.

BOBADILL. I will tell you, sir. Upon my first comming to
the citie, after my long travaile, for knowledge (in   10
that mysterie only) there came three, or foure of 'hem
to me, at a gentlemans house, where it was my chance
to be resident, at that time, to intreat my presence at
their scholes, and with-all so much importun'd me,
that (I protest to you as I am a gentleman) I was   15
asham'd of their rude demeanor, out of all measure :
well, I told 'hem, that to come to a publike schoole,
they should pardon me, it was opposite (in *diameter*[3]) to my humour, but, if so they would give their
attendance at my lodging, I protested to doe them   20
what right or favour I could, as I was a gentleman,
and so forth.

E. KNO'WELL. So, sir, then you tried their skill?

BOBADILL. Alas, soone tried! you shall heare sir. Within
two or three daies after, they came; and, by honestie,   25
faire sir, beleeve mee, I grac't them exceedingly,
shew'd them some two or three tricks of prevention,
have purchas'd 'hem, since, a credit, to admiration!
they cannot denie this : and yet now, they hate mee,
and why? because I am excellent, and for no other   30
vile reason on the earth.

E. KNO'WELL. This is strange, and barbarous! as ever I
heard!

BOBADILL. Nay, for a more instance of their preposter-
ous natures, but note, sir. They have assaulted me   35

---

[2] *punto* : instant; point thrust.   [3] *in diameter* : diametrically;
completely.

some three, foure, five, sixe of them together, as I
have walkt alone, in divers skirts i' the towne, as
Turne-bull, White-chappell, Shore-ditch,[2] which
were then my quarters, and since upon the *Exchange,*
at my lodging, and at my ordinarie : where I have   5
driven them afore me, the whole length of a street,
in the open view of all our gallants, pittying to hurt
them, beleeve me. Yet, all this lenitie will not ore-
come their spleene : they will be doing with a pismier,[4] raysing a hill, a man may spurne abroad,   10
with his foot, at pleasure. By my selfe, I could have
slaine them all, but I delight not in murder. I am loth
to beare any other then this bastinado for 'hem : yet,
I hold it good politie, not to goe disarm'd, for though
I bee skilfull, I may bee oppress'd with multitudes.   15

E. KNO'WELL. I, beleeve me, may you sir : and (in my
    conceit) our whole nation should sustaine the losse
    by it, if it were so.

BOBADILL. Alas, no : what's a peculiar[5] man, to a na-
    tion? not seene.   20

E. KNO'WELL. O, but your skill, sir!

BOBADILL. Indeed, that might be some losse; but, who
    respects it? I will tell you, sir, by the way of private,
    and under seale; I am a gentleman, and live here
    obscure, and to my selfe : but, were I knowne to her   25
    Majestie, and the Lords (observe mee) I would
    under-take (upon this poore head, and life) for the
    publique benefit of the state, not only to spare the
    intire lives of her subjects in generall, but to save the
    one halfe, nay, three parts of her yeerely charge, in   30
    holding warre, and against what enemie soever. And,
    how would I doe it, thinke you?

E. KNO'WELL. Nay, I know not, nor can I conceive.

BOBADILL. Whythus, sir. I would select nineteene,
    more, to my selfe, throughout the land; gentlemen   35
    they should bee of good spirit, strong, and able con-

---

[4] *pismier :* ant.   [5] *peculiar :* private.

stitution, I would choose them by an instinct, a character, that I have : and I would teach these nineteene, the speciall rules, as your *Punto,* your *Reverso,*
your *Stoccata,* your *Imbroccata,* your *Passada,* your
Montanto[3] : till they could all play very neare, or   5
altogether as well as my selfe. This done, say the
enemie were fortie thousand strong, we twentie would
come into the field, the tenth of *March,* or there-
abouts; and wee would challenge twentie of the enemie; they could not, in their honour, refuse us, well,   10
wee would kill them : challenge twentie more, kill
them; twentie more, kill them; twentie more, kill
them too; and thus, would wee kill, every man, his
twentie a day, that's twentie score; twentie score,
that's two hundreth; two hundreth a day, five dayes   15
a thousand; fortie thousand; fortie times five, five
times fortie, two hundreth dayes kills them all up, by
computation. And this, will I venture my poore gentleman-like carcasse, to performe (provided, there
bee no treason practis'd upon us) by faire, and dis-   20
creet manhood, that is, civilly by the sword.

E. KNO'WELL. Why, are you so sure of your hand, Captaine, at all times?

BOBADILL. Tut, never misse thrust, upon my reputation
with you.   25

E. KNO'WELL. I would not stand in Downe-Rights state,
then, an' you meet him, for the wealth of any one
street in *London.*

BOBADILL. Why, sir, you mistake me! if he were here
now, by this welkin,[6] I would not draw my weapon   30
on him! let this gentleman doe his mind : but, I will
bastinado him (by the bright sunne) where-ever I
meet him.

MATTHEW. Faith, and Ile have a fling at him, at my
distance.   DOWNE-RIGHT *walkes over the stage.*   35

[6] *welkin :* sky; heaven.

87

E. KNO'WELL. Gods so', looke, where he is : yonder he
goes.

DOWNE-RIGHT. What peevish luck have I, I cannot meet
with these bragging raskalls?

BOBADILL. It's not he? is it? 5

E. KNO'WELL. Yes faith, it is he.

MATTHEW. Ile be hang'd, then, if that were he.

E. KNO'WELL. Sir, keepe your hanging good, for some
greater matter, for I assure you, that was he.

STEPHEN. Upon my reputation, it was hee. 10

BOBADILL. Had I thought it had beene he, he must not
have gone so : but I can hardly be induc'd, to beleeve, it was he, yet.

E. KNO'WELL. That I thinke, sir. But see, he is come
againe! 15

[*Re-enter* DOWNE-RIGHT.]

DOWNE-RIGHT. O, Pharoahs foot, have I found you?
Come, draw, to your tooles : draw, gipsie, or Ile
thresh you.

BOBADILL. Gentleman of valour, I doe beleeve in thee, 20
heare me—

DOWNE-RIGHT. Draw your weapon, then.

BOBADILL. Tall[7] man, I never thought on it, till now
(body of me) I had a warrant of the peace, served
on me, even now, as I came along, by a water- 25
bearer; this gentleman saw it, Master Matthew.

DOWNE-RIGHT. 'Sdeath, you will not draw, then?

He beates him, and disarmes him : MATTHEW *runnes
away.*

BOBADILL. Hold, hold, under thy favour, forbeare. 30

DOWNE-RIGHT. Prate againe, as you like this, you whoreson foist, you. You'le controll the point, you? Your
consort is gone? had he staid, he had shar'd with you,
sir. [*Exit.*]

BOBADILL. Well, gentlemen, beare witnesse, I was bound 35
to the peace, by this good day.

---

[7] *Tall :* Brave.

E. KNO'WELL. No faith, it's an ill day, Captaine, never
reckon it other : but, say you were bound to the
peace, the law allowes you, to defend your selfe :
that'll prove but a poore excuse.

BOBADILL. I cannot tell, sir. I desire good construction,   5
in faire sort. I never sustain'd the like disgrace (by
heaven) sure I was strooke[8] with a plannet thence,[(4)]
for I had no power to touch my weapon.

E. KNO'WELL. I, like inough, I have heard of many that
have beene beaten under a plannet : goe, get you to   10
a surgean. 'Slid, an' these be your tricks, your *passada's,* and your *mountanto's,* Ile none of them.

                              [*Exit* BOBADILL.]
                    O, manners! that this
age should bring forth such creatures! that Nature   15
should bee at leisure to make 'hem! Come, cousse.

STEPHEN. Masse, Ile ha' this cloke.

E. KNO'WELL. Gods will, 'tis Downe-Right's.

STEPHEN. Nay, it's mine now, another might have tane
up, aswell as I : Ile weare it, so I will.   20

E. KNO'WELL. How, an' he see it? hee'll challenge it,
assure your selfe.

STEPHEN. I, but he shall not ha' it; Ile say, I bought it.

E. KNO'WELL. Take heed, you buy it not, too deare,
cousse.   [*Exeunt.*]   25

Act IV. Scene viii.

[*Enter*] KITELY, WELL-BRED, DAME KITELY,   30
            [*and*] BRIDGET.

[KITELY.] Now, trust me brother, you were much to
                                        blame,
T'incense his anger, and disturbe the peace,
Of my poore house, where there are sentinells   35
That every minute watch, to give alarmes,

---

[8] *strooke :* influenced magically.

Of civill warre, without adjection[1]
Of your assistance, or occasion.

WELL-BRED. No harme done, brother, I warrant you :
since there is no harme done. Anger costs a man
nothing : and a tall man is never his owne man, till   5
he be angrie. To keepe his valure in obscuritie, is to
keepe himselfe, as it were, in a cloke-bag. What's a
musitian, unlesse he play? what's a tall man, unlesse
he fight? For, indeed, all this, my wise brother stands
upon, absolutely : and, that made me fall in with   10
him, so resolutely.

DAME KITELY. I, but what harme might have come of
it, brother?

WELL-BRED. Might, sister? so, might the good warme
clothes, your husband weares, be poyson'd,(1) for   15
any thing he knowes : or the wholesome wine he
drunke, even now, at the table—

KITELY. Now, god forbid : O me. Now, I remember,
My wife drunke to me, last; and chang'd the cup :
And bade me weare this cursed sute to day.   20
See, if heav'n suffer murder undiscovr'd!
I feele me ill; give me some *mithridate*,[2]
Some *mithridate* and oile, good sister, fetch me;
O, I am sicke at heart! I burne, I burne.
If you will save my life, goe, fetch it me.   25

WELL-BRED. O, strange humour! my very breath ha's
poyson'd him.

BRIDGET. Good brother, be content, what doe you
meane?
The strength of these extreme conceits,[3] will kill you.   30

DAME KITELY. Beshrew your heart-bloud, brother Well-
Bred, now;
For putting such a toy into his head.

WELL-BRED. Is a fit *simile*, a toy? will he be poyson'd
with a *simile*? Brother Kitely, what a strange, and   35

ACT IV. SCENE VIII.   [2] *mithridate* : antidote.
[1] *adjection* : addition.   [3] *conceits* : imaginings.

idle imagination is this? For shame, bee wiser. O' my
soule, there's no such matter.

KITELY. Am I not sicke? how am I, then, not poyson'd?
Am I not poyson'd? how am I, then, so sicke?

DAME KITELY. If you be sicke, youre owne thoughts   5
    make sicke.

WELL-BRED. His jealousie is the poyson, he ha's taken.
 [*Enter* BRAYNE-WORME.] *He comes disguis'd like*
    Justice Clements man.

BRAYNE-WORME. Master Kitely, my master, Justice Cle-   10
ment, salutes you; and desires to speake with you,
with all possible speed.

KITELY. No time, but now? when, I thinke, I am sicke?
very sicke! well, I will wait upon his worship.
Thomas, Cob, I must seeke them out, and set 'hem   15
sentinells, till I returne. Thomas, Cob, Thomas.

         [*Exit.*]

WELL-BRED. This is perfectly rare, Brayne-Worme! but
how got'st thou this apparell, of the Justices man?

BRAYNE-WORME. Mary sir, my proper fine pen-man,   20
would needs bestow the grist o'me, at the Wind-Mill,
to hear some martial discourse; where so I marshal'd
him, that I made him drunke, with admiration! &,
because, too much heat was the cause of his distemper, I stript him starke naked, as he lay along asleepe,   25
and borrowed his sute, to deliver this counterfeit message in, leaving a rustie armor, and an old browne
bill[4] to watch him, till my returne : which shall be,
when I ha' pawn'd his apparell, and spent the better
part o' the money, perhaps.   30

WELL-BRED. Well, thou art a successefull merry knave,
Brayne-Worme, his absence will be a good subject
for more mirth : I pray thee, returne to thy yong
master, and will him to meet me, and my sister
Bridget, at the Tower instantly[(2)] : for, here, tell   35
him, the house is so stor'd with jealousie, there is no

---

[4] *bill :* pike.

roome for love, to stand upright in. We must get our
fortunes committed to some larger prison, say; and,
then the Tower, I know no better aire : nor where
the libertie of the house may doe us more present
service. Away.   5

[*Exit* BRAYNE-WORME. *Enter* KITELY *and* CASH.]

KITELY. Come hether, Thomas. Now, my secret's ripe,
And thou shalt have it : lay to both thine eares.
Harke, what I say to thee. I must goe forth, Thomas.
Be carefull of thy promise, keepe good watch,   10
Note every gallant, and observe him well,
That enters in my absence, to thy mistris :
If shee would shew him roomes, the jest is stale,
Follow 'hem, Thomas, or else hang on him,
And let him not goe after; marke their lookes;   15
Note, if shee offer but to see his band,
Or any other amorous toy, about him;
But praise his legge; or foot; or if shee say,
The day is hot, and bid him feele her hand,
How hot it is; ô, that's a monstrous thing!   20
Note me all this, good Thomas, marke their sighes,
And, if they doe but whisper, breake 'hem off :
Ile beare thee out in it. Wilt thou doe this?
Wilt thou be true, my Thomas?
CASH.   As truth's selfe, sir.   25
KITELY. Why, I beleeve thee : where is Cob, now? Cob?

[*Exit* KITELY.]

DAME KITELY. Hee's ever calling for Cob! I wonder,
how hee imployes Cob, so!
WELL-BRED. Indeed, sister, to aske how hee imploies   30
Cob, is a necessarie question for you, that are his
wife, and a thing not very easie for you to be satisfied
in : but this Ile assure you, Cobs wife is an excellent
bawd, sister, and, often-times, your husband hants her
house, mary, to what end, I cannot altogether accuse   35
him, imagine you what you thinke convenient. But,
I have knowne, faire hides have foule hearts, e'er now,
sister.

DAME KITELY. Never said you truer then that, brother, so much I can tell you for your learning. Thomas, fetch your cloke, and goe with me, Ile after him presently : I would to fortune, I could take him there, ifaith. Il'd returne him his owne, I warrant him. 5

[*Exeunt* DAME KITELY *and* CASH.]

WELL-BRED. So, let 'hem goe : this may make sport anon. Now, my faire sister in-law, that you knew, but how happie a thing it were to be faire, and beautiful?

BRIDGET. That touches not me, brother. 10

WELL-BRED. That's true; that's even the fault of it : for, indeede, beautie stands a woman in no stead, unlesse it procure her touching. But, sister, whether it touch you, or no, it touches your beauties; and, I am sure, they will abide the touch[5]; and' they doe not, a 15 plague of all ceruse,[6] say I : and, it touches mee to in part, though not in the—Well, there's a deare and respected friend of mine, sister, stands very strongly, and worthily affected toward you, and hath vow'd to inflame whole bone-fires of zeale, at his heart, in 20 honor of your perfections. I have alreadie engag'd my promise to bring you, where you shall heare him confirme much more. Ned Kno'well is the man, sister. There's no exception against the partie. You are ripe for a husband; and a minutes losse to such an occa- 25 sion, is a great trespasse in a wise beautie. What say you, sister? On my soule hee loves you. Will you give him the meeting?

BRIDGET. Faith, I had very little confidence in mine owne constancie, brother, if I durst not meet a man : 30 but this motion of yours, savours of an old knight-adventurers servant, a little too much, me thinkes.

WELL-BRED. What's that, sister?

BRIDGET. Mary, of the squire.[7]

WELL-BRED. No matter if it did, I would be such an 35

---

[5] *touch :* test.　　　　　　[7] *squire :* pander.
[6] *ceruse :* white lead cosmetic.

one for my friend, but see! who is return'd to hinder
us?

[*Enter* KITELY.]

KITELY. What villanie is this? call'd out on a false mes-
sage?[1]   5

This was some plot! I was not sent for. Bridget,
Where's your sister?

BRIDGET.   I thinke shee be gone forth, sir.

KITELY. How! is my wife gone forth? whether for gods
sake?   10

BRIDGET. Shee's gone abroad with Thomas.

KITELY. Abroad with Thomas? oh, that villaine dors[8]
me.

He hath discover'd all unto my wife!

Beast that I was, to trust him : whither, I pray you.   15
Went shee?

BRIDGET. I know not sir.

WELL-BRED.   Ile tell you, brother,
Whither I suspect shee's gone.

KITELY.   Whither, good brother?   20

WELL-BRED. To Cobs house, I beleeve : but keepe my
counsaile.

KITELY. I will, I will : to Cobs house? doth shee hant
Cobs?

Shee's gone a' purpose, now, to cuckold me,   25
With that lewd raskall, who, to win her favour,
Hath told her all.   [*Exit* KITELY.]

WELL-BRED.   Come, hee's once more gone.
Sister, let's loose no time; th'affaire is worth it.

[*Exeunt.*]   30

ACT IV. SCENE IX.

[*Enter*] MATTHEW [*and*] BOBADILL.[1]

[MATTHEW.] I wonder, Captayne, what they will say   35
of my going away? ha?

[8] *dors :* hoaxes.

BOBADILL. Why, what should they say? but as of a discreet gentleman? quick, warie, respectfull of natures
faire lineaments : and that's all?

MATTHEW. Why, so! but what can they say of your
beating? 5

BOBADILL. A rude part, a touch with soft wood, a kind
of grosse batterie us'd, laid on strongly, borne most
paciently : and that's all.

MATTHEW. I, but would any man have offered it in
Venice? as you say? 10

BOBADILL. Tut, I assure you, no : you shall have there
your *Nobilis,* your *Gentelezza,* come in bravely upon
your *reverse,* stand you close, stand you firme, stand
you faire, save your *retricato*(2) with his left legge,
come to the *assalto*1 with the right, thrust with brave 15
steele, defie your base wood! But, wherefore doe I
awake this remembrance? I was fascinated,2 by Jupiter : fascinated : but I will be un-witch'd, and reveng'd, by law.

MATTHEW. Doe you heare? ist not best to get a warrant, 20
and have him arrested, and brought before Justice
Clement?

BOBADILL. It were not amisse, would we had it.

[*Enter* BRAYNE-WORME *disguised as* FORMALL.]

MATTHEW. Why, here comes his man, let's speake to 25
him.

BOBADILL. Agreed, doe you speake.

MATTHEW. Save you, sir.

BRAYNE-WORME. With all my heart, sir.

MATTHEW. Sir, there is one Downe-Right, hath abus'd 30
this gentleman, and my selfe, and we determine to
make our amends by law; now, if you would doe us
the favour, to procure a warrant, to bring him afore
your master, you shall bee well considered, I assure
you, sir. 35

Act IV. Scene ix.
1 *assalto :* leaping thrust.   2 *fascinated :* bewitched.

BRAYNE-WORME. Sir, you know my service is my living, such favours as these, gotten of my master, is his only preferment,[3] and therefore, you must consider me, as I may make benefit of my place.

MATTHEW. How is that, sir?   5

BRAYNE-WORME. Faith sir, the thing is extraordinarie, and the gentleman may be, of great accompt : yet, bee what hee will, if you will lay mee downe a brace of angells, in my hand, you shall have it, otherwise not.   10

MATTHEW. How shall we doe, Captayne? he askes a brace of angells, you have no monie?

BOBADILL. Not a crosse,[(3)] by fortune.

MATTHEW. Nor I, as I am a gentleman, but two pence, left of my two shillings in the morning for wine, and   15
redish : let's find him some pawne.

BOBADILL. Pawne? we have none to the value of his demand.

MATTHEW. O, yes. I'll pawne this jewell in my eare,[(4)] and you may pawne your silke stockings, and pull up   20
your bootes, they will ne're be mist : It must be done, now.

BOBADILL. Well, an' there be no remedie : Ile step aside, and pull 'hem off.

MATTHEW. Doe you heare, sir? wee have no store of   25
monie at this time, but you shall have good pawnes : looke you, sir, this jewell, and that gentlemans silke stockings, because we would have it dispatcht, e're we went to our chambers.

BRAYNE-WORME. I am content, sir; I will get you the   30
warrant presently, what's his name, say you? Downe-Right?

MATTHEW. I, I, George Downe-Right.

BRAYNE-WORME. What manner of man is he?

MATTHEW. A tall bigge man, sir; hee goes in a cloke,   35

---

[3] *preferment :* wage (*allowed me*).

96

most commonly, of silke russet, laid about with russet
lace.

BRAYNE-WORME. 'Tis very good, sir.

MATTHEW. Here sir, here's my jewell?

BOBADILL. And, here, are stockings.   5

BRAYNE-WORME. Well, gentlemen, Ile procure you this
warrant presently, but, who will you have to serve it?

MATTHEW. That's true, Captaine : that must be consider'd.

BOBADILL. Bodie o'me, I know not! 'tis service of danger?   10

BRAYNE-WORME. Why, you were best get one o' the
varlets o' the citie, a serjeant. Ile appoint you one, if
you please.

MATTHEW. Will you, sir? why, we can wish no better.

BOBADILL. Wee'll leave it to you, sir.   15

          [*Exeunt* BOBADILL *and* MATTHEW.]

BRAYNE-WORME. This is rare! now, will I goe pawne
this cloke of the Justice's mans, at the brokers, for a
varlets sute, and be the varlet my selfe; and get either
more pawnes, or more monie of Downe-Right, for   20
the arrest.   [*Exit.*]

Act IV. Scene x.

      [*Enter*] KNO'WELL.   25

[KNO'WELL.] Oh, here it is, I am glad : I have found it
      now. Ho? who is within, here?

TIB. I am within sir, what's your pleasure?

KNO'WELL. To know, who is within, besides your selfe.

TIB. Why, sir, you are no constable, I hope?   30

KNO'WELL. O! feare you the constable? then, I doubt
      not,
You have some guests within, deserve that feare,
Ile fetch him straight.

      [*Enter* TIB.]   35

TIB.   O' gods name, sir.

KNO'WELL. Goe to. Come, tell me, Is not yong Kno'well,
      here?

TIB. Yong Kno'well? I know none such, sir, o' mine
  honestie!

KNO'WELL. Your honestie? dame, it flies too lightly from
  you :
  There is no way, but, fetch the constable.   5

TIB. The constable? the man is mad, I thinke.   [*Exit.*]
  [*Enter* DAME KITELY *and* CASH.]

CASH. Ho, who keepes house, here?

KNO'WELL. O, this is the female copes-mate[1] of my
  sonne?   10
  Now shall I meet him straight.

DAME KITELY.   Knock, Thomas, hard.

CASH. Ho, good wife?
  [*Re-enter* TIB.]

TIB.   Why, what's the matter with you?   15

DAME KITELY. Why, woman, grieves it you to ope' your
  doore?
  Belike, you get something, to keepe it shut.

TIB. What meane these questions, 'pray yee?

DAME KITELY. So strange you make it? is not my hus-   20
  band, here?

KNO'WELL. Her husband!

DAME KITELY.   My tryed[2] husband, master Kitely.

TIB. I hope, he needes not to be tryed, here.

DAME KITELY. No dame : he do's it not for need, but   25
  pleasure.

TIB. Neither for need, nor pleasure, is he here.

KNO'WELL. This is but a device, to balke me withall.
  [*Enter* KITELY.]
  Soft, who is this? 'Tis not my sonne, disguisd?   30

DAME KITELY. (*Shee spies her husband come : and
  runnes to him.*) O, sir, have I fore-stald your honest
  market?
  Found your close walkes[3]? you stand amaz'd, now,
  doe you?   35

ACT IV. SCENE x.   [2] *tryed :* proved by experience.
[1] *copes-mate :* paramour.   [3] *close walkes :* secret places.

I faith (I am glad) I have smokt you yet at last!
What is your jewell trow? In : come, lets see her;
(Fetch forth your huswife, dame) if shee be fairer,
In any honest judgement, then my selfe,
Ile be content with it : but, shee is change,   5
Shee feedes you fat, shee soothes your appetite,
And you are well? your wife, an honest woman,
Is meat twice sod[4] to you, sir? O, you trecher!
KNO'WELL. Shee cannot counterfeit thus palpably.
KITELY. Out on thy more then strumpets impudence!   10
Steal'st thou thus to thy haunts? and, have I taken
Thy bawd, and thee, and thy companion,
                         Pointing to old KNO'WELL.
This horie-headed letcher, this old goat,
Close at your villanie, and would'st thou 'scuse it,   15
With this stale harlots jest, accusing me?
O, old incontinent, do'st not thou shame,
When all thy powers in chastitie is spent,
To have a mind so hot? and to entice,
And feede th'enticements of a lustfull woman?   20
DAME KITELY. Out, I defie thee, I, dissembling wretch.
KITELY. (*Of* THOMAS.[1], (1)) Defie me, strumpet? aske
               thy pandar, here,
Can he denie it? or that wicked elder?
KNO'WELL. Why, heare you, sir.   25
KITELY.   Tut, tut, tut : never speake.
Thy guiltie conscience will discover thee.
KNO'WELL. What lunacie is this, that hants this man?
KITELY. Well, good-wife Ba'd,[5] Cobs wife; and you,
That make your husband such a hoddie-doddie;(2)   30
And you, yong apple-squire[6]; and old cuckold-maker;
Ile ha' you every one before a Justice :
Nay, you shall answere it, I charge you goe.
KNO'WELL. Marie, with all my heart, sir : I goe willingly.
Though I doe tast this as a trick, put on me,   35

[4] *sod :* boiled.   [6] *apple-squire :* pander.
[5] *Ba'd :* Pun on "bawd."

To punish my impertinent search; and justly :
And halfe forgive my sonne, for the device.

KITELY. Come, will you goe?

DAME KITELY.   Goe? to thy shame, beleeve it.

[*Enter* COB.]

COB. Why, what's the matter, here? What's here to doe?

KITELY. O, Cob, art thou come? I have beene abus'd,
And i' thy house. Never was man so, wrong'd!

COB. Slid, in my house? my master Kitely? Who wrongs
you in my house?

KITELY. Marie, yong lust in old; and old in yong, here :
Thy wife's their bawd, here have I taken 'hem.

COB. (*He falls upon his wife and beates her.*) How?
bawd? Is my house come to that? Am I prefer'd
thether? Did I charge you to keepe your dores shut,
Is'bel? and doe you let 'hem lie open for all commers?

KNO'WELL. Friend, know some cause, before thou beat'st
thy wife,
This's madnesse, in thee.

COB.   Why? is there no cause?

KITELY. Yes, Ile shew cause before the Justice, Cob :
Come, let her goe with me.

COB.   Nay, shee shall goe.

TIB. Nay, I will goe. Ile see, an' you may bee allow'd
to make a bundle o' hempe, o' your right and lawfull
wife thus, at every cuckoldly knaves pleasure. Why
doe you not goe?

KITELY. A bitter queane.[7] Come wee'll ha' you tam'd.

[*Exeunt.*]

ACT IV. SCENE XI.

[*Enter*] BRAYNE-WORME [*disguised as a sergeant.*]

[BRAYNE-WORME.] Well, of all my disguises, yet, now
am I most like my selfe : being in this Serjeants

---

[7] *queane :* whore.

gowne. A man of my present profession, never coun-
terfeits, till hee layes hold upon a debter, and sayes,
he rests him, for then hee brings him to all manner of
unrest. A kinde of little kings wee are, bearing the
diminutive of a mace,(1) made like a yong arti-   5
chocke, that always carries pepper and salt, in it
selfe. Well, I know not what danger I under-goe, by
this exploit, pray heaven, I come well of.

[*Enter* MATTHEW *and* BOBADILL.]

MATTHEW. See, I thinke, yonder is the varlet, by his   10
gowne.

BOBADILL. Let's goe, in quest of him.

MATTHEW. 'Save you, friend, are not you here, by appointment of Justice Clements man?

BRAYNE-WORME. Yes, an't please you, sir : he told me   15
two gentlemen had will'd him to procure a warrant
from his master (which I have about me) to be
serv'd on one Downe-Right.

[*Enter* STEPHEN *in* DOWNE-RIGHT's *cloak.*]

MATTHEW. It is honestly done of you both; and see,   20
where the partie comes, you must arrest : serve it
upon him, quickly, afore hee bee aware—

BOBADILL. Beare backe, master Matthew.

BRAYNE-WORME. Master Downe-Right, I arrest you, i'
the queenes name, and must carry you afore a Justice,   25
by vertue of this warrant.

STEPHEN. Mee, friend? I am no Downe-Right, I. I am
master Stephen, you doe not well, to arrest me, I tell
you, truely : I am in nobodies bonds, nor bookes, I,
would you should know it. A plague on you heartily,   30
for making mee thus afraid afore my time.

BRAYNE-WORME. Why, now are you deceived, gentlemen?

BOBADILL. He weares such a cloke, and that deceived
us : But see, here a1 comes, indeed! this is he, officer.   35

ACT IV. SCENE XI.
1 *a :* he.

[*Enter* DOWNE-RIGHT.]

DOWNE-RIGHT. Why, how now, signior gull! are you turn'd filtcher of late? come, deliver my cloke.

STEPHEN. Your cloke, sir? I bought it, even now, in open market.   5

BRAYNE-WORME. Master Downe-Right, I have a warrant I must serve upon you, procur'd by these two gentle-men.

DOWNE-RIGHT. These gentlemen? these rascals?

BRAYNE-WORME. Keepe the peace, I charge you, in her   10
Majesties name.

DOWNE-RIGHT. I obey thee. What must I doe, officer?

BRAYNE-WORME. Goe before master Justice Clement, to answere what they can object against you, sir. I will use you kindly, sir.   15

MATTHEW. Come, let's before, and make[2] the Justice, Captaine—

BOBADILL. The varlet's a tall man! afore heaven!

[*Exeunt* MATTHEW *and* BOBADILL.]

DOWNE-RIGHT. Gull, you'll gi'me my cloke?   20

STEPHEN. Sir, I bought it, and Ile keepe it.

DOWNE-RIGHT. You will.

STEPHEN. I, that I will.

DOWNE-RIGHT. Officer, there's thy fee, arrest him.

BRAYNE-WORME. Master Stephen, I must arrest you.   25

STEPHEN. Arrest mee, I scorne it. There, take your cloke, I'le none on't.

DOWNE-RIGHT. Nay, that shall not serve your turne, now, sir. Officer, I'le goe with thee, to the Justices : bring him along.   30

STEPHEN. Why, is not here your cloke? what would you have?

DOWNE-RIGHT. I'le ha' you answere it, sir.

BRAYNE-WORME. Sir, Ile take your word; and this gentle-mans, too : for his apparance.   35

DOWNE-RIGHT. I'le ha' no words taken. Bring him along.

[2] *make :* prepare.

BRAYNE-WORME. Sir, I may choose, to doe that : I may
take bayle.

DOWNE-RIGHT. 'Tis true, you may take baile, and choose;
at another time : but you shall not, now, varlet. Bring
him along, or I'le swinge you.   5

BRAYNE-WORME. Sir, I pitty the gentlemans case. Here's
your money againe.

DOWNE-RIGHT. 'Sdeynes, tell not me of my money, bring
him away, I say.

BRAYNE-WORME. I warrant you he will goe with you of   10
himselfe, sir.

DOWNE-RIGHT. Yet more adoe?

BRAYNE-WORME. I have made a faire mash on't.

STEPHEN. Must I goe?

BRAYNE-WORME. I know no remedie, master Stephen.   15

DOWNE-RIGHT. Come along, afore mee, here. I doe not
love your hanging looke behind.

STEPHEN. Why, sir. I hope you cannot hang mee for it.
Can hee, fellow?

BRAYNE-WORME. I thinke not, sir. It is but a whipping   20
matter, sure!

STEPHEN. Why, then, let him doe his worst, I am resolute.   [*Exeunt.*]

25

Act V. Scene i.

[*Enter*] CLEMENT, KNO'WELL, KITELY, DAME KITELY,
TIB, CASH, COB, [*and*] *Servants.*

[CLEMENT.] Nay, but stay, stay, give me leave : my   30
chaire, sirrha. You, master Kno'well, say you went
thither to meet your sonne.

KNO'WELL. I, sir.

CLEMENT. But, who directed you, thither?

KNO'WELL. That did mine owne man, sir.   35

CLEMENT. Where is he?

KNO'WELL. Nay, I know not, now; I left him with your
clarke : And appointed him, to stay here for me.

CLEMENT. My clarke? about what time, was this?

KNO'WELL. Mary, betweene one and two, as I take it.

CLEMENT. And, what time came my man with the false
message to you, master Kitely?

KITELY. After two, sir.   5

CLEMENT. Very good : but, mistris Kitely, how that you
were at Cobs? ha?

DAME KITELY. An' please you, sir, Ile tell you : my
brother, Well-Bred, told me, that Cobs house, was a
suspected place—   10

CLEMENT. So it appeares, me thinkes : but, on.

DAME KITELY. And that my husband us'd thither, daily.

CLEMENT. No matter, so he us'd himselfe well, mistris.

DAME KITELY. True sir, but you know, what growes, by
such hants, often-times.   15

CLEMENT. I see, ranke fruits of a jealous braine, mistris
Kitely : but, did you find your husband there, in that
case, as you suspected?

KITELY. I found her there, sir.

CLEMENT. Did you so? that alters the case. Who gave   20
you knowledge, of your wives being there?

KITELY. Marie, that did my brother Well-Bred.

CLEMENT. How? Well-Bred first tell her? then tell you,
after? where is Well-Bred?

KITELY. Gone with my sister, sir, I know not whither.   25

CLEMENT. Why, this is a meere trick, a device; you are
gull'd in this most grosly, all! alas, poore wench, wert
thou beaten for this?

TIB. Yes, most pittifully, and't please you.

COB. And worthily, I hope : if it shall prove so.   30

CLEMENT. I, that's like, and a piece of a sentence.
[*Enter a* SERVANT.] How now, sir? what's the matter?

SERVANT. Sir, there's a gentleman, i'the court without,
desires to speake with your worship.

CLEMENT. A gentleman? what's he?   35

SERVANT. A souldier, sir, he saies.

CLEMENT. (*He armes himselfe.*) A souldier? take downe
my armor, my sword, quickly : a souldier speake with

me! why, when knaves? come on, come on, hold my
cap there, so; give me my gorget,[1] my sword : stand
by, I will end your matters, anon—Let the souldier
enter, [*Enter* bobadill *and* matthew.] now, sir,
what ha' you to say to me?   5

Act V. Scene ii.

[bobadill.] By your worships favour—   10
clement. Nay, keepe out, sir, I know not your pretence, you send me word, sir, you are a souldier :
why, sir, you shall bee answer'd, here, here be them
have beene amongst souldiers. Sir, your pleasure.
bobadill. Faith, sir, so it is, this gentleman, and my   15
selfe, have beene most uncivilly wrong'd, and beaten,
by one Downe-Right, a course fellow, about the
towne, here, and for mine owne part, I protest, being
a man, in no sort, given to this filthie humour of
quarrelling, he hath assaulted mee in the way of my   20
peace; dispoil'd mee of mine honor; dis-arm'd mee of
my weapons; and rudely, laid me along, in the open
streets : when, I not so much as once offer'd to resist him.
clement. O, gods precious! is this the souldier? here,   25
take my armour of quickly, 'twill make him swoune,
I feare; hee is not fit to looke on't, that will put up a
blow.
matthew. An't please your worship, he was bound to
the peace.   30
clement. Why, and he were, sir, his hands were not
bound, were they?
                    [*Enter a* servant.]
servant. There's one of the varlets of the citie, sir, ha's

Act V. Scene i.
[1] *gorget :* the piece of armor
  protecting the throat.

brought two gentlemen, here, one, upon your worships warrant.

CLEMENT. My warrant?

SERVANT. Yes, sir. The officer say's, procur'd by these
two.   5

CLEMENT. Bid him, come in. [*Exit* SERVANT.] Set by this
picture.[1] [*Enter* DOWNE-RIGHT, STEPHEN, *and* BRAYNE-
WORME.] What, Master Downe-Right! are you
brought at Master Fresh-Waters[2] suite, here!

                                                                      10

ACT V. SCENE III.

[DOWNE-RIGHT.] I faith, sir. And here's another brought
at my suite.   15

CLEMENT. What are you, sir?

STEPHEN. A gentleman, sir. ô, uncle!

CLEMENT. Uncle? who? master Kno'well?

KNO'WELL. I, sir! this is a wise kinsman of mine.

STEPHEN. God's my witnesse, uncle, I am wrong'd here   20
monstrously, hee charges me with stealing of his
cloke, and would I might never stirre, if I did not find
it in the street, by chance.

DOWNE-RIGHT. O, did you find it, now? you said, you
bought it, erewhile.   25

STEPHEN. And, you said, I stole it; nay, now my uncle
is here, I'll doe well inough, with you.

CLEMENT. Well, let this breath a while; you, that have
cause to complaine, there, stand forth : had you my
warrant for this gentlemans apprehension?   30

BOBADILL. I, an't please your worship.

CLEMENT. Nay, doe not speake in passion so : where had
you it?

BOBADILL. Of your clarke, sir.

<hr>

ACT V. SCENE II.   [2] *Fresh-Waters :* Soldier never in
[1] *Picture :* fake (Bobadill).   a foreign country.

CLEMENT. That's well! an' my clarke can make warrants, and my hand not at'hem! Where is the warrant? Officer, have you it?

BRAYNE-WORME. No, sir, your worship's man, master Formall, bid mee doe it, for these gentlemen, and he would be my discharge.[1]   5

CLEMENT. Why, master Downe-Right, are you such a novice, to bee serv'd, and never see the warrant?

DOWNE-RIGHT. Sir. He did not serve it on me.

CLEMENT. No? how then?   10

DOWNE-RIGHT. Mary, sir, hee came to mee, and said, hee must serve it, and hee would use me kindly, and so—

CLEMENT. O, gods pittie, was it so, sir? he must serve it? give me my long-sword there, and helpe me of;   15
so. (*He flourishes over him with his long-sword.*)
Come on, sir varlet, I must cut off your legs, sirrha : nay, stand up, Ile use you kindly; I must cut off your legs, I say.

BRAYNE-WORME. O, good sir, I beseech you; nay, good   20
master Justice.

CLEMENT. I must doe it; there is no remedie. I must cut off your legs, sirrha, I must cut off your eares, you rascall, I must doe it; I must cut off your nose, I must cut off your head.   25

BRAYNE-WORME. O, good your worship.

CLEMENT. Well, rise, how doest thou doe, now? doest thou feele thy selfe well? hast thou no harme?

BRAYNE-WORME. No, I thanke your good worship, sir.

CLEMENT. Why, so! I said, I must cut off thy legs, and   30
I must cut off thy armes, and I must cut off thy head; but, I did not doe it : so, you said, you must serve this gentleman, with my warrant, but, you did not serve him. You knave, you slave, you rogue, doe you

ACT V. SCENE III.
[1] *discharge :* guarantee.

say you must? sirrha, away with him, to the jayle,
Ile teach you a trick, for your *must*, sir.

BRAYNE-WORME. Good sir, I beseech you, be good to me.

CLEMENT. Tell him he shall to the jayle, away with him,
I say.   5

BRAYNE-WORME. Nay, sir, if you will commit mee, it
shall bee for committing more then this : I will not
loose, by my travaile, any graine of my fame certaine.
                              [*He throws off his disguise.*]

CLEMENT. How is this!   10

KNO'WELL. My man, Brayne-Worme!

STEPHEN. O yes, uncle. Brayne-Worme ha's beene with
my cossen Edward, and I, all this day.

CLEMENT. I told you all, there was some device!

BRAYNE-WORME. Nay, excellent Justice, since I have laid   15
my selfe thus open to you; now, stand strong for
mee : both with your sword, and your ballance.

CLEMENT. Bodie o' me, a merry knave! Give me a bowle
of sack : If hee belong to you, master Kno'well, I bespeake your patience.   20

BRAYNE-WORME. That is it, I have most need of. Sir, if
you'll pardon me, only; I'll glorie in all the rest, of my
exploits.

KNO'WELL. Sir, you know, I love not to have my favours
come hard, from me. You have your pardon : though   25
I suspect you shrewdly for being of counsell with
my sonne, against me.

BRAYNE-WORME. Yes, faith, I have, sir; though you re-
tain'd me doubly this morning, for your selfe : first,
as Brayne-Worme; after, as Fitz-Sword. I was your   30
reform'd[1] souldier, sir. 'Twas I sent you to Cobs,
upon the errand, without end.

KNO'WELL. Is it possible! or that thou should'st disguise
thy language so, as I should not know thee?

BRAYNE-WORME. O, sir, this ha's beene the day of my   35
metamorphosis! It is not that shape alone, that I have
runne through, to day. I brought this gentleman,
master Kitely, a message too, in the forme of master

Justices man, here, to draw him out o' the way, as
well as your worship : while master Well-Bred might
make a conveiance of mistris Bridget, to my yong
master.

KITELY. How! my sister stolne away?　　　　　　　　　5

KNO'WELL. My sonne is not married, I hope!

BRAYNE-WORME. Faith, sir, they are both as sure as love,
a priest, and three thousand pound (which is her
portion) can make 'hem : and by this time are readie
to bespeake their wedding supper at the Wind-Mill,　　10
except some friend, here, prevent[2] 'hem, and invite
'hem home.

CLEMENT. Marie, that will I (I thanke thee, for putting
me in mind on't.) Sirrah, goe you, and fetch 'hem
hither, upon my warrant. [*Exit* SERVANT.] Neithers　　15
friends have cause to be sorrie, if I know the yong
couple, aright. Here, I drinke to thee, for thy good
newes. But, I pray thee, what hast thou done with
my man Formall?

BRAYNE-WORME. Faith, sir, after some ceremonie past,　　20
as making him drunke, first with storie, and then with
wine (but all in kindnesse) and stripping him to his
shirt : I left him in that coole vaine, departed, sold
your worships warrant to these two, pawn'd his liverie
for that varlets gowne, to serve it in; and thus have　　25
brought my selfe, by my activitie, to your worships
consideration.

CLEMENT. And I will consider thee, in another cup of
sack. Here's to thee, which having drunke of, this is
my sentence. Pledge me. Thou hast done, or assisted　　30
to nothing, in my judgement, but deserves to bee
pardon'd for the wit o' the offence. If thy master, or
anie man, here, be angrie with thee, I shall suspect
his ingine,[3] while I know him for't. How now? what
noise is that!　　　　　　　　　　　　　　　　　　35

[*Enter a* SERVANT.]

---

[2] *prevent :* anticipate.　　　　　[3] *ingine :* wit; good sense.

SERVANT. Sir, it is Roger is come home.

CLEMENT. Bring him in, bring him in. [*Enter* FORMALL
in armor.] What! drunke in armes, against me? Your
reason, your reason for this.   5

ACT V. SCENE IV.[1]

[FORMALL.] (*To them.*) I beseech your worship to pardon me; I happen'd into ill companie by chance,   10
that cast me into a sleepe, and stript me of all my
clothes—

CLEMENT. Well, tell him, I am Justice Clement, and doe
pardon him : but, what is this to your armour! what
may that signifie?   15

FORMALL. And't please you, sir, it hung up i' the roome,
where I was stript; and I borrow'd it of one o' the
drawers, to come home in, because I was loth, to doe
penance through the street, i' my shirt.

CLEMENT. Well, stand by a while. [*Enter* E. KNO'WELL,   20
WELL-BRED, *and* BRIDGET.] Who be these? O, the
yong companie, welcome, welcome. Gi' you joy.[2]
Nay, mistris Bridget, blush not; you are not so fresh
a bride, but the newes of it is come hither afore you.
Master Bridegroome, I ha' made your peace, give   25
mee your hand : so will I for all the rest; ere you
forsake my roofe.

ACT V. SCENE V.   30

[E. KNO'WELL.] (*To them.*) We are the more bound to
your humanitie, sir.

CLEMENT. Only these two, have so little of man in 'hem,
they are no part of my care.   35

WELL-BRED. Yes, sir, let mee pray you for this gentleman, hee belongs, to my sister, the bride.

CLEMENT. In what place, sir?

WELL-BRED. Of her delight, sir, below the staires, and in
publike : her *poet*, sir.

CLEMENT. A *poet?* I will challenge him my selfe, presently, at *extempore.*

Mount[1] *up thy Phlegon muse, and testifie,* 5
 How Saturne, sitting in an ebon cloud,
Disrob'd his podex[1] *white as ivorie,*
And, through the welkin, thundred all aloud.[1]

WELL-BRED.[1] Hee is not for *extempore*, sir. Hee is all
for the pocket-*muse*, please you command a sight of 10
it.

CLEMENT. Yes, yes, search him for a tast of his veine.

WELL-BRED. You must not denie the Queenes Justice,
Sir, under a writ o' rebellion.

CLEMENT. What! all this verse? Bodie o' me, he carries 15
a whole realme,[2] a common-wealth of paper, in's
hose[2]! let's see some of his subjects!

Unto[2] *the boundlesse Ocean of thy face,*
 Runnes this poore river charg'd with streames of
 eyes.[3] 20

How? this is stolne!

E. KNO'WELL.[3] A *Parodie!* a *parodie!* with a kind of
miraculous gift, to make it absurder then it was.

CLEMENT. Is all the rest, of this batch? Bring me a
torch; lay it together, and give fire. Clense the aire. 25
Here was enough to have infected, the whole citie,
if it had not beene taken in time! See, see, how our
Poets glorie shines! brighter, and brighter! still it in-
creases! ô, now, it's at the highest : and, now, it de-
clines as fast. You may see. *Sic transit gloria mundi.*[3] 30

KNO'WELL. There's an *embleme*[4] for you, sonne, and
your studies!

CLEMENT. Nay, no speech, or act of mine be drawne
against such, as professe it worthily. They are not

ACT V. SCENE v.
[1] *podex :* bottom.   [3] *Sic . . . gloria mundi :* Thus
[2] *hose :* trousers.   passes the glory of the world.

borne everie yeere, as an Alderman. There goes more
to the making of a good *Poet*, then a Sheriffe, Master
Kitely. You looke upon me! though, I live i' the citie
here, amongst you, I will doe more reverence, to him,
when I meet him, then I will to the Mayor, out of   5
his yeere. But, these paper-pedlers! these inke-
dablers! They cannot expect reprehension, or reproch.
They have it with the fact.(5)

E. KNO'WELL. Sir, you have sav'd me the labour of a
defence.   10

CLEMENT. It shall be discourse for supper; betweene
your father and me, if he dare under-take me. But,
to dispatch away these, you signe o'the Souldier, and
picture o' the *Poet* (but, both so false, I will not ha'
you hang'd out at my dore till midnight) while we   15
are at supper, you two shall penitently fast it out in
my court, without; and, if you will, you may pray
there, that we may be so merrie within, as to forgive,
or forget you, when we come out. Here's a third,⁴
because, we tender your safetie, shall watch you, he is 20
provided for the purpose. Looke to your charge, sir.

STEPHEN. And what shall I doe?

CLEMENT. O! I had lost a sheepe, an he had not bleated!
Why, sir, you shall give Master Downe-Right his
cloke : and I will intreat him to take it. A trencher,   25
and a napkin, you shall have, i' the buttrie, and keepe
Cob, and his wife companie, here; whom, I will intreat first to bee reconcil'd : and you to endevour
with your wit, to keepe 'hem so.

STEPHEN. Ile doe my best.   30

COB. Why, now I see thou art honest, Tib, I receive thee
as my deare, and mortall wife, againe.

TIB. And, I you, as my loving, and obedient husband.

CLEMENT. Good complement! It will bee their bridale
night too. They are married anew. Come, I conjure   35
the rest, to put of all discontent. You, Master Downe-

---

⁴ *third :* Formall.

Right, your anger; you, master Kno'well, your cares;
master Kitely, and his wife, their jealousie.
For, I must tell you both, while that is fed,
Hornes i' the mind are worse then o' the head.

KITELY. Sir, thus they goe from me, kisse me, sweet   5
heart.
See,[6] *what a drove of hornes flye, in the ayre,*
Wing'd with my clensed, and my credulous breath!
Watch 'hem, suspicious eyes, watch, where they fall.
See, see! on heads, that thinke th'have none at all!   10
O, what a plenteous world of this, will come!
When ayre raynes hornes, all may be sure of some.
I ha' learned so much verse out of a jealous mans
part, in a play.[6]

CLEMENT. 'Tis well, 'tis well! This night wee'll dedicate   15
to friendship, love, and laughter. Master bridegroome, take your bride, and leade : every one, a fellow. Here is my mistris. Brayne-Worme! to whom all
my addresses of courtship shall have their reference.
Whose adventures, this day, when our grand-children   20
shall heare to be made a fable, I doubt not, but it
shall find both spectators, and applause.   [*Exeunt.*]

THE END.

THE MALCONTENT

BY

JOHN MARSTON

MALCONTENT.

Augmented by *Marston*.

With the Additions played by the Kings
Maiesties seruants.

Written by *Ihon Webster*.

1 6 0 4.

AT LONDON
Printed by V.S. for William Aspley, and
are to be sold at his shop in Paules
Church-yard.

BENJAMINI JONSONIO
POETAE
ELEGANTISSIMO
GRAVISSIMO

AMICO
SUO CANDIDO ET CORDATO,
JOHANNES MARSTON
MUSARUM ALUMNUS

ASPERAM HANC SUAM THALIAM
D. D.[1]

To the Reader.[2]

I am an ill Oratour; and in truth, use to indite more honestly then eloquently, for it is my custome to speake as I thinke, and write as I speake.

In plainenesse therefore understand, that in some things I have willingly erred, as in supposing a Duke of Genoa, and in taking names different from that Citties families: for which some may wittily accuse me; but my defence shall be as honest, as many reproofes unto me have beene most malicious. Since (I hartily protest) it was my care to write so farre from reasonable offence, that even strangers, in whose state I laid my Scene, should not from thence draw any disgrace to any, dead or living. Yet in dispight of my indevors, I understand, some have beene most unadvisedly over-cunning in mis-interpreting me, and with subtilitie (as deepe as hell) have maliciously spread ill rumors, which springing from themselves, might to themselves have heavily returned. Surely I desire to satisfie every firme spirit, who in all his actions,

119

proposeth to himselfe no more ends then God and vertue do,
whose intentions are alwaies simple : to such I protest, that
with my free understanding, I have not glanced at disgrace
of any, but of those, whose unquiet studies labor innovation,
contempt of holy policie, reverent comely superioritie, and
establisht unity : for the rest of my supposed tartnesse, I
feare not, but unto every worthy minde it will be approved
so generall and honest, as may modestly passe with the free-
dome of a Satyre. I would faine leave the paper; onely one
thing afflicts me, to thinke that Scaenes invented, meerely
to be spoken, should be inforcively published to be read, and
that the least hurt I can receive, is to do my selfe the wrong.
But since others otherwise would doe me more, the least in-
convenience is to be accepted. I have my selfe therefore set
forth this Comedie; but so, that my inforced absence must
much relye upon the Printers discretion : but I shall intreate,
slight errors in orthographie may bee as slightly over passed;
and that the unhansome shape which this trifle in reading
presents, may be pardoned, for the pleasure it once afforded
you, when it was presented with the soule of lively action.

Sine aliqua dementia nullus Phoebus.[3]

J. M.

THE
INDUCTION TO
THE MALCONTENT, AND
the additions acted by the
Kings Majesties servants.[1]

Written by *John Webster.*

Enter WILLIAM SLY, *a* TIRE-MAN[1] *following him
with a stoole.*

TIRE-MAN. Sir, the Gentlemen will be angry if you sit
heare.

SLY. Why? we may sit upon the stage at the private   5
house[2] : thou doest not take me for a country gentleman, doest? doest thinke I feare hissing? Ile holde
my life thou took'st me for one of the plaiers.

TIRE-MAN. No sir.

SLY. By gods slid if you had, I would have given you   10
but six pence[2] for your stoole : Let them that have
stale suites, sit in the galleries, hisse at mee : he that
will be laught out of a Taverne or an Ordinarie,[3]
shall seldome feede well or be drunke in good company. Where's Harry Condell, Dick Burbage,[1] and   15
William Sly, let me speake with some of them.

TIRE-MAN. An't please you to go in sir, you may.

SLY. I tell you no; I am one that hath seene this play
often, & can give them intellegence[4] for their action :
I have most of the jeasts heere in my table-booke.[5]   20
Enter SINKLO.[2]

SINKLO. Save you Coose.

SLY. O Coosin, come you shall sit betweene my legges
heare.

SINKLO. No indeede coosin, the audience then will take   25

---

[1] *Tire-man :* Prop-man.
[2] *private house :* Blackfriars
  Theatre.
[3] *Ordinarie :* eating-place.
[4] *intellegence :* direction.
[5] *table-booke :* notebook.

me for a viol de gambo, and thinke that you play
upon me.

SLY. Nay, rather that I worke upon you coose.

SINKLO. We staied for you at supper last night at my
coosin Hony-moones the woollen Draper : After sup-   5
per we drew cuttes for a score of Apricoks, the longest cut stil[6] to draw an Apricoke : by this light t'was
Mistris Franke Hony-moones fortune, still to have the
longest cut : I did measure for the women. What be
these coose?   10

> *Enter* DICK BURBAGE, HARRY CONDELL, [*and*]
> JOHN LOWIN.[3]

SLY. The Plaiers. God save you.

BURBAGE. You are verie welcome.

SLY. I pray you know this Gentleman my coosin, 'tis   15
Master Doomesdaies sonne the userer.

> [*He removes his hat.*]

CONDELL. I beseech you sir be coverd.

SLY. No in good faith for mine ease, looke you my hat's
the handle to this fanne[7] : Gods so,[3] what a   20
beast was I, I did not leave my feather[4] at home.
Well, but Ile take an order with you.

> *Puts his feather in his pocket.*

BURBAGE. Why do you conceale your feather sir?

SLY. Why? do you thinke Ile have jeasts broken upon   25
me in the play to be laught at : this play hath beaten
all your gallants out of the feathers : Blacke friars
hath almost spoild Blacke friars for feathers.[4]

SINKLO. Gods so, I thought 'twas for somewhat our gentlewomen at home counseld me to weare my feather   30
to the play, yet I am loth to spoile it.

SLY. Why coose?

SINKLO. Because I got it in the tilt-yard : there was a
Herald[5] broke my pate for taking it up : but I
have worne it up & downe the Strand, and met him   35
fortie times since, and yet hee dares not challenge it.

---

[6] *stil* : each time.   [7] *fanne* : a very large feather.

SLY. Do you heare sir, this play is a bitter play.

CONDELL. Why sir, tis neither Satyre nor Morall, but the
meane passage of a historie : Yet there are a sort of
discontented creatures that beare a stingelesse envie
to great ones, and these will wrest the doings of any   5
man to their base malitious appliment : but should
their interpretation come to the teste, like your marmoset,[8], [6] they presently turne their teeth to their
taile & eate it.[5]

SLY. I will not go so farre with you, but I say, any man   10
that hath wit, may censure[9] (if he sit in the twelve-
penny roome[10] :) and I say againe, the play is bitter.

BURBAGE. Sir you are like a Patron that presenting a
poore scholler to a benefice, injoynes him not to raile
against any thing that standes within compasse of his   15
Patrons follie : Why should not we injoy the antient
freedome of poesie? Shall we protest to the Ladies
that their painting[11] makes them Angells, or to my
yong gallant, that his expence in the brothell shall
gaine him reputation? No sir, such vices as stand not   20
accountable to law, should be cured as men heale
tetters,[12] by casting inke upon them. Would you be
satisfied in any thing else sir?

SLY. I marry woud I. I would know how you came by
this play?   25

CONDELL. Faith sir the booke was lost, and because twas
pittie so good a play should be lost, we found it and
play it.

SLY. I wonder you would play it, another company having interest in it?   30

CONDELL. Why not *Malevole* in folio[13] with us, as
Jeronimo[6] in Decimo sexto[14], [7] with them. They

---

[8] *marmoset :* small monkey.

[9] *censure :* judge.

[10] *twelve-penny roome :* gallery
box.

[11] *painting :* cosmetics.

[12] *tetters :* scabby sores.

[13] *in folio :* by adults (large
book size).

[14] *in Decimo sexto :* by child
actors (very small book size).

taught us a name for our play, wee call it *One for another*.(8)

SLY. What are your additions?

BURBAGE. Sooth not greatly needefull, only as your sal-let15 to your greate feast, to entertaine a little more   5
time, and to abridge the not received custome(9) of
musicke in our Theater. I must leave you sir.

                                        Exit BURBAGE.[7]

SINKLO. Doth he play the Malcontent?

CONDELL. Yes sir.   10

SINKLO. I durst lay foure of mine eares, the play is not
so well acted as it hath beene.

CONDELL. O no sir, nothing *Ad Parminonis Suem.*(10)

LOWIN. Have you lost your eares(11) sir, that you are
so prodigall of laying them?   15

SINKLO. Why did you aske that friend?

LOWIN. Marry sir because I have heard of a fellow
would offer to lay a hundred pound wager, that was
not worth five bau-bees16 : and in this kinde you
might venter foure of your elbowes : yet God defende   20
your coate should have so many.

SINKLO. Nay truly, I am no great censurer, and yet I
might have beene one of the Colledge of Crittickes
once : my coosin heere hath an excellent memory in-deede sir.   25

SLY. Who I? Ile tell you a strange thing of my selfe, and
I can tell you for one that never studied the art of
memory, tis very strange too.

CONDELL. Whats that sir?

SLY. Why Ile lay a hundred pound Ile walke but once   30
downe by the gold-smiths row in Cheape,17 take no-tice of the signes, and tell you them with a breath
instantly.

LOWIN. Tis verie strange.

SLY. They beginne as the world did, with Adam and   35

---

15 *sallet :* salad.

16 *bau-bees :* Scotch half-pence.

17 *Cheape :* Cheapside, a business thoroughfare.

Eve. Theres in all just five and fiftie.[12] I do use to meditate much when I come to plaies too. What do you thinke might come into a mans head now, seeing all this company?

CONDELL. I know not sir. 5

SLY. I have an excellent thought : if some fiftie of the Grecians that were cramd in the horse belly had eaten garlike, do you not thinke the Trojans might have smelt out their knavery.

CONDELL. Very likely. 10

SLY. By God I would they[8] had, for I love Hector[13] horribly.

SINKLO. O but coose coose.

"Great Alexander when he came to the toombe of
                    Achilles 15
     Spake with a big loude voice, O thou thrice blessed
                    & happy."[14]

SLY. Alexander was an asse to speake so well of a filthy cullion.

LOWIN. Good sir will you leave the stage, Ile helpe you 20 to a private roome.

SLY. Come coose, lets take some Tobacco. Have you never a prologue?

LOWIN. Not any sir.

SLY. Let me see, I will make one extempore. 25

*Come to them and fencing of a congey[18] with
     armes and legges. Be round[19] with them.*

Gentlemen, I could wish for the womens sakes you had all soft cushins : and Gentlewomen, I could wish that for the mens sakes you had all more easie stand- 30 ings. What would they wish more but the play now, and that they shall have instantly.

18 *fencing of a congey :* making   19 *round :* vigorously direct.
an elaborate bow.

Vexat censura
columbas.(1)

ACTUS PRIMUS. SCENA PRIMA.

The vilest out of tune Musicke being heard. 5
Enter BILIOSO *and* PREPASSO.

BILIOSO. Why how now? are ye mad? or drunke? or
both? or what?

PREPASSO. Are ye building *Babilon* there?

BILIOSO. Heere's a noise in Court, you thinke you are in 10
a Taverne, do you not?

PREPASSO. You thinke you are in a brothell house, do
you not? This roome is ill sented.

Enter one with a perfume.

So, perfume, perfume; some upon me I pray thee: 15
The Duke is upon instant entrance; so, make place
there.

SCENA SECUNDA. 20

Enter the Duke PIETRO, FERRARDO, *Count* EQUATO,
Count CELSO *before, and* GUERRINO.

PIETRO. Where breath's that musique?

BILIOSO. The discord rather then the Musique is heard 25
from the Malcontent Malevoles chamber.

FERRARDO. Malevole.

MALEVOLE. (*Out of his chamber.*) Yaugh, godaman
what dost thou there: Dukes *Ganymede*.[1], (1)
Junoes jealous of thy long stockings: shadowe of a 30
woman, what wouldst Weesell? thou lambe a1
Court: what doost thou bleat for? ah[2] you smooth
chind *Catamite*2!

PIETRO. Come downe thou ragged cur, and snarle heere,

ACT I. SCENE II.
1 *a :* of. 2 *Catamite :* Male prostitute.

I give thy dogged sullennes free libertie : trot about
and be-spurtle[3] whom thou pleasest.

MALEVOLE. Ile come among you, you goatish[3] blooded
Toderers,[2] as Gum into Taffata, to fret, to fret :
Ile fall like a spunge into water to sucke up; to sucke   5
up.   *Howle againe.*
Ile go to church and come to you.

PIETRO. This Malevole is one of the most prodigious affections[4] that ever converst with nature; A man, or
rather a monster; more discontent then Lucifer when   10
he was thrust out of the presence, his appetite is un-
satiable as the Grave; as farre from any content, as
from heaven : his highest delight is to procure others
vexation, and therein he thinkes he truly serves
heaven; for 'tis his position, whosoever in this earth   15
can bee contented, is a slave and damn'd; therefore
do's he afflict al in that to which they are most affected[5]; th'Elements struggle within him; his own
soule is at variance within her selfe : his speach is
halter-worthy[6] at all houres : I like him; faith, he   20
gives good intelligence to my spirit, makes me understand those weakenesses which others flattery palli-
ates : harke, they sing.

                                                          25

SCENA TERTIA.

Enter MALEVOLE *after the Song.*

[PIETRO.] See : he comes : now shall you heare the ex-
treamitie of a Malcontent :[1] he is as free as ayre :   30
he blowes over every man. And sir, whence come you
now?

MALEVOLE. From the publike place of much dissimula-
tion, (the Church.)

---

[3] *be-spurtle* : urinate upon.   [5] *affected* : inclined.
[4] *prodigious affections* :   [6] *is halter-worthy* : deserves
passionate dispositions.   hanging.

ACT I. SCENE III

PIETRO. What didst there?

MALEVOLE. Talke with a Usurer : take up at interest.

PIETRO. I wonder what religion thou art of.

MALEVOLE. Of a souldiers religion.

PIETRO. And what doost thinke makes most infidells now? 5

MALEVOLE. Sects, sects, I have seene seeming *Pietie* change her roabe so oft, that sure none but some arch-divell can shape her a Petticote.

PIETRO. O! a religious pollicie. 10

MALEVOLE. But damnation on a politique religion : I am wearie, would I were one of the Dukes houndes now.

PIETRO. But what's the common newes abroad Malevole, thou dogst rumor still? 15

MALEVOLE. Common newes? why common wordes are, God save yee, Fare yee well : common actions, Flattery and Cosenage[1] : common things, Women and Cuckolds : and how do's my little Ferrardo? ah[2] yee lecherous Animall, my little Ferret, he goes suck- 20 ing up and downe the pallace into every hens nest like a Weesell : and to what doost thou addict thy time to now, more then to those Antique painted drabs that are still affected of[2] yong Courtiers, *Flattery, Pride,* and *Venery.* 25

FERRARDO. I studie languages : who doost thinke to be the best linguist of our age?

MALEVOLE. Phew, the Divell, let him possesse thee, hee'le teach thee to speake all languages, most readily and strangely, and great reason mary, hees traveld 30 greatly in the world; & is every where.

FERRARDO. Save i'th Court.

MALEVOLE. I, save i'th Court : (*To* BILIOSO.) and how do's my olde muckhill over-spread with fresh snow :

ACT I. SCENE III.
1 *Cosenage* : Cheating.   2 *affected of* : desired by.

129

thou halfe a man, halfe a goate, al a beast : how do's
thy yong wife, old huddle³?

BILIOSO. Out you improvident rascall.

MALEVOLE. Doe, kicke thou hugely hornd old Dukes
Oxe, good Master make-place.[3]   5

PIETRO. How doost thou live now a daies Malevole?

MALEVOLE. Why like the Knight Sir *Patrik Penlolians*,(1)
with killing a spiders for my Ladies Munkey.

PIETRO. How doost spend the night, I heare thou never
sleep'st?   10

MALEVOLE. O no, but dreame the most fantasticall : O
heaven : O fubbery, fubbery⁴!

PIETRO. Dreame, what dreamst?

MALEVOLE. Why me thinkes I see that *Signior* pawn
his foot-cloth⁵ : that *Metreza* her Plate : this madam   15
takes phisicke : that tother *Mounsieur* may minister
to her : heere is a Pander jeweld : there is a fellow
in shift of Satten this day, that could not shift a shirt
tother night : heere a *Paris* supports that *Hellen* :
there's a Lady *Guinever* beares up that sir *Lancelot*.   20
Dreames, dreames, visions, fantasies, *Chimeraes*, imaginations, trickes, conceits,⁶ (*To* PREPASSO.) Sir *Tris-
tram Trimtram* come a loft Jacke-a-napes with a
whim wham,(2) heere's a Knight of the land of
Catito(3) shall play at trap⁷ with any page in Eu-   25
rope; Do the sword-dance, with any Morris dancer
in Christendome; ride at the Ring(4) till the finne⁸
of his eyes looke as blew as the welkin,⁹ and runne
the wilde-goose chase even with *Pompey the huge*.(5)

PIETRO. You runne.   30

MALEVOLE. To the divell : now *Signor* Guerrino; that
thou from a most pittied prisoner shouldst grow a

---

³ *huddle :* miser.
⁴ *fubbery :* deception.
⁵ *foot-cloth :* ornamental saddle
  cloth.

⁶ *conceits :* illusions.
⁷ *trap :* a boy's game.
⁸ *finne :* lid.
⁹ *welkin :* sky.

most loathd flatterer : Alas poore Celso, thy starr's
opprest, thou art an honest Lord, tis pity.

EQUATO. Ist pitty?

MALEVOLE. I marry ist philosophical Equato, & 'tis pitty
that thou being so excellent a scholler by art, shouldst   5
be so ridiculous a foole by nature : I have a thing to
tell you Duke; bid um avaunt, bid um avaunt.

PIETRO. Leave us, leave us,

              Exeunt all saving PIETRO *and* MALEVOLE.

now sir what ist?   10

MALEVOLE. Duke thou art a *Beco*,[10] a *Cornuto*.[11]

PIETRO. How?

MALEVOLE. Thou art a Cuckold.

PIETRO. Speake; unshale[12] him quicke.

MALEVOLE. With most tumbler-like nimblenes.   15

PIETRO. Who? by whom? I burst with desire.

MALEVOLE. Mendoza is the man makes thee a hornd
beast; Duke 'tis Mendoza cornutes thee.

PIETRO. What conformance[13]; relate, short, short.

MALEVOLE. As a Lawyers beard,   20
  There is an old Crone in the Court, her name is
                    Maquerelle,
  She is my mistris sooth to say, and she doth ever tell
                    me,
Blirt a rime; blirt a rime; Maquerelle is a cunning   25
bawde, I am an honest villaine, thy wife is a close
drab,[14] and thou art a notorious cuckold, farewell
Duke.

PIETRO. Stay, stay.

MALEVOLE. Dull, dull Duke, can lazy patience make   30
lame revenge? O God for a woman to make a man
that which God never created, never made!

PIETRO. What did God never make?

MALEVOLE. A cuckold : To bee made a thing that's hud-

---

[10] *Beco* : Cuckold.   [13] *conformance* : evidence.
[11] *Cornuto* : Horned one.   [14] *close drab* : secret whore.
[12] *unshale* : reveal.

winkt with kindenesse, whilst every rascall philips[15]
his browes; to have a coxcombe with egregious
hornes, pind to a Lords backe, every page sporting
himselfe with delightfull laughter, whilst hee must
be the last must know it; Pistols and Poniards,[16] Pis-   5
tols and Poniards.

PIETRO. Death and damnation!

MALEVOLE . Lightning and thunder!

PIETRO. Vengeance and torture!

MALEVOLE. *Catzo!*[(6)]   10

PIETRO. O revenge!

MALEVOLE. Nay, to select among ten thousand faires,
    A Lady farre inferior to the most,
    In faire proportion both of limbe and soule :
    To take her from austerer check of parents,   15
    To make her his by most devoutfull rightes,
    Make her commandresse of a better essence
    Then is the gorgious world, even[4] of a man.
    To hug her with as rais'd an appetite,
    As usurers do their delv'd up treasury,   20
    (Thinking none tells[17] it but his private selfe,)
    To meete her spirit in a nimble kisse,
    Distilling panting ardor to her hart.
    True to her sheetes, nay diets strong his blood,
    To give her height of *Hymeneall* sweetes.   25

PIETRO. O God!

MALEVOLE. Whilst she lispes, & gives him some court
                       quelquechose[18]
    Made onely to provoke, not satiate :
    And yet even then, the thaw of her delight   30
    Flowes from lewde heate of apprehension,[19]
    Onely from strange imaginations rankenes,
    That formes the adulterers presence in her soule,

---

[15] *philips* : fillips.
[16] *Poniards* : Daggers.
[17] *tells* : counts.

[18] *quelquechose* : trifle.
[19] *apprehension* : mental
    anticipation.

And makes her thinke she clips[20] the foule knaves
               loines.

PIETRO. Affliction to my bloods roote.

MALEVOLE. Nay thinke, but thinke what may proceede
               of this,   5
Adultery is often the mother of incest.

PIETRO. Incest.

MALEVOLE. Yes incest : marke, Mendoza of his wife begets perchance a daughter. Mendoza dies. His son
marries this daughter. Say you? Nay tis frequent, not   10
onely probable, but no question often acted, whilst
ignorance, fearelesse ignorance claspes his owne
seede.

PIETRO. Hydeous imagination!

MALEVOLE. Adultery? why next to the sinne of Symony,   15
'tis the most horride transgression under the cope of
salvation.[21]

PIETRO. Next to Simony?

MALEVOLE. I, next to Symony, in which our men in next
age shall not sinne.   20

PIETRO. Not sinne? Why?

MALEVOLE. Because (thankes to some church-men)
our age will leave them nothing to sinne with. But
adultery! O dulnes! should show[5] exemplary punishment, that intemperate bloods may freeze, but to   25
thinke it. I would dam him and all his generation, my
owne hands should do it; ha, I would not trust heaven
with my vengeance any thing.

PIETRO. Any thing, any thing; Malevole thou shalt see
instantly what temper my spirit holdes; farewell, re-   30
member I forget thee not, farewell.   *Exit* PIETRO.

MALEVOLE. Farewell.
Leane thoughtfulnes, a sallow meditation,
Sucke thy veines drie, distemperance rob thy sleepe,
The hearts disquiet is revenge most deepe.   35

---

[20] *clips* : embraces.   [21] *cope of salvation* : vault of
                                                   heaven.

He that gets blood, the life of flesh but spilles,
But he that breakes hearts peace, the deare soule
kills.
    Well, this disguise doth yet afford me that
Which kings do seldome heare, or great men use,   5
Free speach : and though my state's[6] usurpt,
Yet this affected straine gives me a tongue,
As fetterlesse as is an Emperours.
I may speake foolishly, I knavishly,
Alwaies carelesly, yet no one thinkes it fashion   10
To poize[22] my breath, "for he that laughs and strikes,
Is lightly felt, or seldome strucke againe."
Duke, Ile torment thee : now my just revenge,
From thee than crowne a richer jemme shall part.
Beneath God naught's so deare as a calme heart.   15

Scena quarta.

Enter CELSO.

CELSO. My honor'd Lord.   20
MALEVOLE. Peace, speake low; peace, O Celso, constant
          Lord,
  (Thou to whose faith I onely rest discovered,
  Thou, one of full ten millions of men,
  That lovest vertue onely for it selfe;   25
  Thou in whose hands old *Ops*[1] may put her soule :)
Behold for ever banisht Altofront
This *Genoas* last yeares Duke, O truly noble,
I wanted those old instruments of state,
Dissemblance, and Suspect[2] : I could not time it   30
          Celso,
My throne stood like a point in middest of a circle,
To all of equall neerenes, bore with none :
Raignd all alike, so slept in fearelesse vertue,

22 *poize :* weigh; consider.
  ACT I. SCENE IV.   of harvest.
1 *Ops :* Wife of Cronos, goddess   2 *Suspect :* Suspicion.

Suspectlesse, too suspectlesse : till the croude :
(Still liquorous[3] of untried novelties,)
Impatient with severer government :
Made strong with *Florence :* banisht Altofront.
CELSO. Strong with *Florence,* I, thence your mischiefe   5
             rose,
For when the daughter of the *Florentine*
Was matched once with his Pietro now Duke,
No stratagem of state untride was left, till you of all—
MALEVOLE. Of all was quite bereft,   10
Alas Maria, too close prisoned :
My true faith'd Dutchesse i'th *Citadell.*
CELSO. Ile still adhere, lets mutiny and die.
MALEVOLE. O no, clime not a falling towre Celso,
Tis well held, desperation, no zeale :   15
Hopelesse to strive with fate (peace) Temporize.
Hope, hope, that never forsak'st the wretchedst man,
Yet bidst me live, and lurke in this disguise.
What? play I well the free breath'd discontent?
Why[1] man we are all Philosophical Monarkes   20
Or naturall fooles, Celso, the Courts afiar,
The Dutches sheetes will smoke for't ere it be long :
Impure Mendoza that sharpe nosde Lord, that made
The cursed match linkt *Genoa* with *Florence*
Now brode hornes the Duke, which he now knowes :   25
Discord to Malcontents is very *Manna,*
When the rankes are burst, then scuffle Altofront.[1]
CELSO. I but durst.
MALEVOLE. Tis[2] gone, tis swallowed like a minerall,
Some way 'twill worke, phewt! Ile not shrinke,   30
"Hees resolute who can no lower sinke."[2]
     BILIOSO *Entring,* MALEVOLE *shifteth his speach.*
MALEVOLE. O the father of May-poles, did you never
   see a fellow whose strength consisted in his breath,
   respect in his office, religion on his Lord, and love in   35
   himselfe? why then behold.

---

3 *liquorous :* lecherous; desiring.

BILIOSO. Sinior.

MALEVOLE. My right worshipfull Lord,[3] Your court night-cap makes you have a passing high fore-head.

BILIOSO. I can tell you strange newes, but I am sure you know them already. The Duke speakes much good of you. 5

MALEVOLE. Go to then, and shall you and I now enter into a strict friendship?

BILIOSO. Second one another.

MALEVOLE. Yes. 10

BILIOSO. Do one another good offices.

MALEVOLE. Just, what though I cal'd thee old Oxe, egregious Wittall,[4] Broken-bellied Coward, Rotten Mummy, Yet since I am in favor :

BILIOSO. Words of course, tearmes of disport. His grace 15 presents you by me a chaine, as his gratefull remembrance for—I am ignorant for what, marry yee may impart : Yet howsoever—come—deare friend : Doost know my sonne?

MALEVOLE. Your sonne? 20

BILIOSO. He shall eate wood-cocks, dance jigges, make possets,[5] and play at shuttle-cocke with any yong Lord about the Court : he haz as sweete a Lady too : doost know her little bitch?

MALEVOLE. Tis a dogge man. 25

BILIOSO. Beleeve me, a shee bitch? O tis a good creature, thou shalt be her servant,[1] Ile make thee acquainted with my yong wife too : what, I keepe her not at Court for nothing : Tis growne to supper time, come to my table, that any thing I have standes open to 30 thee.

MALEVOLE. (*To* CELSO.) How smooth to him that is in state of grace,
How servile is the ruggedst Courtiers face.

---

[4] *Wittall :* Cuckold.   [5] *possets :* drinks of milk curdled with wine.

> *What Profit, nay what Nature would keepe downe,*
> *Are heav'd to them, are minions to a crowne.*
> *Envious ambition never sates his thirst,*
> *Till sucking all, he swells, and swells, and burstes.*

BILIOSO. I shall now leave you with my alwaies best   5
wishes, onely let's hold betwixt us a firme correspond-
ence, a mutuall-frendly-reciprocall-kinde of steddie-
unanimous-hartily leagued.—

MALEVOLE. Did your sinniorship ne're see a pigeon
house that was smooth, round, and white without,   10
and full of holes and stinke within, ha ye not old
Courtier?

BILIOSO. O yes, tis the forme the fashion of them all.

MALEVOLE. Adue my true Court-friend, farewell my
deare *Castilio*.(2)   15

CELSO. Yonders Mendoza.   *Exit* BILIOSO.

MALEVOLE. (*Descries* MENDOZA.) True, the privie key.

CELSO. I take my leave, sweete Lord.   *Exit* CELSO.

MALEVOLE. Tis fit, away.
                                                           20

SCENA QUINTA.

Enter MENDOZA *with three or foure suters.*

MENDOZA. Leave your suites with me, I can and will :   25
attend my Secretary, leave me.   [*Exeunt suitors.*]

MALEVOLE. Mendoza, harke yee, harke yee. You are a
treacherous villaine, God b'wy yee.

MENDOZA. Out you base borne rascall.

MALEVOLE. We are all the sonnes of heaven, though a   30
Tripe wife[1] were our mother; ah you whore-sonne
hot reinde[11] he *Marmoset, Egistus*(1) didst ever
heare of one *Egistus?*

MENDOZA. *Gistus?*

Act I. Scene v.
[1] *Tripe wife :* Dresser of tripe.

MALEVOLE. I *Egistus*, he was a filthy incontinent Flesh-
monger, such a one as thou art.
MENDOZA. Out grumbling rogue.
MALEVOLE. *Orestes*,[2] beware *Orestes*.
MENDOZA. Out beggar. 5
MALEVOLE. I once shall rise.
MENDOZA. Thou rise?
MALEVOLE. I at the resurrection.
"No vulgar seede, but once may rise, and shall,
No King so huge, but fore he die, may fall." *Exit.* 10
MENDOZA. Now good *Elizium*, what a delicious heaven
is it for a man to be in a Princes favour : O sweete
God! O pleasure! O fortune! O all thou best of life!
what should I thinke : what say? what do? to be a
favorite? a minion? to have a generall timerous re- 15
spect, observe a man, a statefull silence in his presence, solitarinesse in his absence, a confused hum, and
busie murmure of obsequious suters training[2] him;
the cloth held up, and way proclaimed before him :
Petitionary vassalls licking the pavement with their 20
slavish knees, whilst some odde pallace Lampreels[3]
that ingender with snakes, and are full of eyes on both
sides, with a kinde of insinuated humblenesse, fixe all
their delightes upon his brow : O blessed state, what
a ravishing prospect doth the *Olympus* of favour 25
yeeld! Death, I cornute the Duke : sweete women
most sweete Ladies, nay Angells; by heaven he is
more accursed then a divell that hates you, or is
hated by you, and happier then a God that loves you,
or is beloved by you; you preservers of mankinde, 30
life blood of society, who would live, nay who can
live without you? O Paradice, how majesticall is your
austerer presence? how imperiously chaste is your
more modest face? but O! how full of ravishing
attraction is your prettie, petulant, languishing,[2] 35

[2] *training :* following.   [3] *Lampreels :* Lampreys;
bloodsuckers.

laciviously-composed countenance : these amorous smiles, those soule-warming sparkling glances, ardent as those flames that sing'd the world by heedelesse *Phaeton;*[3] in body how delicate, in soule how wittie, in discourse how pregnant, in life how warie, in 5
favours how juditious, in day how sociable, and in night how? O pleasure unutterable, indeede it is most certaine, one man cannot deserve onely to injoy a beauteous woman : but a Dutchesse? in despight of *Phoebus*[4] Ile write a sonnet instantly in praise of 10
her.   *Exit.*

Scena sexta.

15

Enter ferneze *ushering* aurelia, emilia *and* maquerelle *bearing up her traine,* bianca
attending : all go out but aurelia,
maquerelle *and* ferneze.

aurelia. And ist possible? Mendoza slight me, possible? 20
ferneze. Possible? what can be strange in him that's drunke with favor, Growes insolent with grace? speake Maquerelle, speake.
maquerelle. To speake feelingly, more, more richly in sollide sence then worthlesse wordes, give me those 25
jewells of your eares to receive my inforced dutie, as for my part tis well knowne I can put[1] any thing; can beare patiently with any man : (ferneze *privately feedes* maquerelles *hands with jewells during this speech.*) But when I heard he wronged your 30
pretious sweetenes, I was inforced to take deepe offence; Tis most certaine he loves Emilia with high appetite; and as she told me (as you know we women impart our secrets one to another,) when she repulsed his suite, in that hee was possessed with your indeered 35

Act I. Scene vi.
[1] *put :* bear.

grace : Mendoza most ingratefully renounced all faith
to you.

FERNEZE. Nay, cal'd you, speake Maquerelle, speake.

MAQUERELLE. By heaven—witch : dride bisquet, and
contested blushlesly he lov'd you but for a spurt, or   5
so.

FERNEZE. For maintenance.

MAQUERELLE. Advancement and regard.

AURELIA. O villaine! O impudent Mendoza.

MAQUERELLE. Nay he is the rustiest jawde,[1] the   10
fowlest mouthd knave in railing against our sex : he
will raile against women.

AURELIA. How? how?

MAQUERELLE. I am asham'd to speak't, I.

AURELIA. I love to hate him, speake.   15

MAQUERELLE. Why when Emilia scornde his base un-
steddines the blacke throated rascall scoulded, and
sayde.

AURELIA. What?

MAQUERELLE. Troth 'tis too shamelesse.   20

AURELIA. What said hee?

MAQUERELLE. Why that at foure women were fooles, at
foureteene drabbes, at fortie baudes, at fourescore
witches, and a hundred cattes.

AURELIA. O unlimitable impudencie!   25

FERNEZE. But as for poore Fernezes fixed heart,
Was never shadelesse meadow drier parcht,
Under the scortching heate of heavens dog,[1]
Then is my heart with your inforcing eyes.

MAQUERELLE. A hote simile.   30

FERNEZE. Your smiles have beene my heaven, your
frownes my hell,
O pittie then; Grace should with beautie dwell.

MAQUERELLE. Reasonable perfect by'r lady.

AURELIA. I will love thee, be it but in despight   35
Of that Mendoza : witch! Ferneze : witch!
Ferneze thou art the Dutches favorite,
Be faithfull, private, but tis dangerous.

FERNEZE. *"His love is livelesse, that for love feares breath,*
The worst that's due to sinne, O would 'twere death."

AURELIA. Enjoy my favour, I will be sicke instantly & take phisick, Therefore in deapth of night visite.   5

MAQUERELLE. Visite her chamber, but conditionally, you shall not offend her bed : By this diamond.

FERNEZE. By this diamond. *Gives it to* MAQUERELLE.

MAQUERELLE. Nor tarry longer than you please : By this ruby.   10

FERNEZE. By this ruby.   *Gives againe.*

MAQUERELLE. And that the doore shall not creake.

FERNEZE. And that the doore shall not creake.

MAQUERELLE. Nay but sweare.

FERNEZE. By this purse.   *Gives her his purse.*   15

MAQUERELLE. Go to, Ile keepe your oathes for you : remember, visit.

         Enter MENDOZA *reading a sonnet.*

AURELIA. Dri'd bisquet! looke where the base wretch comes.   20

MENDOZA. *Beauties life, heavens modell, loves Queene.*

MAQUERELLE. That's his Emilia.[2]

MENDOZA. *Natures triumph, best on earth.*

MAQUERELLE. Meaning Emilia.

MENDOZA. *Thou onely wonder that the world hath*   25
seene.

MAQUERELLE. That's Emilia.

AURELIA. Must I then heare her praisde Mendoza?

MENDOZA. Madam, your excellency is gratiously incountred;   30
I have beene writing passionate flashes in honor of.
            Exit FERNEZE.

AURELIA. Out villaine, villaine :
O[3] judgement, where have beene my eyes? what
Bewitched election made me dote on thee?   35
What sorcery made me love thee? but be gone,
Bury thy head : O that I could do more
Then loathe thee : hence worst of ill :

No reason aske, our reason is our will.[3]

                Exit with MAQUERELLE.

MENDOZA. Women? nay furies, nay worse, for they torment onely the bad, but women good and bad. Damnation of mankinde : breath, hast thou praisde them   5
for this? And ist you Ferneze are wrigled into smocke
grace? sit sure, O that I could raile against these
monsters in nature, modells of hell, curse of the earth,
women that dare attempt any thing, and what they
attempt, they care not how they accomplish, without   10
all premeditation or prevention, rash in asking, desperate in working, impatient in suffering, extreame
in desiring, slaves unto appetite, mistrisses in dissembling, only constant in unconstancie, onely perfect in counterfaiting : their wordes are fained, their   15
eyes forged, their sights[2] dissembled, their lookes
counterfait, their haire false, their given hopes deceitfull, their very breath artificiall. *Their blood*[3] *is their
onely God : Bad clothes, and old age, are onely the
divells they tremble at.* That I could raile now!   20

SCENA SEPTIMA.

      Enter PIETRO, *his sword drawne.*   25
PIETRO. A mischiefe fill thy throate, thou fowle jaw'd
           slave : Say thy praiers.
MENDOZA. I ha forgot um.
PIETRO. Thou shalt die.
MENDOZA. So shalt thou; I am heart mad.   30
PIETRO. I am horne mad.
MENDOZA.   Extreame mad?
PIETRO. Monstrously mad.
MENDOZA.   Why?
PIETRO. Why? thou, thou hast dishonoured my bed.   35

----

[2] *sights :* sighs.   [3] *blood :* passion.

MENDOZA. I? come, come, sir,[1] heeres my bare heart
> to thee,
As steddy as is this centre to the glorious world.
And yet harke, thou art a *Cornuto;* but by me?
PIETRO. Yes slave by thee.   5
MENDOZA. Do not, do not with tart and spleenefull
> breath,
Lose[2] him can loose[1] thee; I offend my Duke.
Beare record O ye dumbe and raw-ayrde nights,
How vigilant my sleepelesse eyes have beene,   10
To watch the traitour; record thou spirit of truth,
With what debasement I ha throwne my selfe,
To under offices, onely to learne
The truth, the party, time, the meanes, the place,
By whom, and when, and where thou wert disgrac'd.   15
And am I paid with "slave"? hath my intrusion
To places private, and prohibited,
Onely to observe the closer passages,
Heaven knowes with vowes of revelation,
Made me suspected, made me deemd a villaine?   20
What rogue hath wronged us?
PIETRO. Mendoza, I may erre.
MENDOZA. Erre? tis too milde a name, but erre and erre,
Runne giddy with suspect, for through me thou know
That which most creatures save thy selfe do know :   25
Nay since my service hath so loath'd reject,
Fore Ile reveale, shalt finde them clipt together.
PIETRO. Mendoza, Thou know'st I am a most plaine
breasted man.
MENDOZA. The fitter to make a cuckolde : would your   30
browes were most plaine too.
PIETRO. Tell me, indeede I heard thee raile.
MENDOZA. At women, true, why what cold fleame[2]
> could choose,
Knowing a Lord so honest, vertuous,   35

ACT I. SCENE VII.
[1] *loose :* release.   [2] *fleame :* phlegm.

So boundlesse loving, bounteous, faire-shapt, sweete,
To be contemn'd, abusde, defamde, made cuckold :
Hart, I hate all women for't, sweete sheetes, waxe
lightes, antique bed-postes, cambricke smocks, villanous curtaines, arras pictures, oylde hinges, and all   5
the tongue-tide lascivious witnesses of great creatures
wantonnesse : what salvation can you expect?

PIETRO. Wilt thou tell me?

MENDOZA. Why you may find it your selfe, observe,
observe.   10

PIETRO. I ha not the patience, wilt thou deserve me;
tell, give it.

MENDOZA. Tak't, why Ferneze is the man, Ferneze, Ile
proov't, this night you shall take him in your sheetes,
wilt serve?   15

PIETRO. It will, my bozom's in some peace, till night.

MENDOZA. What?

PIETRO. Farewell.

MENDOZA. God! how weake a Lord are you,
Why do you thinke there is no more but so?   20

PIETRO. Why?

MENDOZA. Nay then will I presume to counsell you,
It should be thus; you with some guard upon the
suddaine
Breake into the Princess[3] chamber, I stay behinde   25
Without the doore, through which he needs must
passe,
Ferneze flies, let him, to me he comes, hee's kild
By me, observe by me, you follow, I raile,
And seeme to save the bodie : Dutches comes   30
On whom (respecting her advanced birth,
And your faire nature,) I know, nay I do know
No violence must be used. She comes, I storme,
I praise, excuse Ferneze, and still maintaine
The Dutches honor, she for this loves me,   35
I honour you, shall know her soule, you mine,
Then naught shall she contrive in vengeance,
(As women are most thoughtfull in revenge)

144

Of her Ferneze, but you shall sooner know't
Then she can think't. Thus shall his death come sure,
Your Dutches braine-caught; so your life secure.

PIETRO. It is too well, my bozome, and my heart,
"*When nothing helpes, cut off the rotten part.*" *Exit.*   5

MENDOZA. "*Who cannot faine friendship, can nere produce the effects of hatred*": Honest foole Duke, subtile lascivious Dutches, seely[3] novice Ferneze; I do
laugh at yee, my braine is in labour till it produce
mischiefe, and I feele sudden throws, proofes sensible,   10
the issue is at hand.

"*As Beares shape yong, so Ile forme my devise,
Which growne prooves horride: vengeance makes
men wise.*"   [*Exit.*]   15

[Scena octava.]

Enter MALEVOLE *and* PASSARELLO.

MALEVOLE. Foole, most happily incountred, canst sing   20
foole?

PASSARELLO. Yes I can sing foole, if youle beare the
burden,[1] and I can play upon instruments, scurvily,
as gentlemen do; O that I had beene gelded, I should
then have beene a fatte foole for a chamber, a squeak-   25
ing foole for a taverne, and a private foole for all the
Ladies.

MALEVOLE. You are in good case since you came to
court foole; what garded,[2] garded!

PASSARELLO. Yes faith, even as footemen and bawdes   30
weare velvet, not for an ornament of Honour, but for
a badge of drudgery: for now the Duke is discontented I am faine to foole him asleepe every night.

MALEVOLE. What are his griefes?

---

[3] *seely* : silly; naive.

Act I. Scene viii.   *pun*).
[1] *burden* : bass part (*with*   [2] *garded* : gaily clothed.

PASSARELLO. He hath sore eies.

MALEVOLE. I never observed so much.

PASSARELLO. Horrible sore eyes; and so hath every
Cuckold, for the rootes of the hornes spring in the
eye-balles, and thats the reason the horne of a cuck-   5
olde is as tender as his eie; or as that growing in the
womans forehead twelve yeeres since, that could not
endure to be toucht.[1] The Duke hangs downe his
head like a columbine.

MALEVOLE. Passarello, why doe great men begge[3]   10
fooles?

PASSARELLO. As the Welchman stole rushes, when there
was nothing else to filch; onely to keepe begging in
fashion.

MALEVOLE. Pue, thou givest no good reason, Thou   15
speakest like a foole.

PASSARELLO. Faith I utter small fragments as your
knight courtes your Citty widow with jingling of his
gilt[1] spurres, advancing his bush colored beard,
and taking Tabacco. This is all the mirrour of their   20
knightly complements[4] : Nay I shall talke when my
toong is a going once; tis like a Citizen on horsebacke,
evermore in a false gallop.

MALEVOLE. And how dooth Maquerelle fare nowa-
dayes?   25

PASSARELLO. Faith I was wont to salute her as our English women are at their first landing in *Flushing;*[2]
I would call her whoore; but now that antiquitie
leaves her as an old peece of plasticke t'work by,[5] I
onely aske hir how her rotten teeth fare every morn-   30
ing, and so leave her : she was the first that ever
invented perfumd smocks for the gentlewomen, and
woollen shooes for feare of creaking : for the visitant,

[3] *begge :* ask guardianship of.
[4] *complements :* accomplish-
ments.

[5] *an old peece of plasticke
t'work by :* an old image to
copy.

she were an excellent Lady, but that hir face peeleth[3] like Muscovie glasse.[6]

MALEVOLE. And how dooth thy olde Lord that hath wit enough to be a flatterer, and conscience enough to be a knave?

PASSARELLO. O excellent, he keepes beside me fifteene jeasters, to instruct him in the Art of fooling, and utters their jeastes in private to the Duke and Dutchesse; heele lie like to your Switzer,[4] or Lawyer; heele be of any side for most mony.

MALEVOLE. I am in haste, be briefe.

PASSARELLO. As your Fidler when he is payd, Heele thrive I warrant you, while your yong courtier stands like Good-friday in Lent, men long to see it, because more fatting dayes come after it, else hees the leanest and pittifulst actor in the whole Pageant; Adew Malevole.

MALEVOLE. O world most vilde,[7] when thy loose vanities Taught by this foole, do make the foole seeme wise!

PASSARELLO. Youle know me againe Malevole.

MALEVOLE. O I, by that velvet.

PASSARELLO. I, as a petti-fogger[5] by his buckram bagge, I am as common in the Court as an hostesses lippes in the countrey; knights, and clownes, and knaves, and all share mee : the Court cannot possibly be without me. Adue Malevole.   *Exeunt severally.*

[6] *Muscovie glasse :* Mica.   [7] *vilde :* vile.

Actus II. Scena i.

Enter MENDOZA *with a sconce,[1] to observe* FERNEZES   5
entrance, who whilest the Act is playing,
enter unbraced,[2] two pages before him with
lights, is met by MAQUERELLE *and convayed*
in. The pages are sent away.

MENDOZA. Hees caught, the woodcockes head is i'th   10
   noose,
Now treads Ferneze in dangerous path of lust,
Swearing his sence is meerely[3] deified.
The foole graspes clouds,(1) and shall beget Cen-
   taures;   15
And now in strength of panting faint delight,
The Goate bids heaven envie him; good Goose,
I can affoorde thee nothing but the poore comfort of
   calamity, Pitty.
"Lust's like the plummets hanging on clocke lines,   20
Wil nere ha done til all is quite undone."
Such is the course salt sallow lust dooth runne,
Which thou shalt trie; Ile be revengde. Duke thy
   suspect,[4]
Dutchesse thy disgrace, Ferneze thy rivallship   25
Shall have swift vengeance; nothing so holy,
No band of nature so strong,
No law of friendship so sacred,
But Ile profane, burst, violate,
Fore Ile indure disgrace, contempt, and povertie :   30
Shall I, whose very humme strooke all heads bare;
Whose face made silence, creaking of whose shooe
Forcde the most private passages flie ope,

ACT II. SCENE i.
[1] *sconce :* lantern.
[2] *unbraced :* without upper
 garment.

[3] *meerely :* completely; purely.
[4] *suspect :* suspicion (*of*
 Mendoza).

Scrape like a servile dogge at some latcht doore?
Learne now to make a leg⁵? and crie, beseech yee,
Pray yee, is such a Lord within? be awde
At some odde Ushers scofft formalitie?
First feare my braines; *Unde cadis non quo re-*   5
    *fert;*⁶, (2)
My heart cries, perish all : how! how! *"What fate*
Can once avoyde revenge, thats desperate,"
Ile to the Duke; if all should ope, if! tush;
"Fortune still dotes on those who cannot blush."   10

Scena secunda.

Enter MALEVOLE *at one doore,* BIANCA, EMILIA *and*   15
    MAQUERELLE *at the other doore.*

MALEVOLE. Blesse yee cast a¹ Ladies : ha *Dipsas,*⁽¹⁾
howe doost thou olde Cole?⁽²⁾

MAQUERELLE. Olde Cole?

MALEVOLE. I olde Cole; mee thinkes thou liest like a   20
brand under billets of greene wood. Hee that will inflame a yong wenches hart, let him lay close to her
an old cole that hath first bin fired, a pandresse, my
halfe burnt lint,² who though thou canst not flame
thy selve, yet arte able to set a thousand virgins ta-   25
pers afire : and how dooth *Janivere*⁽³⁾ thy husband,
my little periwincle, is hee troubled with the cough
of the lungs stil? doos he hawke³ a nights still, he will
not bite.

BIANCA. No by my troth, I tooke him with his mouth   30
emptie of olde teeth.

MALEVOLE. And hee tooke thee with thy belly full of

---

⁵ *make a leg :* bow.
⁶ *Unde cadis . . . refert :*
Whence you fall, not whither
is what matters.

Act II. Scene ii.
¹ *cast a :* set of.
² *lint :* Flax refuse used to start
fires.
³ *hawke :* cough.

yoong bones : Marie[4] he tooke his maime by the
stroke of his enemy.

BIANCA. And I mine by the stroke of my friend.

MALEVOLE. The close stocke[5]! o mortall wench : Lady,
ha ye now no restoratives for your decaied *Jasons?*   5
Looke yee, crabs guts bak'd,[(4)] distild oxe-pith, the
pulverized haires of a lions upper lip, gellie of cocke-
sparrowes, he monkies marrow, or powlder of foxe-
stones. And whither are you ambling now?

BIANCA. To bed, to bed.   10

MALEVOLE. Doe your husbands lie with yee?

BIANCA. That were country fashion yfaith.

MALEVOLE. Ha yee no foregoers about you : come,
whither in good deed law now?

BIANCA. In good indeed law now, to eate the most mi-   15
raculously, admirably, astonishable composd posset[(5)] with three curds, without anie drinke : wil yee
helpe mee with a hee foxe? heeres the Duke.

> *The Ladies goe out.*

MALEVOLE. (*To* BIANCA.) Fride frogs are very good &   20
French-like too.

SCENA TERTIA.

25

Enter Duke PIETRO, *Count* CELSO, *Count* EQUATO,
BILIOSO, FERRARDO, *and* MENDOZA.

PIETRO. The night growes deepe and fowle, what houre
ist?

CELSO. Upon the stroake of twelve.   30

MALEVOLE. Save yee Duke.

PIETRO. From thee : be gone, I doe not love thee, let
mee see thee no more, we are displeased.

MALEVOLE. Why God be with thee, heaven heare my
curse, May thy wife and thee live long together.   35

PIETRO. Be gone sirra.

---

[4] *Marie :* By Mary; marry.   [5] *close stocke :* secret thrust.

MALEVOLE. When *Arthur* first in Court beganne,—
Agamemnon: Menelaus—was ever any Duke a
Cornuto?[1]

PIETRO. Be gone hence.

MALEVOLE. What religion wilt thou be of next? 5

MENDOZA. Out with him.

MALEVOLE. With most servile patience time will come,
When wonder of thy error will strike dumbe,
Thy bezeld[1] sence, slaves I'[2] favour,[1] I mary shall
          he, rise, 10
"Good God! how subtile hell dooth flatter vice,
Mounts him aloft, and makes him seeme to flie,
As Foule the Tortois mockt, who to the skie,
Th'ambitious shell-fish raisde; th'end of all,
Is onely, that from height he might dead fall."[2] 15

BILIOSO. Why when? out yee rogue, be gone ye rascal.

MALEVOLE. I shall now leave yee with all my best
wishes.

BILIOSO. Out ye curre.

MALEVOLE. Onely lets hold together a firme correspond- 20
ence.

BILIOSO. Out.

MALEVOLE. A mutual friendly reciprocall perpetuall
kind of steddie unanimous heartily leagued.

BILIOSO. Hence yee grosse jaw'd pesantly, out, go. 25

MALEVOLE. Adue pigeon house: thou Burre that onely
stickest to nappy fortunes, the Sarpego,[3] the Strangury,[4] an eternall uneffectuall *Priapisme*[3] seise
thee.

BILIOSO. Out rogue. 30

MALEVOLE. Maiest thou be a notorious wittally pander
to thine owne wife, and yet get no office but live to
be the utmost miserie of mankinde, a beggarly cuckold. *Exit.*

ACT II. SCENE III.
1 *bezeld*: intoxicated.   3 *Sarpego*: Ringworm.
2 *I'*: In.   4 *Strangury*: Urinary disorder.

151

PIETRO. It shall be so.

MENDOZA. It must be so, for where great states revenge,
"Tis requisite the partes which pietie,
And soft respect forbeares, be closely dogd,[(4)]
Lay one into his breast shall sleepe with him, 5
Feede in the same dish, runne in selfe[5] faction,
Who may discover any shape of danger;
For once disgracde, displayed in offence,
It makes man blushlesse, and man is (all confesse)
More prone to vengeance than to gratefulnesse. 10
Favours are writ in dust, but stripes[6] we feele,
Depraved nature stamps in lasting steele."

PIETRO. You shall be leagued with the Dutchesse.

EQUATO. The plot is very good.

[PIETRO.][(2)] You shall both kill, and seeme the corse[7] 15
to save.

FERRARDO. A most fine braine tricke.

CELSO. (*Tacitè.[8]*) Of a most cunning knave.

PIETRO. My Lordes, the heavy action we intend,
Is death and shame, two of the ugliest shapes 20
That can confound a soule; thinke, thinke of it :
I strike, but yet like him that gainst stone walles
Directs his shafts, rebounds in his owne face,
My Ladies shame is mine; ô God tis mine.
Therefore I doe conjure all secrecie, 25
Let it be as very little as may be; pray yee, as may be.
Make frightlesse entrance, salute her with soft eyes,
Staine nought with blood, onely Ferneze dies,
But not before her browes : O Gentlemen,
God knowes I love her; nothing else, but this, 30
I am not well. If griefe that suckes veines drie,
Rivels the skinne, casts ashes in mens faces,
Be-dulls the eye, unstrengthens all the blood :
Chance to remoove me to another world,
As sure I once must die : let him succeede : 35

---

[5] *selfe :* the same.   [7] *corse :* body of Ferneze.
[6] *stripes :* wounds.   [8] *Tacitè :* Aside.

I have no childe; all that my youth begot,
Hath bin your loves, which shall inherite me :
Which as it ever shall, I doe conjure it.
Mendoza may succeede, hee's noble borne,
With me of much desert.   5

CELSO. (*Tacitè.*) Much.

PIETRO. Your silence answers I,
I thanke you, come on now : ô that I might die
Before her shame's displayd! would I were forcde
To burne my fathers Tombe, unheale[9] his bones,   10
And dash them in the durt, rather than this :
This both the living and the dead offend :
"Sharpe Surgery where nought but death amends."
                              Exit with the others.
                                                           15

SCENA QUARTA.

Enter MAQUERELLE, EMILIA, *and* BIANCA
with the posset.

MAQUERELLE. Even heere it is, three curdes in three   20
regions individually distinct. Most methodicall according to art compos'd without any drink.

BIANCA. Without any drinke?

MAQUERELLE. Upon my honour, will you sit and eate?

EMILIA. Good, the composure, the receit, how ist?   25

MAQUERELLE. Tis a prettie pearle, by this pearle, (how
doost with me,[1]) thus it is, seaven and thirtie yelkes
of *Barbarie* hennes egges, eighteene spoonefulles and
a halfe of the juyce of cockesparrow bones, one ounce,
three drammes, foure scruples,[2] and one quarter of   30
the sirrop of *Ethiopian* dates, sweetned with three
quarters of a pound of pure candied[1] *Indian
Eringos,*[3, (1)] strewed over with the powder of pearle

---

[9] *unheale :* uncover.
ACT II. SCENE IV.
[1] *how . . . me :* how does it
suit me.

[2] A scruple is one twenty-fourth
of an ounce.
[3] *Indian Eringos :* An
aphrodisiac.

of *America,* amber of *Cataia,*[4] and lambe stones[(2)]
of *Muscovia.*

BIANCA. Trust me the ingredients are very cordiall, and
no question good, and most powerfull in restauration.

MAQUERELLE. I know not what you meane by restaura-   5
tion, but this it doth, it purifieth the blood, smootheth
the skinne, inlifeneth the eye, strengthneth the veines,
mundifieth[5] the teeth, comforteth the stomacke,
fortifieth the backe, and quickneth the wit; that's all.

EMILIA. By my troth I have eaten but two spoonefulls,   10
and me thinkes I could discourse most swiftly and
wittily alreadie.

MAQUERELLE. Have you the art to seeme honest[6]?

BIANCA. I thanke advise and practise.

MAQUERELLE. Why then eate me of this posset, quicken   15
your blood, and preserve your beautie. Do you know
doctor Plaster-face, by this curde, hee is the most
exquisite in forging of veines, sprightning of eyes,
dying of haire, sleeking of skinnes, blushing of
cheekes, surphleing[7] of breastes, blanching and   20
bleaching of teeth that ever made an old Lady gratious by torch-light : by this curd law.

BIANCA. We, we are resolved, what god haz given us
weel cherish.

MAQUERELLE. Cherish any thing saving your husband,   25
keepe him not too high, lest he leape the pale : but
for your beautie, let it be your saint, bequeath two
houres to it every morning in your closet : I ha beene
yong, and yet in my conscience I am not above five
and twentie, but beleeve me, preserve and use your   30
beautie; for youth and beautie once gone, we are like
bee-hives without hony : out a fashion apparell that
no man will weare, therefore use me your beautie.

---

[4] *Cataia :* China.   [7] *surphleing :* painting with
[5] *mundifieth :* cleanses.   cosmetics.
[6] *honest :* chaste.

EMILIA. I but men say.

MAQUERELLE. Men say? let men say what they wil,
life a' woman, they are ignorant of your wants, the
more in yeares, the more in perfection they grow : if
they loose youth & beauty, they gaine wisedome &   5
discretion : But when our beautie fades, goodnight
with us : there cannot be an uglier thing to see, then
an olde woman, from which, O pruning, pinching,
& painting, deliver all sweete beauties.

BIANCA. Harke, musicke.   10

MAQUERELLE. Peace, tis in the Dutches bed-chamber,
good rest most prosperously grac'd Ladies.

EMILIA. Good-night sentinell.[2]

BIANCA. Night deere Maquerelle.

     Exeunt all but MAQUERELLE.   15

MAQUERELLE. May my possets operation send you my
wit & honesty, And me your youth & beauty : the
pleasingst rest.   *Exit* MAQUERELLE.

              20

    SCENA QUINTA.

        A song.
Whilest the song is singing, enter MENDOZA *with his*
sword drawne, standing readie to murder FERNEZE
  as he flies from the Dutches chamber.   25

ALL. [*Within.*] Strike, strike.

AURELIA. [*Within.*] Save my Ferneze, O save my
       Ferneze.
Enter FERNEZE *in his shirt, and is received*
    upon MENDOZAS *sword.*   30

ALL. [*Within.*] Follow, pursue.

AURELIA. [*Within.*] O save Ferneze.

MENDOZA. Pierce, pierce, thou shallow foole drop there.
 "He that attempts a Princes lawlesse love,
 Must have broade hands, close heart, with *Argos*   35
      eyes,[1]
 And backe of *Hercules,* or else he dies."
    Thrusts his rapier in FERNEZE.

Enter AURELIA, *Duke* PIETRO, FERRARDO,
BILIOSO, CELSO, *and* EQUATO.

ALL. Follow, follow.

MENDOZA. Stand off, forbeare, yee most uncivill Lords.

PIETRO. Strike.   5

MENDOZA. Do not; tempt not a man resolved,
   Would you inhumane murtherers more then death?

AURELIA. O poore Ferneze.

MENDOZA. Alas, now all defence too late.

AURELIA.   Hee's dead.   10

PIETRO. I am sory for our shame : go to your bed :
   Weepe not too much, but leave some teares to shed
   When I am dead.

AURELIA. What weepe for thee? my soule no teares shall
                                 finde.   15

PIETRO. Alas, alas, that womens soules are blinde.

MENDOZA. Betray such beautie, murther such youth,
                        contemne civilitie.
   He loves him not that railes not at him.

PIETRO. Thou canst not moove us : we have blood   20
                        ynough.
   And please you Lady we have quite forgot
   All your defects : if not, why then.

AURELIA.   Not.

PIETRO. Not : the best of rest, good night.   25

                Exit PIETRO *with other Courtiers.*

AURELIA. Despight go with thee.

MENDOZA. Madam, you ha done me foule disgrace.
   You have wrongd him much, loves you too much.
   Go to; your soule knowes you have.   30

AURELIA. I thinke I have.

MENDOZA. Do you but thinke so?

AURELIA. Nay, sure I have, my eyes have witnessed
                        thy love :
   Thou hast stoode too firme for me.   35

MENDOZA. Why tell me faire cheekt Lady, who even in
                        tears,
   Art powerfully beauteous, what unadvised passion

Strooke ye into such a violent heate against me?
Speake, what mischiefe wrongd us? what divell in-
                    jur'd us?
Speake.

AURELIA. That thing nere worthy of the name of man;   5
                    Ferneze,
Ferneze swore thou lov'st Emilia,
Which to advance with most reproachfull breath,
Thou both didst blemish and denounce my love.

MENDOZA. Ignoble villaine, did I for this bestride   10
Thy wounded limbes; for this? O God! for this?
Sunke all my hopes, and with my hopes my life,
Ript bare my throte unto the hangmans axe.
Thou most dishonour'd trunke—Emilia.
By life I know her not—Emilia.   15
Did you beleeve him?

AURELIA.   Pardon me, I did.

MENDOZA. Did you? and thereupon you graced him.

AURELIA. I did.

MENDOZA.   Tooke him to favour, nay even clasp'd   20
With him?

AURELIA. Alas I did.

MENDOZA.   This night?

AURELIA.   This night.

MENDOZA. And in your lustfull twines the Duke tooke   25
                    you?

AURELIA. A most sad truth.

MENDOZA. O God! O God! how we dull honest soules,
Heavie brainde men are swallowed in the bogs
Of a deceitfull ground, whilest nimble bloods,   30
Light joynted spirits pent,[1], [1], (2) cut good mens
                    throates,
And scape; alas, I am too honest for this age,
Too full of fleame,[2] and heavie steddinesse :
Stood still whilst this slave cast a noose about me;   35

ACT II. SCENE v.
[1] *pent* : confined.   [2] *fleame* : phlegm.

Nay then to stand in honour of him and her,
Who had even slic'd my heart.

AURELIA. Come, I did erre, and am most sorry, I did
erre.

MENDOZA. Why we are both but dead, the Duke hates   5
us.
"And those whom Princes do once groundly hate,
Let them provide to die as sure as fate,
Prevention[3] *is the heart of pollicie."*

AURELIA. Shall we murder him?   10

MENDOZA. Instantly.

AURELIA. Instantly? before he castes a plot?
Or further blaze my honours much knowne blot?
Lets murther him.

MENDOZA. I would do much for you, will yee marry me?   15

AURELIA. Ile make thee Duke : we are of *Medices.*
Florence our friend in court my faction
Not meanely strengthfull; the Duke then dead,
We well prepard for change : the multitude
Irresolutely reeling, we in force :   20
Our partie seconded, the kingdome mazde,
No doubt of swift successe, all shall be grac'd.

MENDOZA. You do confirme me, we are resolute,
To morrow looke for change, rest confident.
Tis now about the immodest waste[4] of night,   25
The mother of moist dew with pallide light
Spreads gloomie shades about the nummed earth.
Sleepe, sleepe, whilst we contrive our mischiefes
birth;
This man Ile get inhumde; farewell, to bed;   30
I kisse the pillow, dreame, the Duke is dead.

                       Exit AURELIA.

So, so good night, how fortune dotes on impudence,
I am in private the adopted sonne of yon good Prince.
I must be Duke; why if I must, I must,   35
Most seely Lord, name me? O heaven!

---

[3] *Prevention :* Foresight.   [4] *waste :* waist; middle.

I see God made honest fooles, to maintaine crafty
  knaves :
The Dutchesse is wholy mine too; must kill her
  husband
To quit her shame; much; then marry her : I,   5
O I grow prowd in prosperous treachery!
As wrastlers clip, so ile embrace you all,
Not to support, but to procure your fall.
            Enter MALEVOLE.

MALEVOLE. God arrest thee.   10

MENDOZA. At whose suite?

MALEVOLE. At the divels; ah you treacherous damnable
  monster!
How doost? how doost, thou treacherous roague?
Ah yee rascall, I am banisht the Court sirra.   15

MENDOZA. Prethee lets be acquainted, I doe love thee
  faith.

MALEVOLE. At your service, by the Lord law, shall's goe
  to supper, let's be once drunke together, and so unite
  a most vertuously strengthened friendship, shall's   20
  Hugonot,[5] shall's?

MENDOZA. Wilt fall upon my chamber to morrowe
  morne?

MALEVOLE. As a raven to a dunghill; they say theres one
  dead heere, prickt for the pride of the flesh.   25

MENDOZA. Ferneze : there he is, prethee bury him.

MALEVOLE. O most willingly, I mean to turne pure
  Rochel churchman,[6] I.

MENDOZA. Thou churchman! why? why?

MALEVOLE. Because Ile live lazily, raile upon author-   30
  itie, deny kings supremacy in things indifferent, and
  be a Pope in mine owne parish.

MENDOZA. Wherefore doost thou thinke churches were
  made?

MALEVOLE. To scowre plow-shares, I have seene oxen   35

[5] *Hugonot :* Huguenot;   [6] *Rochel churchman :* French
dissenter and rebel.   Protestant.

plow uppe Altares : *Et nunc seges ubi Sion fuit.*[7, (3)]

MENDOZA. Strange.

MALEVOLE. Nay monstrous, I ha seen a sumptuous
steeple turnd to a stincking privie; more beastly, the
sacredst place made a dogges kennell : nay most   5
inhumane, the stoned coffins of long dead christians burst up, and made hogs-troughs—*Hic finis
Priami.*[8, (4)]

Shall I ha some sacke and cheese at thy chamber?
Good night good mischievous incarnate divel, good   10
night Mendoza, ah you inhumane villaine, goodnight,
night fub.[9]

MENDOZA. Good night : to morrow morne.

Exit MENDOZA.

MALEVOLE. I, I will come friendly Damnation, I will   15
come : I doe descry crosse-poynts, honesty and courtship, straddle as farre asunder, as a true Frenchmans
legges.

FERNEZE. O!

MALEVOLE. Proclamations, more proclamations.   20

FERNEZE. O a Surgeon.

MALEVOLE. Heark, lust cries for a Surgeon, what news
from *Limbo*? How dooth the grand cuckolde *Lucifer*?

FERNEZE. O helpe, helpe, conceale and save mee.

FERNEZE *stirres, and* MALEVOLE *helpes him up*   25
and convayes him away.

MALEVOLE. Thy shame more than thy wounds do grieve
me farre,

"Thy wounds but leave upon thy flesh some skarre;
But fame ne're heales, still ranckles[10] worse and   30
worse,

Such is of uncontrolled lust the curse.

Thinke what it is in lawlesse sheetes to lie :

[7] *Et . . . Sion fuit :* Now there
are cornfields where Zion was.

[8] *Hic finis Priami :* This is the
end of Priam.

[9] *fub :* deceiver.

[10] *ranckles :* festers.

But O Ferneze, what in lust to die.
Then thou that shame respects, ô flie converse
With womens eies, and lisping wantonnesse :
Sticke candles gainst a virgine walles white backe,
If they not burne, yet at the least thei'le blacke." 5
Come, ile convey thee to a private port,
Where thou shalt live (ô happy man) from court.
The beautie of the day beginnes to rise,
From whose bright forme Nights heavy shadow flies,
Now ginnes close plots to worke, the Sceane growes 10
    full,
And craves his eies who hath a solide skull. *Exeunt.*

ACTUS III. SCENA I. 15

Enter PIETRO *the Duke,* MENDOZA, *Count* EQUATO
and BILIOSO.

PIETRO. Tis growne to youth of day, how shall wee
    waste this light? 20
My heart's more heavy than a tyrants crowne.
Shall we goe hunt? Prepare for field.   *Exit* EQUATO.
MENDOZA. Would yee could be merry.
PIETRO. Would God I could : Mendoza bid um haste :
                                Exit MENDOZA. 25
I would faine shift place; O vaine reliefe!
*"Sad soules may well change place, but not change
    griefe :"*
As Deere being strucke flie thorow many soiles,[1]
Yet still the shaft stickes fast, so. 30
BILIOSO. A good olde simile, my honest Lord.
PIETRO. I am not much unlike to some sicke man,
    That long desired hurtfull drinke; at last
    Swilles in and drinkes his last, ending at once

ACT III. SCENE I.
[1] *soiles :* watery places (*to
escape detection*).

Both life and thirst : O would I nere had knowne
My owne dishonour! good God that men should
Desire to search out that, which being found, killes all
Their joy of life, to taste the tree of knowledge,
And then be driven from out Paradice.   5
Canst give me some comfort?

BILIOSO. My Lord, I have some bookes which have
beene dedicated to my honor, and I nere read um,
and yet they had verie fine names : *Phisicke for
Fortune :*[1] *Lozinges*[2] *of sanctified sinceritie,* very   10
pretty workes of Curates, Scriveners and Schoole-
maisters. Mary I remember one *Seneca, Lucius
Anaeus*[1] *Seneca.*

PIETRO. Out upon him, he writ of Temperance and
Fortitude, yet lived like a voluptuous epicure, and   15
died like an effeminate coward. Haste thee to *Florence :* heere, take our Letters, see um sealed; away;
report in private to the honored Duke, his daughters
forced disgrace, tell him at length,
We know, too much due complements advance,   20
"Theres nought thats safe and sweete but ignorance."
                              Exit DUKE.
                    Enter BIANCA.[2]

BILIOSO. Madam, I am going Embassador for *Florence,*
twill be great charges to me.   25

BIANCA. No matter my Lord, you have the lease of two
mannors come out[3] next Christmasse; you may lay
your tenants on the greater racke for it : and when
you come home againe, Ile teach you how you shall
get two hundred poundes a yeere by your teeth.   30

BILIOSO. How Madam?

BIANCA. Cut off so much from house-keeping, that which
is saved by the teeth, you know is got by the teeth.

BILIOSO. Fore God, and so I may, I am in wondrous
credite Lady.   35

BIANCA. See the use of flattery, I did ever counsell you

---

[2] *Lozinges :* Lozenges.   [3] *come out :* which expire.

to flatter greatnes, and you have profited well : any
man that will doe so shal be sure to be like your
Scotch Barnacle,(2) now a blocke,4 instantly a
worme, and presently a great goose : (2) this it is to
rot and putrifie in the bosome of greatnes.   5

BILIOSO. Thou arte ever my polititian, O how happy is
that olde Lord that hath a polititian to his yong
Lady! He have fiftie gentlemen shall attend upon
mee; mary the most of them shalbe Farmers sonnes,
because they shall beare their owne charges, and they   10
shall goe appareld thus, in sea-water greene sutes,
ash-color cloakes, wetchet5 stockings, and popinjay
greene feathers, will not the colours doe excellent?

BIANCA. Out upon't, theile looke like Cittizens riding to
their friendes at Whitsontide, their apparell just so   15
many severall parishes.

BILIOSO. Ile have it so, and Passarello my foole shall goe
along with me, mary he shall be in velvet?

BIANCA. A foole in velvet.

BILIOSO. I, tis common for your foole to weare satin,   20
ile have mine in velvet.

BIANCA. What will you weare then my Lord?

BILIOSO. Velvet too, mary it shall be embroidered, because ile differ from the foole somewhat. I am horribly troubled with the gowt, nothing grieves me but   25
that my doctor hath forbidden me wine, and you
know your Ambassador must drinke. Didst thou aske
thy doctor what was good for the gowt?

BIANCA. Yes, hee saide, ease, wine and women, were
good for it.   30

BILIOSO. Nay, thou hast such a witte, what was good to
cure it, said he?

BIANCA. Why the racke : al your Empericks6 could
never do the like cure upon the gowt the racke did

---

4 *blocke :* excrescence of a tree.   6 *Empericks :* Empirics; doctors;
5 *wetchet :* light blue.   charlatans.

in *England :* or your Scotch boote.[7] The French
Harlequin[3] will instruct you.

BILIOSO. Surely I doe wonder, how thou having, for the
most parte of thy life time beene a countrey body,
shouldest have so good a wit.   5

BIANCA. Who I? why I have beene a Courtier thrise two
moneths.

BILIOSO. So have I this twentie yeare, and yet there was
a gentleman usher cald me cocks-coombe tother day,
and to my face too : wast not a backe-biting rascall?   10
I would I were better travaild, that I might have
beene better acquainted with the fashions of severall
country-men : but my Secretary, I thinke he hath
sufficiently instructed me.

BIANCA. How my Lord?   15

BILIOSO. Mary my good Lord quoth hee, your Lordship
shall ever finde amongst a hundred French-men,
fortie hot shottes[8] : amongst a hundred Spaniardes,
threescore bragarts : amongst a hundred Dutch-men,
fourescore drunkardes : amongst a hundred English-   20
men, fourescore and ten mad-men : and amongst an
hundred Welch-men.

BIANCA. What my Lord?

BILIOSO. Fourescore and nineteene gentlemen.[3]

BIANCA. But since you go about a sad[9] imbasie, I would   25
have you go in blacke my Lord.

BILIOSO. Why doost thinke I cannot mourne, unlesse I
weare my hat in cipers[10] like an Aldermans heire,
that's vile, very olde, in faith.

BIANCA. Ile learne of you shortly; O wee should have a   30
fine gallant of you, should not I instruct you : how
will you beare your selfe when you come into the
Duke of *Florence* Court?

BILIOSO. Prowde ynough, and 'twill do well ynough; as

---

[7] *Scotch boote :* instrument of   [9] *sad :* serious; important.
torture.   [10] *cipers :* cypress; crepe.
[8] *hot shottes :* hot-heads.

I walke up and downe the chamber, Ile spit frownes
about me, have a strong perfume in my jerkin, let my
beard grow to make me looke terrible, salute no man
beneath the fourth button, and 'twill do excellent.

BIANCA. But there is a very beautifull Lady there, how   5
will you entertaine her?

BILIOSO. Ile tell you that when the Lady hath enter-
tainde me : but to satisfie thee, heere comes the
foole : foole thou shalt stand for the faire Lady.

Enter PASSARELLO.   10

PASSARELLO. Your foole will stand for your Lady most
willingly and most uprightly.

BILIOSO. Ile salute her in Latine.

PASSARELLO. O your foole can understand no Latine.

BILIOSO. I but your Lady can.   15

PASSARELLO. Why then if your Lady take downe your
foole, your foole will stand no longer for your Lady.

BILIOSO. A pestilent foole : fore God I thinke the world
be turnde up-side downe too.

PASSARELLO. O no sir, for then your Lady, and all the   20
Ladies in the pallace should goe with their heeles
upward, and that were a strange sight you know.

BILIOSO. There be many will repine at my preferment.

PASSARELLO. O I, like the envie of an elder sister that
hath her yonger made a Lady before her.   25

BILIOSO. The Duke is wondrous discontented.

PASSARELLO. I, and more melancholike, then a usurer
having all his mony out at the death of a Prince.

BILIOSO. Didst thou see Madam *Floria* to day?

PASSARELLO. Yes, I found her repairing her face to day,   30
the red upon the white shewed as if her cheekes
should have beene served in for two dishes of Barbaries[11] in stewed broth, and the flesh to them a
wood-cocke.

BILIOSO. A bitter fowle[12] : Come Madam, this night   35

---

[11] *Barbaries :* Barberries.   [12] *fowle : pun on* fowl, fool.

thou shalt injoy me freely, and to morrow for *Florence.*

> *Exit [with* BIANCA].

PASSARELLO. What a naturall foole is hee that would be
a paire of bodies[13] to a womans petti-cote, to bee
trusst[14] and pointed to them. Well, Ile dog my Lord,
and the word is proper : for when I fawne upon him
hee feedes me; when I snap him by the fingers, hee
spittes in my mouth. If a dogges death were not
strangling, I had rather bee one then a serving-man :
for the corruption of coine, is either the generation of
a usurer, or a lowsie beggar.   [*Exit.*]

SCENA SECUNDA.

Enter MALEVOLE *in some freeze*[1] *gowne, whilst*
BILIOSO [*also entering*] *reades his Patent.*

MALEVOLE. I cannot sleepe, my eyes ill neighbouring
                                   lids
Will holde no fellowship : O thou pale sober night,
Thou that in sluggish fumes all sence doost steepe :
Thou that gives all the world full leave to play,
Unbendst the feebled veines of sweatie labour;
The gally-slave, that all the toilesome day,
Tugges at his oare, against the stubburne wave,
Straining his rugged veines, snores fast :
The stooping sithe-man that doth barbe the field
Thou makest winke[2] sure : in night all creatures
                                   sleepe,
Onely the Malcontent, that gainst his fate
Repines and quarrells, alas hee's goodman tell-clocke,
His sallow jaw-bones sinke with wasting mone,
Whilst others beds are downe, his pillowes stone.

ACT III. SCENE II.

13 *bodies :* supports.   1 *freeze :* of coarse wool.
14 *trusst :* tied.   2 *winke :* close his eyes.

BILIOSO. Malevole.

MALEVOLE. (*To* BILIOSO.) Elder of *Israell*,[1] thou hon-
    est defect of wicked nature and obstinate ignorance,
    when did thy wife let thee lie with her?

BILIOSO. I am going Ambassadour to *Florence*.   5

MALEVOLE. Ambassadour? now for thy countries hon-
    our : prethee do not put up mutton & porridge in
    thy cloke-bagge : thy yong Lady wife goes to *Flor-
    ence* with thee too, dooes she not?

BILIOSO. No, I leave her at the pallace.   10

MALEVOLE. At the pallace? now discretion sheelde man,
    for Gods love lets ha no more cuckolds : *Hymen* be-
    ginnes to put off his saffron robe,[2] keepe thy wife
    i'the state of grace, hart a'[1] truth, I would sooner
    leave my Ladie singled in a *Bordello*, then in the   15
    Genoa Pallace,
    Sinne[2] there appearing in her sluttish shape,
    Would soone grow loathsome, even to blushes sence,
    Surfet would cloke intemperate appetite,
    Make the soule scent the rotten breath of lust.   20
    When in an Italian lascivious pallace, a Lady
                    gardianlesse,
    Left to the push of all allurement,
    The strongest incitements to immodestie,
    To have her bound, incensed with wanton sweetes,   25
    Her veines fild hie with heating delicates :
    Soft rest, sweete musicke, amorous Masquerers,
    Lascivious banquets, sinne it selfe gilt o're,
    Strong phantasie tricking up strange delightes,
    Presenting it dressed pleasingly to sence,   30
    Sence leading it unto the soule, confirmed
    With potent example, impudent custome,
    Inticed by that great bawde Opportunitie,
    Thus being preparde, clap to her easie eare,
    Youth in good clothes, well shapt, rich,   35
    Faire-spoken, promising-noble, ardent blood-full,
    Wittie, flattering : *Ulisses* absent,
    O *Ithacan*, chastest *Penelope* hold out![2]

167

BILIOSO. Masse Ile thinke on't, farewell. *Exit* BILIOSO.

MALEVOLE. Farewell, take thy wife with thee, farewell.
To *Florence,* um? it may proove good, it may,
And we may once unmaske our browes.   5

SCENA TERTIA.

Enter Count CELSO.

CELSO. My [1] honourde Lord.   10

MALEVOLE. Celso peace, how ist? speake low, pale
                                        feares
Suspect that hedges, walles and trees have eares :[1]
Speake, how runnes all?

CELSO. I faith my Lord, that beast with many heads   15
The staggering multitude recoiles apace,
Though thorow¹ great mens envie, most mens
                                        malice,
Their much intemperate heate hath banisht you.
Yet now they find envie and mallice neere,   20
Produce faint reformation.
The Duke, the too soft Duke lies as a blocke,
For which two tugging factions seeme to sawe,
But still the yron through the ribbes they draw.

MALEVOLE. I tell thee Celso, I have ever found   25
Thy breast most farre from shifting cowardice
And fearefull basenesse : therefore Ile tell thee Celso,
I finde the winde beginnes to come about,
Ile shift my suite of fortune,
I know the *Florentine* whose onely force,   30
By marrying his prowde daughter to this Prince,
Both banisht me, and made this weake Lord Duke,
Will now forsake them all, be sure hee will :
Ile lie in ambush for conveniencie,
Upon their severance to confirme my selfe.   35

ACT III. SCENE III.
¹ *thorow :* through.

168

CELSO. Is Ferneze interred?

MALEVOLE. Of that at leisure : he lives.

CELSO. But how standes Mendoza, how ist with him?

MALEVOLE. Faith like a paire of snuffers, snibbes[2]
filth in other men, and retaines it in it selfe. 5

CELSO. He doo's flie from publike notice me thinkes, as
a hare do's from houndes, the feete whereon he flies
betraies him.

MALEVOLE. I can tracke him Celso.

O my disguise fooles him most powerfully : 10
For that I seeme a desperate Malcontent,
He faine would claspe with me; he is the true slave
That will put on the most affected grace,
For some vilde second cause.

Enter MENDOZA. 15

CELSO. Hee's heere.

MALEVOLE. Give place. *Exit* CELSO.

Illo, ho, ho, ho, arte there olde true penny?[(1)]
Where hast thou spent thy selfe this morning? I see
flattery in thine eies, and damnation in thy soule. 20
Ha thou huge rascall!

MENDOZA. Thou art very merry.

MALEVOLE. As a scholler *futuens gratis*[3] : How dooth
the divell goe with thee now?

MENDOZA. Malevole, thou art an arrant knave. 25

MALEVOLE. Who I, I have beene a Sergeant man.

MENDOZA. Thou art very poore.

MALEVOLE. As *Job*, an Alcumist, or a Poet.

MENDOZA. The Duke hates thee.

MALEVOLE. As *Irishmen* doe bum-crackes.[(2)] 30

MENDOZA. Thou hast lost his amitie.

MALEVOLE. As pleasing as maids loose their virginitie.

MENDOZA. Would thou wert of a lusty spirit, wold thou
wert noble.

MALEVOLE. Why sure my bloud gives me I am noble, 35

---

[2] *snibbes :* rejects. [3] *futuens gratis :* fornicating
free.

sure I am of noble kinde; for I finde my selfe possessed with all their qualities; love Dogs, Dice, and Drabs, scorne witte in stuffe clothes, have beat my Shoomaker, knockt my Semsters,[4] cuckold my Potecary, and undone my Tayler. Noble, why not? since the Stoicke saide, *Neminem servum non ex regibus, neminem regem non ex servis esse oriundum,*[5, (3)] only busie fortune towses,[6] and the provident chances blends them together; ile give you a similie; Did you ere see a wel with two buckets, whilst one comes up ful to be emptied, another goes downe empty to be filled; such is the state of all humanitie : why looke you, I may be the son of some Duke; for beleeve me, intemperate lascivious bastardy makes Nobilitie doubtfull : I have a lusty daring heart Mendoza.

MENDOZA. Let's graspe, I doe like thee infinitely, wilt inact one thing for me?

MALEVOLE. Shall I get by it? [MENDOZA] (*gives him his purse.*) Commaund me, I am thy slave, beyond death and hell.

MENDOZA. Murther the Duke.

MALEVOLE. My hearts wish, my soules desire, my fantasies dreame, My blouds longing, the onely height of my hopes, how O God how? ô how my united spirites throng together, So strengthen my resolve.

MENDOZA. The Duke is now a hunting.

MALEVOLE. Excellent, admirable, as the divell would have it, lend me, lend me, Rapier, Pistoll, Crossebow; so, so, ile doe it.

MENDOZA. Then we agree.

MALEVOLE. As Lent & fishmongers, come *a cape a pe,*[7] how? inform.

---

[4] *Semsters :* Seamstress.
[5] *Neminem servum . . . oriundum :* There is no slave whose ancestors were not kings, and no king not sprung from slaves.
[6] *towses :* tosses.
[7] *a cape a pe :* completely; from head to foot.

MENDOZA. Know[2] that this weake braind duke, who
                only stands
On *Florence* stilts, hath out of witlesse zeale
Made me his heire, and secretly confirmed
The wreathe to mee after his lifes full poynt.   5
MALEVOLE. Upon what merite?
MENDOZA.   Merite! by heaven I
            horne him,
Onely Fernezes death gave me states life :
Tut we are politique, hee must not live now.[2]   10
MALEVOLE. No reason mary : but how must he die now?
MENDOZA. My utmost project is to murder the Duke,
    that I might have his state, because he makes me his
    heire; to banish the duchesse, that I might be rid
    of a cunning *Lacedemonian*,(4) because I know   15
    Florence will forsake her, and then to marry Maria
    the banished duke Altofronts wife, that her friends
    might strengthen me and my faction; this is all lawe.
MALEVOLE. Do you love Maria?
MENDOZA. Faith no great affection, but as wise men do   20
    love great women, to innoble their bloud, and aug-
    ment their revenew : to accomplish this now, thus
    now. The Duke is in the forrest next the Sea, single
    him, kill him, hurle him in the maine, and proclaime
    thou sawest woolves eate him.   25
MALEVOLE. Um,[3] not so good : mee thinkes when
              he is slaine,
To get some hipocrite, some daungerous wretch
Thats muffled o'er with fained holines,
To sweare he heard the duke on some stiepe cliffe   30
Lament his wifes dishonour, and in an agony
Of his hearts torture hurled his groaning sides
Into the swolne sea : This circumstance
Wel made, sounds probable : and hereupon
The Dutches.   35
MENDOZA.   May well be banished :
O unpeerable invention! rare,
Thou god of pollicie, it honies me.

MALEVOLE. Then feare not for the wife of Altofront,
Ile close[8] to her.[3]

MENDOZA. Thou shalt, thou shalt, our excellencie is
pleased : why wert not thou an Emperour? when we
are Duke, ile make thee some great man sure.   5

MALEVOLE. Nay, make me some rich knave, and ile
make my selfe some great man.

MENDOZA. In[4] thee be all my spirit,
Retaine tenne soules, unite thy virtuall powers;
Resolve, ha, remember greatnes : heart, farewell.   10
"The fate of all my hopes in thee doth dwell."[4]

                                            Exit.

              Enter CELSO.

MALEVOLE. Celso, didst heare? O heaven, didst heare?
Such divelish mischiefe, sufferest thou the world   15
Carowse[5] damnation even with greedie swallow,
And still doost winke, still duz thy vengeance
                              slumber :
"If now thy browes are cleare, when will they
                              thunder!"   20

                        Exit [with CELSO.]

                  SCENA QUARTA
                                            25
Enter PIETRO, FERRARDO, PREPASSO, *and three Pages.*

FERRARDO. The dogges are at a fault.

                  Cornets like hornes.

PIETRO. Would God nothing but the dogges were at it?
let the Deere pursue[1] safely, the dogs follow the   30
game, and doe you follow the dogges; as for me, tis
unfit one beast should hunt an other; I ha one chaseth
me : and't please you, I would be ridde of you a
little.

                                  ACT III. SCENE IV.
[8] *close :* settle matters with.   [1] *pursue :* run away.

                        172

FERRARDO. Would your griefe would as soone leave you
   as we to quietnesse.

                Exeunt [FERRARDO *and* PREPASSO.]

PIETRO. I thanke you; boy, what doost thou dreame of
   now?   5

PAGE. Of a drie summer my Lord, for heere's a hote
   worlde towardes : but my Lord, I had a strange
   dreame last night.

PIETRO. What strange dreame?

PAGE. Why me thought I pleased you with singing, and   10
   then I dreamt you gave me that short sword.

PIETRO. Prettily begd : hold thee, ile proove thy dreame
   true, tak't.   [*Gives him his sword.*]

PAGE. My duetie : but still I dreamt on my Lord, and
   mee thought, and't shall please your excellencie, you   15
   would needs out of your royall bounty give me that
   jewell in your hat.

PIETRO. O thou didst but dreame boy, do not beleeve it,
   dreames proove not alwayes true, they may hold in a
   short sword, but not in a jewell. But now sir, you   20
   dreamt you had pleased mee with singing, make that
   true as I have made the other.

PAGE. Faith my Lord, I did but dreame, and dreames
   you say proove not alwayes true : they may hold in
   a good sword, but not in a good song : the trueth is,   25
   I ha lost my voyce.

PIETRO. Lost thy voyce, how?

PAGE. With dreaming faith, but heere's a couple of
   Syrenicall rascalls shall inchaunt yee : what shall they
   sing my good Lorde?   30

PIETRO. Sing of the nature of women, and then the song
   shall be surely full of varietie; olde crochets and most
   sweete closes,[2] it shalbe humorous, grave, fantastike,
   amorous, melancoly, sprightly, one in all, and all in
   one.   35

PAGE. All in one?

[2] *closes :* concluding rhythm.

PIETRO. Byr lady too many; sing, my speech growes
culpable of unthrifty idlenesse, sing.

SCENA QUINTA   5

Song.
Enter MALEVOLE *with Crossebow and Pistoll.*

[PIETRO.] A, so, so, sing, I am heavie, walke off, I
   shall talke in my sleep; walke off.   *Exeunt Pages.*   10
MALEVOLE. Briefe, briefe, who? the Duke? good heaven
   that fooles should stumble upon greatnesse! do not
   sleepe Duke, give yee good morrow : you must be
   briefe Duke; I am feeed to murther thee, start not :
   Mendoza, Mendoza hired mee, heere's his gold, his   15
   pistoll, crossebow, and sword, tis all as firme as earth :
   O foole, foole, choakt with the common maze of easie
   ideots, Credulitie, make him thine heire : what thy
   sworne murtherer?
PIETRO. O can it be?   20
MALEVOLE. Can?
PIETRO. Discovered he not Ferneze?
MALVOLE. Yes; but why, but why, for love to thee;
   much, much, to be revenged upon his rivall, who had
   thrust his jawes awrie, who being slaine, supposed   25
   by thine owne handes; defended by his sword, made
   thee most loathsome, him most gratious with thy
   loose Princesse, thou closely yeelding egresse and re-
   gresse to her, madest him heire, whose hote unquiet
   lust strait towzde[1] thy sheetes, and now would seize   30
   thy state, polititian, wise man, death to be led to the
   stake like a bull by the hornes, to make even kindnesse
   cutte a gentle throate; life, why art thou nummed?
   thou foggie dulnesse, speake : lives not more faith in

ACT III. SCENE v.
[1] *towzde :* tousled.

a home-thrusting tongue, than in these fencing tip
tap Courtiers?

    Enter CELSO *with a Hermites gowne and beard.*

[PIETRO.][1] Lord Malevole, if this be true.

MALEVOLE. If? come shade thee with this disguise, if?   5
    thou shalt handle it, he shall thanke thee for killing
    thy selfe, come follow my directions, and thou shalt
    see strange sleights.

PIETRO. World whither wilt thou?

MALEVOLE. Why to the divell : come, the morne   10
    growes late, *A stedie quickenes is the soule of state.*
                                           Exeunt.

Actus IV. Scena i.   15

Enter MAQUERELLE *knocking at the Ladies doore.*

MAQUERELLE. Medam, Medam, are you stirring Me-
    dam? if you bee stirring Medam, if I thought I should
    disturbe yee.   20

              [Enter Page.]

PAGE. My Lady is up forsooth.

MAQUERELLE. A pretty boy, faith how old art thou?

PAGE. I thinke foureteene.

MAQUERELLE. Nay, and yee bee in the teenes : are yee   25
    a gentleman borne? do you know me? my name is
    Medam Maquerelle, I lie in the old cunny[1] court.[1]

          Enter BIANCA *and* EMILIA.

See Heere the Ladies.

BIANCA. A faire day to yee Maquerelle.   30

EMILIA. Is the Dutches up yet Sentinell?[1]

MAQUERELLE. O Ladies, the most abhominable mis-
    chance, O deare Ladies, the most piteous disaster,
    Ferneze was taken last night in the Dutches cham-
    ber : alas the Duke catcht him and kild him.   35

Act IV. Scene i.
[1] *cunny court :* women's court.

BIANCA. Was he found in bed?

MAQUERELLE. O no, but the villanous certaintie is, the
doore was not bolted, the tongue-tied hatch held his
peace : so the naked troth is, he was found in his
shirt, whilst I like an arrand beast, lay in the outward   5
chamber, heard nothing, and yet they came by mee in
the dark, and yet I felt them not, like a sencelesse[2]
creature as I was. O beauties, looke to your buske-
pointes,[2] if not chastely, yet charily : be sure the
doore bee bolted : is your Lord gone to *Florence?*   10

BIANCA. Yes Maquerelle.

MAQUERELLE. I hope youle finde the discretion to purchase a fresh gowne for his returne : Now by my
troth beauties I would ha ye once wise : he loves ye,
pish : he is wittie; buble : faire proportioned, meaw :   15
nobly borne, winde : let this be still your fixt position, esteeme me every man according to his good
gifts, and so ye shall ever remaine most deare, and
most worthie to bee most deare Ladies.

EMILIA. Is the Duke returnd from hunting yet?   20

MAQUERELLE. They say not yet.

BIANCA. Tis now in midst of day.

EMILIA. How beares the Dutches with this blemish now?

MAQUERELLE. Faith boldly, strongly defies defame, as
one that haz a Duke to her father. And theres a note   25
to you : be sure of a stowt friend in a corner, that
may alwaies awe your husband. Marke the havior of
the Dutches now : she dares defame, cries "Duke, do
what thou canst, Ile quite[3] mine honour" : nay, as
one confirmed in her owne vertue against ten thou-   30
sand mouthes that mutter her disgrace, shee's presently for dances.

Enter FERRARDO.

BIANCA. For dances?

MAQUERELLE. Most true.   35

---

[2] *buske-pointes :* stays for a
    whale-bone corset.

[3] *quite :* acquit.

EMILIA. Most strange.

[BIANCA.] See, heere's my servant yong Ferardo; how
many servants thinkst thou I have Maquerelle?[3]

MAQUERELLE. The more, the merrier : 'twas well said;
use your servants as you do your smockes, have   5
many, use one, and change often, for thats most
sweete and courtlike.

FERRARDO. Save ye faire Ladies, is the Duke returned?

BIANCA. Sweete sir no voice of him as yet in Court.

FERRARDO. Tis very strange.   10

BIANCA. And how like you my servant Maquerelle?

MAQUERELLE. I thinke he could hardely draw *Ulisses*
bow, but by my fidelitie, were his nose narrower, his
eyes broader, his hands thinner, his lippes thicker, his
legges bigger, his feete lesser, his haire blacker, and 15
his teeth whiter, he were a tollerable sweete youth
yfaith. And he will come to my chamber, I will reade
him the fortune of his beard.   *Cornets sounde.*

FERRARDO. Not yet returnd I feare, but the Dutches ap-
procheth.   20

SCENA SECUNDA.

Enter MENDOZA *supporting the Dutchesse,* [*and*]   25
GUERRINO : *the Ladies that are on the stage rise :*
FERRARDO *Ushers in the Dutches, and then
takes a Lady to treade a measure.*

AURELIA. We will dance, musicke, we will dance.

GUERRINO. *Les quanto*[1] (*Ladie*) *penses bien, passa*   30
regis,[2] or *Biancas* brawle?[3]

AURELIA. We have forgot the brawle.

FERRARDO. So soone? 'tis wonder.

GUERRINO. Why? 'tis but two singles on the left, two on

ACT IV. SCENE II.
[1] *Les quanto :* A courtly dance.
[2] *passa regis :* royal measure.

[3] Biancas *brawle :* French
cotillon. He inquires to display his sophistication.

the right, three doubles forward, a traverse of six
round : do this twice, three singles side, galliard tricke
of twentie, curranto pace;[1] a figure of eight, three
singles broken downe, come up, meete two doubles,
fall backe, and then honour.   5

AURELIA. O *Dedalus!* thy maze,[2] I have quite forgot it.

MAQUERELLE. Trust me so have I, saving the falling
backe, and then honour.

Enter PREPASSO.

AURELIA. Musicke, musicke.   10

PREPASSO. Who saw the Duke? the Duke?

Enter EQUATO.

AURELIA. Musicke.

PREPASSO. The Duke, is the Duke returned?

AURELIA. Musicke.   15

Enter CELSO.

CELSO. The Duke is either quite invisible, or else is not.

AURELIA. Wee are not pleased with your intrusion uppon
our private retirement : wee are not pleased : you
have forgot your selves.   20

Enter a Page.

CELSO. Boy, thy master : where's the Duke?

PAGE. Alas, I left him burying the earth with his spread
joylesse limbes : he told me, he was heavie, would
sleepe, bid mee walke off, for that the strength of   25
fantasie, oft made him talke in his dreames : I straight
obeied, nor ever saw him since : but where so e're he
is, hee's sad.

AURELIA. Musicke, sound high, as is our heart, sound
high.   30

SCENA TERTIA.

Enter MALEVOLE and PIETRO disguised like   35
an Hermite.

MALEVOLE. The Duke, peace, the Duke is dead.

178

AURELIA. Musicke.

MALEVOLE. Is't musicke?

MENDOZA. Give proofe.

FERRARDO. How?

CELSO. Where? 5

PREPASSO. When?

MALEVOLE. Rest in peace as the Duke duz quietly sit :
for my owne part I beheld him but dead; thats all :
mary heere's one can give you a more particular account of him. 10

MENDOZA. Speake holy father, nor let any browe
Within this presence fright thee from the truth :
Speake confidently & freely.

AURELIA.   We attend.

PIETRO. Now had the mounting sunnes al-ripening 15
                    wings
Swept the cold sweat of night from earths danke
                    breast,
When I (whom men call *Hermite* of the Rocke,)
Forsooke my Cell, and clamberd up a cliffe, 20
Against whose Base, the headie *Neptune* dasht
His high curlde browes : there 'twas I easde my
                    limbes,
When loe, my entrailes melted with the moane
Some one, who farre bove me was climbde, did 25
                    make :
I shall offend.

MENDOZA.   Not.

AURELIA.   On.

PIETRO. Me thinks I heare him yet, "O female faith! 30
Go sow the ingratefull sand, and love a woman :
And do I live to be the skoffe of men?
To be the wittall cuckold, even to hugge my poison?
Thou knowest O truth!
Sooner hard steele will melt with Southerne winde; 35
A Sea-mans whistle calme the Ocean;
A towne on fire be extinct with teares,

Then women vow'd to blushlesse impudence,
With sweete behaviour and soft minioning,
Will turne from that where appetite is fixt.
O powerfull blood! how thou doost slave their soule,
I washt an Ethiope, who for recompence,   5
Sullyde my name. And must I then be forc'd
To walke, to live thus blacke : must, must, fie,
He that can beare with must, he cannot die."
With that he sigh'd too passionately deepe,
That the Dull ayre even groan'd : at last he cries,   10
"Sinke shame in seas, sinke deepe enough" : so dies.
For then I viewd his body fall and sowse[1]
Into the fomie maine, O then I saw
That which me thinks I see; it was the Duke,
Whom straight the nicer stomackt sea   15
Belcht up : but then.

MALEVOLE. Then came I in, but las all was too late,
For even straight he sunke.

PIETRO.   Such was the Dukes sad fate.

CELSO. A better fortune to our Duke Mendoza.   20

OMNES. Mendoza!   *Cornets florish.*

MENDOZA. A guard, a guard,

                    Enter a guard.

                              we full of heartie teares,
For our good fathers losse,   25
For so we well may call him :
Who did beseech your loves for our succession,
Cannot so lightly over-jumpe his death,
As leave his woes revengelesse : (*To* AURELIA.)
                    woman of shame,   30
We banish thee for ever to the place,
From whence this good man comes,
Nor permit on death unto the body any ornament :
But base as was thy life, depart away.

AURELIA. Ungratefull.
                                                           35
MENDOZA.   Away.

AURELIA.   Villaine heare me.

MENDOZA.   Be gone.

PREPASSO *and* GERRINO *lead away the Dutches.*
My Lords addresse to[1] publike counsell, 'tis most fit,
The traine of Fortune is borne up by wit.
Away, our presence shall be sudden, haste.
All depart saving MENDOZA, MALEVOLE, *and* PIETRO.   5
MALEVOLE. Now you egregious divell, ha ye murthering
Polititian, how doost Duke? how doost looke now?
brave Duke yfaith.
MENDOZA. How did you kill him?
MALEVOLE. Slatted[2] his braines out, then sowst him   10
in the brinie sea.
MENDOZA. Braind him and drownd him too?
MALEVOLE. O 'twas best, sure worke : *For he that*
strikes a great man, let him strike home, or else 'ware,
hee'le prove no man : shoulder not a huge fellow,   15
unlesse you may be sure to lay him in the kennell.[3]
MENDOZA. A most sound braine-pan. Ile make you both
Emperours.
MALEVOLE. Make us christians, make us christians.
MENDOZA. Ile hoist ye, ye shall mount.   20
MALEVOLE. To the gallowes say ye? Come : *Praemium*
incertum petit certum scelus.[2, 4] How stands the
Progresse?
MENDOZA. Heere, take my ring unto the Citadell,
Have entrance to Maria the grave Dutches   25
Of banisht Altofront. Tell her we love her :
Omit no circumstance to grace our person, (doo't.)
MALEVOLE. Ile make an excellent pander : Duke fare-
well, due, adue Duke.   *Exit* MALEVOLE.
MENDOZA. Take Maquerelle with thee; for 'tis found,   30
None cuttes a diamond, but a diamond.
Hermite, thou art a man for me, my confessor :
O thou selected spirit, borne for my good,

ACT IV. SCENE III.   [2] *Praemium . . . scelus :*
[1] *addresse to :* prepare for.   Uncertain the reward he
                                          seeks, certain the guilt.

Sure thou wouldst make an excellent Elder in a deformed church.

Come, we must be inward, thou and I all one.

PIETRO. I am glad I was ordained for yee.

MENDOZA. Go to then, thou must know that Malevole   5
is a strange villaine : dangerous, very dangerous : you
see how broad a[3] speakes, a grosse jawde rogue, I
would have thee poison him : hee's like a corne upon
my great toe, I cannot go for him : he must be kored
out, he must : wilt doo't, ha?   10

PIETRO. Any thing, any thing.

MENDOZA. Heart of my life, thus then to the Citadell,
Thou shalt consort with this Malevole,
There being at supper, poison him :
It shall be laid upon Maria, who yeelds love, or dies :   15
Skud quicke.

PIETRO. Like lightning.[1] *"Good deedes crawle, but*
mischiefe flies."   *Exit* PIETRO.
Enter MALEVOLE.

MALEVOLE. Your divelships ring haz no vertue, the buffe-   20
captaine, the sallo-westfalian gamon-faced zaza[4] cries,
"Stand out"; must have a stiffer warrant, or no passe
into the Castle of Comfort.

MENDOZA. Command our suddaine Letter : not enter?
sha't,[5] what place is there in *Genoa,* but thou shalt,   25
into my heart, into my very heart : come, lets love,
we must love, we two, soule and body.

MALEVOLE. How didst like the Hermite? a strange Hermite sirrah.

MENDOZA. A dangerous fellow, very perilous : he must   30
die.

MALEVOLE. I, he must die.

MENDOZA. Thoust[6] kil him : we are wise, we must be
wise.

MALEVOLE. And provident.   35

---

[3] *a :* he.   [5] *sha't :* shalt.
[4] *zaza :* Saxon (?).   [6] *Thoust :* Thou must.

MENDOZA. Yea provident; beware an hypocrite.
A Church-man once corrupted, oh avoide
A fellow that makes Religion his stawking horse,[2], (5)
He breedes a plague : thou shalt poison him.
MALEVOLE. Ho, 'tis wondrous necessary : how?   5
MENDOZA. You both go joyntly to the Citadell,
There sup, there poison him : and Maria,
Because shee is our opposite, shall beare
The sad suspect, on which she dies, or loves us.
MALEVOLE. I runne.   *Exit* MALEVOLE.   10
MENDOZA. *We that are great, our sole selfe good still*
                        moves us.
They shall die both, for their deserts craves more
Than we can recompence, their presence still
Imbraides[7] our fortunes with beholdingnesse,   15
Which we abhorre; like deede, not doer : then con-
                        clude,
They live not to cry out "ingratitude."
One sticke burnes tother steele cuts steele alone :
Tis good trust few, but O, tis best trust none.   20
                        Exit MENDOZA.

SCENA QUARTA.
                                                            25

Enter MALEVOLE *and* PIETRO *still disguised,*
at severall doores.
MALEVOLE. How do you? how doost Duke?
PIETRO. O let the last day fall, drop, drop on our cursed
                        heads;   30
Let heaven unclaspe it selfe, vomit forth flames.
MALEVOLE. O do not rant[1] do not turne plaier, there's
more of them than can well live one by another al-
readie. What, art an infidell still?
PIETRO. I am amazde, strucke in a swowne with won-   35
der : I am commanded to poison thee.

7 *Imbraides :* Affronts.

183

MALEVOLE. I am commanded to poison thee at supper.

PIETRO. At supper?

MALEVOLE. In the Citadell.

PIETRO. In the Citadell?

MALEVOLE. Crosse capers, trickes, truth a heaven, hee   5
would discharge us as boyes do elderne gunnes,[1] one
pellet to stricke out another : of what faith art now?

PIETRO. All is damnation, wickednes extreame. There is
no faith in man.

MALEVOLE. In none but usurers and brokers, they de-   10
ceive no man, men take um for blood-suckers, and so
they are : now God deliver me from my friends.

PIETRO. Thy friends?

MALEVOLE. Yes, from my friends, for from mine enemies
ile deliver my selfe. O, cutte-throate friendship is the   15
ranckest vilanie : Marke this Mendoza, marke him for
a villaine; but heaven will send a plague upon him
for a rogue.

PIETRO. O world!

MALEVOLE. World! Tis the only region of death, the   20
greatest shop of the Divell, the cruelst prison of men,
out of the which none passe without paying their
dearest breath for a fee, theres nothing perfect in it,
but extreame extreame calamitie, such as comes
yonder.   25

SCENA QUINTA.

Enter AURELIA, *two Halberds*[1] *before, and twoo*   30
after, supported by CELSO *and* FERRARDO,
AURELIA *in base mourning attire.*

AURELIA. To banishment, ledde on to banishment.

PIETRO. Lady, the blessednesse of repentance to you.

AURELIA. Why? why? I can desire nothing but death,   35

ACT IV. SCENE IV.

[1] *elderne gunnes :* blow guns

Nor deserve any thing but hell.
If heaven should give sufficiencie of grace
To cleere my soule, it would make heaven grace-
lesse :
My sinnes would make the stocke of mercie poore;   5
O they would tire heavens goodnes to reclaime them :
Judgement is just yet from[1] that vast villane : (1)
But sure he shall not misse sad punishment
Fore he shall rule. On to my cell of shame.

PIETRO. My cell tis Lady, where insteede of maskes,   10
Musicke, tilts, tournies, and such courtlike shewes,
The hollow murmure of the checklesse windes
Shall groane againe, whilst the unquiet sea
Shakes the whole rocke with foamy battery :
There Usherlesse the ayre comes in and out :   15
The rheumy vault will force your eyes to weepe,
Whilst you behold true desolation :
A rocky barrennesse shall pierce your eyes,
Where all at once one reaches where he stands,
With browes the roofe, both walles with both his   20
handes.

AURELIA. It is too good, blessed spirite of my Lord,
O in what orbe so ere thy soule is throand,
Beholde me worthily most miserable :
O let the anguish of my contrite spirite   25
Intreate some reconciliation :
If not, ô joy, triumph in my just griefe,
Death is the end of woes, and teares reliefe.

PIETRO. Belike your Lord not lov'd you, was unkinde.

AURELIA. O heaven!   30
As the soule lov'd the body, so lov'd he,
Twas death to him to part my presence,
Heaven to see me pleased :
Yet I, like to a wretch given o'er to hell,
Brake all the sacred rites of marriage,   35

ACT IV. SCENE v.
[1] *yet from :* even from.

To clippe a base ungentle faithlesse villaine.
O God, a very Pagan reprobate :
What should I say? ungratefull, throwes me out,
For whom I lost soule, body, fame and honor :
But tis most fit; why should a better fate   5
Attend on any, who forsake chaste sheetes,
Fly the embrace of a devoted heart,
Joynd by a solemne vow fore God and man,
To taste the brackish bloud of beastly lust,
In an adulterous touch? ô ravenous immodesty,   10
Insatiate impudence of appetite;
Looke, heeres your end, for marke what sap in dust,
What sinne in good, even so much love in lust :
Joy to thy ghost, sweete Lord, pardon to me.

CELSO. Tis the dukes pleasure this night you rest in   15
          court.

AURELIA. Soule lurke in shades, run shame from bright-
          some skies,
In night the blinde man misseth not his eyes.

      Exit [*with* CELSO, FERRARDO, *and* HALBERDIERS.]   20

MALEVOLE. Doe not weepe, kinde cuckolde, take comfort man, thy betters have beene *Beccoes : Agamem-*
non Emperour of all the merry Greekes that tickeled
all the true Troyans, was a *Cornuto :* Prince *Arthur*
that cut off twelve Kings beardes, was a *Cornuto :*   25
Hercules, whose backe bore up heaven, and got forty
wenches with childe in one night.

PIETRO. Nay twas fifty.

MALEVOLE. Faith fortie's enow a'[2] conscience, yet
was a *Cornuto :* patience, mischiefe growes prowde,   30
be wise.

PIETRO. Thou pinchest too deepe, arte too keene upon
me.

MALEVOLE. Tut, a pittifull Surgeon makes a dangerous
sore. Ile tent[2] thee to the ground. Thinkest Ile sus-   35
taine my selfe by flattering thee, because thou art a

---

[2] *tent* : probe.

Prince? I had rather followe a drunkard, and live by licking up his vomite, than by servile flattery.

PIETRO. Yet great men ha doon't.

MALEVOLE. Great slaves feare better than love, borne naturally for a coale-basket,[3] though the common usher of Princes presence, Fortune, hath blindely given them better place, I am vowed to be thy affliction.

PIETRO. Prethee be, I love much misery, and be thou sonne to me.

MALEVOLE. Because you are an usurping Duke.

Enter BILIOSO.

(*To* BILIOSO.) Your Lordship's well returnde from *Florence.*

BILIOSO. Well returnde, I praise my horse.

MALEVOLE. What newes from the Florentines?

BILIOSO. I will conceale the great Dukes pleasure, onely this was his charge, his pleasure is, that his daughter die, Duke Pietro be banished, for publishing[3] his blouds dishonour, and that Duke Altofront be re-accepted : this is all, but I heare Duke Pietro is dead.

MALEVOLE. I, and Mendoza is Duke, what will you do?

BILIOSO. Is Mendoza strongest?

MALEVOLE. Yet he is.

BILIOSO. Then yet Ile holde with him.

MALEVOLE. But if that Altofront should turne strait againe?

BILIOSO. Why then I would turne strait againe.
Tis good runne still with him that haz most might :
I had rather stand with wrong, than fall with right.

MALEVOLE. What religion wil you be of now?

BILIOSO. Of the Dukes religion, when I know what it is.

MALEVOLE. O *Hercules!*

BILIOSO. *Hercules? Hercules* was the sonne of *Jupiter* and *Alkmena.*

5

10

15

20

25

30

35

---

[3] *coale-basket :* To carry coals,
suffer scorn.

MALEVOLE. Your lordship is a very wittall.

BILIOSO. Wittall?

MALEVOLE. I, all-wit.

BILIOSO. *Amphitrio*[2] was a cuckolde.

MALEVOLE. Your lordship sweats, your yong Lady will 5
gette you a cloth for your olde worships browes.
(*Exit* BILIOSO.) Heeres a fellow to be damned, this
is his inviolable maxime, (flatter the greatest, and op-
presse the least:) a whoreson flesh-fly, that still
gnawes upon the leane gawld backes. 10

PIETRO. Why doost then salute him?

MALEVOLE. Yfaith as bawdes goe to church, for fashion
sake: come, be not confounded, thou arte but in danger to loose a dukedome: thinke this: This earth is
the only grave and Golgotha wherein all things that 15
live must rot: tis but the draught wherein the heavenly bodies discharge their corruption, the very muckhill on which the sublunarie orbes cast their excre-
ments: man is the slime of this dongue-pit, and
Princes are the governors of these men: for, for our 20
soules, they are as free as Emperours, all of one peece,
there goes but a paire[3] of sheeres betwixt an Emperor and the sonne of a bagge-piper, onely the dying, dressing, pressing, glossing makes the difference:
now what arte thou like to loose? 25
A Jaylers office to keepe men in bonds,
Whilst toyle and treason, all lifes good confounds.

PIETRO. I heere renounce for ever regencie:
O Altofront, I wrong thee to supplant thy right:
To trip thy heeles up with a divelish slight. 30
For which I now from throne am throwne, world
        tricks abjure:
For vengeance though't comes slow, yet it comes
        sure.
O I am changde; for heerefore the dread power, 35
In true contrition I doe dedicate,
My breath to solitarie holinesse,
My lippes to praier, and my breasts care shall be,

Restoring Altofront to regencie.

MALEVOLE. Thy vowes are heard, and we accept thy
faith.
Undisguiseth himselfe.
Enter FERNEZE *and* CELSO.   5

Banish amazement; come, we foure must stand full
shocke of

Fortune, be not so wonder-stricken.

PIETRO. Dooth Ferneze live?

FERNEZE. For your pardon.   10

PIETRO. Pardon and love, give leave to recollect
My thoughts disperst in wilde astonishment :
My vowes stand fixt in heaven, and from hence
I crave all love and pardon.

MALEVOLE. Who doubts of providence,   15
That sees this change, a heartie faith to all :
He needes must rise, [who] can no lower fall :
For still impetuous vicissitude
Towzeth the world, then let no maze intrude
Upon your spirits : wonder not I rise;   20
For who can sincke, that close can temporize?
The time growes ripe for action, Ile detect
My privatst plot; lest ignorance feare suspect :
Lets close to counsell, leave the rest to fate,
Mature discretion is the life of state.   *Exeunt.*   25

ACTUS V. SCENA I.

Enter BILIOSO *and* PASSARELLO.   30

BILIOSO. Foole, how doost thou like my calfe in a long
stocking?

PASSARELLO. An excellent calfe my Lord.

BILIOSO. This calfe hath beene a reveller this twenty
yeere, when monsieur *Gundi* lay heere Ambassadour,   35
I could have carried a Lady up and downe at armes
end in a platter; and I can tell you there were those
at that time, who to trie the strength of a mans backe,

and his arme, would be coisterd :[1, (1)] I have meas-
ured calves with most of the pallace, and they come
nothing neere mee; besides, I thinke there be not
many armours in the Arsinall will fitte me, especially
for the head-peece. Ile tell thee.   5

PASSARELLO. What my Lord?

BILIOSO. I can eate stewd-broath as it comes seething
off the fire; or a custard, as it comes reeking out of
the oven; and I thinke there are not many Lordes
can doe it : a good pomander[2] a little decayed in the   10
scent, but six graines of muske grownd with rose-
water, and temperd with a little civit, shall fetch her[3]
againe presently.

PASSARELLO. O I, as a bawde with *aqua vitae.*

BILIOSO. And what doost thou raile uppon the Ladies as   15
thou wert wont?

PASSARELLO. I were better roast a live cat, and might
doe it with more safety. I am as secret to th'se'ves[4, [1]]
as their painting : theres Maquerelle oldest bawde,
and a perpetuall beggar. Did you never heare of her   20
tricke to be knowne in the Cittie?

BILIOSO. Never.

PASSARELLO. Why she gets all the Picter-makers to draw
her picture, when they have done, she most courtly
findes fault with them one after another, and never   25
fetcheth them : they in revenge of this, execute her
in Pictures as they doe in *Germanie,* and hang her in
their shops : by this meanes is she better knowne to
the stinkards,[5] then if shee had beene five times
carted.[6]   30

BILIOSO. Fore God an excellent policie.

PASSARELLO. Are there any Revels to night my Lord.

ACT V. SCENE I.
[1] *coisterd* : socially disgraced   [4] *th'se'ves* : their selves.
[2] *pomander* : ball of scents.   [5] *the stinkards* : the rabble.
[3] *fetch her* : restore the   [6] *carted* : punishment for
    pomander.   prostitution.

BILIOSO. Yes.

PASSARELLO. Good my Lord give me leave to breake a
fellows pate that hath abused me.

BILIOSO. Whose pate.

PASSARELLO. Young Ferrardo my Lord.   5

BILIOSO. Take heed hee's very valiant, I have knowne
him fight eight quarrels in five dayes, beleeve it.

PASSARELLO. O is he so great a quarreller? why then
hees an arrant coward.

BILIOSO. How proove you that?   10

PASSARELLO. Why thus, He that quarrels seekes to fight;
and he that seekes to fight, seekes to dye; and he
that seekes to dye, seekes never to fight more; and he
that will quarrell and seekes meanes never to answer
a man more, I thinke hees a coward.   15

BILIOSO. Thou canst proove any thing.

PASSARELLO. Any thing but a ritch knave, for I can
flatter no man.

BILIOSO. Well be not drunke good foole, I shall see you
anon in the presence.   [Exeunt severally.][2]   20

SCENA SECUNDA.

Enter MALEVOLE *and* MAQUERELLE, *at severall*   25
doores opposite, singing.

MALEVOLE. The Dutchman for a drunkard.

MAQUERELLE. The Dane for golden lockes :

MALEVOLE. The Irishman for Usquebath.[1]

MAQUERELLE. The Frenchman for the ([pox]).[1]   30

MALEVOLE. O thou art a blessed creature, had I a modest woman to conceale, I would put her to thy custodie, for no reasonable creature would ever suspect
her to be in thy company : ha, thou art a melodious

ACT V. SCENE II.
1 *Usquebath*: Whisky.

Maquerelle, thou picture of a woman, and substance
of a beast.

> *Enter* PASSARELLO [*with a bowl of wine.*]

MAQUERELLE. O foole will ye be ready anon to go with
me to the revels; the hal will be so pestred anone.   5

PASSARELLO. I as the countrie is with Atturnies.

MALEVOLE. What hast thou there foole.

PASSARELLO. Wine, I have learnt to drink since I went
with my Lord Embassador, Ile drinke to the health
of madam Maquerelle.   10

MALEVOLE. Why thou wast wont to raile uppon her.

PASSARELLO. I but since I borrow'd money of her. Ile
drinke to her health now as gentlemen visit brokers.
Or as knights send venison to the Citty. Eather to
take up more money, or to procure longer forbear-   15
ance.

MALEVOLE. Give me the boule. I drinke a health to
Altofront our deposed duke. [*Drinks.*]

PASSARELLO. Ile take it so? [*Drinks.*] now ile begin a
health to madam Maquerelle.   20

MALEVOLE. Pew I will not pledge her.

PASSARELLO. Why I pledgd your Lord.

MALEVOLE. I care not.

PASSARELLO. Not pledge madam Maquerelle, why then
will I spew up your Lord againe with this fooles fin-   25
ger.

MALEVOLE. Hould Ile take it. [*Drinks.*]

MAQUERELLE. Now thou hast drunke my health; foole
I am friends with thee.

PASSARELLO. Art? art?   30
When Griffon[2] saw the reconciled queane,
    Offeringe about his neck her armes to cast :
He threw of sword and hartes malignant streame,
    And lovely her below the loynes imbrast.
Adew madam Maquerelle.   *Exit* PASSARELLO.   35

---

[2] *Griffon :* A hero in *Orlando
Furioso.*

MALEVOLE. And how doost thou thinke a'[2] this trans-
formation of state now.

MAQUERELLE. Verily very well, for we women alwayes
note, the falling of the one, is the rising of the other :
some must be fatt, some must be leane, some must   5
be fooles, and some must be Lordes, some must be
knaves, and some must be officers : some must be
beggars, some must be Knights : some must be
cuckoldes, and some must be cittizens : as for example, I have two court dogges the most fawning curres,   10
the one called Watch, th'other Catch : now I, like
lady Fortune, sometimes love this dogge, somtimes
raise that dogge, sometimes favour Watch, most
commonly fancie Catch : now that dogge which I
favour I feede, and hee's so ravenous, that what I   15
give he never chawes it, gulpes it downe whole, without any relish of what he haz, but with a greedy expectation of what he shall have : the other dogge,
now :

MALEVOLE. No more dog, sweete Maquerelle, no more   20
dog : and what hope hast thou of the dutchesse
Maria, will shee stoope to the Dukes lewre,[3] will she
cowe thinkst?

MAQUERELLE. Let mee see, where's the signe now? ha
ye ere a calender, where's the signe trow you.   25

MALEVOLE. Signe! why is there any moment in that?

MAQUERELLE. O! beleeve me a most secret power, looke
yee a Chaldean or an Assyrian, I am sure 'twas a
most sweete Jew tolde me, court any woman in the
right signe, you shall not misse : but you must take   30
her in the right vaine then : as when the signe is in
Pisces, a Fishmongers wife is very sociable : in Can-
cer, a Precisians[4] wife is very flexible : in Capricorne,
a Merchants wife hardly holdes out : in Libra, a
Lawyers wife is very tractable, especially, if her hus-   35

---

[3] *lewre :* lure (*for a falcon*).   [4] *Precisians :* Puritan's.

band bee at the terme[5] : onely in Scorpio 'tis very
dangerous medling : haz the Duke sent any jewel, any
rich stones?

Enter Captaine.

MALEVOLE. I, I thinke those are the best signes to take   5
a lady in. By your favour signeor, I must discourse
with the Lady Maria, Altofronts dutches : I must
enter for the Duke.

CAPTAINE. Shee heere shall give you enterview : I received the guardship of this Citadell from the good   10
Altofront, and for his use Ile keep't till I am of no use.

MALEVOLE. Wilt thou? O heavens, that a christian
should be found in a Buffe jerkin! captaine Conscience : I love thee Captaine. (*Exit Captaine.*) We
attend, & what hope hast thou of this Dutches easi-   15
nesse?

MAQUERELLE. Twill goe hard, shee was a colde creature
ever, she hated monkies, fooles, jeasters, & gentle-
men-ushers extreamly : shee had the vilde trick on't,
not onely to be truely modestly honourable in her   20
owne conscience, but she would avoyde the least
wanton carriage that might incurre suspect, as God
blesse me, she had almost brought bed pressing out
of fashion : I could scarse get a fine[6] for the lease of
a Ladies favour once in a fortnight.   25

MALEVOLE. Now in the name of immodesty, how many
maiden-heads hast thou brought to the block?

MAQUERELLE. Let me see : heaven forgive us our misdeeds : Heere's the Dutchesse.

30

SCENA [TERTIA.][1]

Enter MARIA *and Captaine.*

MALEVOLE. God blesse thee Lady.   35
MARIA. Out of thy company.

[5] *at the terme :* away at court.   [6] *fine :* fee.

MALEVOLE. We have brought thee tender of a husband.

MARIA. I hope I have one already.

MAQUERELLE. Nay, by mine honour Madam, as good
ha nere a husband, as a banisht husband, hee's in an
other world now. Ile tell yee Lady, I have heard of a 5
sect that maintained, when the husband was a sleepe,
the wife might lawfully entertaine another man : for
then her husband was as dead, much more when he
is banished.

MARIA. Unhonest creature! 10

MAQUERELLE. Pish, honesty is but an art to seeme so :
pray yee whats honesty? whats constancy? but fables fained, odde old fooles chat, devisde by jealous
fooles, to wrong our liberty.

MALEVOLE. Molly, he that loves thee, is a Duke, Men- 15
doza, he will maintaine thee royally, love thee ar-
dently, defend thee powerfully, marry thee sumptu-
ously, & keep thee in despite of *Rosciclere* or *Donzel
del Phoebo*[1] : thers jewels, if thou wilt, so; if not, so.

MARIA. Captaine, for Gods sake save poore wretchednes 20
From tyranny of lustfull insolence :
Inforce me in the deepest dungeon dwell
Rather then heere, heere round about is hell.
O my dear'st Altofront, where ere thou breath,
Let my soule sincke into the shades beneath, 25
Before I staine thine honor, this thou hast;
And long as I can die, I will live chaste.

MALEVOLE. Gainst him that can inforce, how vaine is
striefe?

MARIA. She that can be enforc'd haz nere a knife? 30
*She that through force her limbes with lust enroules,
Wants* Cleopatres *aspes and* Portiaes *coales.*[2]
God amend you. *Exit with Captaine.*

MALEVOLE. Now the feare of the divell for ever goe

ACT V. SCENE iii.
[1] *Rosciclere, Donzel . . . :*   *Knighthood.*
heroes from *The Mirror of*   [2] *coales :* She swallowed fire.

with thee. Maquerelle I tell thee, I have found an
honest woman, faith I perceive when all is done,
there is of women, as of all other things : some good,
most bad : some saints, some sinners : for as now
adaies, no Courtier but haz his mistris, no Captaine   5
but haz his cockatrice,³ no Cuckold but haz his
hornes, & no foole but haz his feather⁽¹⁾ : even so,
no woman but haz her weakenes & feather too, no
sex⁽²⁾ but haz his : I can hunt the letter no farder :
ô God, how loathsome this toying is to me, that a   10
duke should be forc'd to foole it : well, *Stultorum*
*plena sunt omnia,*⁴, ⁽²⁾ better play the foole Lord,
then be the foole Lord : now, where's your slights
Madam Maquerelle?

MAQUERELLE. Why, are yee ignorant that tis sed, a   15
squemish affected nicenes is naturall to women, and
that the excuse of their yeelding, is onely (forsooth)
the difficult obtaining. You must put her too't :
women are flaxe, and will fire in a moment.

MALEVOLE. Why, was the flax put into thy mouth? &   20
yet thou? thou set fire? thou enflame her?

MAQUERELLE. Marry, but Ile tell yee now, you were too
hot.

MALEVOLE. The fitter to have enflamed the flaxwoman.

MAQUERELLE. You were to boisterous, spleeny, for in-   25
deede.

MALEVOLE. Go, go, thou art a weake pandresse, now I
see.
Sooner earths fire heaven it selfe shall waste,
Then all with heate can melt a minde that's chaste.   30
Go thou the Dukes lime-twig,⁵ Ile make the Duke
turne thee out of thine office. what, not get one touch
of hope, & had her at such advantage.

MAQUERELLE. Now a my conscience, now I thinke in
my discretion, we did not take her in the right signe,   35

³ *cockatrice :* prostitute.   things are full of fools.
⁴ *Stultorum . . . omnia :* All   ⁵ *lime-twig :* snare.

the bloud was not in the true veine, sure.   *Exit.*
                Enter BILIOSO.

BILIOSO. Make way there the Duke returnes from the
inthronment Malevole.

MALEVOLE. Out roage.   5

BILIOSO. Malevole.

MALEVOLE. Hence yee grosse jawd pessantly, out go.

BILIOSO. Nay sweete Malevole, since my returne, I heare
    you are become the thinge I always prophesied
    would be, an advanced virtue, a worthely imployed   10
    faithfulnesse, a man a grace, deere friend. Come;
    what? *Siquoties peccant homines.*[6], [3] If as often
    as courtiers play the knaves honest men should be
    angrie. Why looke yee, we must collouge[7] somtimes,
    forsweare somtimes.   15

MALEVOLE. Be damd somtimes.

BILIOSO. Right *Nemo omnibus horis sapit.*[4] No man
    can be honest at all howers. Necessitie often depraves
    vertue.

MALEVOLE. I will commend thee to the Duke.   20

BILIOSO. Do let us be friends man.

MALEVOLE. And knaves man.

BILIOSO. Right, let us prosper and purchase, our lord-
    ships shall live and our knavery be forgotten.

MALEVOLE. He that by any wayes gets riches his meanes   25
    never shames him.

BILIOSO. True.

MALEVOLE. For impudencie and faithlesnes are the
    maine stayes to greatnesse.

BILIOSO. By the Lord thou art a profound ladd.   30

MALEVOLE. By the Lord thou art a perfect knave. out
    yee antient damnation.[8]

BILIOSO. Peace, peace, and thou wilt not be a freinde

---

[6] *Si . . . homines:* If as often
    as men sin.

[7] *collouge :* intrigue; flatter.

[8] *damnation :* Vice; Devil's
    servant.

to me as I am a knave, be not a knave to me as I am
thy friend and disclose me, peace Cornets.

SCENA [QUARTA.][1]   5

Enter PREPASSO *and* FERRARDO, *two pages with lights,*
CELSO *and* EQUATO, MENDOZA *in Dukes roabs and*
GUERRINO.

MENDOZA. On on, leave us leave us : (*Exeunt all saving*   10
MALEVOLE.) stay, wher is the Hermet?
MALEVOLE. With Duke Pietro, with Duke Pietro.
MENDOZA. Is he dead? is he poysoned?
MALEVOLE. Dead as the Duke is.
MENDOZA. Good, excellent : he will not blabbe, secure-   15
nes lives in secresie; come hether, come hether.
MALEVOLE. Thou hast a certaine strong villanous sent
about thee, my nature cannot indure.
MENDOZA. Sent man? what returnes Maria? what an-
swere to our sute?   20
MALEVOLE. Cold frostie, she is obstinate.
MENDOZA. Then shees but dead, tis resolute, she dies.
Blacke deede onely through blacke deede, safely fles.
MALEVOLE. Pew, *per scelera semper sceleribus tutum*
est iter.[1, (1)]   25
MENDOZA. What art a scholler? art a polititian? sure
thou art an arrand knave.
MALEVOLE. Who I? I have bene twice an under sherife,
man.[2] Well I will go raile upon some great man,
that I may purchase the bastinado, or else go marry   30
some rich *Genoan* lady and instantly go travaile.
MENDOZA. Travaile when thou art married.
MALEVOLE. I tis your yong Lords fashion to do so,
though he was so lasy being a batcheller, that he
would never travaile so farr as the University yet   35

ACT V. SCENE IV.
[1] Translated in previous line.

when he married her tales of,[2] and *Catsoe for Ingland.*

MENDOZA. And why for *Ingland?*

MALEVOLE. Because there is no Brothelhouses there.

MENDOZA. Nor Curtisans? 5

MALEVOLE. Neather; your whore went downe with the
stewes and your punke came up with your Puritan.

MENDOZA. Canst thou impoyson? canst thou impoyson?

MALEVOLE. Excellently, no Jew, Potecary, or Politician
better. Looke ye, here's[3] a box, whom wouldst 10
thou impoison? here's a box which opened, & the
fume taken up in [conduits],[4] thorow which the
braine purges it self, doth instantly for 12. houres
space, bind up all shew of life in a deep cesles sleep :
heres another which being opened under the sleepers 15
nose, choaks at the power of life, kils him sodainely.

MENDOZA. (*Seems to poyson* MALEVOLE.) Ile try experi-
ments, tis good not to be deceived : so, so, *Catzo.*
Who would feare that may destroy,
Death hath no teeth, or tong, 20
And he thats great, to him are slaves
Shame, Murder, fame and wrong. Celso?
Enter CELSO.

CELSO. My honored Lord.

MENDOZA. The[5] good Malevole, that plain-tongued 25
man,
Alas, is dead on sodaine wondrous strangely,
He held in our esteeme good place. Celso
See him buried, see him buried.[5]

CELSO. I shall observe yee. 30

MENDOZA. And Celso, prethee let it be thy care to night
To have some pretty shew, to solemnize
Our high instalement, some musike, maskery :
Weele give faire entertaine unto Maria
The Duches to the banisht Altofront : 35

---

[2] *tales of :* tales off; the account
is closed.

Thou shalt conduct her from the Citadell
Unto the Pallace, thinke on some Maskery.
CELSO. Of what shape, sweete Lord?
MENDOZA. What shape?[6] why any quicke done fiction,
As some brave spirits of the *Genoan* Dukes,   5
To come out of *Elizium* forsooth,
Led in by *Mercury,* to gratulate
Our[7] happy fortune, some such any thing,
Some far-fet tricke, good for Ladies, some stale toy
                          or other,   10
No matter so't bee of our devising.[7]
Do thou prepar't, tis but for a fashion sake,
Feare not, it shall be grac'd man, it shall take.
CELSO. All service.
MENDOZA. All thankes, our hand shall not be close to   15
                thee farewell.
Now is my trechery secure, nor can we fall :
Mischiefe that prospers men do vertue call,
Ile trust no man, he that by trickes gets wreathes,
Keepes them with steele, no man securely breathes,   20
Out of deserved ranckes; the crowde will mutter,
                          foole :
Who cannot beare with spite, he cannot rule,
The chiefest secret for a man of state,
Is, to live sensles of a strenghles hate.   *Exit.* 25
MALEVOLE. (*Starts*[8] *up and speaks.*) Death of the
                damn'd thiefe :
Ile make one i'the maske, thou shalt ha some
Brave spirits of the antique Dukes.
CELSO. My Lord, what strange dilusion?   30
MALEVOLE. Most happy,
Deere Celso, poisond with an empty box?
Ile give thee all anone : my Lady comes to court,
There is a whurle of fate comes tumbling on,
The Castles captaine stands for me, the people   35
Pray for me, and the great leader of
The just stands for me : then courage Celso.[8]
For no disastrous chance can ever move him,

That leaveth nothing but a God above him.

[Exeunt.]

[Scena quinta.]   5

Enter prepasso *and* bilioso, *two pages before them;*
MAQUERELLE, BIANCA *and* EMILIA.

BILIOSO. Make roome there, roome for the Ladies : why
    gentlemen, will not ye suffer the Ladies to be entred   10
    in the great chamber? why gallants? and you sir, to
    droppe your Torch where the beauties must sit too.
PREPASSO. And there's a great fellow playes the knave,
    why dost not strike him?
BILIOSO. Let him play the knave a Gods name, thinkst   15
    thou I have no more wit then to strike a great fellow :
    the musike, more lights, reveling, scaffolds : do you
    heare? let there bee others enow readie at the doore,
    sweare out the divell himself. Lets leave the Ladies,
    and go see if the Lords bee readie for them.   20
                      All save the Ladies depart.
MAQUERELLE. And by my troth Beauties, why do you
    not put you into the fashion, this is a stale cut, you
    must come in fashion : looke ye, you must be all felt,
    fealt and feather, a fealt upon your bare haire : looke   25
    ye, these tiring thinges are justly out of request now :
    and do ye heare? you must weare falling bands,[1] you
    must come into the falling fashion : there is such a
    deale a pinning these ruffes, when the fine cleane
    fall is worth all : and agen, if you should chance to   30
    take a nap in the afternoone, your falling band re-
    quires no poting sticke[2] to recover his forme : be-
    leeve me, no fashion to the falling I say.
BIANCA. And is not *Sinnior S. Andrew* a gallant fellow
    now.   35

Act V. Scene v.
[1] *falling bands :* flat collars.   [2] *poting sticke :* curling stick.

MAQUERELLE. By my maiden-head la, honour and he
agrees aswell together as a satten sute and wollen
stockings.

EMILIA. But is not *Marshall Make-rome* my servant in
reversion, a proper gentleman.   5

MAQUERELLE. Yes in reversion[3] as he had his office, as
in truth he hath all things in reversion : hee haz his
Mistris in reversion, his cloathes in reversion, his wit
in reversion : and indeede is a suter to me, for my
dogge in reversion : but in good verity la, he is as   10
proper a gentleman in reversion as : and indeede, as
fine a man as may be, having a red beard and a pair
of warpt[1] legges.

BIANCA. But I faith I am most monstrously in love with
Count Quidlibet-in-Quodlibet,[1] is he not a pretty   15
dapper unydle[2] gallant?

MAQUERELLE. He is even one of the most busy fingered
Lordes, he will put the beauties to the squeake most
hiddeously.

[*Enter* BILIOSO.]   20

BILIOSO. Roome, make a lane there, the Duke is entring :
stand handsomely for beauties sake, take up the
Ladyes there. So, cornets, cornets.

                                                                        25

SCENA [SEXTA.][1]

Enter PREPASSO, *joynes to* BILIOSO, *two pages and
lights,* FERRARDO, MENDOZA, *at the other doore two
pages with lights, and the Captaine leading in*   30
MARIA, *the Duke meetes* MARIA,
*and closeth with her, the
rest fall backe.*

MENDOZA. Madam, with gentle eare receive my sute,
A kindomes safety should o'er paize[1] slight rites,   35

ACT V. SCENE VI.
[3] *in reversion :* by inheritance.   [1] *o'er paize :* outweigh.

Marriage is meerely Natures policy :
Then, since unlesse our royall beds be joynd,
Danger and civill tumult frights the state.
Be wise as you are faire, give way to fate.

MARIA. What wouldst thou, thou affliction to our house?　　5
Thou ever divell, twas thou that banishedst
My truely noble Lord.

MENDOZA. I?

MARIA. I, by thy plottes, by thy blacke stratagems,
Twelve Moones have suffred change since I beheld　　10
The loved presence of my deerest Lord.
O thou far worse than death, he parts but soule
From a weake body : but thou, soule from soule
Disseverest, that which Gods owne hand did knit.
Thou scant of honor, full of divelish wit.　　15

MENDOZA. Weele checke your too intemperate lavish-
　　　　　　　　　　　　　　nesse.
I can and will.

MARIA.　　　　What canst?

MENDOZA. Go to, in banishment thy husband dies.　　20

MARIA. *He ever is at home that's ever wise,*

MENDOZA. Youst[2] never meete more, reason should love
　　　　　　　　　　　　　　controule,

MARIA. Not meete?
Shee that deere loves, her love's still in her soule.　　25

MENDOZA. You are but a woman Lady, you must yeeld,

MARIA. O save me thou innated bashfulnes,
Thou onely ornament of womans modesty.

MENDOZA. Modesty? Death Ile torment thee.

MARIA. Do, urge all torments, all afflictions trie,　　30
Ile die my Lords, as long as I can die.

MENDOZA. Thou obstinate, thou shalt die. Captaine, that
　　　　　　　　　　　　　　Ladies life
Is forfeited to Justice, we have examined[2] her,
And we do finde, she hath impoysoned　　35
The reverend Hermit : therefore we commaund

---

[2] *Youst :* You must.

Severest custodie. Nay, if youle dooe's no good,
Youst dooe's no harme, a Tirants peace is bloud.

MARIA. O thou art mercifull, O gratious divell,
Rather by much let me condemned be
For seeming murder, than be damn'd for thee.   5
Ile mourne no more, come girt my browes with
       floures,
Revell and daunce; soule, now thy wish thou hast,
Die like a Bride, poore heart thou shalt die chast.
    Enter AURELIA *in mourning habit.*   10

AURELIA. *Life is a frost of coulde felicitie,*
And death the thaw of all our vanity.[1]
Wast not an honest Priest that wrote so?

MENDOZA. Who let her in?

BILIOSO.   Forbeare.   15

PREPASSO.   Forbeare.

AURELIA. *Alas calamity, is every where.*
Sad miserie dispight your double doores,
Will enter even in court.

BILIOSO.   Peace.   20

AURELIA. I ha done? one word, take heede, I ha done.
    Enter MERCURIE *with lowde musicke.*

MERCURIE. Cillenian *Mercurie,* the God of ghosts,
From gloomie shades that spread the lower coasts,
Calls foure high famed *Genoan* Dukes to come   25
And make this presence their *Elizium :*
To passe away this high triumphall night,
With song and daunces, courts more soft delight.

AURELIA. Are you God of ghosts, I have a sute depend-
ing in hell betwixt me and my conscience, I would   30
faine have thee helpe me to an advocate.

BILIOSO. *Mercurie* shall be your lawyer, Lady.

AURELIA. Nay faith, *Mercurie* haz too good a face, to
be a right lawyer.

PREPASSO. Peace, forbeare : *Mercurie* presents the   35
maske.
    Cornets: The Song to the Cornets, which playing,

the maske enters. MALEVOLE, PIETRO, FERNEZE,
and CELSO *in white robes, with Dukes Crownes
upon lawrell wreathes, pistolets and
short swords under their robes.*

MENDOZA. Celso, Celso, court[3] Maria for our love;   5
Lady, be gratious, yet grace.
    MALEVOLE *takes his wife to daunce.*
MARIA. With me Sir?
MALEVOLE. Yes, more loved then my breath : With you
       Ile dance.   10
MARIA. Why then you dance with death,
But come Sir, I was nere more apt to mirth.
*Death gives eternity a glorious breath :
O, to die honourd, who would feare to die.*
MALEVOLE. *They die in feare, who live in villany.*   15
MENDOZA. Yes beleeve him, Lady, and be rulde by him.
PIETRO. Madam, with me?
   PIETRO *taks his wife* AURELIA *to dance.*
AURELIA.   Wouldst then be miserable?
PIETRO. I neede not wish.   20
AURELIA. O yet forbeare my hand, away, fly, fly,
O seeke not her, that onely seekes to die.
PIETRO. Poore loved soule.
AURELIA.   What, wouldst court misery?
PIETRO. Yes.   25
AURELIA. Sheele come too soone, O my griev'd heart!
PIETRO. Lady, ha done, ha done.
Come, lets dance, be once from sorrow free.
AURELIA. Art a sad man.
PIETRO.   Yes sweet.   30
AURELIA.   Then weele agree.
  FERNEZE *takes* MAQUERELLE, *and* CELSO, BIANCA :
   *then the Cornets sound the measure,
one change and rest.*
FERNEZE. (*To* BIANCA.) Beleeve it Lady, shall I sweare,   35
let me injoy you in private, and Ile mary you by my
soule.

BIANCA. I had rather you would sweare by your body :
I thinke that would prove the more regarded othe
with you.

FERNEZE. Ile sweare by them both, to please you.

BIANCA. O, dam them not both to please me, for Gods   5
sake.

FERNEZE. Faith, sweet creature, let me injoy you to
night, and Ile mary you to morow fortnight, by my
troth la.

MAQUERELLE. On his troth la, beleeve him not, that   10
kinde of cunnicatching³ is as stale as *Sir Oliver An-
choves* perfumde jerken : promise of matrimony by a
yong gallant, to bring a virgin Lady into a fooles
paradise : make her a great woman, and then cast
her off : tis as common as naturall to a Courtier, as   15
jelosie to a Citizen, gluttony to a Puritan, wisdome to
an Alderman, pride to a Tayler, or an empty hand-
basket to one of these sixpeny damnations⁴ : of his
troth la, beleeve him not, traps to catch polecats.

MALEVOLE. (*To* MARIA.) Keepe your face constant, let   20
no suddaine passion speake in your eies.

MARIA. O my Altofront.

PIETRO. [*To* AURELIA.]   A tyrants jelosies
Are very nimble, you receive it all.

AURELIA. (AURELIA *to* PIETRO.) My heart, though not   25
my knees, doth umbly fall,
Lowe as the earth to thee.

[MALEVOLE.]⁽⁴⁾ Peace, next change, no words.

MARIA. Speach to such, ay, O what will affordes?

Cornets sound the measure over againe : which   30
danced they unmaske.

MENDOZA. Malevole?

MALEVOLE. No.

They environ MENDOZA, *bending their*
Pistolles on him.   35

---

³ *cunnicatching* : fool-
   exploiting.

⁴ *sixpeny damnations* : cheapest
   prostitute.

MENDOZA. Altofront, Duke Pietro, Ferneze, hah?

ALL. Duke Altofront, Duke Altofront.

    Cornets a florish. They seize upon MENDOZA.

MENDOZA. Are we surprizde? what strange delusions
        mocke   5

 Our sences, do I dreame? or have I dreamt,

 This two dayes space? where am I?

MALEVOLE. Where an arch-vilaine is.

MENDOZA. O lend me breath, till I am fit to die.

 For peace with heaven, for your owne soules sake, 10

 Vouchsafe me life.

PIETRO. Ignoble villaine, whom neither heaven nor hell,

 Goodnesse of God or man, could once make good.

MALEVOLE. Base treacherous wretch, what grace canst
        thou expect   15

 That hast growne impudent in gracelesnesse.

MENDOZA. O life!

MALEVOLE.   Slave, take thy life.

 Wert thou defenced through blood and woundes,

 The sternest horror of a civell fight.   20

 Would I atcheeve thee : but prostrat at my feete

 I scorne to hurt thee : tis the heart of slaves

 That daines to triumph over peasants graves.

 For such thou art, since birth doth neere inrole

 A man mong monarkes, but a glorious soule. 25

 O I have seene strange accidents of state,

 The flatterer like the Ivy clip the Oke,

 And wast it to the hart : lust so confirm'd

 That the black act of sinne it selfe not shamd

 To be termde Courtship.   30

 O they that are as great as be their sinnes,

 Let them remember that th'inconstant people,

 Love many Princes meerely for their faces,

 And outward shewes : and they do covet more

 To have a sight of these then of their vertues, 35

 Yet thus much let the great ones still conceale,

 When they observe not Heavens imposd conditions,

 They are no Kings, but forfeit their commissions.

MAQUERELLE. O good my Lord, I have lived in the
Court this twenty yeare, they that have beene olde
Courtiers and come to live in the Cittie, they are
spighted at and thrust to the wals like Apricokes,
good my Lord.   5

BILIOSO. My Lord, I did know your Lordship in this
disguise, you heard me ever say if Altofront did returne I would stand for him : besides twas your Lordships pleasure to call me Wittoll and Cuckold; you
must not thinke but that I knew you I would have   10
put it up so patiently.

MALEVOLE. (*To* PIETRO *&* AURELIA.) You o'er-joy'd spir-
       its wipe your long wet eyes,
Hence with this man : an Eagle takes not flies.

                              Kicks out MENDOZA.   15
(*To* PIETRO *&* AURELIA.) You to your vowes : (*To*
   MAQUERELLE.) And thou unto the suburbs.[2]
(*To* BILIOSO.) You to my worst frend I would hardly
       give :
Thou art a perfect olde knave, all pleased live.   20
(*To* CELSO *& the Captain*.) You two unto my breast :
       (*To* MARIA.) thou to my hart.
The rest of idle actors idly part,
And as for me I here assume my right,
To which I hope all's pleasd : to all goodnight.   25
           Cornets a florish. Exeunt omnes.
                   FINIS.

                                                           30
An imperfect Ode, being but one staffe, spoken by
            the Prologue.

To wreast each hurtlesse thought to private sence,
   Is the foule use of ill bred Impudence :   35
       Immodest censure now growes wilde,
            all over-running.
       Let Innocence be nere so chast,

                   208

> Yet at the last
> She is defild.
> With too nice-brained cunning.
> O you of fairer soule
> controule   5
> With an Herculean arme
> this harme :
> And once teach all olde freedome of a pen,
> Which still must write of fooles, whilst writes of men.
>   10

Epilogus.

Your modest scilence, full of heedy stillnesse,
Makes me thus speake : A voluntary illnesse   15
Is meerely sensles, but unwilling error,
Such as proceedes from too rash youthfull fervour,
May well be cald a fault but not a sinne,
Rivers take names from Fountes where they begin.
  Then let not too severe an eye peruse,   20
The slighter brakes[1] of our reformed Muse,
Who could her selfe, hir selfe of faultes detect,
But that she knowes tis easie to correct.
Though some mens labour : troth to erre is fit,
  As long as wisdom's not professd, but wit.   25
Then till an others[2] happier Muse appeares,
Till his Thalia feast your learned eares,
To whose desertfull Lampes pleasd fates impart.
Art above Nature, Judgment above Art,
  Receive this peece which hope, nor feare yet   30
    daunteth,
  He that knows most, knows most how much he
    wanteth.

FINIS.   35

EPILOGUE
[1] *brakes :* flaws.   [2] *an others :* Ben Jonson's.

THE WHITE DEVIL

BY

JOHN WEBSTER

THE
WHITE DIVEL,

OR,

The Tragedy of *Paulo Giordano
Ursini*, Duke of *Brachiano*,

With

The Life and Death of Vittoria
Corombona the famous
Venetian Curtizan.

Acted by the Queenes Maiesties Seruants.

Written by IOHN WEBSTER.

Non inferiora secutus.

LONDON,
Printed by *N.O.* for *Thomas Archer*, and are to be sold
at his Shop in Popes head Pallace, neere the
Royall Exchange. 1612.

To the Reader

*In publishing this Tragedy, I do but challenge to my selfe
that liberty, which other men have tane before mee; not that
I affect praise by it, for,* nos haec novimus esse nihil,[1] *onely
since it was acted, in so dull a time of Winter, presented in so
open and blacke*[1] *a Theater,*[2] *that it wanted (that which is
the onely grace and setting out of a Tragedy) a full and understanding Auditory: and that since that time I have
noted, most of the people that come to that Play-house, resemble those ignorant asses (who visiting Stationers shoppes
their use is not to inquire for good bookes, but new bookes)
I present it to the generall veiw with this confidence.*

Nec Rhoncos metues, maligniorum,
Nec Scombris tunicas, dabis molestas.[3]

*If it be objected this is no true Drammaticke Poem, I shall
easily confesse it,* non potes in nugas dicere plura meas : Ipse
ego quam dixi,[4] *willingly, and not ignorantly, in this kind
have I faulted : for should a man present to such an Auditory,
the most sententious Tragedy that ever was written, observing all the critticall lawes, as heighth of stile; and gravety of
person; inrich it with the sententious* Chorus, *and as it were
life'n Death, in the passionate and waighty* Nuntius : *yet
after all this divine rapture,* O dura messorum ilia,[5] *the
breath that comes from the uncapable multitude, is able to
poison it, and ere it be acted, let the Author resolve to fix to
every scaene, this of* Horace,

Haec hodie Porcis comedenda relinques.[6]

---

[1] *nos haec . . . nihil :* we realize that these things are nothing.

[2] *a Theater :* The Red Bull.

[3] *Nec Rhoncos . . . dabis molestas :* You [my book] shall not
fear the snouts of the malicious, / Nor provide wrapping paper for
mackerel.

[4] *Ipse . . . dixi :* You cannot say more against my trifles than I
myself have said.

[5] *O . . . ilia :* O how strong are the stomachs of peasants.

[6] *Haec . . . relinques :* These you will leave for the pigs to eat
today.

To those who report I was a long time in finishing this Tragedy, I confesse I do not write with a goose-quill, winged with two feathers, and if they will needes make it my fault, I must answere them with that of Eurypides *to* Alcestides, *a Tragicke Writer:* Alcestides *objecting that* Eurypides *had onely in three daies composed three verses, whereas himselfe had written three hundreth: Thou telst truth, (quoth he) but heres the difference, thine shall onely bee read for three daies, whereas mine shall continue three ages.*

Detraction is the sworne friend to ignorance: For mine owne part I have ever truly cherisht my good opinion of other mens worthy Labours, especially of that full and haightned stile of Maister Chapman. *The labor'd and understanding workes of Maister* Johnson: *The no lesse worthy composures of the both worthily excellent Maister* Beamont, *& Maister* Fletcher: *And lastly (without wrong last to be named) the right happy and copious industry of Master* Shake-speare, *Master* Decker, *& Master* Heywood, *wishing what I write may be read by their light: Protesting, that, in the strength of mine owne judgement, I know them so worthy, that though I rest silent in my owne worke, yet to most of theirs I dare (without flattery) fix that of* Martiall.

—non norunt, Haec monumenta mori.[7]

[7] *non . . . Haec . . . mori:* these monuments do not know how to die.

[DRAMATIS PERSONAE.

MONTICELSO, *a cardinal, afterwards Pope Paul IV.*

FRANCISCO DE MEDICIS, *Duke of Florence; in Act V disguised as* MULINASSAR, *a Moor.*

BRACHIANO, *otherwise Paulo Giordano Ursini, Duke of Brachiano; husband of Isabella and later of Vittoria.*

GIOVANNI, *his son by Isabella.*

LODOVICO, *a count, in love with Isabella.*

ANTONELLI, } *friends of Lodovico.*
GASPARO,

CARLO, } *attendants of Brachiano but secretly in league with*
PEDRO, } *the Duke of Florence.*

CAMILLO, *first husband of Vittoria, cousin of Monticelso.*

HORTENSIO, *an officer of Brachiano's household.*

MARCELLO, *brother of Vittoria, attendant of the Duke of Florence.*

FLAMINEO, *his younger brother, secretary of Brachiano.*

CARDINAL OF ARRAGON.

JULIO, *a doctor.*

ISABELLA, *first wife of Brachiano, sister of the Duke of Florence.*

VITTORIA COROMBONA, *a Venetian lady; wife first of Camillo and afterwards of Brachiano.*

CORNELIA, *mother of Vittoria, Marcello, and Flamineo.*

ZANCHE, *a Moor; servant of Vittoria.*

MATRON, *of a House of Convertites.*

Ambassadors, Courtiers, Lawyers, Officers, Physicians, Conjuror, Armorer, Attendants (including Jaques, a Moor; Christophero; Guid-antonio).]

[THE SCENE
ROME—PADUA.]

THE TRAGEDY
OF PAULO GIORDANO
Ursini Duke of Brachiano, and Vittoria Corombona.

[ACT I. SCENE I.]

Enter Count LODOVICO, ANTONELLI *and* GASPARO.

LODOVICO. Banisht?

ANTONELLI.   It greev'd me much to heare the
                sentence.   5

LODOVICO. Ha, Ha, ô *Democritus* thy Gods[1]
    That governe the whole world! Courtly reward,
    And punishment. Fortun's a right whore.
    If she give ought, she deales it in smal percels,
    That she may take away all at one swope.   10
    This tis to have great enemies, God quite[1] them :
    Your woolfe no longer seemes to be a woolfe
    Then when shees hungry.[2]

GASPARO.   You terme those enemies
    Are men of Princely ranke.   15

LODOVICO.   Oh I pray for them.
    The violent thunder is adored by those
    Are pasht in peeces by it.

ANTONELLI.   Come my Lord,
    You are justly dom'd;[3] looke but a little backe   20
    Into your former life : you have in three yeares
    Ruin'd the noblest Earldome.

GASPARO.   Your followers
    Have swallowed you like Mummia,[4] and being sicke

ACT I. SCENE I.

[1] *quite* : requite; repay.

[2] *Your woolfe . . . hungry:*
    Successful wolves are given

another name.

[3] *dom'd :* judged; sentenced.

[4] *Mummia :* Mummy, taken as
    a medicine.

With such unnaturall and horrid Phisicke
Vomit you up ith kennell.[5]

ANTONELLI.   All the damnable degrees
Of drinkings have you[1] staggerd through; one
                  Cittizen   5
Is Lord of two faire Manors, cald you master,
Only for Caviare.[2]

GASPARO.   Those noblemen
Which were invited to your prodigall feastes,
Wherin the Phaenix scarce could scape your throtes, 10
Laugh at your misery, as fore-deeminge you :
An idle Meteor[3] which drawne forth the earth
Would bee soone lost ith aire.

ANTONELLI.   Jeast upon you,
And say you were begotten in an Earthquake,   15
You have ruin'd such faire Lordships.

LODOVICO.   Very good,
This Well goes with two buckets, I must tend[6]
The powring out of eather.[4]

GASPARO.   Worse then these, 20
You have acted, certaine Murders here in Rome,
Bloody and full of horror.

LODOVICO.   Las they were flea-bytinges :
Why tooke they not my head then?

GASPARO.   O my Lord 25
The law doth somtimes mediate,[5] thinkes it good
Not ever to steepe violent sinnes in blood,
This gentle pennance may both end your crimes,
And in the example better these bad times.

LODOVICO. So, but I wonder then some great men scape 30
This banishment,[6] ther's Paulo Giordano Orsini,
The Duke of Brachiano, now lives in Rome,
And by close pandarisme seekes to prostitute
The honour of Vittoria Corombona,
Vittoria, she that might have got my pardon   35
For one kisse to the Duke.

[5] *kennell :* gutter.   [6] *tend :* await.

ANTONELLI.   Have a full man within you,
Wee see that Trees beare no such pleasant fruite
There where they brew first, as where they are new
                              set.[7]
Perfumes the more they are chaf'd the more they   5
                              render
Their pleasing sents, and so affliction
Expresseth vertue, fully, whether trew,
Or ells adulterate.
LODOVICO.   Leave your painted comforts,   10
Ile make Italian cut-works in their guts
If ever I returne.
GASPARO.   O Sir.
LODOVICO.   I am patient,
I have seene some ready to be executed   15
Give pleasant lookes, and money, and growne familiar
With the knave hangman, so do I, I thanke them,
And would account them nobly mercifull
Would they dispatch me quicklie,—
ANTONELLI.   Fare you well,   20
Wee shall find time I doubt not to repeale
Your banishment.
          Enter [Sennet and sound trumpets.][2]
LODOVICO.   I am ever bound to you :
This is the worlds almes; pray make use of it,   25
Great men sell sheep, thus to be cut in peeces,
When first they have shorne them bare and sold their
                    fleeces.   *Exeunt.*

                                                      30
               [ACT I. SCENE II.]

     Enter BRACHIANO, CAMILLO, FLAMINEO, VITTORIA
            COROMBONA [*and attendants.*]
BRACHIANO. Your best of rest.   35
VITTORIA.   Unto my Lord the Duke,
The best of wellcome, More lights, attend the Duke.
          [*Exeunt* CAMILLO *and* VITTORIA.]

BRACHIANO. Flamineo.

FLAMINEO.   My Lord.

BRACHIANO.   Quite lost Flamineo.

FLAMINEO. Pursew your noble wishes, I am prompt

  As lightning to your service, ô my Lord!   5

  (*Whisper*) The faire Vittoria, my happy sister

  Shall give you present audience; gentlemen

  Let the caroach[1] go on, and tis his pleasure

  You put out all your torches and depart.

                     [*Exeunt attendants.*]   10

BRACHIANO. Are wee so happy.

FLAMINEO.   Can't be otherwise?

  Observ'd you not to night my honor'd Lord

  Which way so ere you went shee threw her eyes,

  I have dealt already with her chamber-maid   15

  Zanche the More, and she is wondrous proud

  To be the agent for so high a spirit.

BRACHIANO. Wee are happie above thought, because

               'bove merrit.

FLAMINEO. 'bove merrit! wee may now talke freely :   20

  'bove merrit; what ist you doubt, her coynesse, thats

  but the superficies of lust most women have; yet

  why should Ladyes blush to heare that nam'd, which

  they do not feare to handle?[(1)] O they are polli-

  ticke, They know our desire is increas'd by the   25

  difficultie of injoying; whereas[[1]] satiety is a blunt,

  weary and drowsie passion,[(2)] if the buttery[(3)]

  hatch at Court stood continually open their would be

  nothing so passionat crouding, nor hot suit after the

  beverage,—   30

BRACHIANO. O but her jealous husband.

FLAMINEO. Hang him, a guilder that hath his braynes

  perisht with quicke-silver is not more could in the

  liver.[2, (4)] The great Barriers[3] moulted not more

Act I. Scene ii.   less nature.

[1] *caroach :* large coach.   [3] *Barriers :* between duelists on

[2] A cold liver meant a passion-   foot.

feathers(5) then he hath shed haires, by the confession of his doctor. An Irish gamster that will play himselfe naked, and then wage all downeward, at hazard, is not more venterous.(6) So un-able to please a woman that like a dutch doublet all his 5
backe is shrunke into his breeches.
Shrowd you within this closet, good my Lord,
Some tricke now must be thought on to devide
My brother in law from his faire bed-fellow,—

BRACHIANO. O should she faile to come,— 10

FLAMINEO. I must not have your Lordship thus unwisely amorous, I my selfe have loved a lady and peursued her with a great deale of under-age protestation, whom some 3. or 4. gallants that have enjoyed would with all their harts have bin glad to have 15
bin rid of. Tis just like a summer bird-cage in a garden, the birds that are without, despaire to get in, and the birds that are within despaire and are in a consumption for feare they shall never get out :(7)
away away my Lord.   [*Exit* BRACHIANO.] 20
              Enter CAMILLO.
[*Aside.*] See here he comes; this fellow by his apparell
Some men would judge a pollititian,
But call his wit in question you shall find it 25
Merely an Asse in's foot cloath,4 How now brother!
What travailing(8) to bed to your kind wife?

CAMILLO. I assure you brother no, My voyage lyes
More northerlie, in a farre colder clime,
I do not well remember I protest when I last lay with 30
              her.

FLAMINEO. Strange you should loose your Count.

CAMILLO. Wee never lay together but eare morning
Their grew a flaw5 betweene us.

---

4 *foot cloath :* ornamental
  saddle-cloth.

5 *flaw :* squall; disagreement;
  crack.

FLAMINEO.   T'had byn your part
    To have made up that flaw.

CAMILLO.   Trew, but shee loathes
    I should be seene in't.

FLAMINEO.   Why Sir, what's the matter?   5

CAMILLO. The Duke your maister visits me I thanke him,
    And I perceave how like an earnest bowler
    Hee very passionatelie leanes that way,
    He should have his boule runne—

FLAMINEO. I hope you do not thinke—   10

CAMILLO. That noble men boule bootie[6]? Faith his
               cheeke
    Hath a most excellent Bias,[7] it would faine
    Jumpe(9) with my mistris.

FLAMINEO.   Will you be an asse.   15
    Despight your[2] *Aristotle* or a Cocould
    Contrary to your *Ephemerides*[8]
    Which shewes you under what a smiling planet
    You were first swadled,—

CAMILLO.   Pew wew, Sir tell not me   20
    Of planets nor of *Ephemerides*.
    A man may be made Cocould in the day time
    When the Stars eyes are out.

FLAMINEO.   Sir God boy[9] you,
    I do commit you to your pittifull pillow   25
    Stuft with horne-shavings.(10)

CAMILLO.   Brother.

FLAMINEO.   God refuse me
    Might I advise you now your onlie course
    Weare to locke up your wife.   30

CAMILLO.   'Tweare very good.

FLAMINEO. Bar her the sight of revels.

CAMILLO.   Excellent.

[6] *boule bootie* : cheat at bowling.

[7] *Bias* : Weighted cheek of bowling ball.

[8] *Contrary . . . Ephemerides* : Despite learning or astrological prediction.

[9] *boy* : be with.

FLAMINEO. Let her not go to Church, but like a hounde
   In Leon[10] at your heeles.

CAMILLO.   Tweare for her honour.

FLAMINEO. And so you should be certayne in one fort-
                            night,   5
   Despight her chastity or innocence
   To bee Cocoulded, which yet is in suspence.
   This is my counsell and I aske no fee for't.

CAMILLO. Come you know not where my night-cap
   wringes mee.   10

FLAMINEO. Weare it ath' old fashion, let your large
   eares[11] come through, it will be more easy, nay I
   will be bitter, barre your wife of her entertaynment :
   women are more willinglie & more gloriouslie chast,
   when they are least restrayned of their libertie.[12]   15
   It seems you would be a fine Capricious Mathematically[13] jealous Coxcombe, take the height of
   your owne hornes with a *Jacobs* staffe[11] afore they
   are up. These polliticke inclosures for paltry mutton,[14] makes more rebellion in the flesh then all   20
   the provocative electuaries[12] Doctors have uttered
   sence last Jubilee.[15]

CAMILLO. This doth not phisicke me.

FLAMINEO. It seems you are Jealous, ile shew you the
   error of it by a familiar example, I have seene a paire   25
   of spectacles fashiond with such perspective art, that
   lay downe but one twelve pence ath'bord twill appeare as if there were twenty, now should you weare
   a paire of these spectacles, and see your wife tying
   her shooe, you would Imagine twenty hands were   30
   taking up of your wives clothes, and this would put
   you into a horrible causlesse fury,—

CAMILLO. The fault there Sir is not in the eye-sight.

FLAMINEO. True, but they that have the yellow Jaun-

---

[10] *In Leon :* On a leash.
[11] *Jacobs staffe :* Instrument for
measuring heights.

[12] *electuaries :* medicinal fruit
mixtures; aphrodisiacs.

deise, thinke all objects they looke on to bee yellow.[16] Jealousy is worser, her fits present to a man, like so many bubles in a Bason of water, twenty severall crabbed faces, many times makes his owne shadow his cocould-maker. 5

Enter [VITTORIA] COROMBONA.

See she comes, what reason have you to be jealous of this creature? what an ignorant asse or flattering knave might he be counted, that should write sonnets to her eyes, or call her brow the snow of Ida,[17] 10 or Ivorie of Corinth, or compare her haire to the blacke birds bill, when 'tis liker the blacke[18] birds feather. This is all : Be wise, I will make you freinds and you shall go to bed together, marry looke you, it shall not be your seeking, do you stand upon that by 15 any meanes, walk you a loofe, I would not have you seene in't,—sister (my Lord attends you in the banquetting house), your husband is wondrous discontented.

VITTORIA. I did nothing to displease him, I carved[19] 20 to him at supper-time.

FLAMINEO. (You need not have carved him infaith, they say he is a capon already, I must now seemingly fall out with you.) Shall a gentleman so well descended as Camillo.—(a lousy slave that within this twenty 25 yeares rode with the blacke guard[20] in the Dukes cariage mongst spits and dripping-pannes.)

CAMILLO. Now he begins to tickle her.

FLAMINEO. An excellent scholler, (one that hath a head fild with calves braynes without any sage in them),— 30 come crouching in the hams to you for a nights lodging—(that hath an itch in's hams, which like the fier at the glasse house[21] hath not gone out this seaven yeares)—is hee not a courtly gentleman,— (when he weares white sattin one would take him by 35 his blacke mussel[13] to be no other creature, then a

13 *mussel :* muzzle.

maggot), you are a goodly Foile, I confesse, well set
out—(but coverd with a false stone, yon conterfaite
dyamond).

CAMILLO. He will make her know what is in mee.

FLAMINEO. [*Aside to* VITTORIA.] Come, my Lord at- 5
tends you, thou shalt go to bed to my Lord.

CAMILLO. Now he comes to't.

FLAMINEO. With a relish as curious as a vintner going
to taste new wine, [*To* CAMILLO.] I am opening your
case hard. 10

CAMILLO. A vertuous brother a my credit.

FLAMINEO. He will give thee a ringe with a philosophers
stone[22] in it.

CAMILLO. Indeede I am studying Alcumye.

FLAMINEO. Thou shalt lye in a bed stuft with turtles 15
feathers, swoone in perfumed lynnen like the fellow
was smothered in roses,[23] so perfect shall be thy
happinesse, that as men at Sea thinke land and trees
and shippes go that way they go, so both heaven and
earth shall seeme to go your voyage.[24] Shal't 20
meete him, tis fixt, with nayles of dyamonds to inevitable necessitie.[25]

VITTORIA. [*Aside to* FLAMINEO.] How shals rid him
hence?

FLAMINEO. (I will put brees[14, 26] in's tayle, set him 25
gadding presentlie), [*To* CAMILLO.] I have almost
wrought her to it, I find her comming, but might I
advise you now for this night I would not lye with
her, I would crosse her humor to make her more
humble. 30

CAMILLO. Shall I, shall I?

FLAMINEO. It will shew in you a supremacie of Judgement.

CAMILLO. Trew, and a mind differing from the tumultu-
ary opinion, for *que negata grata.*[15] 35

---

[14] *brees* : gadfly.   [15] *que . . . grata* : things
refused are desired.

FLAMINEO. Right, you are the Adamant[27] shall draw
her to you, though you keepe distance of :

CAMILLO. A philosophicall reason.

FLAMINEO. Walke by her a'the noble mans fashion, and
tell her you will lye with her at the end of the   5
Progresse.[16]

CAMILLO. Vittoria, I cannot be induc'd, or as a man
would say incited.

VITTORIA. To do what Sir?

CAMILLO. To lye with you to night; your silkeworme   10
useth to fast every third day, and the next following
spinnes the better. To morrow at night I am for you.

VITTORIA. Youle spinne a faire thread, trust to't.

FLAMINEO. But do you heare, I shall have you steale to
her chamber about midnight.   15

CAMILLO. Do you thinke so, why looke you brother,
because you shall not thinke ile gull you, take the key,
locke me into the chamber, and say you shall be sure
of me.

FLAMINEO. Introth I will, ile be your jaylor once, But   20
have you nere false dore?

CAMILLO. A pox on't, as I am a Christian; tell mee to
morrow how scurvelie shee takes my unkind parting.

FLAMINEO. I will.

CAMILLO. Didst thou not marke the jeast of the silke-   25
worme? good night; in faith I will use this tricke
often,—

FLAMINEO. Do, do, do.   *Exit* CAMILLO.
So now you are safe. Ha ha ha, thou intanglest thy
selfe in thine owne worke like a silke-worme.[28]   30
       Enter BRACHIANO.
Come sister, darkenesse hides your blush, women are
like curst dogges, civilitie keepes them tyed all day
time, but they are let loose at midnight, then they do
most good or most mischeefe[29]—my Lord, my   35
Lord!

[16] *Progresse :* Visit.

BRACHIANO. Give credit[17] : I could wish time would
                stand still
And never end this enterview this hower,
But all delight doth it selfe soon'st devour.

ZANCHE *brings out a Carpet, Spreads it and layes*   5
   on it two faire Cushions. Enter CORNELIA
         [*behind, listening.*]
Let me into your bosome happy Ladie,
Powre out in stead of eloquence my vowes,
Loose[30] me not Madam, for if you forego me   10
I am lost eternallie.

VITTORIA.   Sir in the way of pittie
I wish you hart-hole.

BRACHIANO.   You are a sweet Phisition.

VITTORIA. Sure Sir a loathed crueltie in Ladyes   15
Is as to Doctors many funeralls :
It takes away their credit.

BRACHIANO.   Excellent Creature.
Wee call the cruell fayre, what name for you
That are so mercifull?   20

ZANCHE.   See now they close.

FLAMINEO. Most happie union.

CORNELIA. [*Aside.*] My feares are falne upon me, oh
            my heart!
My sonne the pandar : now I find our house   25
Sinking to ruine. Earth-quakes leave behind,
Where they have tyrannised, iron, or lead, or stone,
But woe to ruine : violent lust leaves none.

BRACHIANO. What valew is this Jewell.

VITTORIA.   Tis the ornament   30
Of a weake fortune.

BRACHIANO. In sooth ile have it; nay I will but change
My Jewell for your Jewell.

FLAMINEO.   Excellent,
His Jewell for her Jewell, well put in Duke.   35

BRACHIANO. Nay let me see you weare it.

[17] *Give credit :* Believe me.

VITTORIA. Heare sir.

BRACHIANO. Nay lower, you shall weare my Jewell
    lower.

FLAMINEO. That's better : she must weare his Jewell
    lower.   5

VITTORIA. To passe away the time I'le tell your grace,
    A dreame I had last night.

BRACHIANO. Most wishedly.

VITTORIA. A foolish idle dreame,
    Me thought I walkt about the mid of night,   10
    Into a Church-yard, where a goodly $Eu^{(31)}$ Tree
    Spred her large roote in ground, under that $Eu,^{(31)}$
    As I sat sadly leaning on a grave,
    Checkered with crosse-sticks,$^{(32)}$ their came steal-
        ing in   15
    Your Dutchesse and my husband, one of them
    A picax bore, th'other a Rusty spade,
    And in rough termes they gan to challenge me,
    About this $Eu.^{(31)}$

BRACHIANO. That Tree.   20

VITTORIA. This harmelesse $Eu.^{(31)}$
    They told me my entent was to root up
    That well-growne $Eu,^{(31)}$ and plant i'th steed of it
    A withered blacke-thorne,$^{(33)}$ and for that they
        vow'd   25
    To bury me alive : my husband straight
    With picax gan to dig, and your fell[18] Dutchesse
    With shovell, like a fury, voyded out
    The earth & scattered bones, Lord how me thought
    I trembled, and yet for all this terror   30
    I could not pray.

FLAMINEO. No the divell was in your dreame.

VITTORIA. When to my rescue there arose me thought
    A whirlewind, which let fall a massy arme
    From that strong plant,   35
    And both were strucke dead by that sacred Eu

18 *fell :* fierce.

In that base shallow grave that was their due.
FLAMINEO. Excellent Divell.
    Shee hath taught him in a dreame
    To make away his Dutchesse and her husband.
BRACHIANO. Sweetly shall I enterpret this your dreame,   5
    You are lodged within his armes who shall protect
             you,
    From all the feavers of a jealous husband,
    From the poore envy[34] of our flegmaticke Dutch-
             esse,   10
    I'le seate you above law and above scandall,
    Give to your thoughts the invention of delight
    And the fruition, nor shall government
    Divide me from you longer then a care
    To keepe you great : you shall to me at once,   15
    Be Dukedome, health, wife, children, friends and all.
CORNELIA. [*Coming forward.*] Woe to light hearts : they
             still forerun our fall.
FLAMINEO. What fury rais'd thee up? away, away!
                          Exit ZANCHE.   20
CORNELIA. What make you heare my Lord this dead of
             night?
    Never dropt meldew on a flower here,
    Till now.
FLAMINEO. I pray will you go to bed then,   25
    Least you be blasted.
CORNELIA.   O that this faire garden,
    Had all poysoned hearbes of *Thessaly,*[35]
    At first bene planted, made a nursery
    For witch-craft; rather a buriall plot,   30
    For both your Honours.
VITTORIA.   Dearest mother heare me.
CORNELIA. O thou dost make my brow bend to the
             earth,
    Sooner then nature; see the curse of children,   35
    In life they keepe us frequently[36] in teares,
    And in the cold grave leave[3] us in pale feares.
BRACHIANO. Come, come, I will not heare you.

VITTORIA.   Deere my Lord.

CORNELIA. Where is thy Dutchesse now adulterous
        Duke?

  Thou little dreamd'st this night shee is come to *Rome*.

FLAMINEO. How? come to *Rome*,—   5

VITTORIA.   The Dutchesse,—

BRACHIANO.   She had bene better,—

CORNELIA. The lives of Princes should like dyals
        move,[37]

  Whose regular example is so strong,   10

  They make the rimes by them go right or wrong.

FLAMINEO. So, have you done?

CORNELIA.   Unfortunate Camillo.

VITTORIA. I do protest if any chast deniall,

  If any thing but bloud could have alayed   15

  His long suite to me,—

CORNELIA.   I will joyne[38] with thee,

  To the most wofull end ere mother kneel'd,

  If thou dishonour thus thy husbands bed,

  Bee thy life short as are the funerall teares   20

  In great mens,—

BRACHIANO.   Fye, fye, the womans mad.

CORNELIA. Bee thy act *Judas-like* : betray in kissing;

  Maiest thou be envied during his short breath,

  And pittied like a wretch after his[4] death.   25

VITTORIA. O me accurst.   *Exit* VITTORIA.

FLAMINEO. Are you out of your wits? my Lord

  Ile fetch her backe againe?

BRACHIANO.   No I'le to bed.

  Send Doctor Julio to me presently;   30

  Uncharitable woman thy rash tongue

  Hath rais'd a fearefull and prodigious[39] storme,

  Bee thou the cause of all ensuing harme :

                     Exit BRACHIANO.

FLAMINEO. Now, you that stand so much upon your   35
        honour,

  Is this a fitting time a night thinke you,

  To send a Duke home without ere a man :

I would faine know where lies the masse of wealth
Which you have whoorded for my maintenance,
That I may beare my beard out of the levell
Of my Lords Stirop.

CORNELIA.   What? because we are poore, 5
 Shall we be vitious?

FLAMINEO.   Pray what meanes have you
 To keepe me from the gallies, or the gallowes?
 My father prov'd himselfe a Gentleman,
 Sold al's land, and like a fortunate fellow, 10
 Died ere the money was spent. You brought me up,
 At *Padua* I confesse, where I protest
 For want of meanes, the University judge me,
 I have bene faine to heele my Tutors stockings
 At least seven yeares : Conspiring with a beard 15
 Made me a Graduate, then to this Dukes service,(40)
 I visited the Court, whence I return'd :
 More courteous, more letcherous by farre,
 But not a suite the richer, and shall I,
 Having a path so open and so free 20
 To my preferment, still retaine your milke
 In my pale forehead? no this face of mine
 I'le arme and fortefie with lusty wine,
 'Gainst shame and blushing.

CORNELIA. O that I ne're had borne thee,— 25

FLAMINEO.   So would I.
 I would the common'st Courtezan in *Rome*,
 had bene my mother rather then thy selfe.
 Nature is very pitifull[5] to whoores
 To give them but few children, yet those children 30
 Plurality of fathers, they are sure
 They shall now want. Go, go,
 Complaine unto my great Lord Cardinall,
 Yet may be he will justifie the act.
 Lycurgus wondred much men would provide 35
 Good stalions for their Mares, and yet would suffer
 Their faire wives to be barren.

CORNELIA. Misery of miseries.   *Exit* CORNELIA.

FLAMINEO. The Dutchesse come to Court, I like not that,
Wee are ingag'd to mischiefe and must on.
As Rivers to finde out the Ocean
Flow with crooke bendings beneath forced bankes,[41]
Or as wee see to aspire some mountaines top,   5
The way ascends not straight, but Imitates
The suttle fouldings of a Winters snake,[42]
So who knowes policy and her true aspect,
Shall finde her waies winding and indirect.   *Exit.*
                                                        10

[ACT II. SCENE i.]

Enter FRANCISCO DE MEDICIS, *Cardinall*
MONTICELSO, MARCELLO, ISABELLA, *young*   15
GIOVANNI, *with little* JAQUES *the Moore.*

FRANCISCO. Have you not seene your husband since you
                    arived?
ISABELLA. Not yet sir.
FRANCISCO.   Surely he is wondrous kind,—   20
If I had such a Dove-house as Camillo's
I would set fire on't, wer't but to destroy
The Pole-cats[1] that haunt to't,—my sweet cossin.
GIOVANNI. Lord unkle you did promise mee a horse
And armour.   25
FRANCISCO.   That I did my pretty cossin,
Marcello see it fitted.
MARCELLO.   My Lord the Duke is here.
FRANCISCO. Sister away, you must not yet bee seene.
ISABELLA. I do beseech you   30
Intreate him mildely, let not your rough tongue
Set us at louder variance, all my wrongs
Are freely pardoned, and I do not doubt
As men to try the precious Unicornes horne[2]
Make of the powder a preservative Circle   35
And in it put a spider, so these armes
Shall charme his poyson, force it to obeying
And keepe him chast from an infected straying.

233

FRANCISCO. I wish it may. Be gone.   *Exit* [ISABELLA.]
     Enter BRACHIANO, *and* FLAMINEO.
Void the chamber, [*Exeunt* FLAMINEO, MARCELLO,
                         GIOVANNI, *and* JAQUES.]
You are welcome, will you sit, I pray my Lord   5
Bee you my Orator, my hearts too full,
I'le second you anon.
MONTICELSO.   E're I beginne
Let me entreat your grace forgo all passion
Which may be raised by my free discourse.   10
BRACHIANO. As silent as i'th Church—you may proceed.
MONTICELSO. It is a wonder to your noble friends,
That you [that] have[1] as 'twere entred the world,
With a free Scepter in your able hand,
And have to th'use of nature well applyed   15
High gifts of learning, should in your prime-age
Neglect your awfull throne, for the soft downe
Of an insatiate bed. oh my Lord,
The Drunkard after all his lavish cuppes,
Is dry, and then is sober, so at length,   20
When you awake from this lascivious dreame,
Repentance then will follow; like the sting
Plac't in the Adders tayle[3] : wretched are Princes
When fortune blasteth but a pretty flower
Of their unweldy crownes; or ravesheth   25
But one pearle from their Scepter : but alas!
When they to wilfull shipwrake loose good Fame
All Princely titles perish with their name.
BRACHIANO. You have said my Lord,—
MONTICELSO.   Inough to give you tast   30
How farre I am from flattering your greatnesse?
BRACHIANO. Now you that are his second, what say you?
Do not like yong hawkes fetch a course about,
Your game flies faire and for you,—
FRANCISCO.   Do not feare it;   35
I'le answere you in your owne hawking phrase,
Some Eagles that should gaze upon the Sunne
Seldome soare high, but take their lustfull ease,

Since they from dunghill birds their prey can ceaze,
You know Vittoria,—
BRACHIANO.   Yes.
FRANCISCO.   You shift your shirt there
When you retire from Tennis.   5
BRACHIANO.   Happely.[4]
FRANCISCO. Her husband is Lord of a poore fortune
Yet she wears cloth of Tissue,[5]
BRACHIANO.   What of this?
Will you urge that my good Lord Cardinall   10
As part of her confession at next Shrift,
And know from whence it sailes.
FRANCISCO.   She is your Strumpet,
BRACHIANO. Uncivill sir ther's Hemlocke in thy breath
And that blacke slander, were she a whore of mine   15
All thy loud Cannons, and thy borrowed Switzers,[6]
Thy Gallies, nor thy sworne confederates,
Durst not supplant her.
FRANCISCO.   Let's not talke on thunder,
Thou hast a wife, our sister, would I had given   20
Both her white hands to death, bound and lockt fast
In her last winding sheete, when I gave thee
But one.
BRACHIANO. Thou hadst given a soule to God then.[7]
FRANCISCO.   True, 25
Thy ghostly father with al's absolution,
Shall ne're do so by thee.
BRACHIANO.   Spit thy poyson,
FRANCISCO. I shall not need, lust carries her sharpe
                              whippe   30
At her owne girdle, looke to't for our anger
Is making thunder-bolts.
BRACHIANO.   Thunder? infaith,
They are but crackers.[8]
FRANCISCO.   Wee'le end this with the 35
                              Cannon.
BRACHIANO. Thou'lt get nought by it but iron in thy
                              wounds,

And gunpowder in thy nostrels.

FRANCISCO.   Better that

Then change perfumes for plaisters,[1]

BRACHIANO.   Pitty on thee,

   'Twere good you'ld shew your slaves or men con-   5
           demn'd

   Your new plow'd[9] fore-head; defiance, and I'le
           meete theè,

   Even in a thicket of thy ablest men.

MONTICELSO. My Lords, you shall not word it any   10
           further

   Without a milder limit.

FRANCISCO.   Willingly.

BRACHIANO. Have you proclaimed a Triumph that you
           baite   15

   A lyon thus.

MONTICELSO. My Lord.

BRACHIANO.   I am tame, I am tame sir.

FRANCISCO. We send, unto the Duke for conference

   Bout leavyes 'gainst the Pyrates, my Lord Duke   20

   Is not at home, we come our selfe in person,

   Still my Lord Duke is busied, but we feare

   When Tyber to each proling[10] passenger

   Discovers flockes of wild-duckes.[11] then my Lord—

   'Bout moulting[12] time, I meane—wee shall be   25
           certaine

   To finde you sure enough and speake with you.

BRACHIANO.   Ha?

FRANCISCO. A meere tale of a tub,[13] my wordes are
           idle,   30

   But to expresse the Sonnet by naturall reason,

   When Stagges grow melancholike[14] you'le finde
           the season.

           Enter GIOVANNI.

ACT II. SCENE I.
[1] *change perfumes for plaisters :*
need medicine after lechery.

MONTICELSO. No more my Lord, heare comes a Cham-
                   pion, [15]
  Shall end the difference betweene you both,
  Your sonne the Prince Giovanni; see my Lords
  What hopes you store in him, this is a casket   5
  For both your Crowns, & should be held like deere :
  Now is he apt for knowledge, therefore know
  It is a more direct and even way
  To traine to vertue those of Princely bloud,
  By examples then by precepts : if by examples   10
  Whom should he rather strive to imitate
  Then his owne father [16] : be his patterne then,
  Leave him a stocke of vertue that may last,
  Should fortune rend his sailes, and split his mast.
BRACHIANO. Your hand boy—growing to souldier.   15
GIOVANNI.   Give me a pike.
FRANCISCO. What practising your pike so yong, faire
                  cous.
GIOVANNI. Suppose me one of *Homers* frogges, [17] my
                  Lord,   20
  Tossing my bul-rush thus, pray sir tell mee
  Might not a child of good descretion
  Be leader to an army :
FRANCISCO.   Yes cousin a yong Prince
  Of good descretion might.   25
GIOVANNI.   Say you so,
  Indeed I have heard 'tis fit a Generall [18]
  Should not endanger his owne person oft
  So that he make a noyse, when hee's a horsebacke
  Like a danske [19] drummer, ô 'tis excellent.   30
  Hee need not fight, me thinkes his horse as well
  Might lead an army for him; [18] if I live
  I'le charge the French foe, in the very front
  Of all my troupes, the formost man.
FRANCISCO.   What, what,   35
GIOVANNI. And will not bid my Souldiers up and follow
  But bid them follow me.
BRACHIANO.   Forward Lap-wing.

He flies with the shell on's head.[20]

FRANCISCO.   Pretty cousin.

GIOVANNI. The first yeare unkle that I go to warre,
All prisoners that I take I will set free
Without their ransome.   5

FRANCISCO.   Ha, without their ransome,
How then will you reward your souldiers
That tooke those prisoners for you.

GIOVANNI.   Thus my Lord,
I'le marry them to all the wealthy widowes   10
That fals that yeare.

FRANCISCO.   Why then the next yeare following
You'le have no men to go with you to warre.

GIOVANNI. Why then I'le presse the women to the war,
And then the men will follow.   15

MONTICELSO.   Witty Prince.

FRANCISCO. See a good habite makes a child a man,
Whereas a bad one makes a man a beast :
Come you and I are friends.

BRACHIANO.   Most wishedly,   20
Like bones which broke in sunder and well set
Knit the more strongly.

FRANCISCO. [*To servant off-stage.*] Call Camillo hither.
You have received the rumor, how Count Lodowicke
Is turn'd a Pyrate.[21]   25

BRACHIANO.   Yes.

FRANCISCO.   We are now preparing,
Some shippes to fetch him in :
                    [*Enter* ISABELLA.]
                                    behold your Dutchesse.   30
Wee now will leave you and expect from you
Nothing but kind intreaty.

BRACHIANO.   You have charm'd mee.
                    Exeunt FRANCISCO, MONTICELSO,
                                    [*and*] GIOVANNI.   35
You are in health we see.

ISABELLA.   And above health
To see my Lord well,—

BRACHIANO.   So—I wonder much,
  What amorous whirlewind hurryed you to *Rome*.
ISABELLA. Devotion my Lord.
BRACHIANO.   Devotion?[22]
  Is your soule charg'd with any grievous sinne?   5
ISABELLA. 'Tis burdened with too many, and I thinke
  The oftner that we cast our reckonings up,
  Our sleepes will be the sounder.
BRACHIANO.   Take your chamber.
ISABELLA. Nay my deere Lord I will not have you angry,   10
  Doth not my absence from you two moneths,
  Merit one kisse?
BRACHIANO.   I do not use to kisse,
  If that will dispossesse your jealousy,
  I'le sweare it to you.   15
ISABELLA.   O my loved Lord,
  I do not come to chide; my jealousy,
  I am to learne[23] what that *Italian* meanes,
  You are as welcome to these longing armes,
  As I to you a Virgine.   20
BRACHIANO.   O your breath,
  Out upon sweete meates, and continued Physicke.
  The plague is in them.
ISABELLA.   You have oft for these two lippes
  Neglected *Cassia*[2] or the naturall sweetes   25
  Of the Spring-violet, they are not yet much whith-
                      ered;
  My Lord I should be merry, these your frownes
  Shew in a Helmet lovely, but on me,
  In such a peacefull enterveiw me thinkes   30
  They are too too roughly knit.
BRACHIANO.   O dissemblance.
  Do you bandy factions[3] 'gainst me? have you learn't,
  The trick of impudent basenes to complaine
  Unto your kindred?   35

---

[2] *Cassia* : fragrant plant.   [3] *bandy factions* : work in
                                         league.

ISABELLA.   Never my deere Lord.

BRACHIANO. Must I be haunted out, or was't your trick
   To meete some amorous gallant heere in Rome
   That must supply our discontinuance?

ISABELLA. I pray sir burst my heart, and in my death   5
   Turne to your antient pitty, though not love.

BRACHIANO. Because your brother is the corpulent[24]
                  Duke,
   That is the great Duke, S'death I shall not shortly
   Rackit away five hundreth Crownes at Tenis,   10
   But it shall rest upon record : I scorne him
   Like a shav'd[25] Pollake, all his reverent wit
   Lies in his wardrope, hee's a discret fellow
   When hee's made up in his roabes of state,
   Your brother the great Duke, because h'as gallies,   15
   And now and then ransackes a Turkish flye-boate,[4]
   (Now all the hellish furies take his soule,)
   First made this match; accursed be the Priest
   That sang the wedding Masse, and even my Issue.

ISABELLA. O too too far you have curst.   20

BRACHIANO.   Your hand I'le kisse,
   This is the latest ceremony of my love,
   Hence-forth I'le never lye with thee, by this,
   This wedding-ring : I'le ne're more lye with thee.
   And this divorce shall be as truely kept,   25
   As if the Judge had doom'd it : fare you well,
   Our sleeps are sever'd.

ISABELLA.   Forbid it the sweet union
   Of all things blessed; why the Saints in heaven
   Will knit their browes at that.   30

BRACHIANO.   Let not thy love,
   Make thee an unbeleever, this my vow,
   Shall never on my soule bee satisfied
   With my repentance : let thy brother rage
   Beyond a horred tempest or sea-fight,   35

[4] *Turkish flye-boate :* small, fast
   boat.

My vow is fixed.

ISABELLA.   O my winding sheet,
Now shall I need thee shortly, deere my Lord,
Let me heare once more, what I would not heare,
Never?   5

BRACHIANO. Never!

ISABELLA. O my unkind Lord may your sins find mercy,
As I upon a woefull widowed bed,
Shall pray for you, if not to turne your eyes,
Upon your wretched wife, and hopefull sonne,   10
Yet that in time you'le fix them upon heaven.

BRACHIANO. No more, go, go, complaine to the great
Duke.

ISABELLA. No my deere Lord, you shall have present
witnesse,   15
How I'le worke peace betweene you, I will make
My selfe the author of your cursed vow.
I have some cause to do it, you have none,
Conceale it I beseech you, for the weale
Of both your Dukedomes, that you wrought the   20
meanes
Of such a separation, let the fault
Remaine with my supposed jealousy,
And thinke with what a pitteous and rent heart,
I shall performe this sad insuing part.   25

    Enter FRANCISCO, FLAMINEO, MONTICELSO, [*and*]
                MARCELLO.

BRACHIANO. Well, take your course; my honourable
brother.

FRANCISCO. Sister, this is not well my Lord, why sister,   30
She merits not this welcome.

BRACHIANO.   Welcome say?
Shee hath given a sharpe welcome.

FRANCISCO.   Are you foolish?
Come dry your teares, is this a modest course.   35
To better what is nought, to raile and weepe?
Grow to a reconcilement, or by heaven,

I'le nere more deale betweene you.
ISABELLA.   Sir you shall not,
No though Vittoria upon that condition
Would become honest.
FRANCISCO.   Was your husband loud,   5
Since we departed.
ISABELLA.   By my life sir no,
I sweare by that I do not care to loose.
Are all these ruines of my former beauty,
Laid out for a whores triumph?   10
FRANCISCO.   Do you heare?
Looke upon other women, with what patience
They suffer these slight wrongs, with what justice
They study to requite them, take that course.
ISABELLA. O that I were a man, or that I had power   15
To execute my apprehended(26) wishes,
I would whip some with scorpions.(27)
FRANCISCO.   What? turn'd fury?
ISABELLA. To dig the strumpets eyes out, let her lye
Some twenty monethes a dying, to cut off   20
Her nose and lippes, pull out her rotten teeth,
Preserve her flesh like *Mummia*, for trophies
Of my just anger : Hell to my affliction
Is meere snow-water : by your favour sir,
Brother draw neere, and my Lord Cardinall,   25
Sir let me borrow of you but one kisse,
Hence-forth I'le never lye with you, by this,
This wedding ring.
FRANCISCO.   How? nere more lie with him,—
ISABELLA. And this divorce shall be as truly kept,   30
As if in thronged Court, a thousand eares
Had heard it, and a thousand Lawyers hands,
Seal'd to the separation.
BRACHIANO.   Nere lie with me?
ISABELLA. Let not my former dotage,   35
Make thee an unbelever, this my vow
Shall never on my soule be satisfied

With my repentance, *manet alta mente repos-*
            tum.[5], [2], (28)

FRANCISCO. Now by my birth you are a foolish, mad,
And jealous woman.

BRACHIANO.   You see 'tis not my seeking.   5

FRANCISCO. Was this your circle of pure Unicornes
            horne,
You said should charme your Lord; now hornes upon
            thee,
For jealousy deserves them, keepe your vow,   10
And take your chamber.

ISABELLA.   No sir I'le presently to *Padua,*
I will not stay a minute.

MONTICELSO.   O good Madame.

BRACHIANO. 'Twere best to let her have her humor,   15
Some halfe daies journey will bring downe her
            stomacke,
And then she'le turne in post.[6]

FRANCISCO.   To see her come,
To my Lord Cardinall for a dispensation   20
Of her rash vow will beget excellent laughter.

ISABELLA. "Unkindnesse do thy office, poore heart
            breake,
Those are the killing greifes which dare not
            speake." (29)   *Exit* 25
            Enter CAMILLO.

MARCELLO. Camillo's come my Lord.

FRANCISCO. Where's the commission?

MARCELLO.   Tis here.

FRANCISCO. Give me the Signet.   30

FLAMINEO. [*To* BRACHIANO.] My Lord do you marke
their whispering, I will compound a medicine out of
their two heads, stronger then garlick, deadlier then

---

[5] *manet . . . repostum :* it shall   of my mind.
remain stored up in the depths   [6] *in post :* in haste.

stibium,[7] the Cantarides[8] which are scarce seene to
sticke upon the flesh when they work to the heart,
shall not do it with more silence or invisible cunning.

Enter DOCTOR [JULIO.]

BRACHIANO. About the murder.   5

FLAMINEO. They are sending him to *Naples,* but I'le
send him to *Candy,*[9, (30)] here's another property[10]
to.

BRACHIANO. O the Doctor,—

FLAMINEO. A poore quackesalving knave, my Lord, one   10
that should have bene lasht for's letchery, but that
he confest a judgement, had an execution laid upon
him,[11] and so put the whip to a *non-plus.*

DOCTOR JULIO. And was cosin'd,[12] my Lord, by an ar-
ranter knave then my selfe, and made pay all the   15
coulourable execution.

FLAMINEO. He will shoot pils into a mans guts, shall
make them have more ventages then a cornet or a
lamprey, hee will poyson a kisse, and was once
minded, for his Master-peece, because *Ireland* breeds   20
no poyson,[(31)] to have prepared a deadly vapour
in a *Spaniards* fart[(32)] that should have poison'd all
Dublin.

BRACHIANO. O Saint *Anthony* fire :[(33)]

DOCTOR JULIO. Your Secretary is merry my Lord.   25

FLAMINEO. O thou cursed antipathy to nature, looke his
eye's bloud-shed like a needle a Chirurgeon stitcheth
a wound with, let me embrace thee toad, & love thee
ô thou abhominable lothsome gargarisme,[13] that will
fetch up lungs, lights, heart, and liver by scruples.[14]   30

BRACHIANO. No more, I must employ thee honest
Doctor,

[7] *stibium* : antimony.
[8] *Cantarides* : Spanish fly.
[9] *Candy* : To death (Crete).
[10] *property* : instrument; villain.
[11] *had an execution laid upon him* : had himself imprisoned for debt.
[12] *cosin'd* : cheated by someone who collected the false debt.
[13] *gargarisme* : gargle.
[14] *scruples* : very small portions.

You must to *Padua* and by the way,
Use some of your skil for us.

DOCTOR JULIO.   Sir I shall.

BRACHIANO. But for Camillo?

FLAMINEO. He dies this night by such a polliticke   5
                   straine,
Men shall suppose him by's owne engine[15] slaine.
But for your Dutchesse death.

DOCTOR JULIO.   I'le make her sure—

BRACHIANO. Small mischiefes are by greater made   10
            secure.

FLAMINEO. Remember this you slave, when knaves
come to preferment they rise as gallouses[34] are
raised i'th low countries, one upon another's[3]
shoulders.   15

                        Exeunt [BRACHIANO, FLAMINEO,
                            and DOCTOR JULIO.]

MONTICELSO. Here is an Embleme nephew pray peruse
it.
'Twas throwne in at your window,—   20

CAMILLO.   At my window?
Here is a Stag my Lord hath shed his hornes,
And for the losse of them the poore beast weepes—
The word *Inopem me copia fecit.*[16, (35)]

MONTICELSO.   That is.   25
Plenty of hornes hath made him poore of hornes.

CAMILLO. What should this meane.

MONTICELSO.   Ile tell you, 'tis given out
You are a Cocould.

CAMILLO.   Is it given out so?   30
I had rather such report as that my Lord,
Should keepe within dores.

FRANCISCO.   Have you any children?

CAMILLO. None my Lord.

FRANCISCO.   You are the happier—   35

---

[15] *engine :* contrivance.
[16] *Inopem . . . fecit :*

Abundance has made me
poor.

Ile tell you a tale.

CAMILLO.   Pray my Lord.

FRANCISCO.   An old tale.[36]

Upon a time *Phoebus* the God of light
Or him wee call the Sunne would neede be married.   5
The Gods gave their consent, and *Mercury*
Was sent to voice it to the generall world.
But what a pitious cry their straight arose
Amongst Smiths, & Felt-makers, Brewers & Cooks.
Reapers and Butter-women, amongst Fishmongers   10
And thousand other trades, which are annoyed
By his excessive heate; twas lamentable.
They came to *Jupiter* all in a sweat
And do forbid the banes; a great fat Cooke
Was made their Speaker, who intreates of *Jove*   15
That *Phoebus* might bee guelded, for if now
When there was but one Sunne, so many men
We are like to perish by his violent heate.
What should they do if hee were married
And should beget more, and those children   20
Make fier-workes like their father? so say I,
Only I will apply it to your wife,
Her issue should not providence prevent it
Would make both nature, time, and man repent it.

MONTICELSO. Looke you cossin.   25
Go change the aire for shame : see if your absence,
Will blast your *Cornucopia;* Marcello
Is chosen with you joint commissioner
For the relieving our Italian coast
From pirats.   30

MARCELLO. I am much honord int.

CAMILLO.   But sir
Ere I returne the Stagges hornes may be sprouted,
Greater then these are shed.

MONTICELSO.   Do not feare it,   35
I'le bee your ranger.

CAMILLO.   You must watch i'th nights,
Then's the most danger.

FRANCISCO.   Farewell good Marcello.
 All the best fortunes of a Souldiers wish,
 Bring you a ship-board.
CAMILLO. Were I not best now I am turn'd Souldier,
 E're that I leave my wife, sell all shee hath,   5
 And then take leave of her?
MONTICELSO.   I expect good from you,
 Your parting is so merry.
CAMILLO. Merry my Lord, a'th Captaines humor right.
 I am resolved to be drunke this night.   10
       Exit [CAMILLO *with* MARCELLO.]
FRANCISCO. So, 'twas well fitted, now shall we descerne,
 How his wisht absence will give violent way,
 To Duke Brachiano's lust,—
MONTICELSO.   Why that was it;   15
 To what scorn'd purpose else should we make choice
 Of him for a sea Captaine? and besides,
 Count Lodowicke which was rumor'd for a pirate,
 Is now in *Padua*.
FRANCISCO.   Is't true?   20
MONTICELSO.   Most certaine.
 I have letters from him, which are suppliant
 To worke his quicke repeale from banishment,
 He meanes to adresse himselfe for pention,
 Unto our sister[17] Dutchesse.   25
FRANCISCO.   O 'twas well.
 We shall not want his absence past six daies,
 I faine would have the Duke Brachiano run
 Into notorious scandale, for their's nought
 In such curst dotage, to repaire his name,   30
 Onely the deepe sence of some deathlesse shame.
MONTICELSO. It may be objected I am dishonourable,
 To play thus with my kinsman, but I answere,
 For my revenge I'de stake a brothers life,
 That being wrong'd durst not avenge himselfe.   35

[17] *sister :* general courtesy
form.

FRANCISCO. Come to 'observe this Strumpet.

MONTICELSO.   Cursse of greatnes,

Sure hee'le not leave her.

FRANCISCO.   There's small pitty in't :

Like mistle-tow on seare Elmes spent by weather,   5

Let him cleave to her and both rot together.

Exeunt.

[ACT II. SCENE II.]   10

Enter BRACHIANO *with one in the habite of a Conjurer.*

BRACHIANO. Now sir I claime your promise, 'tis dead

midnight,

The time prefixt to shew me by your Art,   15

How the intended murder of Camillo,

And our loathed Dutchesse grow to action.

CONJUROR. You have won me by your bounty to a

deed,

I do not often practise, some there are,   20

Which by Sophisticke tricks, aspire that name

Which I would gladly loose, of Nigromancer;

As some that use to juggle upon cardes,[1]

Seeming to conjure, when indeed they cheate.

Others that raise up their confederate spirits,   25

'Bout wind-mils,[2] and indanger their owne neckes,

For making of a squib, and some their are

Will keepe a curtall[3] to shew juggling trickes(1)

And give out 'tis a spirit : besides these

Such a whole reame(2) of Almanacke-makers,   30

figure-flingers,

Fellowes indeed that onely live by stealth,

Since they do meerely lie about stolne goods,

ACT II. SCENE II.

[1] *juggle upon cardes :* use cards   [2] *wind-mils :* wild schemes.
for magic.   [3] *curtall :* bob-tailed horse.

Thei'd make men thinke the divell were fast and loose,
With speaking fustian Lattine : pray sit downe,
Put on this night-cap sir, 'tis charm'd, and now
I'le shew you by my strong-commanding Art
The circumstance that breakes your Dutchesse heart.　　5

A Dumbe Shew. [3]

Enter suspiciously, JULIO *and* CHRISTOPHERO, *they draw
a curtaine wher* BRACHIANO's *picture is, they put on
spectacles of glasse, which cover their eyes and
noses, and then burne perfumnes afore the picture,*　　10
*and wash the lips of the picture, that done, quenching
the fire, and putting off their spectacles they depart
laughing.*

Enter ISABELLA *in her night-gowne as to bed-ward, with
lights after her,* Count LODOVICO, GIOVANNI, GUID-　　15
ANTONIO *and others waighting on her, shee kneeles
downe as to prayers, then drawes the curtaine of the
picture, doe's three reverences to it, and kisses it
thrice, shee faints and will not suffer them to come
nere it, dies, sorrow exprest in* GIOVANNI *and in* Count　　20
LODOVICO, *shees conveid out solemnly.*

BRACHIANO. Excellent, then shee's dead,—

CONJUROR.　　　　　　　　　　She's poysoned,
By the fum'd picture, 'twas her custome nightly,
Before shee went to bed, to go and visite　　25
Your picture, and to feed her eyes and lippes
On the dead shadow; Doctor Julio
Observing this, infects it with an oile
And other poison'd stuffe, which presently
Did suffocate her spirits.　　　　　　　　　30

BRACHIANO.　　　　　Me thought I saw,
Count Lodowicke there.

CONJUROR.　　　　　　He was, and by my art
I finde hee did most passionately doate
Upon your Dutchesse; now turne another way,　　35
And view Camillo's farre more polliticke fate,
Strike louder musicke from this charmed ground,
To yeeld, as fits the act, a Tragicke sound.

The Second Dumbe Shew.[4]

Enter FLAMINEO, MARCELLO, CAMILLO, *with foure more*
as Captaines, they drinke healths and dance, a vaut-
ing horse is brought into the roome, MARCELLO *and*
two more whisper'd out of the roome, while FLAMINEO   5
and CAMILLO *strip themselves into their shirts, as to*
vault, complement who shall beginne, as CAMILLO
is about to vault, FLAMINEO *pitcheth him upon his*
necke, and with the help of the rest, wriths his necke
about, seemes to see if it be broke, and layes him   10
foulded double as 'twere under the horse, makes
shewes to call for helpe. MARCELLO *comes in, laments,*
sends for the Cardinall [MONTICELSO] *and* Duke
[FRANCISCO,] *who comes forth with armed men, won-*
der at the act, commands the bodie to be carried   15
home, apprehends FLAMINEO, MARCELLO, *and the*
rest, and go as 'twere to apprehend VITTORIA.

BRACHIANO. 'Twas quaintly done, but yet each circum-
               stance,
  I tast not fully.   20
CONJUROR.   O 'twas most apparant,
  You saw them enter charged with their deepe helthes
  To their boone voyage,[5] and to second that,
  Flamineo cals to have a vaulting horse
  Maintaine their sport. The vertuous Marcello,   25
  Is innocently plotted forth the roome,
  Whilst your eye saw the rest, and can informe you
  The engine of all.
[BRACHIANO.][11] It seemes Marcello, and Flamineo
  Are both committed.   30
CONJUROR.   Yes, you saw them guarded,
  And now they are come with purpose to apprehend
  Your Mistresse, faire Vittoria; wee are now
  Beneath her roofe : 'twere fit we instantly
  Make out by some backe posterne :   35
BRACHIANO.   Noble friend.
  You bind me ever to you, this shall stand
  As the firme seale annexed to my hand.

It shall inforce a payment.
CONJUROR.   Sir I thanke you.
                                        Exit BRACHIANO.
Both flowers and weedes, spring when the Sunne is
          warme,   5
And great men do great good, or else great harme.
                                        Exit CONJUROR.

[ACT III. SCENE I.]   10

Enter FRANCISCO, *and* MONTICELSO, [*with*] *their*
          Chancellor and Register
FRANCISCO. You have dealt discreetly to obtain the
          presence,   15
Of all the grave Leiger Embassadours[1]
To heare Vittorias triall.
MONTICELSO.   'Twas not ill,
For sir you know we have nought but circumstances
To charge her with, about her husbands death,   20
Their approbation therefore to the proofes
Of her blacke lust, shall make her infamous
To all our neighbouring Kingdomes,—I wonder
If Brachiano will be here.
FRANCISCO.   O fye 'twere impudence too palpable.   25
                                        [*Exeunt.*]
Enter FLAMINEO *and* MARCELLO *guarded, and a*
          Lawyer.
LAWYER. What are you in by the weeke[1]? so I will try
now whether thy wit be close prisoner, mee thinke's   30
none should sit upon thy sister but old whoore-
maisters,—[2]
FLAMINEO. Or cocoulds, for your cocould is your most
terrible tickler of letchery : whoore-maisters would

ACT III. SCENE I.
[1] *in by the weeke :* deeply
    trapped.

serve, for none are judges at tilting, but those that
have bene old Tilters.

LAWYER. My Lord Duke and shee have bene very
private :

FLAMINEO. You are a dull asse, 'tis threatned they have   5
bene very publicke.

LAWYER. If it can be proved they have but kist one another.

FLAMINEO. What then?

LAWYER. My Lord Cardinall will ferit them,—   10

FLAMINEO. A Cardinall I hope will not catch conyes.[2]

LAWYER. For to sowe kisses (marke what I say) to
sowe kisses, is to reape letchery, and I am sure a
woman that will endure kissing is halfe won.

FLAMINEO. True, her upper part by that rule,—if you   15
will win her nether part to, you know what followes.

LAWYER. Harke the Embassadours are lighted,—

FLAMINEO. [*Aside.*] I do put on this feigned Garbe of
                 mirth,
To gull suspition.   20

MARCELLO.   O my unfortunate sister!
I would my daggers point had cleft her heart
When she first saw Brachiano : You 'tis said,
Were made his engine, and his stauking horse
To undo my sister.   25

FLAMINEO.   I made a kind of path
To her & mine owne preferment.

MARCELLO.   Your ruine.

FLAMINEO. Hum! thou art a souldier,
Followest the great Duke, feedest his victories,   30
As witches do their serviceable spirits,
Even with thy prodigall bloud;[3] what hast got?
But like the wealth of Captaines, a poore handfull,
Which in thy palme thou bear'st, as men hold water—
Seeking to gripe it fast, the fraile reward   35
Steales through thy fingers.[4]

---

[2] *conyes :* rabbits; women.

MARCELLO.　　　　　Sir,
FLAMINEO.　　　　　　　Thou hast scarce maintenance
　To keepe thee in fresh shamoyes.(5)
MARCELLO.　　　　　　　　Brother.
FLAMINEO.　　　　　　　　　　Heare me,　　5
　And(6) thus when we have even powred ourselves,
　Into great fights, for their ambition
　Or idle spleene, how shall we find reward,
　But as we seldome find the mistle-towe
　Sacred to physicke : Or the builder Oke,　　　　10
　Without a Mandrake by it, so in our quest of gaine.
　Alas the poorest of their forc'd dislikes
　At a limbe proffers,3 but at heart it strikes :
　This is lamented doctrine.(6)
MARCELLO.　　　　　Come, come.　　　　15
FLAMINEO. When age shall turne thee,
　White as a blooming hauthorne,—
MARCELLO.　　　　　　　I'le interrupt you.
　For love of vertue beare an honest heart,
　And stride over every polliticke respect,　　　　20
　Which where they most advance they most infect.
　Were I your father, as I am your brother,
　I should not be ambitious to leave you
　A better patrimony.
FLAMINEO.　　　　I'le think on't,　　　25
　　　Enter Savoy [Ambassador.]
　　　　　　　　The Lord Embassadors.
　Here there is a passage of the Lieger Embassa-
　dours over the Stage severally. Enter French
　　　　　Embassadour.[1]　　　30
LAWYER. O my sprightly Frenchman, do you know him,
　he's an admirable Tilter.(7)
FLAMINEO. I saw him at last Tilting, he shewed like a
　peuter candlesticke fashioned like a man in armour,

---

3 *proffers :* feints (*as in
　duelling*).

houlding a Tilting staffe in his hand, little bigger then
a candle of twelve i'th pound.

LAWYER. O but he's an excellent horseman.

FLAMINEO. A lame one in his lofty trickes,(8) hee
sleepes a horsebacke like a poulter,—4   5
      Enter English and Spanish [Ambassadors.]

LAWYER. Lo you my Spaniard.

FLAMINEO. He carries his face in's ruffe, as I have seene
a serving-man carry glasses in a cipres5 hat-band,
monstrous steddy for feare of breaking, He lookes   10
like the claw of a blacke-bird, first salted and then
broyled in a candle.   *Exeunt.*

[ACT III. SCENE II.]   15

THE ARAIGNEMENT OF VITTORIA.

Enter FRANCISCO, MONTICELSO, *the sixe lieger Embassadours*, BRACHIANO, VITTORIA, [ZANCHE, FLAMINEO,
      MARCELLO], *Lawyer, and a guard.*   20

MONTICELSO. Forbeare my Lord, here is no place
                        assign'd[1] you,
      This businesse by his holinesse is left
      To our examination.

BRACHIANO.   May it thrive with you.   25
                  Laies a rich gowne under him.

FRANCISCO. A Chaire there for his Lordship.

BRACHIANO. Forbeare your kindnesse, an unbidden
                        guest
      Should travaile as dutch-women go to Church :   30
      Beare their stooles with them.

MONTICELSO.   At your pleasure Sir.
      Stand to the table gentlewoman[2] : now Signior
      Fall to your plea.

---

4 *poulter :* poulterer; seller of   5 *cipres :* crepe.
   poultry.

[LAWYER.] *Domine Iudex converte oculos in hanc*
        pestem mulierum corruptissimam.[1]

VITTORIA. Whats he?

FRANCISCO.   A Lawyer, that pleades against you.

VITTORIA. Pray my Lord, Let him speake his usuall   5
                tongue
Ile make no answere else.

FRANCISCO.   Why you understand lattin.

VITTORIA. I do Sir, but amongst this auditory
    Which come to heare my cause, the halfe or more   10
    May bee ignorant in't.

MONTICELSO.   Go on Sir:

VITTORIA.   By your favour,
    I will not have my accusation clouded,
    In a strange tongue: All this assembly   15
    Shall heare what you can charge mee with.

FRANCISCO.   Signior,
    You need not stand on't much; pray change your
                language.[3]

MONTICELSO. Oh for God sake: gentlewoman, your   20
                credit
    Shall bee more famous by it.

LAWYER.   Well then have at you.

VITTORIA. I am at the marke Sir, Ile give aime to you,
    And tell you how neare you shoote.   25

LAWYER. Most literated Judges, please your Lordships,
    So to connive your Judgements to the view
    Of this debausht and diversivolent[2] woman
    Who such a blacke concatenation
    Of mischiefe hath effected, that to exterpe   30
    The memory of't, must be the consummation
    Of her and her projections—[1]

VITTORIA.   What's all this?

ACT III. SCENE II.

[1] *Domine . . . corruptissimam:*   rupted of women.
    O Lord, turn your eyes on   [2] *diversivolent:* wishing to
    this plague, the most cor-   cause division.

LAWYER. Hould your peace,
Exorbitant sinnes must have exulceration.(2)
VITTORIA. Surely my Lords this lawier here hath swal-
lowed
Some Poticaryes bils, or proclamations.   5
And now the hard and undegestable wordes,
Come up like stones wee use give Haukes for phisicke.
Why this is welch to Lattin.
LAWYER.   My Lords, the woman
Know's not her tropes nor figures, nor is perfect   10
In the accademick derivation
Of Grammaticall elocution.
FRANCISCO.   Sir your paynes
Shall bee well spared, and your deepe eloquence
Bee worthely applauded amongst those   15
Which understand you.
LAWYER.   My good Lord.
FRANCISCO. (FRANCISCO *speakes this as in scorne.*) Sir,
Put up your papers in your fustian³ bag,
Cry mercy Sir, tis buckeram,(3) and accept   20
My notion of your learn'd verbosity.
LAWYER. I most graduatically(4) thanke your Lordship.
I shall have use for them elsewhere.   [*Exit.*]
MONTICELSO. I shall bee playner with you, and paint out
Your folies in more naturall red and white,   25
Then that upon your cheeke.
VITTORIA.   O you mistake.
You raise a blood as noble in this cheeke
As ever was your mothers.
MONTICELSO. I must spare you till proofe cry whore to   30
that;
Observe this creature here my honoured Lords,
A woman of a most prodigious spirit
In her effected.(5)
VITTORIA.   Honorable my Lord,   35

³ *fustian :* coarse cloth;
bombastic language.

It doth not sute a reverend Cardinall
To play the Lawier thus.

MONTICELSO. Oh your trade instructs your language!
You see my Lords what goodly fruict she seemes,
Yet like those apples travellers report   5
To grow where *Sodom* and *Gomora* stood.
I will but touch her and you straight shall see
Sheele fall to soote and ashes.[6]

VITTORIA.   Your invenom'd
Poticary should doo't—   10

MONTICELSO.   I am resolved.
Were there a second Paradice to loose
This Devell would betray it.

VITTORIA.   O poore charity!
Thou art seldome found in scarlet.[7]   15

MONTICELSO. Who knowes not how, when severall night
                    by night
Her gates were choak'd with coaches, and her roomes
Out-brav'd the stars with severall kind of lights,
When shee did counterfet a Princes Court.   20
In musicke banquets and most ryotous surfets
This whore, forsooth, was holy.

VITTORIA.   Ha? whore—what's that?

MONTICELSO. Shall I expound whore to you?[8] sure I
                    shal;   25
Ile give their perfect character.[9] They are first,
Sweete meates which rot the eater: In mans nostrill
Poison'd perfumes. They are coosning Alcumy,
Shipwrackes in Calmest weather! What are whores?
Cold Russian winters, that appeare so barren,   30
As if that nature had forgot the spring.
They are the trew matteriall fier of hell,
Worse then those tributes ith low countries payed,
Exactions upon meat, drinke, garments, sleepe.[10]
I even on mans perdition, his sin.   35
They are those brittle evidences of law
Which forfait all a wretched mans estate
For leaving out one sillable.[11] What are whores?

They are those flattering bels have all one tune :
At weddings, and at funerals, your ritch whores
Are only treasuries by extortion fild,
And emptied[4] by curs'd riot. They are worse,
Worse then dead bodies, which are beg'd at gallowes   5
And wrought upon by surgeons, to teach man
Wherin hee is imperfect. Whats a whore?
Shees like the guilty conterfetted coine
Which who so eare first stampes it brings[5] in
       trouble   10
All that receave it.
VITTORIA.   This carracter scapes me.
MONTICELSO. You gentlewoman?
 Take from all beasts, and from all mineralls
 Their deadly poison—   15
VITTORIA.   Well what then?
MONTICELSO.   Ile tell thee
 Ile find in thee a Poticaries shop
 To sample them all.
FRENCH AMBASSADOR. Shee hath lived ill.   20
ENGLISH AMBASSADOR. Trew, but the Cardinals too bitter.
MONTICELSO. You know what Whore is; next the devell,
     Adultry,
 Enters the devell, murder.
FRANCISCO.   Your unhappy husband   25
 Is dead.
VITTORIA. O hee's a happy husband
 Now hee owes Nature nothing.
FRANCISCO. And by a vaulting engine.
MONTICELSO.   An active plot—   30
 Hee jumpt into his grave.
FRANCISCO.   What a prodigy wast,
 That from some two yardes height a slender man
 Should breake his necke!
MONTICELSO.   Ith'rushes.   35
FRANCISCO.   And what's more,
 Upon the instant loose all use of speach,

All vitall motion, like a man had laine
Wound up[4] three dayes. Now marke each circum-
stance.
MONTICELSO. And looke upon this creature was his wife.
Shee comes not like a widow : shee comes arm'd   5
With scorne and impudence : Is this a mourning
habit?
VITTORIA. Had I forknowne his death as you suggest,
I would have bespoke my mourning.
MONTICELSO. O you are conning.   10
VITTORIA. You shame your wit and Judgement
To call it so; What is my just defence
By him that is my Judge cal'd impudence?
Let mee appeale then from this Christian Court
To the uncivill[12] Tartar.   15
MONTICELSO.   See my Lords.
Shee scandals our proceedings.
VITTORIA.   Humbly thus,
Thus low, to the most worthy and respected
Leigier Embassadors, my modesty   20
And womanhood I tender; but withall
So intangled in a cursed accusation
That my defence of force like *Perseus*,[13]
Must personate masculine vertue—to the point![14]
Find mee but guilty, sever head from body :   25
Weele part good frindes : I scorn to hould my life
At yours or any mans intreaty, Sir.
ENGLISH AMBASSADOR. Shee hath a brave spirit.
MONTICELSO. Well, well, such counterfet Jewels
Make trew ones[6] oft suspected.   30
VITTORIA.   You are deceaved.
For know that all your strickt combined[15] heads,
Which strike against this mine of diamondes,
Shall prove but glassen hammers, they shall breake,

---

[4] *Wound up :* For burial, in a
shroud.

These are but faigned shadowes of my evels.
Terrify babes, my Lord, with painted devils,
I am past such needlesse palsy, for your names,
Of Whoore and Murdresse they proceed from you,   5
As if a man should spit against the wind,
The filth returne's in's face.

MONTICELSO. Pray you Mistresse satisfy me one ques-
                tion :
Who lodg'd beneath your roofe that fatall night
Your husband brake his necke?   10

BRACHIANO.   That question
Inforceth me breake silence, I was there.

MONTICELSO. Your businesse?

BRACHIANO.   Why I came to comfort her,
And take some course for setling her estate,   15
Because I heard her husband was in debt
To you my Lord.

MONTICELSO.   He was.

BRACHIANO.   And 'twas strangely fear'd,
That you would cosen her.   20

MONTICELSO.   Who made you over-seer?

BRACHIANO. Why my charity, my charity, which should
               flow
From every generous and noble spirit,
To orphans and to widdows.   25

MONTICELSO.   Your lust.

BRACHIANO. Cowardly dogs barke loudest. Sirrah Priest,
Ile talke with you hereafter,—Do you heare?
The sword you frame of such an excellent temper,
I'le sheath in your owne bowels :   30
There are a number of thy coate resemble
Your common post-boyes.[5]

MONTICELSO.   Ha?

BRACHIANO. Your mercinary post-boyes,
Your letters carry truth, but 'tis your guise   35

[5] *post-boyes :* lying news-
  mongers.

To fill your mouths[7] with grosse and impudent
         lies.
                    [*He is about to go.*]
SERVANT. My Lord your gowne.
BRACHIANO. Thou liest, 'twas my stoole.[6, (16)]   5
  Bestow't upon thy maister that will challenge
  The rest a'th houshold-stuffe—for Brachiano
  Was nere so beggarly, to take a stoole
  Out of anothers lodging : let him make
  Valence for his bed on't, or a demy foote-cloth,   10
  For his most reverent moile,[7] Monticelso,
  Nemo me Impune lacessit[8, (17)]   *Exit* BRACHIANO.
MONTICELSO. Your Champions gon.
VITTORIA.   The wolfe may prey the better.
FRANCISCO. My Lord there's great suspition of the 15
         murder,
  But no sound proofe who did it : for my part
  I do not thinke she hath a soule so blacke
  To act a deed so bloudy; if shee have,
  As in cold countries husband-men plant Vines,   20
  And with warme bloud manure them, even so
  One summer she will beare unsavory fruite,
  And ere next spring wither both branch and roote.
  The act of bloud let passe, onely descend,
  To matter of incontinence.   25
VITTORIA.   I decerne poison,
  Under your guilded pils.
MONTICELSO. Now the Duke's gone, I wil produce a
         letter,
  Wherein 'twas plotted, he[8] and you should meete, 30
  At an Appoticaries summer-house,[(18)]
  Downe by the river Tiber : veiw't my Lords :
  Where after wanton bathing and the heat
  Of a lascivious banquet,—I pray read it,
  I shame to speak the rest.   35

---

[6] He had only his cloak to sit on.   [8] *Nemo . . . lacessit :* No one
[7] *moile :* mule.   hurts me without hurt.

VITTORIA.   Grant I was tempted,
Temptation to lust proves not the act,
Casta est quam nemo rogavit,[9]
You reade his hot love to me, but you want
My frosty answere.   5
MONTICELSO.   Frost i'th dog-daies![19] strange!
VITTORIA. Condemne you me for that the Duke did
                              love mee,
So may you blame some faire and christall river
For that some melancholike distracted man,   10
Hath drown'd himselfe in't.[20]
MONTICELSO.   Truly drown'd indeed.
VITTORIA. Summe up my faults I pray, and you shall
                              finde,
That beauty and gay clothes, a merry heart,   15
And a good stomacke to feast, are all,
All the poore crimes that you can charge me with :
Infaith my Lord you might go pistoll flyes,
The sport would be more noble.
MONTICELSO.   Very good.   20
VITTORIA. But take you your course, it seemes you have
                              beggerd me first
And now would faine undo me; I have houses,
Jewels, and a poore remnant of Crusado's,[21]
Would those would make you charitable.   25
MONTICELSO.   If the devill
Did ever take good shape behold his picture.
VITTORIA. You have one vertue left,
You will not flatter me.
FRANCISCO.   Who brought this letter?   30
VITTORIA. I am not compel'd to tell you.
MONTICELSO. My Lord Duke sent to you a thousand
                              duckets,
The twelfth of August.

[9] *Casta . . . rogavit :* She is
chaste whom no man has
solicited.

262

VITTORIA.   'Twas to keepe your cosen
　From prison, I paid use[10] for't.

MONTICELSO.   I rather thinke
　'Twas Interest for his lust.

VITTORIA. Who saies so but your selfe? if you bee my   5
　　　　　accuser
　Pray cease to be my Judge, come from the Bench,
　Give in your evidence 'gainst me, and let these
　Be moderators : my Lord Cardinall,
　Were your intelligencing[11] eares as long   10
　As to my thoughts, had you an honest tongue
　I would not care though you proclaim'd them all.

MONTICELSO. Go to, go to.
　After your goodly and vaine-glorious banquet,
　I'le give you a choake peare.[(22)]   15

VITTORIA.   A' your owne grafting?

MONTICELSO. You were borne in *Venice*, honourably
　　　　　descended,
　From the Vittelli;[(23)] 'twas my cossins fate,—
　Ill may I name the hower—to marry you,   20
　Hee bought you of your father.

VITTORIA.   Ha?

MONTICELSO. Hee spent there in six monthes,
　Twelve thousand Dukets, and to my acquaintance
　Receiv'd in dowry with you not one *Julio*[12] :[(24)]   25
　'Twas a hard peny-worth, the ware being so light,
　I yet but draw the curtaine—now to your picture,
　You came from thence a most notorious strumpet,
　And so you have continued.

VITTORIA.   My Lord.   30

MONTICELSO. Nay heare me,
　You shall have time to prate—my Lord Brachiano,
　Alas I make but repetition,[9]
　Of what is ordinary and Ryalto talke,[(25)]
　And ballated,[(26)] and would bee plaid a'th stage,   35

---

[10] *use* : usury; interest.   [12] *Julio* : coin worth about an
[11] *intelligencing* : spying.   English sixpence.

But that vice many times findes such loud freinds,
That Preachers are charm'd silent.
You Gentlemen Flamineo and Marcello,
The Court hath nothing now to charge you with,
Onely you must remaine upon your suerties,   5
For your appearance.

FRANCISCO.   I stand for Marcello.

FLAMINEO. And my Lord Duke for me.

MONTICELSO. For you Vittoria, your publicke fault,
Joyn'd to th'condition of the present time,   10
Takes from you all the fruits of noble pitty.
Such a corrupted triall have you made
Both of your life and beauty, and bene stil'd
No lesse in ominous fate then blasing starres
To Princes; heare's your sentence, you are confin'd,   15
Unto[10] a house of convertites and your baud—

FLAMINEO. [*Aside.*] Who I?

MONTICELSO.   The Moore.

FLAMINEO. [*Aside.*]   O I am a sound man againe.

VITTORIA. A house of convertites, what's that?   20

MONTICELSO.   A house
Of penitent whoores.

VITTORIA.   Do the Noblemen in Rome,
Erect it for their wives, that I am sent
To lodge there?   25

FRANCISCO.   You must have patience.

VITTORIA. I must first have vengeance.
I faine would know if you have your salvation
By patent,[(27)] that you proceed thus.

MONTICELSO.   Away with her.   30
Take her hence.

VITTORIA. A rape, a rape![(28)]

MONTICELSO.   How?

VITTORIA.   Yes you have ravisht justice,
Forc't her to do your pleasure.   35

MONTICELSO.   Fy shee's mad.

VITTORIA. Dye with those pils in your most cursed
mawe,[11]

Should bring you health, or while you sit a'th Bench,
Let your owne spittle choake you.

MONTICELSO.   She's turn'd fury.

VITTORIO. That the last day of judgement may so find
                    you,   5
And leave you the same devill you were before,—
Instruct me some good horse-lech[29] to speak
                    Treason,
For since you cannot take my life for deeds,
Take it for wordes; ô womans poore revenge   10
Which dwels but in the tongue,—I will not weepe,
No I do scorne to call up one poore teare
To fawne on[12] your injustice,—beare me hence,
Unto this house of—what's your mittigating Title?

MONTICELSO. Of convertites.   15

VITTORIA. It shal not be a house of convertites—
My minde shall make it honester to mee
Then the Popes Pallace, and more peaceable
Then thy soule, though thou art a Cardinall;
Know this, and let it somewhat raise your spight,   20
Through darkenesse Diamonds spred their ritchest
                    light.

                              Exit VITTORIA.

                    Enter BRACHIANO.

BRACHIANO. Now you and I are friends sir, wee'le shake   25
                    hands,
In a friends grave, together, a fit place,
Being the embleme of soft peace t'attone[30] our
                    hatred.

FRANCISCO. Sir, what's the matter?   30

BRACHIANO. I will not chase more bloud from that lov'd
                    cheeke,
You have lost too much already, fare-you-well.[31]
                                        [*Exit.*]

FRANCISCO. How strange these words sound? what's the   35
                    interpretation?

FLAMINEO. [*Aside.*] Good, this is a preface to the discovery of the Dutches death : Hee carries it well :

because now I cannot counterfeit a whining passion
for the death of my Lady, I will faine a madde
humor for the disgrace of my sister, and that will
keepe off idle questions; Treasons tongue hath a villanous palsy[32] in't, I will talk to any man, heare   5
no man, and for a time appeare a polliticke mad-man.
                                                    [*Exit.*]
         Enter GIOVANNI, [*and*] Count LODOVICO.

FRANCISCO. How now my Noble cossin, what in blacke?

GIOVANNI. Yes Unckle, I was taught to imitate you   10
  In vertue, and you must imitate mee
  In couloures for your garments,—my sweete mother
  Is,—

FRANCISCO. How? Where?

GIOVANNI. Is there,—no yonder; indeed sir I'le not tell   15
                you,
  For I shall make you weepe.

FRANCISCO.   Is dead.

GIOVANNI. Do not blame me now,
  I did not tell you so.   20

LODOVICO.   She's dead my Lord.

FRANCISCO. Dead?

MONTICELSO.   Blessed Lady;
  Thou art now above thy woes,—
  Wilt please your Lordships to with-draw a little?   25

GIOVANNI. What do the dead do, uncle? do they eate,
  Heare musicke, goe a hunting, and bee merrie,
  As wee that live?

FRANCISCO. No cose; they sleepe.

GIOVANNI.   Lord, Lord, that I were dead,   30
  I have not slept these six nights. When doe they
                wake?

FRANCISCO. When God shall please.

GIOVANNI.[13]   Good God let her sleepe ever.
  For I have knowne her wake an hundreth nights,   35
  When all the pillow, where shee laid her head,
  Was brine-wet with her teares. I am to complaine
                to you Sir.

Ile tell you how they have used her now shees dead :
They wrapt her in a cruell fould of lead,
And would not let mee kisse her.
FRANCISCO.   Thou didst love her.
GIOVANNI. I have often heard her say shee gave mee   5
         sucke,
And it should seeme by that shee deerely lov'd mee,
Since Princes seldome doe it.
FRANCISCO. O, all of my poore sister that remaines!
Take him away for Gods sake.   10
MONTICELSO.   How now my Lord?
FRANCISCO. Beleeve mee I am nothing but her grave,
And I shall keepe her blessed memorie,
Longer then thousand Epitaphs.   *[Exeunt.]*
                                        15

[ACT III. SCENE III.]

Enter FLAMINEO *as distracted,* [*followed*
     by MARCELLO *and* LODOVICO.]   20
FLAMINEO. Wee indure the strokes like anviles or hard
         steele,
Till paine it selfe make us no paine to feele.
Who shall doe mee right now? Is this the end of
service? Ide rather go weede garlicke; travaile   25
through France, and be mine owne ostler; weare
sheepe-skin lininges; or shoos that stinke of blacking;
bee entred into the list of the fourtie thousand pedlars in Poland.[1]
       Enter SAVOY [AMBASSADOR.]   30
Would I had rotted in some Surgeons house at Venice, built upon the Pox as well as on piles,[2] ere I
had serv'd Brachiano.
SAVOY AMBASSADOR. You must have comfort.
FLAMINEO. Your comfortable wordes are like honie.   35
They rellish well in your mouth that's whole; but in
mine that's wounded they go downe as if the sting
of the Bee were in them. Oh they have wrought their

purpose cunningly, as if they would not seeme to doe
it of malice. In this a Polititian imitates the devill, as
the devill imitates a Cannon.[1] Wheresoever he
comes to doe mischiefe, he comes with his backside
towardes you.   5

   Enter the FRENCH [AMBASSADOR.]

FRENCH AMBASSADOR. The proofes are evident.

FLAMINEO. Proofe! 'twas corruption. O Gold, what a
God art thou! and ô man, what a devill art thou to be
tempted by that cursed Minerall! Yon diversivolent   10
Lawyer; marke him, knaves turne informers, as mag-
gots turne to flies, you may catch gudgions[1] with
either. A Cardinall; I would hee would heare mee,
theres nothing so holie but mony will corrupt and
putrifie it, like vittell under the line.[2]   15

   [*Enter* ENGLISH AMBASSADOR.]

You are happie in England, my Lord; here they sell
justice with those weights they presse men to death
with.[3] O horrible salarie!

ENGLISH AMBASSADOR. Fie, fie, Flamineo.   20

FLAMINEO. Bels nere ring well, till they are at their full
pitch,[4] And I hope yon Cardinall shall never have
the grace to pray well, till he come to the scaffold.

   [*Exeunt* AMBASSADORS.]

If they were rackt now to know the confederacie! But   25
your Noblemen are priviledged from the racke; and
well may. For a little thing would pull some of them
a peeces afore they came to their arraignement.
Religion; oh how it is commeddled with policie. The
first bloudshed in the world happened about reli-   30
gion.[5] Would I were a Jew.

MARCELLO. O, there are too many.

FLAMINEO. You are deceiv'd. There are not Jewes
enough; Priests enough, nor gentlemen enough.

MARCELLO. How?   35

ACT III. SCENE III.   [2] *vittell . . . line*: food at the
[1] *gudgions*: small fish; fools.   equator.

FLAMINEO. Ile prove it. For if there were Jewes enough,
  so many Christians would not turne usurers; if Preists
  enough, one should not have sixe Benefices; and if
  gentlemen enough, so many earlie mushromes,[6]
  whose best growth sprang from a dunghill, should   5
  not aspire to gentilitie. Farewell. Let others live by
  begging. Bee thou one of them; practize the art of
  Wolnor[3] in England to swallow all's given thee;[7]
  And yet let one purgation make thee as hungrie
  againe as fellowes that worke in saw-pit. Ile go heare   10
  the scritch-owle.   *Exit.*
LODOVICO. [*Aside.*] This was Brachiano's Pandar, and
                              'tis strange
  That in such open and apparant guilt
  Of his adulterous sister, hee dare utter   15
  So scandalous a passion. I must wind him.
                  Enter FLAMINEO.
FLAMINEO. [*Aside.*] How dares this banisht Count re-
                              turne to Rome,
  His pardon not yet purchast?[8] I have heard   20
  The deceast Dutchesse gave him pension,
  And that he came along from Padua
  I'th' traine of the yong Prince. There's somewhat in't.
  Phisitians, that cure poisons, still doe worke
  With counterpoisons.   25
MARCELLO.   Marke this strange incounter.
FLAMINEO. The God of Melancholie turne thy gall to
                              poison,
  And let the stigmaticke[9] wrincles in thy face,
  Like to the boisterous waves in a rough tide   30
  One still overtake an other.
LODOVICO.   I doe thanke thee
  And I doe wish ingeniously[10] for thy sake
  The dog-daies all yeare long.
FLAMINEO.   How crokes the raven?   35

[3] *Wolnor:* a Windsor chorister
  who ate anything offered him.

Is our good Dutchesse dead?
LODOVICO.   Dead.
FLAMINEO.   O fate!
Misfortune comes like the Crowners[4] businesse,
Huddle upon huddle.   5
LODOVICO.   Shalt thou & I joyne house-
keeping?
FLAMINEO. Yes, content.
Let's bee unsociably sociable.
LODOVICO. Sit some three daies together, and discourse.   10
FLAMINEO. Onely with making faces;
Lie in our clothes.
LODOVICO.   With faggots for our pillowes.
FLAMINEO. And bee lowsie.
LODOVICO. In taffeta lininges; that's gentile[11] melan-   15
                    cholie,
Sleepe all day.
FLAMINEO. Yes : and like your melancholike hare[12]
Feed after midnight.
          Enter ANTONELLI [*and* GASPARO *laughing.*]   20
Wee are observed : see how yon couple greve.
LODOVICO. What a strange creature is a laughing foole,
As if man were created to no use
But onely to shew his teeth.
FLAMINEO.   Ile tell thee what,   25
It would doe well in stead of looking glasses
To set ones face each morning by a sawcer[13]
Of a witches congealed bloud.
LODOVICO.   Pretious girne,[5] rogue.[2]
Weel never part.   30
FLAMINEO.   Never : till the beggerie of Courtiers,
The discontent of church-men, want of souldiers,
And all the creatures that hang manacled,
Worse then strappado'd,[6] on the lowest fellie[7]
Of fortunes wheele be taught in our two lives   35

---

[4] *Crowners :* Coroner's.
[5] *girne :* snarl; grimace.
[6] *strappado'd :* hung up by the

hands tied behind the back.
[7] *fellie :* spoke.

To scorne that world which life of meanes deprives.
ANTONELLI. My Lord, I bring good newes. The Pope
    on's death-bed,
 At th'earnest suit of the great Duke of Florence,
 Hath sign'd your pardon, and restor'd unto you—   5
LODOVICO. I thanke you for your news. Look up againe
 Flamineo, see my pardon.
FLAMINEO.   Why do you laugh?
 There was no such condition in our convenant.
LODOVICO.   Why?   10
FLAMINEO. You shall not seeme a happier man then I,
 You know our vow sir, if you will be merry,
 Do it i'th like posture, as if some great man
 Sate while his enemy were executed :
 Though it be very letchery unto thee,   15
 Doo't with a crabbed Polititians face.
LODOVICO. Your sister is a damnable whore.
FLAMINEO.   Ha?
LODOVICO. Looke you; I spake that laughing.
FLAMINEO. Dost ever thinke to speake againe?   20
LODOVICO. Do you heare?
 Wil't sel me fourty ounces of her bloud,
 To water a mandrake?
FLAMINEO.   Poore Lord, you did vow
 To live a lowzy creature.   25
LODOVICO.   Yes;
FLAMINEO.   Like one
 That had for ever forfaited the day-light,
 By being in debt,—
LODOVICO.   Ha, ha!   30
FLAMINEO. I do not greatly wonder you do breake : [14]
 Your Lordship learn't long since. But Ile tell you,—
LODOVICO. What?
FLAMINEO.   And't shall sticke by you.
LODOVICO. I long for it.   35
FLAMINEO. This laughter scurvily becomes your face,
 If you will not be melancholy, be angry.
           Strikes him.

See, now I laugh too.

MARCELLO. You are to blame, Ile force you hence.

LODOVICO. Unhand me : *Exit* MARCELLO *&* FLAMINEO.
 That ere I should be forc't to right my selfe,
 Upon a Pandar.   5

ANTONELLI. My Lord.

LODOVICO. H'had bene as good met with his fist a thun-
        derbolt.

GASPARO. How this shewes!

LODOVICO. Uds'death, how did my sword misse him? 10
 These rogues that are most weary of their lives,
 Still scape the greatest dangers,—
 A pox upon him : all his reputation;
 Nay all the goodnesse of his family;
 Is not worth halfe this earthquake.   15
 I learnt it of no fencer to shake thus;
 Come, I'le forget him, and go drinke some wine.

               Exeunt.

[ACT IV. SCENE I.]   20

Enter FRANCISCO *and* MONTICELSO.

MONTICELSO. Come, come my Lord, untie your foulded
        thoughts,
 And let them dangle loose as a bride's[1] haire.(1) 25
 Your sister's poisoned.

FRANCISCO.   Farre bee it from my thoughts
 To seeke revenge.

MONTICELSO.   What, are you turn'd all marble?

FRANCISCO. Shall I defye him, and impose a warre 30
 Most burthensome on my poore subjects neckes,
 Which at my will I have not power to end?
 You know; for all the murders, rapes, and thefts,
 Committed in the horred lust of warre,
 He that unjustly caus'd it first proceed,   35
 Shall finde it in his grave and in his seed.

MONTICELSO. That's not the course I'de with you : pray,
        observe me,

We see that undermining more prevailes
Then doth the Cannon.[2] Beare your wrongs con-
      ceal'd,
And, patient as the Tortoise, let this Cammell
Stalke o're your back unbruis'd : sleep with the Lyon,   5
And let this brood of secure foolish mice
Play with your nosthrils, till the time bee ripe
For th'bloudy audit, and the fatall gripe :
Aime like a cunning fowler, close one eie,
That you the better may your game espy.   10
FRANCISCO. Free me my innocence; from treacherous
      actes :
I know ther's thunder yonder : and I'le stand,
Like a safe vallie, which low bends the knee
To some aspiring mountaine : since I know   15
Treason, like spiders weaving nets for flies,
By her foule worke is found, and in it dies.
To passe away these thoughts, my honour'd Lord,
It is reported you possesse a booke
Wherein you have quoted, by intelligence,[1]   20
The names of all notorious offenders
Lurking about the Citty,—
MONTICELSO.   Sir I do;
And some there are which call it my blacke booke :(2)
Well may the title hold : for though it teach not   25
The Art of conjuring, yet in it lurke,
The names of many devils.
FRANCISCO.   Pray let's see it.
MONTICELSO. I'le fetch it to your Lordship.
                    Exit MONTICELSO.   30
FRANCISCO.   Monticelso,
I'le not trust thee, but in all my plots
I'le rest as jealous as a Towne besieg'd.
Thou canst not reach what I intend to act.
Your flax soone kindles, soone is out againe,   35

Act IV. Scene i.
[1] *intelligence :* spying.

But gold slow heats,[3] and long will hot remaine.
Enter MONTICELSO, *presents* FRANCISCO *with a booke.*
MONTICELSO. 'Tis here my Lord.
FRANCISCO. First your Intelligencers pray let's see.
MONTICELSO. Their number rises strangely,   5
 And some of them
 You'd take for honest men.
 Next are Pandars.
 These are your Pirats : and these following leaves,
 For base rogues that undo yong Gentlemen   10
 By taking up commodities : for pollitick bank-
    roupts :[3]
 For fellowes that are bawdes to their owne wives,
 Onely to put off[2] horses and slight jewels,
 Clockes, defac't plate, and such commodities,   15
 At birth of their first children.
FRANCISCO.   Are there such?
MONTICELSO. These are for Impudent baudes,
 That go in mens apparell : for usurers
 That share with scriveners for their good report- 20
    age :[4]
 For Lawyers that will antedate their writtes :
 And some Divines you might find foulded there;
 But that I slip them o're for conscience sake.
 Here is a generall catalogue of knaves.   25
 A man might study all the prisons o're,
 Yet never attaine this knowledge.
FRANCISCO.   Murderers.
 Fould downe the leafe I pray,
 Good my Lord let me borrow this strange doctrine. 30
MONTICELSO. Pray use't my Lord.
FRANCISCO.   I do assure your Lordship,
 You are a worthy member of the State,
 And have done infinite good in your discovery
 Of these offendors.   35

[2] *put off :* sell at exorbitant
prices.

MONTICELSO.   Some-what Sir.

FRANCISCO.   O God!

  Better then tribute of wolves paid in *England*.[5]

  'Twill hang their skinnes o'th hedge.

MONTICELSO.   I must make bold   5

  To leave your Lord-ship.

FRANCISCO.   Deerely sir, I thanke you,

  If any aske for me at Court, report

  You have left me in the company of knaves.

                  Exit MONTICELSO.   10

  I gather now by this, some cunning fellow

  That's my Lords Officer, and that lately skipt

  From a Clerkes deske up to a Justice chaire,

  Hath made this knavish summons; and intendes,

  As th'Irish rebels wont were to sell heads,   15

  So to make prize of these.[6] And thus it happens,

  Your poore rogues pay for't, which have not the
                  meanes

  To present bribe in fist : the rest o'th'band

  Are raz'd out of the knaves record; or else   20

  My Lord he winkes at them with easy will,

  His man growes rich, the knaves are the knaves still.

  But to the use I'le make of it; it shall serve

  To point me out a list[4] of murderers,

  Agents for any villany. Did I want   25

  Ten leash[7] of Curtisans, it would furnish me;

  Nay lawndresse three Armies. That in so[5] little
                  paper

  Should lie th'undoing of so many men!

  'Tis not so big as twenty declarations.[3]   30

  See the corrupted use some make of bookes :

  Divinity, wrested by some factious bloud,

  Draws swords, swels battels, & orethrowes all good.

  To fashion my revenge more seriously,

  Let me remember my dead sisters face :   35

[3] *declarations* : public
  proclamations.

Looke for her picture : no; I'le close mine eyes,
And in a melancholicke thought I'le frame
Her figure 'fore me.

      Enter ISABELLA's *Ghost.*

           Now I—ha't[6]—how strong   5
Imagination workes! how she can frame
Things which are not! me thinks she stands afore me;
And by the quicke Idea of my minde,
Were my skill pregnant, I could draw her picture.
Thought, as a subtile Jugler, makes us deeme   10
Things, supernaturall, which have cause
Common as sickenesse. 'Tis my melancholy,
How cam'st thou by thy death?—how idle am I
To question mine owne idlenesse?—did ever
Man dreame awake till now?—remove this object—   15
Out of my braine with't : what have I to do
With tombes, or death-beds, funerals, or teares,
That have to meditate upon revenge?   *Exit ghost.*
So now 'tis ended, like an old wives story.
States-men thinke often they see stranger sights   20
Then mad-men. Come, to this waighty businesse.
My Tragedy must have some idle mirth in't,
Else it will never passe. I am in love,
In love with Corombona; and my suite
Thus haltes to her in verse.—   *he writes.* 25
I have done it rarely : ô the fate of Princes!
I am so us'd to frequent flattery,
That being alone I now flatter my selfe;
But it will serve, 'tis seal'd; beare this

          Enter servant.   30

To th'house of Convertites; and watch your leisure
To give it to the hands of Corombona,
Or to the Matron, when some followers
Of Brachiano may be by. Away.   *Exit servant.*
He that deales all by strength, his wit is shallow :   35
When a mans head goes through each limbe will
        follow.
The engine for my busines, bold Count Lodowicke :

'Tis gold must such an instrument procure,
With empty fist no man doth falcons lure. [8]
Brachiano, I am now fit for thy encounter.
Like the wild Irish I'le nere thinke thee dead,
Till I can play at footeball with thy head.   5
Flectere si nequeo superos, Acheronta movebo. [4,9]
                                                    Exit.

[ACT IV. SCENE ii.]
                                                         10
Enter the Matron, and FLAMINEO.
MATRON. Should it be knowne the Duke hath such re-
                              course,
To your imprison'd sister, I were like
T'incur much damage by it.   15
FLAMINEO.   Not a scruple.
The Pope lies on his death-bed, [1] and their heads
Are troubled now with other businesse
Than guarding of a Ladie.
                    Enter Servant.   20
SERVANTS. [*Aside.*] Yonder's Flamineo in conference
With the Matrona. [*To the Matron.*] Let mee speake
                         with you.
I would intreat you to deliver for mee
This letter to the faire Vittoria.   25
MATRON. I shall Sir.
                    Enter BRACHIANO.
SERVANT.   With all care and secrecie,
Hereafter you shall know mee, and receive
Thankes for this curtesie   [*Exit.*]   30
FLAMINEO.   How now? what's that?
MATRON. A letter.
FLAMINEO.   To my sister : Ile see't delivered.
BRACHIANO. What's that you read Flamineo?

---

4 *Flectere . . . movebo :* If I
   cannot prevail on the
   heavens, I will move hell.

FLAMINEO. Looke.

BRACHIANO. Ha? "To the most unfortunate his best respected Vittoria—"
Who was the messenger?

FLAMINEO. I know not. 5

BRACHIANO. No! Who sent it?

FLAMINEO. Ud's foot you speake, as if a man
Should know what foule is coffind[2] in a bak't meate
Afore you cut it up.

BRACHIANO. Ile open't, were't her heart. What's heere 10
subscribed?
Florence? This jugling is grosse and palpable.
I have found out the conveyance;[3] read it, read it.

FLAMINEO. (*Reades the letter.*)
Your teares Ile turne to triumphes, bee but mine. 15
Your prop is fall'n; I pittie that a vine
Which Princes heretofore have long'd to gather,
Wanting supporters, now should fade and wither.
Wine yfaith, my Lord, with lees would serve his turne.
Your sad imprisonement Ile soone uncharme, 20
And with a princelie uncontrolled arme
Lead you to Florence, where my love and care
Shall hang your wishes in my silver haire,
A halter on his strange aequivocation.[1]
Nor for my yeares returne mee the sad willow,[4] 25
Who prefer blossomes before fruit that's mellow.
Rotten on my knowledge with lying too long i'th bed-
straw.[5]
And all the lines of age this line convinces :[6]
The Gods never wax old, no more doe Princes. 30
A pox on't—teare it, let's have no more Atheists[7]
For Gods sake.

BRACHIANO. Udsdeath, Ile cut her into Atomies
And let th'irregular[8] North-winde sweepe her up

ACT IV. SCENE II.
[1] *aequivocation :* playing with
words.

And blow her int' his nosthrils. Where's this whore?

FLAMINEO. That?[1] what doe you call her?

BRACHIANO. Oh, I could bee mad,
Prevent the curst disease shee'l bring mee to;
And teare my haire off. Where's this changeable   5
    stuffe?

FLAMINEO. Ore head and eares in[2] water[9], I assure
    you,
Shee is not for your wearing.

BRACHIANO.   In you Pandar?   10

FLAMINEO. What mee, my Lord, am I your dog?

BRACHIANO. A bloud-hound : doe you brave? doe you
    stand[10] mee?

FLAMINEO. Stand you? let those that have diseases run;
I need no plaisters.   15

BRACHIANO.   Would you bee kickt?

FLAMINEO. Would you have your necke broke?
I tell you Duke, I am not in Russia;
My shinnes must be kept whole.[11]

BRACHIANO.   Do you know mee?   20

FLAMINEO. O my Lord! methodically.[12]
As in this world there are degrees of evils :
So in this world there are degrees of devils.
You'r a great Duke; I your poore secretarie.
I doe looke now for a Spanish fig, or an Italian sallet   25
    daily.[2]

BRACHIANO. Pandar, plie your convoy, and leave your
    prating.

FLAMINEO. All your kindnesse to mee is like that miserable curtesie of *Polyphemus* to *Ulisses,* you reserve   30
mee to be devour'd last, you would dig turves out of
my grave to feed your Larkes : that would bee musicke to you.[13] Come, Ile lead you to her.

BRACHIANO. Do you face mee?

FLAMINEO. Sir I would not go before a Pollitique enemie   35

---

[2] Expect to be poisoned.

with my backe towards him, though there were behind mee a whirle-poole.

Enter VITTORIA *to* BRACHIANO *and* FLAMINEO.

BRACHIANO. Can you read Mistresse? looke upon that
                        letter;   5
There are no characters nor Hieroglyphicks.
You need no comment, I am growne your re-
                      ceiver,[14]—
Gods pretious[15] you shall be a brave great Ladie,
A statelie and advanced whore.   10
VITTORIA.   Say Sir?
BRACHIANO. Come, come, let's see your Cabinet, dis-
                      cover
Your treasurie of love-letters. Death and furies,
Ile see them all.   15
VITTORIA.   Sir, upon my soule,
I have not any. Whence was this directed?
BRACHIANO. Confusion on your politicke ignorance.

                      [*Gives her the letter.*]
You are reclaimed; are you? Ile give you the bels   20
And let you flie to the devill.
FLAMINEO.   Ware hawke,[3, (16)] my Lord.
VITTORIA. Florence! This is some treacherous plot, my
                      Lord,—
To mee, he nere was thought on I protest,   25
So much as in my sleepe.
BRACHIANO.   Right : they are plots.
Your beautie! ô, ten thousand curses on't.
How long have I beheld the devill in christall?[17]
Thou hast lead mee, like an heathen sacrifice,   30
With musicke, and with fatall yokes of flowers
To my eternall ruine. Woman to man
Is either a God or a wolfe.[18]
VITTORIA.   My Lord.
BRACHIANO.   Away.   35

3 *Ware hawke :* Control her
  with a lure.

We'll bee as differing as two Adamants;[19]
The one shall shunne the other. What? dost weepe?
Procure but ten of thy dissembling trade,
Yee'ld[3] furnish all the Irish funeralls
With howling, past wild Irish.[20]   5
FLAMINEO.   Fie, my Lord.
BRACHIANO. That hand, that cursed hand, which I have
                              wearied
With doting kisses! O my sweetest Dutchesse
How lovelie art thou now! [*To* VITTORIA.] Thy loose   10
                              thoughtes
Scatter like quicke-silver, I was bewitch'd;
For all the world speakes ill of thee.
VITTORIA.   No matter.
Ile live so now Ile make that world recant   15
And change her speeches. You did name your
                              Dutchesse.
BRACHIANO. Whose death God pardon.
VITTORIA. Whose death God revenge
On thee most godlesse Duke.   20
FLAMINEO.   Now for two[4] whirlewindes.
VITTORIA. What have I gain'd by thee but infamie?
Thou hast stain'd the spotlesse honour of my house,
And frighted thence noble societie :
Like those, which sicke oth' Palsie, and retaine   25
Ill-senting foxes 'bout them,[21] are still shun'd
By those of choicer nosthrills. What doe you call this
                              house?
Is this your palace? did not the Judge stile it
A house of penitent whores? who sent mee to it?   30
Who hath the honour to advance Vittoria
To this incontinent colledge? is't not you?
Is't not your high preferment? Go, go brag
How many Ladies you have undone, like mee.
Fare you well Sir; let me heare no more of you.   35
I had a limbe corrupted to an ulcer,
But I have cut it off[22] : and now Ile go
Weeping to heaven on crutches. For your giftes,

I will returne them all; and I do wish
That I could make you full Executor
To all my sinnes,—ô that I could tosse my selfe
Into a grave as quickly : for all thou art worth
Ile not shed one teare more;—Ile burst first.　　　5

She throwes her selfe upon a bed.

BRACHIANO. I have drunke Lethe.
Vittoria? My dearest happinesse? Vittoria?
What doe you aile my Love? why doe you weepe?
VITTORIA. Yes, I now weepe poniardes,[4] doe you see?　10
BRACHIANO. Are not those matchlesse eies mine?
VITTORIA.　　　　　　　　　　I had rather,
They were not matches.
BRACHIANO.　　　　　　Is not this lip mine?
VITTORIA. Yes : thus to bite it off, rather than give it　15
thee.
FLAMINEO. Turne to my Lord, good sister.
VITTORIA. Hence you Pandar.
FLAMINEO. Pandar! Am I the author of your sinne?
VITTORIA. Yes : Hee's a base theif that a theif lets in.　20
FLAMINEO. Wee're blowne up, my Lord,—
BRACHIANO. Wilt thou heare mee?
Once to bee jealous of thee, is t'expresse
That I will love thee everlastingly.
And never more bee jealous.　　　　　　　　　25
VITTORIA.　　　　　　　　O thou foole,
Whose greatnesse hath by much oregrowne thy wit!
What dar'st thou doe, that I not dare to suffer,
Excepting to bee still thy whore? for that,
In the seas bottome sooner thou shalt make　　　30
A bonefire.
FLAMINEO. O, no othes for gods sake.
BRACHIANO. Will you heare mee?
VITTORIA.　　　　　　　　Never.
FLAMINEO. What a damn'd impostume[5] is a womans　35
will?

---

[4] *poniardes :* daggers.　　　[5] *impostume :* festering sore.

Can nothing breake it? [*Aside.*] fie, fie, my Lord.
Women are caught as you take Tortoises,
Shee must bee turn'd on her backe. [*To* VITTORIA.]
        Sister, by this hand
I am on your side. Come, come, you have wrong'd   5
        her.
What a strange credulous man were you, my Lord,
To thinke the Duke of Florence would love her?
[*Aside.*] Will any Mercer take an others ware
When once 'tis tows'd and sullied? [*To* VITTORIA.]   10
        And yet, sister,
How scurvily this frowardnesse becomes you?
[*Aside.*] Yong Leverets stand not long;[23] and
        womens anger
Should, like their flight, procure a little sport;   15
A full crie for a quarter of an hower;
And then bee put to th' dead quat.[6]

BRACHIANO.   Shall these eies,
Which have so long time dwelt upon your face,
Be now put out?   20

FLAMINEO.   No cruell Land-ladie ith'world,
Which lends[5] forth grotes[7] to broome-men, &
        takes use for them,
Would doe't.
Hand her, my Lord, and kisse her : be not like   25
A ferret to let go your hold with blowing.[8]

BRACHIANO. Let us renew right handes.

VITTORIA.   Hence.

BRACHIANO. Never shall rage, or the forgetfull wine,[24]
Make mee commit like fault.   30

FLAMINEO. Now you are ith' way ont, follow 'thard.

BRACHIANO. Bee thou at peace with mee; let all the
        world
Threaten the Cannon.

---

[6] *quat :* squat (*hunting term*),   [8] A superstition : blowing on a
  cowering at bay.   ferret will make it release its
[7] *grotes :* very small coins.   teeth from anything.

FLAMINEO. Marke his penitence.
Best natures doe commit the grossest faultes,
When they're giv'n ore to jealosie; as best wine
Dying makes strongest vinneger. Ile tell you;
The Sea's more rough and raging then calme rivers,   5
But nor so sweet nor wholesome. A quiet woman
Is a still water under a great bridge.
A man may shoot her safely.(25)
VITTORIA. O yee dissembling men!
FLAMINEO. Wee suckt that, sister,   10
From womens brestes, in our first infancie.
VITTORIA. To ad miserie to miserie.
BRACHIANO. Sweetest.
VITTORIA. Am I not low enough?
I, I, your good heart gathers like a snow-ball   15
Now your affection's cold.
FLAMINEO. Ud'foot, it shall melt,
To a hart againe, or all the wine in Rome
Shall run o'th lees for't.
VITTORIA. Your dog or hawke should be rewarded better   20
Then I have bin. Ile speake not one word more.
FLAMINEO. Stop her mouth,
With a sweet kisse, my Lord.
So now the tide's turne'd the vessel's come about
Hee's a sweet armefull. O wee curl'd-haird men   25
Are still(26) most kind to women. This is well.
BRACHIANO. That you should chide thus!
FLAMINEO. O, sir, your little chimnies
Doe ever cast most smoke. I swet for you.
Couple together with as deepe a silence,   30
As did the Grecians in their wodden horse.
My Lord supplie your promises with deedes.
You know that painted meat no hunger feedes.
BRACHIANO. Stay, ingratefull Rome!
FLAMINEO. Rome! it deserves to be cal'd Barbarie, for   35
our villainous usage.
BRACHIANO. Soft; the same project which the Duke of
Florence,

(Whether in love or gullerie[9] I know not)
Laid downe for her escape, will I pursue.

FLAMINEO. And no time fitter than this night, my Lord;
The Pope being dead; and all the Cardinals entred
The Conclave for th'electing a new Pope;   5
The Cittie in a great confusion;
Wee may attire her in a Pages suit,
Lay her post-horse, take shipping, and amaine
For Padua.

BRACHIANO. Ile instantly steale forth the Prince Gio-   10
    vanni,
And make for Padua. You two with your old Mother
And yong Marcello that attendes on Florence,
If you can worke him to it, follow mee.
I will advance you all : for you Vittoria,   15
Thinke of a Dutchesse title.

FLAMINEO.   Lo you sister.
    Stay, my Lord; I'le tell you a tale. The crocodile,
which lives in the river *Nilus*, hath a worme breds
i'th teeth of't, which puts it to extreame anguish : a   20
little bird, no bigger then a wren, is barbor-surgeon
to this crocodile; flies into the jawes of't; pickes out
the worme; and brings present remedy. The fish,
glad of ease but ingratefull to her that did it, that
the bird may not talke largely of her abroad for non   25
payment, closeth her chaps intending to swallow her,
and so put her to perpetuall silence. But nature loath-
ing such ingratitude, hath arm'd this bird with a
quill or pricke on the head, top o'th which wounds
the crocodile i'th mouth; forceth her open her bloudy   30
prison; and away flies the pretty tooth-picker from
her cruell patient.[27]

BRACHIANO. Your application is, I have not rewarded
The service you have done me.

FLAMINEO.   No, my Lord;   35
You sister are the crocodile : you are blemisht in your

9 *gullerie :* as a trap.

fame, My Lord cures it. And though the comparison
hold not in every particle; yet observe, remember,
what good the bird with the pricke i'th head hath
done you; and scorne ingratitude.[28]

[*Aside.*] It may appeare to some ridiculous   5
Thus to talke knave and madman; and sometimes
Come in with a dried sentence,[10] stuft with sage.
But this allowes my varying of shapes.
Knaves do grow great by being great mens apes.

                              [*Exeunt.*]   10

[ACT IV. SCENE III.][(1)]

Enter LOVODICO, GASPARO, *and sixe Embassadours.*   15
At another dore [FRANCISCO] *the Duke of
Florence.*

FRANCISCO. So, my Lord, I commend your diligence—
Guard well the conclave, and, as the order is,
Let none have conference with the Cardinals.   20
LODOVICO. I shall, my Lord : roome for the Embassa-
                              dors,—
GASPARO. They're wondrous brave[1] to day : why do
                    they weare
These severall habits?   25
LODOVICO.   O sir, they'r Knights
Of severall Orders.
That Lord i'th blacke cloak with the silver crosse
Is Knight of *Rhodes;* the next Knight of S. *Michael;*[(2)]
That of the golden fleece;[(3)] the *French-man* there   30
Knight of the Holy-Ghost;[(4)] my Lord of *Savoy*
Knight of th'Annuntiation;[(5)] the *Englishman*
Is Knight of th'honoured Garter,[(6)] dedicated
Unto their Saint, S. *George.* I could describe to you
Their severall institutions, with the lawes   35

                              ACT IV. SCENE III.
[10] *dried sentence :* proverb.   [1] *brave :* dressed up.

Annexed to their Orders; but that time
Permits not such discovery.
FRANCISCO.   Where's Count Lodowicke?
LODOVICO. Here my Lord.
FRANCISCO.   'Tis o'th point of dinner time,   5
Marshall the Cardinals service,
LODOVICO.   Sir I shall.
Enter servants with severall dishes covered.
Stand, let me search your dish, who's this for?
SERVANT. For my Lord Cardinall Monticelso.   10
LODOVICO. Whose this?
SERVANT. For my Lord Cardinall of *Burbon.*
FRENCH AMBASSADOR. Why doth he search the dishes?
                to observe
What meate[2] is drest?   15
ENGLISH AMBASSADOR. No Sir, but to prevent,
Least any letters should be convei'd in
To bribe or to sollicite the advancement
Of any Cardinall; when first they enter
'Tis lawfull for the Embassadours of Princes   20
To enter with them, and to make their suit
For any man their Prince affecteth[3] best;
But after, till a generall election,
No man may speake with them.
LODOVICO. You that attend on the Lord Cardinals   25
Open the window,(7) and receive their viands.
                     [*Window opens.*]
A CONCLAVIST.[1] You must returne the service; the
               Lord Cardinals(8)
Are busied 'bout electing of the Pope,   30
They have given o're scrutinie, and are fallen
To admiration.[4]
LODOVICO.   Away, away.
FRANCISCO. I'le lay a thousand Duckets you here news
Of a Pope presently, Hearke; sure he's elected,   35

---

[2] *meate* : food.   [4] *admiration* : adoration.
[3] *affecteth* : likes.

Behold! my Lord of *Arragon* appeares,
On the Church battlements.
>   [*The*] CARDINAL [OF ARRAGON *appears*] *on the*
>   *Terrace.*[2]

ARRAGON. *Denuntio vobis gaudium magnum. Reveren-*   5
dissimus Cardinalis Lorenso de Monticelso *electus*
est in sedem Apostolicam, & elegit sibi nomen Paulum
quartum.

OMNES. *Vivat sanctus Pater Paulus Quartus.*[5, (9)],
>   [*Enter servant.*]   10

SERVANT. Vittoria my Lord—
FRANCISCO. Wel : what of her?
SERVANT.   Is fled the Citty,—
FRANCISCO.   Ha?
SERVANT. With Duke Brachiano.   15
FRANCISCO.   Fled? Where's the Prince Giovanni?
SERVANT. Gone with his father.
FRANCISCO. Let the Matrona of the Convertites
Be apprehended : fled—ô damnable! [*Exit servant.*]
How fortunate are my wishes. Why? 'twas this   20
I onely laboured. I did send the letter
T'instruct him what to doe. Thy fame, fond Duke,
I first have poison'd; directed thee the way
To marrie a whore; what can be worse? This followes.
The hand must act to drowne the passionate tongue,   25
I scorne to weare a sword and prate of wrong.
>   *Enter* MONTICELSO *in state.*

MONTICELSO. *Concedimus vobis Apostolicam benedic-*
>   *tionem & remissionem peccatorum.*[6]
>   [FRANCISCO *whispers to him.*]   30

My Lord reportes Vittoria Corombona

---

[5] *Denuntio . . . Quartus :* I
announce to you tidings of
great joy. The Most Reverend
Cardinal Lorenzo de Monticelso has been elected to the
Apostolic See, and has chosen
the title Paul IV.
ALL. Long live the Holy
Father Paul IV.

[6] *Concedimus . . . peccatorum :*
We grant you the Apostolic
blessing and remission of sins.

Is stol'ne from forth the house of Convertites
By Brachiano, and they're fled the Cittie.
Now, though this bee the first daie of our seate,
Wee cannot better please the divine power,
Than to sequester from the holie Church   5
These cursed persons. Make it therefore knowne,
Wee doe denounce excommunication
Against them both : all that are theirs in Rome
Wee likewise banish. Set on.

> *Exeunt [all except* FRANCISCO   10
> *and* LOVODICO.]

FRANCISCO. Come deare Lodovico.
You have tane the sacrament to prosecute
Th'intended murder.

LODOVICO.   With all constancie.   15
But, Sir, I wonder you'l ingage your selfe,
In person, being a great Prince.

FRANCISCO.   Divert mee not.
Most of his Court are of my faction,
And some are of my councell. Noble freind,   20
Our danger shall be 'like in this designe,
Give leave, part of the glorie may bee mine.

> *Exit* FRANCISCO.
> *Enter* MONTICELSO.

MONTICELSO. Why did the Duke of Florence with such   25
                    care
Labour your pardon? say.

LODOVICO. Italian beggars will resolve you that
Who, begging of an almes, bid those they beg of
Doe good for their owne sakes; or't may bee   30
Hee spreades his bountie with a sowing hand,
Like Kinges, who many times give out of measure;
Not for desert so much as for their pleasure.

MONTICELSO. I know you're cunning. Come, what devill
                    was that   35
That you were raising?[3]

LODOVICO.   Devill, my Lord?

MONTICELSO.   I aske you.

How doth the Duke imploy you, that his bonnet
Fell with such complement unto his knee,
When hee departed from you?
LODOVICO.   Why, my Lord,
Hee told mee of a restie Barbarie horse   5
Which he would faine have brought to the carreere,
The 'sault, and the ring galliard.⁷ Now, my Lord,
I have a rare French Rider.
MONTICELSO.   Take you heede :
Least the Jade breake your necke. Doe you put mee   10
off
With your wild horse-trickes? Sirra you doe lie.
O, thou'rt a foule blacke cloud, and thou do'st threat
A violent storme.
LODOVICO.   Stormes are i'th aire, my Lord;   15
I am too low to storme.
MONTICELSO.   Wretched creature!
I know that thou art fashion'd for all ill,
Like dogges, that once get bloud, they'l ever kill.
About some murder? wa'st not?   20
LODOVICO.   Ile not tell you;
And yet I care not greatly if I doe;
Marry with this preparation. Holie father,
I come not to you as an Intelligencer,
But as a penitent sinner. What I utter   25
Is in confession meerely; which you know
Must never bee reveal'd.
MONTICELSO.   You have oretane mee.
LODOVICO. Sir I did love Brachiano's Dutchesse deerely;
Or rather I pursued her with hot lust,   30
Though shee nere knew on't. Shee was poyson'd;
Upon my soule shee was : for which I have sworne
T'avenge her murder.
MONTICELSO.   To the Duke of Florence?
LODOVICO. To him I have.   35

⁷ *galliard :* standard exercise
movements.

MONTICELSO.   Miserable Creature!
   If thou persist in this, 'tis damnable.
   Do'st thou imagine thou canst slide on bloud
   And not be tainted with a shamefull fall?
   Or like the blacke, and melancholicke Eugh-tree,[8]   5
   Do'st thinke to roote thy selfe in dead mens graves,
   And yet to prosper? Instruction to thee
   Comes like sweet showers to over-hardned ground :
   They wet, but peirce not deepe. And so I leave thee
   Withall the Furies hanging bout thy necke,   10
   Till by thy penitence thou remove this evill,
   In conjuring from thy breast that cruell Devill.
                            Exit MONTICELSO.
LODOVICO. I'le give it o're. He saies 'tis damable :
   Besides I did expect his suffrage,   15
   By reason of Camillo's death.
       *Enter servant & * FRANCISCO. [LODOVICO *retires.*]
FRANCISCO. Do you know that Count?
SERVANT.   Yes, my Lord.
FRANCISCO. Beare him these thousand Duckets to his   20
                 lodging;
   Tell him the Pope hath sent them. Happily
   That will confirme him more then all the rest. [*Exit.*]
SERVANT. Sir.
LODOVICO. To me sir?   25
SERVANT. His holinesse hath sent you a thousand
                 Crownes,
   And will you if you travaile, to make him
   Your Patron for intelligence.
LODOVICO.   His creature ever to bee commanded.   30
                        [*Exit servant.*]
   Why now 'tis come about. He rail'd upon me;
   And yet these Crownes were told out and laid ready,
   Before he knew my voiage. O the Art,
   The modest forme of greatnesse! that do sit   35

[8] *Cf.* Eu; Yew (I. ii. 11, p. 229.)

Like Brides at wedding dinners, with their looks[4]
               turn'd
From the least wanton jests, their puling stomacke
Sicke of the modesty, when their thoughts are loose,
Even acting of those hot and lustfull sports   5
Are to ensue about midnight : such his cunning!
Hee soundes my depth thus with a golden plummet,
I am doubly arm'd now. Now to th'act of bloud,
There's but three furies found in spacious hell;
But in a great mans breast three thousand dwell.   10
                                [*Exit.*]

[ACT V. SCENE I.]

15

A passage over the stage of BRACHIANO, FLAMINEO,
MARCELLO. HORTENSIO, [VITTORIA] COROMBONA,
CORNELIA, ZANCHE *and others.* [FLAMINEO
and HORTENSIO *remain.*][1]

FLAMINEO. In all the weary minutes of my life,   20
Day nere broke up till now. This mariage
Confirmes me happy.
HORTENSIO.   'Tis a good assurance.
Saw you not yet the Moore that's come to Court?
FLAMINEO. Yes, and confer'd with him i'th Dukes closet,   25
I have not seene a goodlier personage,
Nor ever talkt with man better experienc't
In State-affares or rudiments of warre.
Hee hath by report, serv'd the *Venetian*
In *Candy*[2] these twice seven yeares, and bene cheife   30
In many a bold designe.
HORTENSIO.   What are those two,
That beare him company?
FLAMINEO. Two Noblemen[3] of *Hungary*, that living
in the Emperours service as commanders, eight yeares   35
since, contrary to the expectation of all the Court
entred into religion, into the strickt order of Ca-

puchins⁽⁴⁾ : but being not well setled in their un-
dertaking they left their Order and returned to Court :
for which being after troubled in conscience, they
vowed their service against the enemies of Christ;
went to *Malta;* were there knighted; and in their re-   5
turne backe, at this great solemnity, they are resolved
for ever to forsake the world, and settle themselves
here in a house of Capuchines in *Padua.*

HORTENSIO. 'Tis strange.

FLAMINEO. One thing makes it so. They have vowed   10
for ever to weare next their bare bodies those coates
of maile they served in.

HORTENSIO. Hard penance. Is the Moore a Christian?

FLAMINEO.   Hee is.

HORTENSIO. Why proffers hee his service to our Duke?   15

FLAMINEO. Because he understands ther's like to grow
Some warres betweene us and the Duke of Florence,
In which hee hopes imployment.
I never saw one in a sterne bold looke
Weare more command, nor in a lofty phrase   20
Expresse more knowing, or more deepe contempt
Of our slight airy Courtiers. Hee talkes
As if hee had travail'd all the Princes Courts
Of Christendome; in all things strives t'expresse,
That all that should dispute with him may know,   25
Glories, like glow-wormes, a farre off shine bright
But lookt to neare, have neither heat nor light.
The Duke.

Enter BRACHIANO, [FRANCISCO *Duke of*] *Florence*
disguised like Mulinassar; LODOVICO, ANTONELLI,   30
[AND] GASPARO [*disguised*], [*with* CARLO *and*
PEDRO], FARNESE *bearing their*
swordes and helmets.

BRACHIANO. You'are nobly welcome. Wee have heard at
full   35
Your honourable service 'gainst the Turke.
To you, brave Mulinassar, wee assigne

A competent pension : and are inly sorrow,[1]
The vowes of those two worthie gentlemen,
Make them incapable of our proffer'd bountie.
Your wish is you may leave your warlike swordes
For Monuments in our Chappell. I accept it   5
As a great honour done mee, and must crave
Your leave to furnish out our Dutchesse revells.
Onely one thing, as the last vanitie
You ere shall view, denie mee not to stay
To see a Barriers prepar'd to night;   10
You shall have private standings : It hath pleas'd
The great Ambassadours of severall Princes
In their returne from Rome to their owne Countries
To grace our marriage, and to honour mee
With such a kind of sport.   15
FRANCISCO.   I shall perswade them
    To stay, my Lord.
[BRACHIANO.] Set on there to the presence.[5]

                           Exeunt BRACHIANO, FLAMINEO,
                                    and [HORTENSIO.][1]   20
            The conspirators here imbrace.
CARLO. Noble my Lord, most fortunately wellcome,
    You have our vowes seal'd with the sacrament
    To second your attempts.
PEDRO.   And all thinges readie.   25
    Hee could not have invented his owne ruine,
    Had hee despair'd—with more proprietie.
LODOVICO. You would not take my way.
FRANCISCO.   'Tis better ordered.
LODOVICO. T'have poison'd his praier booke, or a paire[6]   30
                    of beades,
    The pummell of his saddle, his looking-glasse,
    Or th'handle of his racket, ô that, that!
    That while he had bin bandying at Tennis,

ACT V. SCENE I.
[1] *are inly sorrow :* acceptable
form for "sorry."

                         294

He might have sworne himselfe to hell, and strooke
His soule into the hazzard![2, (7)] O my Lord!
I would have our plot bee ingenious,
And have it hereafter recorded for example
Rather than borrow example.   5
FRANCISCO.   There's no way
More speeding than this thought on.
LODOVICO.   On then.
FRANCISCO. And yet mee thinkes that his revenge is
                              poore,   10
Because it steales upon him like a theif,—
To have tane him by the Caske in a pitcht feild,[3]
Led him to Florence!
LODOVICO.   It had bin rare.—And there
Have crown'd him with a wreath of stinking garlicke.   15
T'have showne the sharpnesse of his government;
And rancknesse of his lust. Flamineo comes.
                    Exeunt [all except FRANCISCO.][2]
          Enter FLAMINEO, MARCELLO, and ZANCHE.
MARCELLO. Why doth this devill haunt you? say.   20
FLAMINEO.   I know not.
For by this light I doe not conjure for her.
Tis not so great a cunning as men thinke
To raise the devill : for heeres one up allreadie,
The greatest cunning were to lay him downe.   25
MARCELLO. Shee is your shame.
FLAMINEO.   I prethee pardon her.
In faith you see, women are like to burres;
Where their affection throwes them, there they'l
                              sticke.   30
ZANCHE. That is my Country-man, a goodly person;
When hee's at leisure Ile discourse with him
In our owne language.
FLAMINEO.   I beseech you doe,—
                              Exit ZANCHE.   35

[2] *hazzard* : a wall opening in   [3] *feild* : by the helmet in open
court tennis.   combat.

295

How is't brave souldier; ô that I had seene
Some of your iron daies! I pray relate
Some of your service to us.

FRANCISCO. 'Tis a ridiculous thing for a man to bee his
owne Chronicle; I did never wash my mouth with   5
mine owne praise for feare of getting a stincking
breath.

MARCELLO. You're too Stoicall. The Duke will expect
other discourse from you—

FRANCISCO. I shall never flatter him, I have studied man   10
too much[3] to do that : What difference is betweene the Duke and I? no more than betweene two
brickes; all made of one clay. Onely 't may bee one
is plac't on the top of a turret; the other in the bottom
of a well by meere chance; if I were plac't as high   15
as the Duke, I should sticke as fast; make as faire a
shew; and beare out weather equally.

FLAMINEO. [*Aside.*] If this souldier had a patent to beg
in Churches, then hee would tell them stories.

MARCELLO. I have bin a souldier too.   20

FRANCISCO. How have you thriv'd?

MARCELLO. Faith poorely.

FRANCISCO. That's the miserie of peace. Onely outsides
are then respected : As shippes seeme verie great
upon the river, which shew verie little upon the Seas :   25
So some men i'th Court seeme *Colossusses* in a chamber, who if they came into the feild would appeare
pittiful Pigmies.

FLAMINEO. Give mee a faire roome yet hung with Arras,(8) and some great Cardinall to lug mee by th'   30
eares as his endeared Minion.

FRANCISCO. And thou maist doe, the devill knowes what
vilanie.

FLAMINEO. And safely.

FRANCISCO. Right; you shall see in the Countrie in har-   35
vest time, pigeons, though they destroy never so
much corne, the farmer dare not present the fowling
peece to them! why? because they belong to the Lord

296

of the Mannor; whilest your poore sparrowes that belong to the Lord of heaven, they go to the pot for't.

FLAMINEO. I will now give you some polliticke instruction. The Duke saies hee will give you pension; that's
but bare promise : get it under his hand.[4] For I have   5
knowne men that have come from serving against the
Turke; for three or foure moneths they have had pension to buy them new woodden legges and fresh
plaisters; but after 'twas not to bee had. And this
miserable curtesie shewes, as if a Tormenter should   10
give hot cordiall drinkes to one three quarters dead
o'th' racke, onely to fetch the miserable soule againe
to indure more dogdaies.   [*Exit* FRANCISCO.]

   Enter HORTENSIO, *a yong Lord*, ZANCHE,
        and two more.   15

How now, Gallants; what are they readie for the
Barriers?

YOUNG LORD. Yes : the Lordes are putting on their
armour.

HORTENSIO. What's hee?   20

FLAMINEO. A new up-start : one that sweares like a
Falckner, and will lye in the Dukes eare day by day
like a maker of Almanacks; And yet I knew him since
hee came to th' Court smell worse of sweat than an
under-tennis-court keeper.   25

HORTENSIO. Looke you, yonder's your sweet Mistresse.

FLAMINEO. Thou art my sworne brother, I'le tell thee,
I doe love that Moore, that Witch very constrain-
edly : shee knowes some of my villany; I do love her,
just as a man holds a wolfe by the eares. But for   30
feare of turning upon mee, and pulling out my
throate, I would let her go to the Devill.

HORTENSIO. I heare she claimes marriage of thee.

FLAMINEO. 'Faith, I made to her some such darke promise, and in seeking to flye from't I run on, like a   35
frighted dog with a bottle at's taile, that faine would

---

[4] *under his hand :* in writing.

bite it off and yet dares not looke behind him. Now
my pretious Gipsie!

ZANCHE. I, your love to me rather cooles then heates.

FLAMINEO. Marry, I am the sounder, lover, we have
many wenches about the Towne heate too fast.   5

HORTENSIO. What do you thinke of these perfum'd Gallants then?

FLAMINEO. Their sattin cannot save them. I am confi-
dent
They have a certaine spice of the disease,   10
For they that sleep with dogs, shall rise with fleas.

ZANCHE. Beleeve it! A little painting and gay clothes,
Make you loath me.

FLAMINEO. How? love a Lady for painting or gay apparell? I'le unkennell one example more for thee.   15
Esop had a foolish dog that let go the flesh to catch
the shadow. I would have Courtiers bee better *Diners.*

ZANCHE. You remember your oathes.

FLAMINEO. Lovers oathes are like Marriners prayers,
uttered in extremity; but when the tempest is o're,   20
and that the vessell leaves tumbling, they fall from
protesting to drinking. And yet amongst Gentlemen
protesting and drinking go together, and agree as
well as Shooemakers and West-phalia bacon. They
are both drawers on : for drinke drawes on protesta-   25
tion; and protestation drawes on more drinke. Is not
this discourse better now then the morality[4] of
your sun-burnt Gentleman.

Enter CORNELIA.

CORNELIA. Is this your pearch, you haggard?[5, (9)] flye   30
to th'stewes.[6]   [*Strikes* ZANCHE.]

FLAMINEO. You should be clapt by th'heeles now :
strike i'th Court![(10)]   [*Exit* CORNELIA.]

ZANCHE. She's good for nothing but to make her maids,

---

[5] *haggard :* female hawk;   [6] *stewes :* brothels.
strumpet.

Catch cold a nights; they dare not use a bedstaffe,[11]
For feare of her light fingers.

MARCELLO.   You're a strumpet.
An impudent one.   [*Kicks* ZANCHE.]

FLAMINEO. Why do you kicke her? say,   5
Do you thinke that she's like a walnut-tree?
Must she be cudgel'd ere shee beare good fruite?

MARCELLO. Shee brags that you shall marry her.

FLAMINEO.   What then?

MARCELLO. I had rather she were pitcht upon a stake 10
In some new-seeded garden, to affright
Her fellow crowes thence.

FLAMINEO.   You're a boy, a foole,
Be guardian to your hound, I am of age.

MARCELLO. If I take her neere you I'le cut her throate. 15

FLAMINEO. With a fan of feathers?

MARCELLO.   And for you, I'le whip
This folly from you.

FLAMINEO.   Are you cholericke?
I'le purg't with Rubarbe.   20

HORTENSIO.   O your brother!

FLAMINEO.   Hang him.
Hee wrongs me most that ought t'offend mee least,—
I do suspect my mother plaid foule play,
When she conceiv'd thee.   25

MARCELLO.   Now by all my hopes,
Like the two slaughtred sonnes of *Oedipus*,
The very flames of our affection,
Shall turne two[5] waies.[12] Those words I'le make
      thee answere   30
With thy heart bloud.

FLAMINEO.   Doe like the geesse in the prog-
     resse,[7]
You know where you shall finde mee. [*Exit.*]

MARCELLO.   Very good, 35

[7] *Doe . . . progresse:* Follow
 me like a goose.

299

And thou[13] beest a noble friend, beare him my
         sword,
And bid him fit the length on't.

YOUNG LORD.   Sir I shall.
               [Exeunt all except ZANCHE.*]*   5
   Enter FRANCISCO *the Duke of Florence*
        [disguised as Mulinassar].

ZANCHE. *[Aside.]* He comes. Hence petty thought of
         my disgrace,—
[To FRANCISCO.*]* I neere lov'd my complexion till   10
         now,
Cause I may boldly say without a blush,
I love you.

FRANCISCO. Your love is untimely sowen,
Ther's a Spring at Michaelmas,[14] but 'tis but a   15
        faint one,
I am suncke in yeares, and I have vowed never to
        marry.

ZANCHE. Alas! poore maides get more lovers then husbands, Yet you may mistake my wealth. For, as when   20
Embassadours are sent to congratulate Princes, there's
commonly sent along with them a rich present; so
that though the Prince like not the Embassadours
person nor words, yet he likes well of the present-
ment. So I may come to you in the same maner, &   25
be better loved for my dowry then my vertue.

FRANCISCO. I'le thinke on the motion.

ZANCHE. Do, I'le now detaine you no longer. At your
better leasure I'le tell you things shall startle your
bloud.
                             30
Nor blame me that this passion I reveale;
Lovers dye inward that their flames conceale,

[FRANCISCO.][6] Of all intelligence this may prove the
         best,
Sure I shall draw strange fowle from this foule nest.   35
                     [Exeunt.]

[Act V. Scene ii.]

Enter MARCELLO *and* CORNELIA.   5

CORNELIA. I heare a whispering all about the Court,
    You are to fight, who is your opposite?
    What is the quarrell?

MARCELLO.   'Tis an idle rumour.

CORNELIA. Will you dissemble? sure you do not well   10
    To fright me thus, you never look thus pale,
    But when you are most angry. I do charge you
    Upon my blessing; nay I'le call the Duke,
    And he shall schoole you.

MARCELLO.   Publish not a feare   15
    Which would convert to laughter; 'tis not so,—
    Was not this Crucifix my fathers?[1]

CORNELIA.   Yes.

MARCELLO. I have heard you say, giving my brother
                 sucke,   20
    Hee tooke the Crucifix betweene his hands,

          Enter FLAMINEO.

    And broke a limbe off.

CORNELIA.   Yes : but 'tis mended.

FLAMINEO. I have brought your weapon backe.   25

     FLAMINEO *runnes* MARCELLO *through.*

CORNELIA. Ha, O my horrour!

MARCELLO. You have brought it home indeed.

CORNELIA. Helpe, oh he's murdered.

FLAMINEO. Do you turne your gaule up[1]? I'le to sanc-   30
             tuary,
    And send a surgeon to you.   [*Exit.*]

    Enter CARLO, HORTENSIO, [*and*] PEDRO.

HORTENSIO.   How? o'th ground?

MARCELLO. O mother now remember what I told,   35

Act V. Scene ii.
[1] *gaule up :* vomit blood.

Of breaking off the Crucifix : farewell—
There are some sinnes which heaven doth duly
                    punish,
In a whole family. This it is to rise
By all dishonest meanes. Let all men know   5
That tree shall long time keepe a steddy foote
Whose branches spread no wilder then the roote.
                                      [*Dies.*]

CORNELIA. O my perpetuall sorrow!

HORTENSIO.   Vertuous Marcello.   10
Hee's dead : pray leave him Lady; come, you shall.

CORNELIA. Alas he is not dead : hee's in a trance. Why
here's no body shall get any thing by his death. Let
me call him againe for Gods sake.

CARLO. I would you were deceiv'd.   15

CORNELIA. O you abuse mee, you abuse me, you abuse
me. How many have gone away thus for lacke of
tendance; reare up's head, reare up's head; His bleeding inward will kill him.

HORTENSIO. You see hee is departed.   20

CORNELIA. Let mee come to him; give mee him as hee
is, if hee bee turn'd to earth; let mee but give him
one heartie kisse, and you shall put us both into one
coffin : fetch a looking glasse, see if his breath will
not staine it; or pull out some feathers from my pil-   25
low, and lay them to his lippes, will you loose him
for a little paines taking?

HORTENSIO. Your kindest office is to pray for him.

CORNELIA. Alas! I would not pray for him yet. Hee may
live to lay mee ith' ground, and pray for mee, if you'l   30
let mee come to him.

    Enter BRACHIANO *all armed, save the beaver,*[2]
        with FLAMINEO, [FRANCISCO *disguised as*
        Mulinassar, LODOVICO *disguised, and a Page*].

BRACHIANO. Was this your handy-worke?   35

[2] *beaver* : face-piece of the
helmet.

FLAMINEO. It was my misfortune.

CORNELIA. Hee lies, hee lies, hee did not kill him : these
have kill'd him, that would not let him bee better
look't to.

BRACHIANO. Have comfort my greiv'd Mother. 5

CORNELIA. O you scritch-owle.

HORTENSIO. Forbeare, good Madam.

CORNELIA. Let mee goe, let mee goe.

Shee runes to FLAMINEO *with her knif drawne
and comming to him lets it fall.* 10

The God of heaven forgive thee. Do'st not wonder
I pray for thee? Ile tell thee what's the reason,
I have scarce breath to number twentie minutes;
Ide not spend that in cursing. Fare thee well—
Halfe of thy selfe lies there : and maist thou live 15
To fill an howre-glasse with his mouldred ashes,
To tell how thou shouldst spend the time to come
In blest repentance.

BRACHIANO.   Mother, pray tell mee
How came hee by his death? what was the quarrell? 20

CORNELIA. Indeed my yonger boy presum'd too much
Upon his manhood; gave him bitter wordes;
Drew his sword first; and so I know not how,
For I was out of my wits, hee fell with's head
Just in my bosome. 25

PAGE. This is not trew Madam.

CORNELIA.   I pray thee peace.
One arrow's graz'd[2] allready; it were vaine
T'lose this : for that will nere bee found againe.

BRACHIANO. Go, beare the bodie to Cornelia's lodging : 30
And wee commaund that none acquaint our Dutch-
esse
With this sad accident : for you Flamineo,
Hearke you, I will not graunt your pardon.

FLAMINEO.   No? 35

BRACHIANO. Onely a lease of your life. And that shall last
But for one day. Thou shalt be forc't each evening
To renew it, or be hang'd.

FLAMINEO. At your pleasure.

LODOVICO *sprinckles* BRACHIANO's *bever with*
a poison.[3]

Your will is law now, Ile not meddle with it.

BRACHIANO. You once did brave mee in your sisters   5
          lodging;

I'le now keepe you in awe for't. Where's our beaver?

FRANCISCO. [*Aside.*] Hee cals for his destruction. Noble
          youth,

I pitty thy sad fate. Now to the barriers.   10

This shall his passage to the blacke lake further,

The last good deed hee did, he pardon'd murther.

                    (*Exeunt.*)

          15

[ACT V. SCENE III.]

Charges and shoutes, They fight at Barriers; first
single paires, then three to three.

Enter BRACHIANO *&* FLAMINEO *with others*   20
[*including* VITTORIA, GIOVANNI, *and* FRANCISCO
disguised as Mulinassar].

BRACHIANO. An Armorer? uds'death an Armorer?

FLAMINEO. Armorer; where's the Armorer?

BRACHIANO. Teare off my beaver.   25

FLAMINEO.   Are you hurt, my Lord?

BRACHIANO. O my braine's on fire,

          Enter Armorer.

                The helmet is poison'd.

ARMORER. My Lord upon my soule.   30

BRACHIANO.   Away with him to torture.

          [*Exit Armorer guarded.*]

There are some great ones that have hand in this,

And neere about me.

VITTORIA.   O my loved Lord, poisoned?   35

FLAMINEO. Remove the barre :[1] heer's unfortunate
          revels,

Call the Physitions;

Enter 2 Physitians.
a plague upon you;
Wee have to much of your cunning here already.
I feare the Embassadours are likewise poyson'd.

BRACHIANO. Oh I am gone already : the infection   5
Flies to the braine and heart. O thou strong heart!
There's such a covenant 'tweene the world and it,
They're loath to breake.

GIOVANNI.   O my most loved father!

BRACHIANO. Remove the boy away,—   10
Where's this good woman? had I infinite worlds
They were too little for thee. Must I leave thee?[2]
What say yon scritch-owles, is the venomne mor-
                    tall?[3]

PHYSICIAN. Most deadly.   15

BRACHIANO.   Most corrupted pollitick hangman!
You kill without booke; but your art to save
Failes you as oft, as great mens needy friends.
I that have given life to offending slaves
And wretched murderers, have I not power   20
To lengthen mine owne a twelve-month?
[*To* VITTORIA.] Do not kisse me, for I shall poyson
                    thee.[4]
This unction is sent from the great Duke of Florence.

FRANCISCO. Sir bee of comfort.   25

BRACHIANO. O thou soft naturall death, that art joint-
                    twin,
To sweetest slumber : no rough-bearded Comet,
Stares on thy milde departure : the dull Owle
Beates not against thy casement : the hoarse wolfe   30
Sents not thy carion. Pitty windes thy coarse,
Whilst horrour waights on Princes.

VITTORIA.   I am lost for ever.

BRACHIANO. How miserable a thing it is to die,
'Mongst women howling!   35
    [*Enter* LODOVICO *and* GASPARO *disguised.*][1]
                    What are those?

FLAMINEO.   Franciscans.[5]

305

They have brought the extreame unction.

BRACHIANO. On paine of death, let no man name death
           to me,
  It is a word infinitely terrible,—
  Withdraw into our Cabinet. 5

                       Exeunt [all] but FRANCISCO
                               and FLAMINEO.

FLAMINEO. To see what solitarinesse is about dying
  Princes. As heretofore they have unpeopled Townes;
  divorst friends, and made great houses unhospitable : 10
  so now, ô justice! where are their flatterers now?
  Flatterers are but the shadowes of Princes bodies, the
  least thicke cloud makes them invisible.

FRANCISCO. There's great moane made for him.

FLAMINEO. 'Faith, for some few howers salt water will 15
  runne most plentifully in every Office o'th Court. But
  beleeve it; most of them do but weepe over their step-
  mothers graves.

FRANCISCO. How meane you?

FLAMINEO. Why? They dissemble, as some men doe that 20
  live within compasse o'th verge.[1, (6)]

FRANCISCO. Come you have thriv'd well under him.

FLAMINEO. 'Faith, like a wolfe[(7)] in a womans breast;
  I have beene fed with poultry;[(8)] but for money,
  understand me, I had as good a will to cosen him, 25
  as e're an Officer of them all. But I had not cunning
  enough to doe it.

FRANCISCO. What did'st thou thinke of him; 'faith speake
  freely.

FLAMINEO. Hee was a kinde of States-man, that would 30
  sooner have reckond how many Cannon bullets he
  had discharged against a Towne, to count his expence
  that way, than how many of his valiant and deserving subjects hee lost before it.

FRANCISCO. O, speake well of the Duke. 35

ACT V. SCENE III.   within twelve miles of the
[1] *within . . . verge :* area   king's court.

FLAMINEO. I have done. Wilt heare some of my Court
wisedome?
> *Enter* LODOVICO [*disguised as before*].
To reprehend Princes is dangerous : and to over-
commend some of them is palpable lying.   5
FRANCISCO. How is it with the Duke?
LODOVICO.   Most deadly ill.
Hee's fall'n into a strange distraction.
Hee talkes of Battailes and Monopolies,
Levying of taxes, and from that descends   10
To the most brain-sicke language. His minde fastens
On twentie severall objects, which confound
Deepe Sence with follie. Such a fearefull end
May teach some men that beare too loftie crest,
Though they live happiest, yet they dye not best.   15
Hee hath conferr'd the whole State of the Dukedome
Upon your sister, till the Prince arrive
At mature age.
FLAMINEO.   There's some good lucke in that yet.
FRANCISCO. See heere he comes.   20
> *Enter* BRACHIANO, *presented in a bed,* VITTORIA *and*
> *others* [*including* GASPARO *disguised as before*].
                    There's death in's face allready.
VITTORIA. O my good Lord!
BRACHIANO.   Away, you have abus'd mee.   25
                (*These speeches are severall*
                kinds of distractions and in
                the action should apeare so.)
You have convayd coyne forth our territories;
Bought and sold offices; oppres'd the poore,   30
And I nere dreampt on't. Make up your accountes;
Ile now bee mine owne Steward.
FLAMINEO.   Sir, have patience.
BRACHIANO. Indeed I am too blame.
For did you ever heare the duskie raven   35
Chide blacknesse? or wast ever knowne, the divell
Raild against cloven Creatures.
VITTORIA.   O my Lord!

BRACHIANO. Let mee have some quailes to supper.

FLAMINEO. Sir, you shal.

BRACHIANO. No : some fried dog-fish. Your Quailes[9]
    feed on poison,—
That old dog-fox, that Polititian Florence,— 5
Ile forsweare hunting and turne dog-killer;
Rare! Ile bee frindes with him. for marke you, sir,
    one dog
Still sets another a barking : peace, peace,
Yonder's a fine slave come in now. 10

FLAMINEO. Where?

BRACHIANO. Why there.
In a blew bonnet, and a paire of breeches
With a great codpeece. Ha, ha, ha,
Looke you his codpeece is stucke full of pinnes 15
With pearles o'th head of them.[10] Doe not you
    know him?

FLAMINEO. No, my Lord.

BRACHIANO. Why 'tis the Devill.
I know him by a great rose[11] he weares on's shooe 20
To hide his cloven foot. Ile dispute with him.
Hee's a rare linguist.[12]

VITTORIA. My Lord heer's nothing.

BRACHIANO. Nothing? rare! nothing! when I want monie,
Our treasurie is emptie; there is nothing, 25
Ile not bee us'd thus.

VITTORIA. O! 'ly still, my Lord.

BRACHIANO. See, see, Flamineo that kill'd his brother
Is dancing on the ropes there : and he carries
A monie-bag in each hand, to keepe him even, 30
For feare of breaking's necke. And there's a Lawyer
In a gowne whipt[2] with velvet, stares and gapes
When the mony will fall. How the rogue cuts capers!
It should have bin in a halter.
'Tis there; what's shee? 35

FLAMINEO. Vittoria, my Lord.

----

[2] *whipt :* trimmed intricately.

BRACHIANO. Ha, ha, ha. Her haire is sprinckled with
Arras powder,[13] that makes her looke as if she had
sinn'd in the Pastrie. What's hee?

FLAMINEO. A Divine my Lord.

BRACHIANO. Hee will bee drunke : Avoid him : th'   5
                 argument
Is fearefull when Church-men stagger in't.
Looke you; six gray rats that have lost their
                 tailes,[14]
Crall up the pillow, send for a Rat-catcher.   10
Ile doe a miracle : Ile free the Court
From all foule vermin. Where's Flamineo?

FLAMINEO. I doe not like that hee names mee so often,
Especially on's death-bed : 'tis a signe
I shall not live long : see hee's neere his end.   15

BRACHIANO *seemes heare neare his end,* LODOVICO *&*
GASPARO *in the habit of Capuchins, present him in*
his bed with a Crucifix and hallowed candle.

LODOVICO. Pray give us leave; *Attende Domine*
                Brachiane,[3]   20

FLAMINEO. See, see, how firmely hee doth fixe his eye
Upon the Crucifix.

VITTORIA.   O hold it constant.
It settles his wild spirits; and so his eies
Melt into teares.   25

LODOVICO. (*By the crucifix.*) *Domine Brachiane, solebas*
in bello tutus esse tuo clypeo, nunc hunc clypeum
hosti tuo opponas infernali.

GASPARO. (*By the Hallowed taper.*) *Olim hasta valuisti*
in bello; nunc hanc sacram hastam vibrabis contra   30
hostem animarum.

LODOVICO. *Attende Domine Brachiane si nunc quoque*
probas ea quae acta sunt inter nos, flecte caput in
dextrum.

GASPARO. *Esto securus Domine Brachiane : cogita quan-*   35

---

[3] *Attende . . . Brachiane :*
Hear, Lord Brachiano.

*tum habeas meritorum—denique memineris meam
animam pro tua oppignoratam si quid esset periculi.*

LODOVICO. *Si nunc quoque probas ea quae acta sunt in-
ter nos, flecte caput in laevum.*[4],[15]
Hee is departing : pray stand all apart,   5
And let us onely whisper in his eares
Some private meditations, which our order
Permits you not to heare.

               Heare the rest being departed
           LODOVICO *and* GASPARO *discover*   10
                       themselves.

GASPARO.   Brachiano.
LODOVICO. Devill Brachiano. Thou art damn'd.
GASPARO.   Perpetually.
LODOVICO. A slave condemn'd, and given up to the   15
               gallowes
Is thy great Lord and Master.
GASPARO.   True : for thou
Art given up to the devill.
LODOVICO.   O you slave!   20
You that were held the famous Pollititian;
Whose art was poison.
GASPARO.   And whose conscience[16] murder.
LODOVICO. That would have broke your wives necke
               downe the staires   25
Ere she was poison'd.[17]

[4] *Domine Brachiane . . . in
laevum :* Lord Brachiano, you
were accustomed to be protected in war by your shield;
now this shield you will op-
pose to your infernal enemy.
Once with a spear you overcame in war; now this holy
spear you will brandish
against the enemy of souls.
LODOVICO. Hear, Lord Bra-
chiano, if you now also approve what has been per-
formed among us, turn your
head to the right. GASPARO.
Be assured, Lord Brachiano :
consider how many good
deeds you have done—finally
remember that my soul is
pledged for yours if there may
be any danger. LODOVICO. If
now you also approve what
has been performed among
us, turn your head to the left.

GASPARO.   That had your villanous sallets.

LODOVICO. And fine imbrodered bottles, and perfumes
 Equally mortall with a winter plague.

GASPARO. Now there's Mercarie.[5]

LODOVICO.   And copperesse[6]—   5

GASPARO.   And quicke-silver.[7, (18)]

LODOVICO. With other develish potticarie stuffe
 A melting in your polliticke braines : do'st heare?

GASPARO. This is Count Lodovico.

LODOVICO.   This Gasparo. 10
 And thou shalt die like a poore rogue.

GASPARO.   And stinke
 Like a dead flie-blowne dog.

LODOVICO.   And be forgotten
 Before thy funerall sermon. 15

BRACHIANO.   Vittoria?
 Vittoria!

LODOVICO.   O the cursed devill,
 Come to himselfe againe. Wee are undone.

    Enter VITTORIA *and the attendants.* 20

GASPARO. [*Aside.*] Strangle him in private. [*To* VIT-
  TORIA.] What? will you call him againe
 To live in treble torments? for charitie,
 For Christian charitie, avoid the chamber.

     [*Exeunt* VITTORIA *and attendants.*] 25

LODOVICO. You would prate, Sir. This is a true-love knot
 Sent from the Duke of Florence.

     BRACHIANO *is strangled.*

GASPARO.   What is it done?

LODOVICO. The snuffe[(19)] is out. No woman-keeper i'th 30
  world,
 Though shee had practis'd seven yere at the Pest-
  house,[(20)]
 Could have done't quaintlyer. My Lordes hee's dead.

---

[5] *Mercarie :* Wild mercury
 plant.

[6] *copperesse :* sulphate of
 copper.

[7] *quicke-silver :* mercury.

[*Enter* VITTORIA, FRANCISCO *disguised,* FLAMINEO,
            and attendants.]

OMNES. Rest to his soule.

VITTORIA.   O mee! this place is hell.

                              Exit VITTORIA [*and others,*   5
                              except LODOVICO, FRANCISCO,
                                        and FLAMINEO.]

FRANCISCO. How heavily shee takes it.

FLAMINEO.   O yes, yes;

Had women navigable rivers in their eies   10
They would dispend them all; surely I wonder
Why wee should wish more rivers[21] to the Cittie,
When they sell water so good cheape.[22] Ile tell thee,
These are but Moonish shades of greifes or feares,
There's nothing sooner drie than womens teares.   15
Why heere's an end of all my harvest, hee has given
                    mee nothing—
Court promises! Let wise men count them curst
For while you live hee that scores best paies worst.

FRANCISCO. Sure, this was Florence doing.   20

FLAMINEO.   Very likelie.

Those are found waightie strokes which come from
                    th'hand,
But those are killing strokes which come from th'head.
O the rare trickes of a Machivillian![23]   25
Hee doth not come like a grosse plodding slave
And buffet you to death : No, my quaint knave,
Hee tickles you to death; makes you die laughing;
As if you had swallow'd downe a pound of saffron—
You see the feat, 'tis practis'd in a trice   30
To teach Court-honestie, it jumpes[24] on Ice.

FRANCISCO. Now have the people libertie to talke
And descant[25] on his vices.

FLAMINEO.   Miserie of Princes,

That must of force bee censur'd by their slaves!   35
Not onely blam'd for doing things are ill,
But for not doing all that all men will.
One were better be a thresher.

Uds'death, I would faine speake with this Duke yet.

FRANCISCO. Now hee's dead?

FLAMINEO. I cannot conjure; but if praiers or oathes
Will get to th'speech of him : though forty devils
Waight on him in his livery of flames,   5
I'le speake to him, and shake him by the hand,
Though I bee blasted.   *Exit* FLAMINEO.

FRANCISCO.   Excellent Lodovico!
What? did you terrifie him at the last gaspe?

LODOVICO. Yes; and so idely, that the Duke had like   10
T'have terrified us.

FRANCISCO.   How?
                    Enter [ZANCHE] *the Moore.*

LODOVICO. You shall heare that heareafter,—
See! yon's the infernall, that would make up sport.   15
Now to the revelation of that secret,
Shee promi'st when she fell in love with you.

FRANCISCO. You're passionately met in this sad world.

ZANCHE. I would have you look up, Sir; these Court
                    teares   20
Claime not your tribute to them. Let those weepe
That guiltily pertake in the sad cause.
I knew last night by a sad dreame I had
Some mischiefe would insue; yet to say truth
My dreame most concern'd you.   25

LODOVICO.   Shal's fall a dreaming?

FRANCISCO. Yes, and for fashion sake Ile dreame with
                    her.

ZANCHE. Mee thought sir, you came stealing to my bed.

FRANCISCO. Wilt thou beleeve me sweeting; by this light   30
I was a dreampt on thee too : for me thought
I saw thee naked.

ZANCHE.   Fy sir! as I told you,
Me thought you lay downe by me.

FRANCISCO.   So drempt I;   35
And least thou should'st take cold, I cover'd thee
With this Irish mantle.[26]

ZANCHE.   Verily I did dreame,

You were somewhat bold with me; but to come to't.
LODOVICO. How? how? I hope you will not go to it here.
FRANCISCO. Nay : you must heare my dreame out.
ZANCHE.   Well, sir, forth.
FRANCISCO. When I threw the mantle ore thee, thou   5
          didst laugh
Exceedingly me thought.
ZANCHE.   Laugh?
[FRANCISCO.][2]   And cridst out,
The haire did tickle thee.   10
ZANCHE.   There was a dreame indeed.
LODOVICO. Marke her I prethee, shee simpers like the
          suddes
A Collier hath bene washt in.
ZANCHE. Come, sir; good fortune tends you; I did tell   15
          you
I would reveale a secret,—Isabella
The Duke of Florence sister was impoison'd,
By a 'fum'd(27) picture : and Camillo's necke
Was broke by damn'd Flamineo; the mischance   20
Laid on a vaulting horse.
FRANCISCO.   Most strange!
ZANCHE.   Most true.
LODOVICO. The bed of snakes is broke.
ZANCHE. I sadly do confesse I had a hand   25
In the blacke deed.
FRANCISCO.   Thou kepts their counsell,
ZANCHE.   Right,
For which, urg'd with contrition, I intend
This night to rob Vittoria.   30
LODOVICO.   Excellent penitence!
Usurers dreame on't while they sleepe out Sermons.
ZANCHE. To further our escape, I have entreated
Leave to retire me, till the funerall,
Unto a friend i'th country. That excuse   35
Will further our escape. In coine and jewels
I shall, at least, make good unto your use
An hundred thousand crowns.

FRANCISCO.   O noble wench!

LODOVICO. Those crownes we'le share.

ZANCHE.   It is a dowry,

Me thinkes, should make that sun-burnt proverbe false,   5

And wash the Ethiop white.[28]

FRANCISCO.   It shall, away!

ZANCHE. Be ready for our flight.

FRANCISCO.   An howre 'fore day.

                           Exit the Moore.   10

O strange discovery! why till now we knew not
The circumstance of either of their deaths.

                    Enter Moore.

ZANCHE. You'le waight about midnight
In the Chappel.   15

FRANCISCO.   There.   [*Exit* ZANCHE.]

LODOVICO. Why now our action's justified,

FRANCISCO.   Tush for justice.

What harmes it Justice? we now, like the partridge
Purge the disease with lawrell:[29] for the fame   20
Shall crowne the enterprise and quit the shame.

                           Exeunt.

[Act V. Scene iv.]   25

     Enter FLAMINEO *and* GASPARO *at one dore,*
         another way GIOVANNI *attended.*

GASPARO. The yong Duke: Did you e're see a sweeter
Prince?   30

FLAMINEO. I have knowne a poore womans bastard better favor'd,—this is behind him: Now, to his face all
comparisons were hatefull: Wise was the Courtly
Peacocke, that being a great Minion, and being compar'd for beauty, by some dottrels[1] that stood by, to   35

Act V. Scene iv.
[1] *dottrels :* simpletons; plovers.

the Kingly Eagle, said the Eagle was a farre fairer
bird then herselfe, not in respect of her feathers, but
in respect of her long Tallants. (1) His will grow
out in time,—
My gratious Lord.   5
GIOVANNI.   I pray leave mee Sir.
FLAMINEO. Your Grace must be merry: 'tis I have
cause to mourne, for wot you what said the little boy
that rode behind his father on horsebacke?
GIOVANNI. Why, what said hee?   10
FLAMINEO. When you are dead father (said he) I hope
then I shall ride in the saddle, O 'tis a brave thing
for a man to sit by himselfe : he may stretch him-
selfe in the stirrops, looke about, and see the whole
compasse of the Hemisphere; you're now, my Lord,   15
ith saddle.
GIOVANNI. Study your praiers, sir, and be penitent,
'Twere fit you'd thinke on what hath former bin,
I have heard griefe nam'd the eldest child of sinne.
           Exit GIOVANNI [*and all except* FLAMINEO].   20
FLAMINEO. Study my praiers? he threatens me divinely,
I am falling to peeces already, I care not, though,
like *Anacharsis*(2) I were pounded to death in a
mortar. And yet that death were fitter for Usurers
gold and themselves to be beaten together, to make   25
a most cordiall chullice² for the devill.
He hath his unckles villanous looke already,
In decimo[1] *sexto.*(3)
                 Enter Courtier.
                 Now sir, what are you?   30
COURTIER. It is the pleasure sir, of the yong Duke
That you forbeare the Presence, and all roomes
That owe him reverence.
FLAMINEO.   So, the wolfe and the raven
Are very pretty fools when they are yong.   35
Is it your office, sir, to keepe me out?

² *chullice* : broth.

COURTIER. So the Duke wils.

FLAMINEO. Verely, Maister Courtier, extreamity is not
to bee used in all offices : Say that a gentlewoman
were taken out of her bed about midnight, and committed to Castle Angelo, to the Tower yonder,[4]   5
with nothing about her, but her smocke : would it
not shew a cruell part in the gentleman porter to lay
clame to her upper garment, pull it ore her head
and eares; and put her in nak'd?

COURTIER. Very good : you are merrie.   *Exit.*   10

FLAMINEO. Doth hee make a Court ejectment of mee?
A flaming firebrand[5] casts more smoke without a
chimney, then withint. Ile smoore³ some of them.

    Enter [FRANCISCO *Duke of*] *Florence,*
      [*disguised as Mulinassar*].   15

How now? Thou art[2] sad.

FRANCISCO. I met even now with the most pitious sight.

FLAMINEO. Thou metst another heare—a pittifull
Degraded Courtier.

FRANCISCO.   Your reverend mother   20
Is growne a very old woman in two howers.
I found them winding of Marcello's coarse;
And there is such a solemne melodie
'Tweene dolefull songes, teares, and sad elegies :
Such, as old grandames, watching by the dead,   25
Were wont t'out-weare the nights with; that beleeve
        mee
I had no eies to guide mee forth the roome,
They were so ore-charg'd with water.

FLAMINEO.   I will see them.   30

FRANCISCO. 'Twere much uncharety in you : for your
        sight
Will adde unto their teares.

FLAMINEO.   I will see them.

They are behind the travers. Ile discover   35

---

³ *smoore :* suffocate.

Their superstitious howling.

> [*Draws the traverse*(6) *curtain.*]
> CORNELIA, *the Moore and 3. other Ladies*
> *discovered, winding* MARCELLO'*s Coarse.*
> *A song.*   5

CORNELIA. This rosemarie is wither'd, pray get fresh;
I would have these herbes grow up in his grave
When I am dead and rotten. Reach the bayes,
Il tye a garland heere about his head:
'Twill keepe my boy from lightning.(7) This sheet   10
I have kept this twentie yere, and everie daie
Hallow'd it with my praiers, I did not thinke
Hee should have wore it.

ZANCHE.   Looke you; who are yonder?
CORNELIA. O reach mee the flowers.   15
ZANCHE. Her Ladiships foolish.
[LADY.][3]   Alas! her grief
Hath turn'd her child againe.
CORNELIA.   You're very wellcome.
There's Rosemarie for you, and Rue(8) for you,   20

> (*To* FLAMINEO.)

Hearts-ease(9) for you. I pray make much of it.
I have left more for my selfe.
FRANCISCO.   Ladie, who's this?
CORNELIA. You are, I take it, the grave-maker.   25
FLAMINEO.   So.
ZANCHE. 'Tis Flamineo.
CORNELIA. Will you make mee such a foole? heere's a
> white hand :
Can bloud so soone bee washt out? Let mee see,   30
When scritch-howles croke upon the chimney tops,
And the strange Cricket ith oven singes and hoppes,
When yellow spots doe on your handes appeare,
Bee certaine then you of a Course⁴ shall heare.
Out upon't, how 'tis speckled! h'as handled a   35
> toad(10) sure.

---

⁴ *Course* : Like "coarse"; corpse.

Couslep-water[11] is good for the memorie :
Pray buy mee 3. ounces of't.

FLAMINEO. I would I were from hence.

CORNELIA.   Do you heere, sir?
Ile give you a saying which my grandmother   5
Was wont, when she heard the bell tolle, to sing
Ore unto her lute.

FLAMINEO.   Doe and you will, doe.

(CORNELIA *doth this in severall formes of distraction.*)

CORNELIA. *Call for the Robin-Red-brest and the wren,*   10
Since ore shadie groves they hover,
And with leaves and flowres doe cover
The friendlesse bodies of unburied men.[12]
Call unto his funerall Dole
The Ante, the field-mouse, and the mole   15
To reare him hillockes, that shall keepe him warme,
And (when gay tombes are rob'd) sustaine no harme,
But keepe the wolfe far thence : that's foe to men,
For with his nailes hee'l dig them up agen.[13]
They would not bury him 'cause hee died in a   20
                   quarrell
But I have an answere for them.
Let holie Church receive him duly
Since hee payd the Church tithes truly.
His wealth is sum'd, and this is all his store :   25
This poore men get; and great men get no more.
Now the wares are gone, wee may shut up shop.[14]
Blesse you all good people,—

                Exeunt CORNELIA, [ZANCHE,]
                      and Ladies.   30

FLAMINEO. I have a strange thing in mee, to th' which
I cannot give a name, without it bee
Compassion, I pray leave mee.   *Exit* FRANCISCO.
This night Ile know the utmost of my fate,
Ile bee resolv'd what my rich sister meanes   35
T'assigne mee for my service : I have liv'd
Riotously ill, like some that live in Court.
And sometimes, when my face was full of smiles

Have felt the mase[15] of conscience in my brest.
Oft gay and honour'd robes those tortures trie,
"Wee thinke cag'd birds sing, when indeed they crie."
   Enter BRACHIANO's *Ghost. In his leather Cassock*
    & breeches, bootes, [and] a cowle; [in his hand]   5
      a pot of lilly-flowers with a scull in't.[16]
Ha! I can stand thee. Neerer, neerer yet.
What a mockerie hath death made of thee? thou
     look'st sad.[17]
In what place art thou? in yon starrie gallerie,   10
Or in the cursed dungeon? No? not speake?
Pray, Sir, resolve mee, what religions best
For a man to die in? or is it in your knowledge
To answere mee how long I have to live?
That's the most necessarie question.   15
Not answere? Are you still like some great men
That onely walke like shadowes up and downe,
And to no purpose : say :—
    The Ghost throwes earth upon him and
        shewes him the scull.   20
What's that? O fatall! hee throwes earth upon mee.
A dead mans scull beneath the rootes of flowers.
I pray speake Sir; our Italian Church-men
Make us beleve, dead men hold conference
With their familiars, and many times   25
Will come to bed to them, and eat with them.
                     Exit Ghost.
Hee's gone; and see, the scull and earth are vanisht.
This is beyond melancholie. I doe dare my fate
To doe its worst. Now to my sisters lodging,   30
And summe up all these horrours; the disgrace
The Prince threw on mee; next the pitious sight
Of my dead brother; and my Mothers dotage;
And last this terrible vision. All these
Shall with Vittoria's bountie turne to good,   35
Or I will drowne this weapon in her blood. *Exit.*

[Act V. Scene v.]

Enter FRANCISCO, LODOVICO, *and* HORTENSIO   5
[overhearing them].

LODOVICO. My Lord upon my soule you shall no further :
    You have most ridiculously ingag'd your selfe
    Too far allready. For my part, I have payd
    All my debts, so if I should chance to fall   10
    My Creditours fall not with mee; and I vow
    To quite¹ all in this bold assemblie
    To the meanest follower. My Lord leave the Cittie,
    Or Ile forsweare the murder.
FRANCISCO.   Farewell Lodovico.   15
    If thou do'st perish in this glorious act,
    Ile reare unto thy memorie that fame
    Shall in the ashes keepe alive thy name.
                  [Exeunt FRANCISCO *and*
                        LODOVICO *severally.]*   20
HORTENSIO. There's some blacke deed on foot. Ile pres-
                ently
    Downe to the Citadell, and raise some force.
    These strong Court factions that do brooke no checks,
    In the cariere⁽¹⁾ of't breake the Riders neckes.   25
                              [Exit.]

[Act V. Scene vi.]

                                     30

Enter VITTORIA *with a booke in her hand,* ZANCHE,
    [and] FLAMINEO *following them.*⁽¹⁾
FLAMINEO. What are you at your prayers? Give o're.
VITTORIA.   How Ruffin?⁽²⁾
FLAMINEO. I come to you 'bout worldly businesse :   35

    ACT V. SCENE v.
¹ *quite :* repay.

Sit downe, sit downe : Nay stay blouze,[1] you may
　　　　　　　heare it,
The dores are fast inough.

VITTORIA. 　　　　　　　Ha, are you drunke?

FLAMINEO. Yes, yes, with wormewood water, you shall　　5
　　　　　　　tast
Some of it presently.

VITTORIA. 　　　　　　What intends the fury?

FLAMINEO. You are my Lords Executrix, and I claime
Reward, for my long service.　　　　　　　10

VITTORIA. 　　　　　　　For your service?

FLAMINEO. Come therfore heere is pen and Inke, set
　　　　　　　downe
What you will give me. 　　　　　　*She writes.*

VITTORIA. There,—　　　　　　　15

FLAMINEO. 　　　　Ha! have you done already?
'Tis a most short conveyance.

VITTORIA. 　　　　　　　I will read it.
[*Reads.*] *I give that portion to thee, and no other*
Which Caine gron'd under having slaine his brother.　　20

FLAMINEO. A most courtly Pattent to beg by.[3]

VITTORIA. You are a villaine.

FLAMINEO. Is't come to this? they say affrights cure
　　　　　　　agues :
Thou hast a Devill in thee; I will try　　　　　　　25
If I can scarre him from thee : Nay sit still :
My Lord hath left me yet two case of Jewels[4]
Shall make me scorne your bounty; you shall see
　　　　　　　them. 　　　　　　　[*Exit.*]

VITTORIA. Sure hee's distracted.　　　　　　　30

ZANCHE. 　　　　　　　O he's desperate—
For your owne safety give him gentle language.
　　　He enters with two case of pistols.

FLAMINEO. Looke, these are better far at a dead lift,[2]

ACT V. SCENE VI.

[1] *blouze* : red-faced wench　　　[2] *at a dead lift* : in an
　(*ironic for Zanche*).　　　　　　　emergency.

322

Then all your jewell house.

VITTORIA.   And yet mee thinkes,
These stones have no faire lustre, they are ill set.

FLAMINEO. I'le turne the right side towards you : you
                     shall see   5
How they will sparkle.

VITTORIA.   Turne this horror from mee :
What do you want? what would you have mee doe?
Is not all mine, yours? have I any children?

FLAMINEO. Pray thee good woman doe not trouble mee   10
With this vaine wordly businesse; say your prayers,
I made a vow to my deceased Lord,
Neither your selfe, nor I should out-live him,
The numbring of foure howers.

VITTORIA.   Did he enjoyne it?   15

FLAMINEO. He did, and 'twas a deadly jealousy,
Least any should enjoy thee after him;
That urg'd him vow me to it : For my death—
I did propound it voluntarily, knowing
If hee could not be safe in his owne Court   20
Being a great Duke, what hope then for us?

VITTORIA. This is your melancholy and dispaire.

FLAMINEO.   Away,
Foole, thou art to thinke that Polititians
Do use to kill the effects of injuries   25
And let the cause live : shall we groane in irons,
Or be a shamefull and a waighty burthen
To a publicke scaffold? This is my resolve
I would not live at any mans entreaty
Nor dye at any's bidding.   30

VITTORIA.   Will you heare me?

FLAMINEO. My life hath done service to other men,
My death shall serve mine owne turne; make you
                 ready—

VITTORIA. Do you meane to die indeed?   35

FLAMINEO.   With as much pleasure
As e're my father gat me.

VITTORIA. [*Aside.*] Are the dores lockt?

ZANCHE. [*Aside.*] Yes Madame.

VITTORIA. Are you growne an Atheist? will you turne
your body,
Which is the goodly pallace of the soule   5
To the soules slaughter house? ô the cursed Devill
Which doth present us with all other sinnes
Thrice candied ore; Despaire with gaule and *stibium*,
Yet we carouse it off; [5] [*Aside.*] Cry out for helpe,—
Makes us forsake that which was made for Man,   10
The world, to sinke to that was made for devils,
Eternall darkenesse.

ZANCHE.   Helpe, helpe.

FLAMINEO.   I'le stop your throate
With Winter plums,[3]   15

VITTORIA.   I prethee yet remember,
Millions are now in graves, which at last day
Like Mandrakes shall rise shreeking.

FLAMINEO.   Leave your prating,
For these are but grammaticall laments,   20
Feminine arguments, and they move me
As some in Pulpits move their Auditory
More with their exclamation then sence
Of reason, or sound Doctrine. [6]

ZANCHE.   [*Aside.*] Gentle Madam   25
Seeme to consent, onely perswade him teach
The way to death; let him dye first.

VITTORIA. [*Aside.*] 'Tis good, I apprehend it,—
[*To* FLAMINEO.] To kill one's selfe is meate that we
                    must take   30
Like pils, not chew't, but quickly swallow it, [7]
The smart a'th wound, or weakenesse of the hand
May else bring trebble torments.

FLAMINEO.   I have held it
A wretched and most miserable life,   35
Which is not able to dye.

[3] *Winter plums :* Hard pellets.

VITTORIA. O but frailty!
Yet I am now resolv'd, farewell affliction;
Behold Brachiano, I that while you liv'd
Did make a flaming Altar of my heart
To sacrifice unto you; Now am ready   5
To sacrifice heart and all. Fare-well Zanche.
ZANCHE. How Madam! Do you thinke that I'le out-live
                    you?
Especially when my best selfe Flamineo
Goes the same voiage.   10
FLAMINEO. O most loved Moore!
ZANCHE. Onely by all my love let me entreat you;
Since it is most necessary none of us
Do violence on our selves; let you or I
Be her sad taster; teach her how to dye.   15
FLAMINEO. Thou dost instruct me nobly, take these
                    pistols,
Because my hand is stain'd with bloud already :
Two of these you shall levell at my brest,
Th'other gainst your owne, and so we'le dye,(8)   20
Most equally contented : But first sweare
Not to out-live me.
VITTORIA & ZANCHE. Most religiously.
FLAMINEO. Then here's an end of me : fare-well day-
                    light   25
And ô contemtible Physike! that dost take
So long a study, onely to preserve
So short a life, I take my leave of thee.
                Shewing the pistols.
These are two cupping-glasses,(9) that shall draw   30
All my infected bloud out,
Are you ready?
BOTH. Ready.
FLAMINEO. Whither shall I go now? O *Lucian* thy ridic-
ulous Purgatory—to finde *Alexander* the great cobling 35
shooes, *Pompey* tagging points, and *Julius Caesar*
making haire buttons, *Haniball* selling blacking, and
Augustus crying garlike, *Charlemaigne* selling lists by

the dozen, and King *Pippin* crying Apples in a cart
drawn with one horse.[10]
Whether I resolve to Fire, Earth, Water, Aire,
Or all the Elements by scruples; I know not
Nor greatly care,—Shoote, shoote,   5
Of all deaths the violent death is best,
For from our selves it steales our selves so fast
The paine once apprehended is quite past.

> *They shoot and run to him*
> *& tread upon him.*   10

VITTORIA. What, are you drop't?

FLAMINEO. I am mixt with Earth already: As you are
                              Noble
Performe your vowes, and bravely follow mee.

VITTORIA. Whither—to hell?   15

ZANCHE.   To most assured damnation.

VITTORIA. O thou most cursed devill.

ZANCHE.   Thou art caught—

VITTORIA. In thine owne Engine,[11]—I tread the fire out
That would have bene my ruine.   20

FLAMINEO. Will you be perjur'd? what a religious oath
was Stix[4] that the Gods never durst sweare by and
violate? ô that wee had such an oath to minister, and
to be so well kept in our Courts of Justice.

VITTORIA. Thinke whither thou art going.   25

ZANCHE.   And remember
What villanies thou hast acted.

VITTORIA.   This thy death,
Shall make me like a blazing ominous starre,
Looke up and tremble.   30

FLAMINEO.   O I am caught with a springe!

VITTORIA. You see the Fox comes many times short
                              home,
'Tis here prov'd true.

FLAMINEO.   Kild with a couple of braches.[5]   35

---

[4] *Stix :* the infernal river Styx.   [5] *with . . . braches :* by a
                                        couple of bitches.

VITTORIA. No fitter offring for the infernall furies
  Then one in whom they raign'd while hee was living.
FLAMINEO. O the waies darke and horrid! I cannot see,
  Shall I have no company?
VITTORIA.   O yes thy sinnes,   5
  Do runne before thee to fetch fire from hell,
  To light thee thither.
FLAMINEO. O I smell soote, most stinking soote, the
                      chimne is a fire,
  My livers purboil'd like scotch holly-bread[6];   10
  There's a plumber, laying pipes in my guts, it scalds;
  Wilt thou out-live mee?
ZANCHE.   Yes, and drive a stake
  Through thy body; for we'le give it out,
  Thou didst this violence upon thy selfe.[12]   15
FLAMINEO. O cunning Devils! now I have tri'd your love,
  And doubled all your reaches.[13] I am not wounded :
              FLAMINEO riseth.
  The pistols held no bullets : 'twas a plot
  To prove your kindnesse[14] to mee; and I live   20
  To punish your ingratitude; I knew
  One time or other you would finde a way
  To give me a strong potion,—ô Men
  That lye upon your death-beds, and are haunted
  With howling wives, neere trust them, they'le re-   25
                      marry
  Ere the worme peirce your winding sheete : ere the
                      Spider
  Make a thinne curtaine for your Epitaphes.
    How cunning you were to discharge? Do you prac-   30
  tise at the Artillery yard?[15] Trust a woman? never,
  never; Brachiano bee my president : we lay our soules
  to pawne to the Devill for a little pleasure, and a
  woman makes the bill of sale. That ever man should
  marry! For one *Hypermnestra*[16] that sav'd her   35

---

[6] *holly-bread* : holy bread of
the Eucharist.

Lord and husband, forty nine of her sisters cut their
husbands throates all in one night. There was a shole
of vertuous horse-leeches.[7]

Here are two other Instruments.[17]

 Enter LODOVICO, [*and*] GASPARO [*disguised as*   5
  Capuchins, with] PEDRO, [*and*] CARLO.

VITTORIA.   Helpe, helpe.

FLAMINEO. What noise is that? hah? falce keies i'th
    Court.

LODOVICO. We have brought you a Maske.[18]   10

FLAMINEO.   A matachine[8] it seemes,
 By your drawne swords. Church-men turn'd revellers.

[CARLO.][1] Isabella, Isabella!

LODOVICO. Doe you know us now?

        [They throw off their   15
         disguises.]

FLAMINEO.   Lodovico and Gasparo.

LODOVICO. Yes and that Moore the Duke gave pention to
 Was the great Duke of Florence.

VITTORIA.   O wee are lost.   20

FLAMINEO. You shall not take Justice from forth my
    hands,
 O let me kill her.—Ile cut my safty
 Through your coates of steele : Fate's a Spaniell,
 Wee cannot beat it from us :[19] what remaines   25
    now?
 Let all that doe ill, take this president :
 Man may his Fate foresee, but not prevent.
 And of all Axiomes this shall winne the prise,
 'Tis better to be fortunate then wise.   30

GASPARO. Bind him to the pillar.[20]

VITTORIA.   O your gentle pitty!
 I have seene a black-bird that would sooner fly
 To a mans bosome, then to stay the gripe
 Of the feirce Sparrow-hawke.[21]   35

GASPARO.   Your hope deceives you.

---

[7] *horse-leeches :* blood-suckers.   [8] *matachine :* sword dance.

VITTORIA. If Florence be ith Court, would hee would
                 kill mee.

GASPARO. Foole! Princes give rewards with their owne
                 hands,

But death or punishment by the handes of others.   5

LODOVICO. Sirha you once did strike mee,—Ile strike you
Into the Center.

FLAMINEO. Thoul't doe it like a hangeman; a base
                 hangman;

Not like a noble fellow, for thou seest   10
I cannot strike againe.

LODOVICO.   Dost laugh?

FLAMINEO. Wouldst have me dye, as I was borne, in
                 whining?

GASPARO. Recommend your selfe to heaven.   15

FLAMINEO. Noe I will carry mine owne commendations
                 thither.

LODOVICO. Oh could I kill you forty times a day
And us't foure yeere together; 'tweare too little :
Nought greev's but that you are too few to feede   20
The famine of our vengeance. What dost thinke on?

FLAMINEO. Nothing; of nothing : leave thy idle ques-
                 tions,

I am ith way to study a long silence,
To prate were idle, I remember nothing.   25
Thers nothing of so infinit vexation
As mans owne thoughts.

LODOVICO.   O thou glorious strumpet,
Could I devide thy breath from this pure aire
When't leaves thy body, I would sucke it up   30
And breath't upon some dunghill.

VITTORIA.   You, my Deaths man;
Me thinkes thou doest not looke horrid enough,
Thou hast too[2] good a face to be a hang-man,—
If thou be doe thy office in right forme;   35
Fall downe upon thy knees and aske forgivenesse.

LODOVICO. O thou hast bin a most prodigious comet,
But Ile cut of your traine : kill the Moore first.

VITTORIA. You shall not kill her first. behould my breast,
    I will be waited on in death; my servant
    Shall never go before mee.

GASPARO.   Are you so brave.

VITTORIA. Yes I shall wellcome death   5
    As Princes doe some great Embassadors;
    Ile meete thy weapon halfe way.

LODOVICO.   Thou dost tremble,
    Mee thinkes feare should dissolve thee into ayre.

VITTORIA. O thou art deceiv'd, I am too true a woman :   10
    Conceit[22] can never kill me : Ile tell thee what,
    I will not in my death shed one base teare,
    Or if looke pale, for want of blood, not feare.

CARLO. Thou art my taske, blacke fury.

ZANCHE.   I have blood   15
    As red as either of theirs; wilt drinke some?
    'Tis good for the falling sicknesse :[23] I am proud
    Death cannot alter my complexion,
    For I shall neere looke pale.

LODOVICO.   Strike, strike,   20
    With a Joint motion.   *They strike them.*

VITTORIA.   'Twas a manly blow—
    The next thou giv'st, murder some sucking Infant,
    And then thou wilt be famous.

FLAMINEO.   O what blade ist?   25
    A Toledo, or an English Fox.[24]
    I ever thought a Cutler should distinguish
    The cause of my death, rather then a Doctor.
    Search my wound deeper : tent[9] it with the steele
    That made it.   30

VITTORIA.   O my greatest sinne lay in my blood.
    Now my blood paies for't.

FLAMINEO.   Th'art a noble sister—
    I love thee now; if woeman[25] doe breed man
    Shee ought to teach him manhood : Fare thee well.   35

[9] *tent :* probe.

Know many glorious woemen that are fam'd
For masculine vertue, have bin vitious—
Onely a happier silence did betyde them—
Shee hath no faults, who hath the art to hide them.

VITTORIA. My soule, like to a ship in a blacke storme,   5
Is driven I know not whither.

FLAMINEO.   Then cast ancor.
"Prosperity doth bewitch men seeming cleere,
But seas doe laugh, shew white, when Rocks are
          neere.   10
Wee cease to greive, cease to be fortunes slaves,
Nay cease to dye by dying." Art thou gonne
And thou[26] so neare the bottome : falce reporte
Which saies that woemen vie with the nine Muses
For nine tough durable lives : I doe not looke   15
Who went before, nor who shall follow mee;
Noe, at my selfe I will begin and end.
"While we looke up to heaven wee confound
Knowledge with knowledge." ô I am in a mist.

VITTORIA. "O happy they that never saw the Court,   20
Nor ever knew great Man but by report."
                     VITTORIA *dyes.*

FLAMINEO. I recover like a spent taper, for a flash
And instantly go out.
Let all that belong to Great men remember th'ould   25
wives tradition, to be like the Lyons ith Tower on
Candlemas day, to mourne if the Sunne shine, for
feare of the pittifull remainder of winter to come.[27]
'Tis well yet there's some goodnesse in my death,
My life was a blacke charnell : I have cought   30
An everlasting could. I have lost my voice
Most irrecoverably : Farewell glorious villaines,
"This busie trade of life appeares most vaine,
Since rest breeds rest, where all seeke paine by
          paine."[28]   35
Let no harsh flattering Bels resound my knell,
Strike thunder, and strike lowde to my farewell.
                       Dyes.

ENGLISH AMBASSADOR. [*Within.*] This way, this way,
     breake ope the doores, this way.
LODOVICO. Ha, are wee betraid?
  Why then lets constantly dye all together,
  And having finisht this most noble deede,   5
  Defy the worst of fate; not feare to bleed.
     Enter ENGLISH AMBASSADOR *and* GIOVANNI
         [*with soldiers*].
ENGLISH AMBASSADOR. Keepe backe the Prince, shoot,
     shoot,—   10
       [*Soldiers shoot* LODOVICO.]
LODOVICO. O I am wounded.
  I feare I shall be tane.
GIOVANNI.   You bloudy villaines,
  By what authority have you committed   15
  This Massakre?
LODOVICO.   By thine.
GIOVANNI.   Mine?
LODOVICO.   Yes, thy unckle
  Which is a part of thee enjoyn'd us to't.   20
  Thou knowst me I am sure, I am Count Lodowicke,
  And thy most noble unckle in disguise
  Was last night in thy Court.
GIOVANNI.   Ha!
CARLO.   Yes, that Moore   25
  Thy father chose his pentioner.
GIOVANNI.   He turn'd murderer;
  Away with them to prison, and to torture;
  All that have hands in this, shall tast our justice,
  As I hope heaven.   30
LODOVICO.   I do glory yet,
  That I can call this act mine owne : For my part,
  The racke, the gallowes, and the torturing wheele
  Shall bee but sound sleepes to me; here's my rest—
  "I limb'd[10] this night-peece and it was my best."   35
GIOVANNI. Remove the bodies, see my honoured Lord,

---

[10] *limb'd :* limned; painted.

What use you ought make of their punishment.
Let guilty men remember their blacke deedes,
Do leane on crutches, made of slender reedes.

[*Exeunt.*]

5

Instead of an Epilogue onely this of *Martial* sup-
plies me.

Haec fuerint nobis praemia si placui.[11]   10

For the action of the play, twas generally well, and
I dare affirme, with the Joint testimony of some of
their owne quality, (for the true imitation of life,
without striving to make nature a monster)[29] the
best that ever became them : whereof as I make a   15
generall acknowledgement, so in particular I must
remember the well approved industry of my freind
Maister Perkins,[12] and confesse the worth of his action did Crowne both the beginning and end.

FINIS.

[11] *Haec . . . placui :* These things will be our reward if I have pleased.

[12] *Maister Perkins :* Richard Perkins, who probably played Flamineo.

BUSSY D'AMBOIS

BY

GEORGE CHAPMAN

Bussy D'Ambois:

A TRAGEDIE:

As it hath been often Acted with great Applause.

Being much corrected and amended by the Author before his death,

LONDON:
Printed by *A. N.* for *Robert Lunne.*
1641.

HENRY III, *King of France.*
MONSIEUR, *brother of the king.*
DUKE OF GUISE.
COUNT OF MONTSURRY.
BUSSY D'AMBOIS.
BARRISOR,
L'ANOU, } *adversaries of Bussy.*
PYRHOT,
BRISAC,
MELYNELL, } *friends of Bussy.*
FRIAR *(and his* UMBRA*).*
MAFFE, *steward to Monsieur.*
NUNTIUS.
BEHEMOTH,
CARTOPHYLAX, } *spirits.*
MURDERERS.
ELENOR, *Duchess of Guise.*
TAMYRA, *Countess of Montsurry.*
MADAME DE BEAUPRE, *niece of Elenor.*
ANNABELLE, *maid to Elenor.*
PERO, *maid to Tamyra.*
CHARLOTTE, *maid to Madame de Beaupre.*
        Courtiers, Pages, Servants, and Spirits.]

[THE SCENE
PARIS.]

PROLOGUE

Not out of confidence that none but wee
Are able to present this Tragedie,
Nor out of envie at the grace of late
It did receive, nor yet to derogate
From their deserts, who give out boldly, that   5
They move with equall feet on the same flat;
Neither for all, nor any of such ends,
Wee offer it, gracious and noble friends,
To your review, wee farre from emulation
(And charitably judge from imitation)   10
With this work entertaine you, a peece knowne
And still beleev'd in Court to be our owne.
To quit our claime, doubting our right or merit,
Would argue in us poverty of spirit
Which we must not subscribe to : *Field*[1] is gone   15
Whose Action first did give it name, and one[2]
Who came the neerest to him, is denide
By his gray beard to shew the height and pride
Of *D'Ambois* youth and braverie; yet to hold
Our title still a foot, and not grow cold   20
By giving it o'er, a third man[3] with his best
Of care and paines defends our interest;
As *Richard*[4] he was lik'd, nor doe wee feare,
In personating *D'Ambois,* hee'le appeare
To faint, or goe lesse, so your free consent   25
As heretofore give him encouragement.

PROLOGUE.
[1] *Field :* Nathan Field.
[2] *one :* Joseph Taylor.
[3] *man :* Eliard Swanston.
[4] *Richard :* Shakespeare's
        Richard III.

Actus primi. Scena prima.

Enter bussy d'ambois *poore.*   5

bussy. Fortune, not Reason, rules the state of things,
Reward goes backwards, Honor on his head;
Who is not poore, is monstrous; only Need
Gives forme and worth to every humane seed.
As Cedars beaten with continuall[1] stormes,(1)   10
So great men flourish; and doe imitate
Unskilfull statuaries, who suppose
(In forming[2] a Colossus) if they make him
Stroddle enough, stroot,1 and look bigg, and gape,
Their work is goodly : so men meerely great[3]   15
(In their affected gravity of voice,
Sowernesse of countenance, manners cruelty,
Authority, wealth, and all the spawne of Fortune)
Think they beare all the Kingdomes worth before
                              them;   20
Yet differ not from those Colossick Statues,
Which with Heroique formes without o'er-spread,
Within are nought but morter, flint and lead.
Man is a Torch borne in the winde; a Dreame
But of a shadow, summ'd2 with all his substance;   25
And as great Seamen using all their wealth[4]
And skills in *Neptunes* deepe invisible pathes,
In tall ships richly built and ribd with brasse,
To put a Girdle round about the world,(1)
When they have done it (comming neere their   30
                              Haven)
Are faine[5] to give a warning peece,3 and call
A poore staid fisher-man, that never past
His Countries sight, to waft and guide them in :
So when we wander furthest through the waves   35

ACT I. SCENE i.   2 *summ'd* : clothed.
1 *stroot* : strut.   3 *peece* : cannon shot.

Of Glassie Glory and the Gulfes of State,
Topt with all Titles, spreading all our reaches,
As if each private Arme would sphere the earth,[6]
Wee must to vertue for her guide resort,
Or wee shall shipwrack in our safest Port.   5

                              Procumbit.[4]

          [*Enter*] MONSIEUR *with two Pages.*

[MONSIEUR.] There is no second place in Numerous
                              State
That holds more than a Cypher : In a King   10
All places are contain'd. His words and looks
Are like the flashes and the bolts of *Jove*,
His deeds inimitable, like the Sea
That shuts still as it opes, and leaves no tracts,
Nor prints of President[5] for meane[7] mens facts :[6]   15
There's but a Thred betwixt me and a Crowne;
I would not wish it cut, unlesse by nature;
Yet to prepare me for that possible[8] Fortune,
Tis good to[9] get resolved spirits about mee.
I follow'd D'Ambois to this greene Retreat;   20
A man of spirit beyond the reach of feare,
Who (discontent with his neglected worth)
Neglects the light, and loves obscure Abodes;
But hee is young and haughty, apt to take
Fire at advancement, to beare state, and flourish;   25
In his Rise therefore shall my bounties shine :
None lothes the world so much, nor loves to scoffe it,
But gold and grace will make him surfet of it.
What, D'Ambois?

BUSSY.   He sir.   30

MONSIEUR.   Turn'd to Earth, alive?
Up man, the Sunne shines on thee.

BUSSY.   Let it shine.
I am no mote to play in't, as great men are.

MONSIEUR. Callest[10] thou men great in state, motes in   35

---

[4] *Procumbit :* He prostrates   [5] *President :* Precedent.
    himself.   [6] *facts :* deeds.

342

                    the sunne?[2]
They say so that would have thee freeze in shades,
That (like the grosse Sicilian Gurmundist)
Empty their Noses in the Cates[7] they love,
That none may eat but they. Do thou but bring   5
Light to the Banquet Fortune sets before thee
And thou wilt loath leane Darknesse like thy Death.
Who would beleeve thy mettall could let sloth
Rust and consume it? If *Themistocles*
Had liv'd obscur'd thus in th'Athenian state,   10
Xerxes had made both him and it his slaves.
If brave *Camillus* had lurckt so in Rome,
He had not five times beene Dictator there,
Nor foure times triumpht. If *Epaminondas*
(Who liv'd twice twenty yeeres obscur'd in Thebs)   15
Had liv'd so still,[8] he had beene still unnam'd,
And paid his Country nor himselfe their right :
But putting forth his strength, he rescu'd both
From imminent ruine; and like burnisht Steele,
After long use he shin'd; for as the light   20
Not only serves to shew, but render us
Mutually profitable; so our lives
In acts exemplarie, not only winne
Our selves good Names, but doe[11] to others give
Matter for vertuous Deeds, by which wee live.[2]   25
BUSSY. What would you wish me?[12]

MONSIEUR.   Leave the troubled streames,
And live where[13] Thrivers doe, at the Well head.
BUSSY. At the Well head? Alas what should I doe
With that enchanted Glasse? See devils there?   30
Or (like a strumpet) learne to set my looks
In an eternall Brake,[9] or practise jugling,[10]
To keepe my face still fast, my heart still loose;
Or beare (like Dames Schoolmistresses their Riddles)
Two Tongues, and be good only for a shift;   35

---

[7] *Cates :* Delicacies.   [9] *Brake :* Vise; mask.
[8] *still :* always.   [10] *jugling :* trickery.

343

Flatter great Lords, to put them still in minde
Why they were made Lords : or please humor-
 ous[14] Ladies
With a good carriage, tell them idle Tales,
To make their Physick work; spend a mans life 5
In sights and visitations, that will make
His eyes as hollow as his Mistresse heart :
To doe none good, but those that have no need;
To gaine being forward, though you break for haste
All the Commandements ere you break your fast; 10
But Beleeve backwards, make your Period
And Creeds last Article, "I beleeve in God" :
And (hearing villanies preacht t'unfold[3] their
 Art)[15]
Learne to commit them, 'Tis a great mans Part. 15
Shall I learne this there?
MONSIEUR.   No, thou needst not learne,
Thou hast the Theorie, now goe there and practise.
BUSSY. I, in a thrid-bare suit; when men come there,
They must have high Naps,[11] and goe from thence 20
 bare :
A man may drowne the parts[12] of ten rich men
In one poore suit, Brave Barks, and outward Glosse
Attract Court Loves,[16] be in parts ne're so grosse.
MONSIEUR. Thou shalt have Glosse enough, and all things 25
 fit
T'enchase in all shew thy long smothered spirit :
Be rul'd by me then. The old[17] Scythians
Painted blinde Fortunes powerfull hands with
 wings,[4] 30
To shew her gifts come swift and suddenly,
Which if her Favorite be not swift to take,
He loses them for ever. Then be wise :[18]
Stay but a while here, and I'le send to thee.
   Exit MONSIEUR [*with Pages.*] *Manet* BUSSY. 35

---

[11] *Naps :* New, rich clothing. [12] *parts :* talents.

BUSSY. What will he send? some Crowns? It is to sow
     them
 Upon my spirit, and make them spring a Crowne
 Worth Millions of the seed Crownes he will send.
 Like[19] to disparking[13] noble Husbandmen,   5
 Hee'll put his Plow into me, Plow me up :
 But his unsweating thrift[5] is policie,[19]
 And learning-hating policie is ignorant
 To fit his seed-land soyl;[20] a smooth plain ground
 Will never nourish any politick seed;   10
 I am for honest Actions, not for great :
 If I may bring up a new fashion,
 And rise in Court for[21] vertue; speed his plow :
 The King hath knowne me long as well as hee,
 Yet could my Fortune never fit the length   15
 Of both their understandings till this houre.
 There is a deepe nicke in times restlesse wheele
 For each mans good, when which nicke comes it
     strikes;
 As Rhetorick, yet workes not perswasion,   20
 But only is a meane to make it worke :
 So no man riseth by his reall merit,
 But when it cries Clincke in his Raisers spirit.
 Many will say, that cannot rise at all,
 Mans first houres rise is first step to his fall :   25
 I'le venture that; men that fall low must die,
 As well as men cast head long from the skie.
     Enter MAFFE.
MAFFE. Humor of Princes! Is this wretch[22] indu'd
 With any merit worth a thousand Crownes?   30
 Will my Lord have me be so ill a Steward
 Of his Revenue, to dispose a summe
 So great with so small cause as shewes in him?
 I must examine this : Is your name D'Ambois?
BUSSY. Sir.   35

13 *disparking :* plowing up
 parks.

MAFFE.   Is your name D'Ambois?

BUSSY.   Who have we here?

  Serve you the Monsieur?

MAFFE.   How?

BUSSY.   Serve you the Monsieur?   5

MAFFE. Sir, y'are very hot. I doe serve[23] the
                          Monsieur;

  But in such place[24] as gives me the Command

  Of all his other servants :[24] And because

  His Graces pleasure is, to give your good   10

  His Passe[14, 25] through my Command, Me thinks
                you might

  Use me with more respect.[26]

BUSSY.   Crie you mercy.

  Now you have opened my dull eies, I see you;   15

  And would be glad to see the good you speake of :

  What might I call your name?

MAFFE.   Monsieur Maffe.

BUSSY. Monsieur Maffe? Then good Monsieur Maffe,

  Pray let me know you better.   20

MAFFE.   Pray doe so,

  That you may use me better. For your selfe,

  By your no better outside, I would judge you

  To be some[27] Poet; Have you given my Lord

  Some Pamphlet?   25

BUSSY.   Pamphlet?

MAFFE.   Pamphlet sir, I say.

BUSSY. Did your great Masters goodnesse[28] leave the
                good

  That is to passe your charge, to my poore use,   30

  To your discretion?

MAFFE.   Though he did not sir,

  I hope 'tis no rude[29] office to aske reason,

  How that his Grace gives me in charge goes from me?

BUSSY. That's very perfect sir.   35

MAFFE.   Why very good sir;

---

14 *His Passe :* Its passage.

I pray then give me leave : If for no Pamphlet,
May I not know what other merit in you,
Makes his compunction willing to relieve you?
BUSSY. No merit in the world sir.
MAFFE.   That is strange.   5
Y'are a poore souldier, are you?
BUSSY.   That I am sir.
MAFFE. And have Commanded?
BUSSY.   I, and gone without sir.(6)
MAFFE. [Aside.] I see the man : A hundred Crownes   10
            will make him
Swagger, and drinke healths to his Graces[30]
            bountie;
And sweare he could not be more bountifull.
So there's nine hundred Crounes sav'd; here tall15   15
            souldier
His grace hath sent you a whole hundred Crownes.
BUSSY. A hundred sir? Nay doe his Highnesse right;
I know his hand is larger, and perhaps
I may deserve more than my outside shewes :   20
I am a Poet,[31], (7) as I am a Souldier,
And I can Poetise; and (being well encourag'd)
May sing his fame for giving; yours for delivering
(Like a most faithfull Steward) what he gives.
MAFFE. What shall your subject be?   25
BUSSY.   I care not much.
If to his bounteous Grace[32] I sing the praise,
Of faire great Noses, (8) And to you of long
                              ones.[33]
What Qualities have you sir (beside your chaine16   30
And velvet Jacket) Can your worship dance?
MAFFE. A pleasant[34] fellow faith : It seemes my
                              Lord
Will have him for his Jester; And by'r lady[35]
Such men are now no fooles, 'Tis a Knights place :   35

15 *tall* : brave.   16 *chaine* : a steward's
                              insignium.

If I (to save his Grace[36] some Crounes) should
        urge him
T'abate his Bountie, I should not be heard;
I would to heaven I were an errant Asse,
For then I should be sure to have the Eares   5
Of these great men, where now their Jesters have
        them :
'Tis good to please him, yet Ile take no notice
Of his Preferment, but in policie
Will still be grave and serious, lest he thinke   10
      I feare his woodden dagger :[9] Here sir Ambo,
BUSSY. How,[38] Ambo sir?
MAFFE.   Is[37] not your name Ambo?
BUSSY. You call'd me lately D'Amboys, has your Worship
So short a head?   15
MAFFE.   I cry thee mercy D'Amboys.[38]
A thousand Crownes I bring you from my Lord;
If you be thriftie and[39] play the good husband,
        you may make
This a good standing living. 'Tis a Bountie,   20
His Highnesse might perhaps have bestow'd better.
BUSSY. Goe, y'are a Rascall; hence, Away you Rogue.
MAFFE. What meane you sir?
BUSSY.   Hence; prate no more;
Or by thy villans bloud thou prat'st thy last :   25
A Barbarous Groome, grudge at his masters Bountie :
But since I know he would as much abhorre
His hinde should argue what he gives his friend,
Take that Sir, [*He strikes him.*] for your aptnesse to
        dispute.   *Exit.* 30
MAFFE. These Crownes are set[40] in bloud, bloud be
        their fruit.   *Exit.*

ACT I. SCENE II

[SCENA SECUNDA.]

[Enter] HENRY, GUISE, MONTSURRY, ELENOR,   5
TAMYRA, BEAUPRE, PERO, CHARLOTTE, PYRA,
[and] ANNABELLE.

HENRY. Duchesse of Guise, your Grace is much enricht,
In the attendance of that[1] English virgin,[1]
That will initiate her Prime of youth,   10
(Dispos'd to Court conditions) under the hand[2]
Of your prefer'd instructions and Command,
Rather than any in the English Court,
Whose Ladies are not matcht in Christendome,
For gracefull and confirm'd behaviours;   15
More than the Court where they are bred is equall'd.
GUISE. I like not their Court-fashion,[3] it is too crest-
                        falne,
In all observance; making Demi-gods[4]
Of their great Nobles; and of their old Queene   20
An ever-yong, and most immortall Goddesse.[1]
MONTSURRY. No[5] question shee's the rarest Queene
                        in Europe.[1]
GUISE. But what's that to her Immortality?[5]
HENRY. Assure you Cosen Guise, so great a Courtier,   25
So full of majestie and Roiall parts,
No Queene in Christendome may vaunt[6] her selfe,
Her Court approves it. That's a Court indeed;
Not[2] mixt with Clowneries[7] us'd in common
                        houses;   30
But, as Courts should be th'abstracts of their king-
                        domes,
In all the Beautie, State, and Worth they hold;
So is hers, amplie, and by her inform'd.[2]
The world is not contracted in a man,   35

ACT I. SCENE II.
[1] virgin : Annabelle.   [2] inform'd : given form.

349

With more proportion and expression,
Than in her Court, her Kingdome : Our French Court
Is a meere mirror of confusion to it :
The King and subject, Lord and every slave,
Dance a continuall Haie;[3] Our Roomes of State,   5
Kept like our stables; no place more observ'd
Than a rude Market-place :[(2)] and though our
                      Custome
Keepe this assur'd confusion[8] from our eyes,
'Tis nere the lesse essentially unsightly,   10
Which they would soone see, would they change their
                      forme
To this of ours, and then compare them both;
Which we must not affect,[4] because in Kingdomes,
Where the Kings change doth breed the Subjects   15
                      terror,
Pure Innovation is more grosse than error.
MONTSURRY. No Question we shall se them imitate
(Though a farre off) the fashions of our Courts,
As they have ever Ap't us in attire;   20
Never were men so weary of their skins,
And apt to leape out of themselves as they;
Who when they travell[5] to bring forth rare men,
Come home delivered of a fine French suit :
Their Braines lie with their Tailors, and get babies   25
For their most compleat issue; Hee's sole heire[9]
To all the morall vertues, that first greetes
The light with a new fashion, which becomes them
Like Apes, disfigur'd with the attires of men.
HENRY. No Question they much wrong their reall worth,   30
In affectation of outlandish Scumme;
But they have faults, and we more;[10] They foolish-
                    proud,
To jet[6] in others plumes so haughtely;[11]
We proud, that they are proud of foolerie,   35

---

[3] *Haie* : Common rural dance.   [5] *travell : pun on* "travail."
[4] *affect :* wish.   [6] *jet :* strut.

Holding our worthes more compleat for their
 vaunts.[12]
Enter monsieur [*and*] d'ambois.

monsieur. Come mine owne sweet heart I will enter[7]
 thee.   5

Sir, I have brought a Gentleman to court;[13]
And pray, you would vouchsafe to doe him grace.

henry. D'Ambois,[14] I thinke.

bussy.   That's still my name, my Lord,
Though I be something altered in attire.   10

henry. We[15] like your alteration, and must tell
 you,[14]

We[16] have expected th'offer of your service;
For we (in feare to make mild vertue proud)
Use not to seeke her out in any man.   15

bussy. Nor doth she use to seeke out any man :
They that will winne, must wooe her.[17]

monsieur. I[18] urg'd her modestie in him, my Lord,
And gave her those Rites, that he sayes shee merits.

henry. If you have woo'd and won, then Brother weare 20
 him.

     [henry *and* guise *begin a game of chess.*]

monsieur. Th'art mine, sweet heart;[19] See here's the
 Guises Duches;

The Countesse of Montsurry,[20] Beaupre;   25
Come I'le enseame[8] thee. Ladies, y'are too many
To be in Counsell : I have here a friend,
That I would gladly enter in your Graces.[18]

bussy. 'Save you Ladyes.[21]

elenor. If you enter him in our Graces, my Lord,[22] 30
me thinkes by his blunt behaviour, he should come
out of himselfe.

tamyra. Has he never been Courtier, my Lord?

monsieur. Never, my Lady.

beaupre. And why did the Toy take him in th'head 35
now?

---

[7] *enter :* introduce to the king.   [8] *enseame :* introduce.

BUSSY. Tis leape yeare,[3] Lady, and therefore very good to enter a Courtier.

HENRY. Marke[23] Duchesse of Guise, there is one is not bashfull.

ELENOR. No my Lord, he is much guilty of the bold extremity.[23] 5

TAMYRA. The man's a Courtier at first sight.

BUSSY. I can sing prick song,[9] Lady, at first sight; and why not be a Courtier as suddenly?

BEAUPRE. Here's a Courtier rotten before he be ripe. 10

BUSSY. Thinke me not impudent, Lady, I am yet no Courtier, I desire to be one, and would gladly take entrance (Madam) under your Princely Colours.[24]

Enter BARRISOR, L'ANOU, [*and*] PYRHOT.

ELENOR. Soft[25] sir, you must rise by degrees, first 15
being the servant of some common Lady or Knights wife, then a little higher to a Lords wife; next a little higher to a Countesse; yet a little higher to a Duchesse, and then turne the ladder.[10]

BUSSY. Doe you allow a man then foure mistresses, when 20
the greatest Mistresse is alowed but three servants?

ELENOR. Where did you find that statute sir?

BUSSY. Why be judged by the Groome-porters.[11]

ELENOR. The Groome-porters?

BUSSY. I Madam, must not they judge of all gamings 25
i'th' Court?[25]

ELENOR. You talke like a gamester.

[GUISE *comes forward.*]

GUISE. Sir, know you me?

BUSSY. My Lord? 30

GUISE. I know not you : Whom doe you serve?

BUSSY. Serve, my Lord?

GUISE. Go to Companion; Your Courtship's too saucie.

BUSSY. [*Aside.*] Saucie? Companion? Tis the Guise, but

[9] *prick song :* from written music.

[10] *turne the ladder :* be hanged.

[11] *Groome-porters :* Court officials of gaming.

yet those termes might have been spar'd of the
Guiserd.[12] Companion? He's jealous by this light : are
you blind of that side Duke?[26] Ile to her againe
for that. [*To the Duchess.*] Forth princely Mistresse,[27] for the honour of Courtship. Another   5
Riddle.[28]

GUISE. Cease your Courtshippe, or by heaven Ile cut
your throat.

BUSSY. Cut my throat? cut a whetstone; young[29]
Accius Noevius,[(4)] doe as much with your tongue   10
as he did with a Rasor; cut my throat?

BARRISOR. What[30] new-come Gallant have wee heere,
that dares mate[13] the Guise thus?

L'ANOU. Sfoot[14] tis D'Ambois; The Duke mistakes him
(on my life) for some Knight of the new edition.[(5)]   15

BUSSY. Cut my throat? I would the King fear'd thy cutting of his throat no more than I feare thy cutting
of mine.[30]

GUISE. Ile[32] doe't by this hand.[31]

BUSSY.   That hand dares not doe't;   20
Y'ave cut too many throats already Guise,
And robb'd the Realme of many thousand Soules,
More precious than thine owne.[(6)] Come Madam,
                    talk on;
Sfoot, can you not talk? Talk on I say.   25
Another riddle.[33]

PYRHOT.   Here's some strange distemper.[32]

BARRISOR. Here's a sudden transmigration with D'Ambois, out of the Knights Ward,[15] into the Duches
bed.   30

L'ANOU. See what a Metamorphosis a brave[16] suit can
work.

PYRHOT. Slight[17] step to the Guise and discover him.

---

[12] *Pun on* "gizzard"; throat.
[13] *mate :* challenge.
[14] *Sfoot :* By God's foot.
[15] *Knights Ward :* A section of
the Counter, debtor's prison.
[16] *brave :* colorful.
[17] *Slight :* By God's light.

BARRISOR. By no meanes, let the new suit work, wee'll
see the issue.

GUISE. Leave your Courting.[34]

BUSSY. I will not. I say Mistresse, and I will stand unto
it, that if a woman may have three servants, a man   5
may have threescore Mistresses.

GUISE. Sirrha, Ile have you whipt out of the Court for
this insolence.

BUSSY. Whipt?[7] Such another syllable out a th'-
presence, if thou dar'st for thy Dukedome.   10

GUISE. Remember, Poultron.

MONSIEUR. Pray thee forbeare.

BUSSY. Passion of death! Were not the King here, he
should strow the Chamber like a rush.[8]

MONSIEUR. But leave Courting his wife then.   15

BUSSY. I wil not; Ile Court her in despight of him. Not
Court her! Come Madam, talk on; Feare me nothing :
[*To* GUISE.] Well mai'st thou drive thy Master from
the Court; but never D'Ambois.

MONSIEUR. His great heart will not down, tis like the Sea 20
That partly by his owne internall heat,
Partly the starrs' daily and nightly motion,
Their heat[35] and light, and partly of the place
The divers frames,[18, (9)] but[36] chiefly by the
                               Moone,   25
Bristled with surges, never will be wonne,
(No, not when th'hearts of all those powers are burst)
To make retreat into his setled home,
Till he be crown'd with his owne quiet fome.

HENRY. You have the Mate. Another.   30

GUISE. No more.

Flourish short.[37] *Exit* GUISE, *after him the King,*
                MONSIEUR whispering.

BARRISOR. Why here's the Lion skar'd with the throat of
a dunghill Cock; a fellow that has newly shak'd off   35

---

18 *divers frames :* varying
shapes.

his shackles; Now does he crow for that victory.

L'ANOU. Tis one of the best Jiggs[19] that ever was acted.

PYRHOT. Whom does the Guise suppose him to be troe?[20]

L'ANOU. Out of doubt, some new denizond Lord;[(10)] and thinks that suit newly drawne[38] out a th'-Mercers books.   5

BARRISOR. I have heard of a fellow, that by a fixt imagination looking upon a Bulbaiting, had a visible paire of hornes grew out of his forhead : and I beleeve this Gallant overjoyed with the conceit of Monsieurs cast[21] suit, imagines himself to be the Monsieur.   10

L'ANOU. And why not? as well as the Asse, stalking in the Lions case,[22] bare himselfe like a Lion, braying[39] all the huger beasts out of the Forrest?[(11)]   15

PYRHOT. Peace, he looks this way.

BARRISOR. Marrie let him look sir; what will you say now if the Guise be gone to fetch a blanquet[23] for him?

L'ANOU. Faith I beleeve it for his honour sake.[40]   20

PYRHOT. But, if D'Ambois carrie it cleane?

Exeunt Ladies.[41]

BARRISOR. True, when he curvets in the blanquet.

PYRHOT. I marrie sir.

L'ANOU. Sfoot, see how he stares on's.   25

BARRISOR. Lord blesse us, let's away.

BUSSY. Now sir, take your full view : how does the Object please ye?

BARRISOR. If you aske my opinion sir, I think your suit fits as well as if't had beene made for you.   30

BUSSY. So sir, and was that the subject of your ridiculous joylity?

L'ANOU. What's that to you sir?

---

[19] *Jiggs :* Musical farces.
[20] *troe :* Do you think?
[21] *cast :* discarded.

[22] *case :* skin.
[23] *to fetch a blanquet :* (to toss *Bussy in*).

355

BUSSY. Sir, I have observ'd all your fleerings; and resolve your selves yee shall give a strickt account for't.

Enter BRISAC [*and*] MELYNELL.

BARRISOR. O[42] miraculous jealousie![43] Doe you think your selfe such a singular subject for laughter, 5 that none can fall into the matter of[44] our merriment but you?[42]

L'ANOU. This jealousie of yours sir, confesses some close defect in your selfe, that wee never dream'd of.[45]

PYRHOT. Wee held discourse of a perfum'd Asse, that be- 10 ing disguis'd in[47] a Lions case, imagin'd himself a Lion : I hope that toucht not you.[46]

BUSSY. So, sir : Your descants[24] doe marvellous well fit this ground,[25] we shall meet where your Buffonly laughters will cost ye the best blood in your bodies. 15

BARRISOR. For lifes sake let's be gone; hee'll kill's outright else.[48]

BUSSY. Goe at your pleasures, Ile be your Ghost to haunt you, and yee sleepe an't, hang me.

L'ANOU. Goe, goe sir, Court your Mistresse. 20

PYRHOT. And be advis'd : we shall have odds against you.

BUSSY. Tush, valour stands not in number : Ile maintaine it, that one man may beat three boyes.

BRISAC. Nay, you shall have no ods of him in number 25 sir : hee's a Gentleman as good as the proudest of you, and yee shall not wrong him.

BARRISOR. Not sir.

MELYNELL. Not sir : Though he be not so rich, hee's a better man than the best of you; And I will not en- 30 dure it.

L'ANOU. Not you sir?

BRISAC. No sir, nor I.

BUSSY. I should thank you for this kindnesse, if I thought

---

[24] *descants :* musical counterpoint.

[25] *Pun on* "ground bass" *or* "melody" *and* "place."

these perfum'd musk-Cats (being out of this priviledge) durst but once mew at us.

BARRISOR. Does your confident spirit doubt that sir? Follow us[49] and try.

L'ANOU. Come sir, wee'll lead you a dance.   *Exeunt.*   5
                    Finis Actus Primi.

ACTUS SECUNDI. SCENA PRIMA.
                                                                    10
          [*Enter*] HENRY, GUISE, MONTSURRY, *and*
                    Attendants.[1]

HENRY. This desperate quarrel sprung out of their envies
     To D'Ambois sudden bravery,[1] and great spirit.
GUISE. Neither is worth their envie.   15
HENRY.   Lesse than either
     Will make the Gall of Envie overflow;
     She feeds on outcast entrailes like a Kite :
     In which foule heape, if any ill lies hid,
     She sticks her beak into it, shakes it up,   20
     And hurl's it all abroad, that all may view it.
     Corruption is her Nutriment; but touch her
     With any precious oyntment, and you kill her :
     Where[2] she finds any filth in men, she feasts,
     And with her black throat bruits it through the world   25
     (Being sound and healthfull).[1] But if she but taste
     The slenderest pittance of commended vertue,
     She surfets of it, and is like a flie,
     That passes all the bodies soundest parts,
     And dwels upon the sores; or if her squint eie   30
     Have power to find none there, she forges some :
     She makes that crooked ever which is strait;
     Call's Valour giddinesse, Justice Tyrannie :
     A wise man may shun her, she not her selfe;
     Whither soever she flies from her Harmes,   35

ACT II. SCENE I.
1 *bravery* : flaring up.

357

She beares her Foe still claspt in her own Armes :
And therefore cousen Guise let us avoid her.
Enter NUNTIUS.

NUNTIUS. What *Atlas* or *Olympus* lifts his head
   So farre past Covert,[2] that with aire enough   5
   My words may be inform'd? And from their[3]
               height
   I may be seene, and heard through all the world?
   A tale so worthy, and so fraught with wonder,
   Sticks in my jawes, and labours with event.   10
HENRY. Com'st thou from D'Ambois?
NUNTIUS.   From him, and the rest
   His friends and enemies; whose sterne fight I saw,
   And heard their words before, and in the fray.
HENRY. Relate at large what thou hast seene and heard.   15
NUNTIUS. I saw fierce D'Ambois, and his two brave
           friends
   Enter the Field, and at their heeles their foes;
   Which were the famous souldiers, Barrisor,
   L'Anou, and Pyrhot, great in deeds of Armes :   20
   All which arriv'd at the evenest peece of earth
   The field afforded; The three Challengers
   Turn'd head, drew all their rapiers, and stood ranckt :
   When face to face the three Defendants met them,
   Alike prepar'd, and resolute alike,   25
   Like bonfires of Contributorie wood,
   Every mans look shew'd, Fed with eithers spirit,
   As one had beene a mirror to another,
   Like formes of life and death each took from
          other;[2]   30
   And so were life and death mixt at their heights,
   That you could see no feare of death, for life;
   Nor love of life, for death : But in their browes
   Pyrrho's Opinion[3] in great letters shone;
   That life and death in all respects are one.   35
HENRY. Past there no sort of words at their encounter?

[2] *Covert :* Trees and forest.

NUNTIUS. As *Hector,* twixt the Hosts of Greece and Troy,
  (When *Paris* and the Spartane King should end
  The nine yeares warre) held up his brasen launce
  For signall, that both Hosts should cease from
                    Armes,[4]   5
  And heare him speak : So Barrisor (advis'd[3])
  Advanc'd his naked Rapier twixt both sides,
  Ript up[4] the Quarrell, and compar'd six lives,
  Then laid in ballance with six idle words,
  Offer'd remission and contrition too;   10
  Or else that he and D'Ambois might conclude
  The others dangers. D'Ambois lik'd the last;
  But Barrisors friends (being equally engag'd
  In the maine Quarrell) never would expose
  His life alone, to that they all deserv'd.   15
  And (for the other offer of remission)
  D'Ambois (that like a Lawrell put in fire,
  Sparkl'd[4] and spit) did much much more than
                    scorne,
  That his wrong should incense him so like chaffe,   20
  To goe so soone out; and like lighted paper,
  Approve his spirit at once both fire and ashes :
  So drew they lots, and in them Fates appointed,
  That Barrisor should fight with firie D'Ambois;
  Pyrhot with Melynell; with Brisac L'Anou :   25
  And then like flame and Powder they commixt,
  So spritely, that I wisht they had beene spirits,
  That the ne're shutting wounds, they needs must open,
  Might as they open'd, shut, and never kill :
  But D'Ambois sword (that lightned as it flew)   30
  Shot like a pointed Comet at the face
  Of manly Barrisor; and there it stucke :
  Thrice pluckt he[5] at it, and thrice drew on thrusts,
  From him, that of himselfe[6] was free as fire;

---

[3] *advis'd* : deliberately.   [4] *Ript up* : Reviewed the back-
                                           ground of.

Who[7] thrust still as he[7] pluckt, yet (past
    beliefe!)
He[8] with his subtile eye, hand, body, scap't;
At last the deadly bitten point tugg'd off,
On fell his yet undaunted Foe[9] so fiercely,   5
That (only made more horrid with his wound)
Great D'Ambois shrunke, and gave a little ground;
But soone return'd, redoubled in his danger,
And at the heart of Barrisor seal'd his anger :
Then, like as in Arden I have seene an Oke   10
Long shooke with tempests, and his loftie toppe
Bent to his root, which being at length made loose
(Even groaning with his weight) he gan to Nodde
This way and that : as loth his curled Browes
(Which he had oft wrapt in the skie with stormes)   15
Should stoope : and yet, his radicall fivers[5] burst,
Storme-like he fell, and hid the feare-cold Earth,
So fell stout Barrisor, that had stood the shocks
Of ten set Battels in your Highnesse warre,
'Gainst the sole souldier of the world, Navarre.[10]   20
GUISE. O pitious and horrid murther!
MONTSURRY.[5]   Such a life
Me thinks had mettall in it to survive
An age of men.
HENRY.   Such, often soonest end.   25
Thy felt report cals on, we long to know
On what events the other have arriv'd.
NUNTIUS. Sorrow and fury, like two opposite fumes,
Met in the upper Region of a Cloud,
At the report made by this Worthies fall,   30
Brake from the earth, and with them rose Revenge,
Entring with fresh powers his two noble friends;
And under that ods fell surcharg'd Brisac,
The friend of D'Ambois, before fierce L'Anou;
Which D'Ambois seeing, as I once did see   35

---

[5] *fivers :* fibers; roots.

In my young travels through Armenia,
An angrie Unicorne in his full cariere
Charge with too swift a foot[6] a Jeweller,
That watcht him for the Treasure of his brow;
And ere he could get shelter of a tree,   5
Naile him with his rich Antler to the Earth : [11]
So D'Ambois ranne upon reveng'd L'Anou,
Who eying th'eager point borne in his face,
And giving backe, fell back, and in his fall
His foes uncurbed sword stopt in his heart :   10
By which time all the life strings of the tw'other[7]
Were cut, and both fell as their spirit[8] flew
Upwards : and still hunt Honour at the view. [12]
And now (of all the six) sole D'Ambois stood
Untoucht, save only with the others bloud.   15

HENRY. All slaine outright but hee?[9]
NUNTIUS.   All slaine outright but he,
Who kneeling in the warme life of his friends,
(All freckled[10] with the bloud his Rapier raind)
He kist their pale lips,[11] and bade both farewell;   20
And see the bravest man the French earth beares.
    Enter MONSIEUR [*and*] D'AMBOIS, *bare[-headed.]*

BUSSY. Now is the time, y'are Princely vow'd my friend,
Performe it Princely, and obtaine my pardon.
MONSIEUR. Else Heaven forgive not me : Come on brave   25
                 friend.
                 [*They kneel before the King.*]
If ever Nature held her selfe her owne,
When the great Triall of a King and subject
Met in one bloud, both from one belly springing :   30
Now prove her vertue and her greatnesse One,
Or make the t'one the greater with the t'other,
(As true Kings should) and for your brothers love,
(Which is a speciall species of true vertue)
Doe that you could not doe, not being a King. [13]   35
HENRY. Brother I know your suit; these wilfull murthers
Are ever past our pardon.
MONSIEUR.   Manly slaughter

Should never beare th'account of wilfull murther;
It being a spice of[6] justice, where with life
Offending past law, equall life is laid
In equall balance, to scourge that offence
By law of reputation, which to men   5
Exceeds all positive law, and what that leaves
To true mens valours (not prefixing rights
Of satisfaction, suited to their wrongs)
A free mans eminence may supply and take.

HENRY. This would make every man that thinks him   10
                              wrong'd,
Or is offended, or in wrong or right,
Lay on this violence, and all vaunt themselves,
Law-menders and supplyers though meere Butchers;
Should this fact (though of justice) be forgiven?   15

MONSIEUR. O no, my Lord; it would make Cowards
                              feare
To touch the reputations of true[12] men,
When only they are left to impe[7] the law,
Justice will soone distinguish murtherous minds   20
From just revengers : Had my friend beene slaine,
(His enemy surviving) he should die,
Since he had added to a murther'd fame
(Which was in his intent) a murthered man;
And this had worthily beene wilfull murther :   25
But my friend only sav'd his fames deare life,
Which is above life, taking th'under value,
Which in the wrong it did was forfeit to him;
And in this fact only preserves a man
In his uprightnesse; worthy to survive   30
Millions of such as murther men alive.

HENRY. Well brother, rise, and raise your friend withall
From death to life : and D'Ambois, let your life
(Refin'd by passing through this merited death)
Be purg'd from more such foule pollution;   35

---

[6] *spice of* : kind of.   [7] *impe* : mend.

362

Nor on your scape, nor valour more presuming,
To be againe so daring.[13]

BUSSY.   My Lord,
I lothe as much a deed of unjust death,
As law it selfe doth; and to Tyrannise,   5
Because I have a little spirit to dare,
And power to doe, as to be Tyranniz'd;
This is a grace that (on my knees redoubled)
I crave to double this my short lifes gift.
And shall your royall bountie Centuple,   10
That I may so make good what law[14] and nature
Have given me for my good : since I am free,
(Offending no Just law) let no law make
By any wrong it does, my life her slave :
When I am wrong'd and that law failes to right me,   15
Let me be King my selfe (as man was made)
And doe a justice that exceeds the law :
If my wrong passe the power of single valour
To right and expiate; then be you my King,
And doe a Right, exceeding Law and Nature :   20
Who to himselfe is law, no law doth need,
Offends no Law,[15] and is a King indeed.(14)

HENRY. Enjoy what thou intreat'st, we give but ours.[16]
BUSSY. What you have given, my Lord, is ever yours,[16]
                    Exit Rex cum MONTSURRY.   25
GUISE. Who would[17] have pardon'd such a murther?
                                          Exit.

MONSIEUR. Now vanish horrors into Court attractions,
For which let this balme make thee fresh and faire.
And[18] now forth with thy service to the Duchesse,   30
As my long love will to Montsurrys Countesse. *Exit.*
BUSSY. To whom my love hath long been vow'd in heart,
Although in hand for shew I held the Duchesse.
And now through bloud and vengeance, deeds of
                                          height,   35
And hard to be atchiev'd, tis fit I make
Attempt of her perfection, I need feare

363

No check in his Rivality, since her vertues
. Are so renown'd, and hee of all Dames hated.[18]

Exit.

[SCENA SECUNDA.][1]

Enter MONSIEUR, TAMYRA, *and* PERO *with a Booke.*

MONSIEUR. Pray thee regard thine owne good, if not
          mine,   10
And cheere my Love for that; you doe not know
What you may be by me, nor what without me;
I may have power t'advance and pull downe any.
TAMYRA. That's not my study. One way I am sure
   You shall not pull downe me; my husbands height   15
Is crowne to all my hopes, and his retiring
To any meane state, shall be my aspiring :
Mine honour's in mine owne hands, spite of kings.
MONSIEUR. Honour, what's that? your second mayden-
          head :   20
And what is that? a word; the word is gone,
The thing remaines; the Rose is pluckt, the stalk
Abides : an easie losse where no lack's found.
Beleeve it, there's as small lack in the losse,
As there is pain ith'losing : Archers ever   25
Have two strings to a bow, and shall great *Cupid*
(Archer of Archers both in men and women)
Be worse provided than a common Archer?
A Husband and a Friend all wise Wives have.
TAMYRA. Wise wives they are that on such strings de-   30
          pend,
With a firme husband joyning a lose[2] friend.
MONSIEUR. Still you stand on your husband, so doe all
The common sex of you, when y're encounter'd
With one ye cannot fancie : all men know   35
You live in Court here by your owne election,
Frequenting all our common[3] sports and triumphs,
All the most youthfull company of men :

And wherefore doe you this? To please your husband?
Tis grosse and fulsome : if your husbands pleasure
Be all your Object, and you ayme at Honour,
In living close to him, Get you from Court,
You may have him at home : these common Put-ofs   5
Your common women serve : "my honour? husband?"
Dames maritorious,[1],(1) ne're were meritorious :
Speak plaine, and say "I doe not like you Sir,
Y'are an ill-favour'd fellow in my eye"
And I am answer'd.   10

TAMYRA.   Then I pray be you[4] answer'd :
For in good faith my Lord I doe not like you
In that sort you like.

MONSIEUR.   Then have at you here :
Take (with a politique hand) this rope of Pearle;   15
And though you be not amorous, yet be wise :
Take me for wisedom; he that you can love
Is nere the further from you.

TAMYRA.   Now it comes
So ill prepar'd, that I may take a poyson   20
Under a medicine as good cheap[2] as it :
I will not have it were it worth the world.

MONSIEUR. Horror of death : could I but please your
                 eye,
You would give me the like, ere you would loose me :   25
Honour and husband?

TAMYRA.   By this light my Lord.
Y'are a vile fellow : and Ile tell the King
Your occupation of dishonouring Ladies
And of his Court : a Lady cannot live   30
As she was borne, and with that sort of pleasure
That fits her state, but she must be defam'd
With an infamous Lords detraction :
Who would endure the Court if these attempts,

ACT II. SCENE II.

[1] *maritorious :* overconscious of   [2] *as good cheap :* for as good a
their husbands.   bargain.

Of open and profest lust must be borne?
Whose there? come on Dame,[3] you are at your book
When men are at your Mistresse; have I taught you
Any such waiting womans quality?[(2)]

MONSIEUR. Farewell "good husband."   5

TAMYRA.   Farewell wicked Lord.

                        Exit MONSIEUR.

         Enter MONTSURRY.

MONTSURRY. Was not the Monsieur here?

TAMYRA.   Yes, to good purpose.   10
And your cause is as good to seek him too,
And haunt his company.

MONTSURRY.   Why, what's the matter?

TAMYRA. Matter of death, were I some husbands wife :
I cannot live at quiet in my chamber   15
For opportunities almost to rapes
Offerd me by him.

MONTSURRY.   Pray thee beare with him :
Thou know'st he is a Bachelor, and a Courtier,
I, and a Prince : and their prerogatives[(3)]   20
Are, to their lawes, as to their pardons are
Their reservations, after Parliaments,
One quits another : forme gives all their essence :
The Prince doth high in vertues reckoning stand
That will entreat a vice, and not command :   25
So farre beare with him : should another man
Trust to his priviledge, he should trust to death :
Take comfort then (my comfort) nay triumph,
And crown thy selfe, thou part'st with victory :
My presence is so onely deare to thee,   30
That other mens appeare worse than they be.
For this night yet, beare with my forced absence :
Thou know'st my businesse; and with how much
                weight,
My vow hath charged it.   35

TAMYRA.   True my Lord, and never

[3] *Dame :* Pero.

My fruitlesse love shall let[4] your serious honour,[5]
Yet, sweet Lord, do not stay, you know my soule
Is so long time without me, and I dead
As you are absent.

MONTSURRY.　　　　By this kisse, receive　　　　　5
My soule for hostage, till I see my love.

TAMYRA. The morne shall let me see you.

MONTSURRY.　　　　　　　　With the sunne
Ile visit thy more comfortable beauties.

TAMYRA. This is my comfort, that the sunne hath left　10
The whole worlds beauty ere my sunne leaves me.

MONTSURRY. Tis late night now indeed : farewell my
　　　　　　　　light.　　　　　　　*Exit.*

TAMYRA. Farewell my light and life : But not in him,
In[6] mine owne dark love and light bent to an-　15
　　　　　other.[6]
Alas, that in the wave[7] of our affections
We should supply it with a full dissembling,
In which each youngest Maid is grown a Mother,
Frailty is fruitfull, one sinne gets another :　　　　20
Our loves like sparkles are that brightest shine,
When they goe out; most vice shewes most divine :
Goe Maid, to bed, lend me your book I pray :
Not like your selfe, for forme, Ile this night trouble
None of your services : Make sure the dores,　　　25
And call your other fellowes to their rest.

PERO. I will, [*Aside.*] yet I will watch to know why
　　　　　　　　you watch.　　　　　　　*Exit.*

TAMYRA. Now all yee[8] peacefull regents of the night,
Silently-gliding exhalations,[5]　　　　　　　　30
Languishing windes, and murmuring falls of waters,
Sadnesse of heart, and ominous securenesse,
Enchantments, dead sleepes, all the friends of rest,
That ever wrought upon the life of man,
Extend your utmost strengths; and this charm'd houre　35
Fix like the Center :(4) make the violent wheeles

----

[4] *let :* obstruct.　　　　　[5] *exhalations :* meteors.

Of Time and Fortune stand; and Great Existens
(The Makers treasurie) now not seeme to be,
To all but my approaching friends and me :
They come, alas they come, feare, feare and hope
Of one thing, at one instant fight in me :   5
I love what most I loath, and cannot live
Unlesse I compasse that which[9] holds my death :
For lifes meere death loving one that loathes me,[10]
And he I love, will loath me when he sees
I flie my sex, my vertue, my Renowne,   10
To runne so madly on a man unknowne.

                    The Vault opens.[11]

See,[12] see a Vault is opening that was never
Knowne to my Lord and husband, nor to any
But him that brings the man I love, and me;   15
How shall I looke on him? how shall I live
And not consume in blushes, I will in;[12]
And cast my selfe off, as I ne're had beene.[6, (5)]

                        Exit.[13]

      Ascendit FRIAR *and* D'AMBOIS.   20

FRIAR.[14] Come worthiest sonne, I am past measure
             glad,
That you (whose worth I have approv'd so long)
Should be the Object of her fearefull love;
Since both your wit and spirit can adapt   25
Their full force to supply her utmost weaknesse :
You know [her] worths[15] and vertues, for Report
Of all that know, is to a man a knowledge :
You know besides, that our affections storme,
Rais'd in our bloud, no Reason can reforme.   30
Though she seeke then their satisfaction,
(Which she must needs, or rest unsatisfied)
Your judgement will esteeme her peace thus wrought,
Nothing lesse deare, than if your selfe had sought :
And (with another colour,[7] which my Art   35

---

[6] *And cast . . . had beene :*   [7] *colour :* pretence.
  Commit myself recklessly.

Shall teach you to lay on) your selfe must seeme
The onely agent, and the first Orbe move,[16], (6)
In this our set, and cunning world of Love.
BUSSY. Give me the colour (my most honour'd Father)
And trust my cunning then to lay it on.   5
FRIAR. Tis this, good sonne; Lord Barrisor (whom you
                    slew)
Did love her dearely, and with all fit meanes
Hath urg'd his acceptation, of all which
Shee keepes one letter written in his blood :   10
You must say thus then, that you heard from mee
How much her selfe was toucht in conscience
With a Report (which is in truth disperst)
That your maine quarrell grew about her love,
Lord Barrisor imagining your Courtship   15
Of the great Guises Duchesse in the Presence,
Was by you made to his elected Mistresse;
And so made me your meane now to resolve her,
Chosing (by my direction) this nights depth.
For the more cleare avoiding of all note   20
Of your presumed presence, and with this
(To cleare her hands of such a Lovers blood) (7)
She will so kindly thank and entertaine you,
(Me thinks I see how) I, and ten to one,
Shew you the confirmation in his blood,   25
Lest you should think report, and she did faine,
That you shall so have circumstantiall meanes,
To come to the direct, which must be used :
For the direct is crooked; Love comes flying;
The height of love is still wonne with denying.   30
BUSSY. Thanks honoured Father.
FRIAR.   Shee must never know
That you know any thing of any love (8)
Sustain'd on her part : For learne this of me;
In any thing a woman does alone,   35
If she dissemble, she thinks tis not done;
If not dissemble, nor a little chide,
Give her her wish, she is not satisfi'd;

To have a man think that she never seekes,
Does her more good than to have all she likes :
This frailty sticks in them beyond their sex;
Which to reforme, reason is too perplex : [9]
Urge reason to them, it will doe no good;   5
Humour (that is the charriot of our food
In every body) must in them be fed,
To carrie their affections by it bred.
Stand close.

      Enter TAMYRA *with a Book.*[17]   10

TAMYRA. Alas, I feare my strangenesse[8] will retire him :
If he goe back, I die; I must prevent it,
And cheare his onset with my sight at least,
And that's the most; though every step he takes
Goes to my heart, Ile rather die than seeme   15
Not to be strange to that I most esteeme.

FRIAR. Madam.

TAMYRA.   Ah!

FRIAR.   You will pardon me, I hope,
That, so beyond your expectation,   20
(And at a time for visitants so unfit)
I (with my noble friend here) visit you :
You know that my accesse at any time
Hath ever beene admitted; and that friend
That my care will presume to bring with me,   25
Shall have all circumstance of worth in him,
To merit as free welcome as my selfe.

TAMYRA. O Father, but at this suspicious houre
You know how apt best men are to suspect us,
In any cause, that makes suspicious[18] shadow   30
No greater than the shadow of a haire :
And y'are to blame : what though my Lord and
              husband
Lie forth to night? and since I cannot sleepe
When he is absent, I sit up to night,   35
Though all the dores are sure, and all our servants

---

[8] *strangenesse* : aloofness.

As sure bound with their sleepes; yet there is one
That wakes[19] above, whose eye no sleepe can
    binde :
He sees through dores, and darknesse, and our
    thoughts;   5
And therefore as we should avoid with feare,
To think amisse our selves before his search;
So should we be as curious[9] to shunne
All cause that other think not ill of us.

BUSSY. Madam, 'tis farre from that : I only heard   10
By this my honour'd Father, that your conscience
Made some deepe scruple[20] with a false report;
That Barrisors blood should something touch your
    honour,[21]
Since he imagin'd I was courting you,   15
When I was bold to change words with the Duchesse,
And[22] therefore made his quarrell, his long love
And service, as I heare, being deepely vowed
To your perfections, which my ready presence[22]
Presum'd on with my Father at this season,   20
For the more care of your so curious honour,
Can well resolve your Conscience, is most false.

TAMYRA. And is it therefore that you come good sir?
Then crave I now your pardon and my Fathers,
And sweare your presence does me so much good,[23]   25
That all I have it bindes to your requitall :
Indeed sir, 'tis most true that a report
Is spread, alleadging that his love to me
Was reason of your quarrell, and because
You shall not think I faine it for my glory,   30
That he importun'd me for his Court service,
I'le shew you his own hand, set down in blood
To that vaine purpose : Good sir, then come in.
Father I thank you now a thousand fold.
                Exit TAMYRA *and* D'AMBOIS.[24]   35

---

[9] *curious :* scrupulous.

FRIAR. May it be worth it to you honour'd daughter.
            Descendit FRIAR.
      Finis Actus Secundi.

5

    ACTUS TERTII. SCENA PRIMA.

Enter D'AMBOIS [*and*] TAMYRA, *with a Chaine of*
Pearle.

BUSSY. Sweet[1] Mistresse cease, your conscience is too   10
            nice,¹
    And bites too hotly of the Puritane spice.[1]
TAMYRA. O my deare servant, in thy close embraces,
    I have set open all the dores of danger
    To my encompast honour, and my life :   15
    Before I was secure against death and hell;
    But now am subject to the heartlesse feare,
    Of every shadow, and of every breath,
    And would change firmnesse with an aspen leafe :
    So confident a spotlesse conscience is;   20
    So weake a guilty : O the dangerous siege
    Sinne layes about us? and the tyrannie
    He exercises when he hath expugn'd :²
    Like to the horror of a Winters thunder,
    Mixt with a gushing storme, that suffer nothing   25
    To stirre abroad on earth, but their own rages,
    Is sinne, when it hath gathered head above us,
    No roofe, no shelter can secure us so,
    But he will drowne our cheeks in feare or woe.
BUSSY. Sin is a coward Madam, and insults   30
    But on our weaknesse, in his truest valour : (1)
    And so our ignorance tames us, that we let
    His shadows fright us : and like empty clouds
    In which our faulty apprehensions forge
    The formes of Dragons, Lions, Elephants,   35

ACT III. SCENE I.   ² *expugn'd :* conquered by
¹ *nice :* sensitive.   force.

When they hold no proportion : the slie charmes
Of the witch policy makes him, like a Monster
Kept onely to shew men for Servile[2] money :
That false hagge often paints him in[3] her cloth
Ten times more monstrous than he is in troth :   5
In three of us, the secret of our meeting,
Is onely guarded, and three friends as one
Have ever beene esteem'd : as our three powers[3]
That in one soule,[4] are, as one united :
Why should we feare then? for my selfe[5] I sweare   10
Sooner shall torture be the Sire to pleasure,
And health be grievous to one[6] long time sick,
Than the deare jewell of your fame in me,
Be made an out-cast to your infamy;
Nor shall my value (sacred to your vertues)   15
Onely give free course to it, from my selfe :
But make it flie out of the mouthes of Kings
In golden vapours, and with awfull wings.

TAMYRA. It rests as all Kings seales were set in thee.
Now[7] let us call my Father, whom I sweare   20
I could extreamly chide, but that I feare
To make him so suspicious of my love
Of which (sweet servant) doe not let him know
For all the world.

BUSSY.   Alas! he will not think it?   25

TAMYRA. Come then—ho? Father, ope, and take your
                        friend.

Ascendit FRIAR.

FRIAR. Now honour'd daughter, is your doubt resolv'd.

TAMYRA. I Father, but you went away too soone.   30

FRIAR. Too soone?

TAMYRA.   Indeed you did, you should have stayed;
Had not your worthy friend beene of your bringing,
And that containes all lawes to temper me,

---

[3] *three powers* : Vegetative,
Sensory, and Reasoning
faculties.

Not all the fearefull danger that besieged us,
Had aw'd my throat from exclamation.

FRIAR. I know your serious disposition well.
Come sonne the morne comes on.

BUSSY.   Now honour'd Mistresse   5
Till farther service call, all blisse supply you.

TAMYRA. And you this chaine of pearle, and my love
                    onely.[7]

> *Descendit* FRIAR *and* D'AMBOIS.

It is not I, but urgent destiny,   10
That (as great States-men for their generall end
In politique justice, make poore men offend)
Enforceth my offence to make it just :
What shall weak Dames doe, when th'whole work of
                    Nature   15
Hath a strong finger in each one of us?
Needs must that sweep away the silly cobweb
Of our still-undone labours; that layes still
Our powers to it : as to the line, the stone,
Not to the stone, the line should be oppos'd.[8], (2)   20
We cannot keepe our constant course in vertue :
What is alike at all parts? every day
Differs from other : every houre and minute :
I, every thought in our false clock of life,
Oft times inverts the whole circumference :   25
We must be sometimes one, sometimes another :
Our bodies are but thick clouds to our soules;
Through which they cannot shine when they desire :
When all the starres, and even the sunne himselfe,
Must stay the vapours times that he exhales   30
Before he can make good his beames to us :
O how can we, that are but motes to him,
Wandring at randon in his ordered rayes,
Disperse our passions fumes, with our weak labours,
That are more thick and black than all earths   35
                    vapours?

> *Enter* MONTSURRY.

MONTSURRY. Good day, my love : what up and ready[4]
        too!
TAMYRA. Both, (my deare Lord) not all this night
        made I
My selfe unready, or could sleep a wink.   5
MONTSURRY. Alas, what troubled my true Love? my
        peace,
From being at peace within her better selfe?
Or how could sleepe forbeare to seize thine eyes[9]
When he might challenge them as his just prise?   10
TAMYRA. I am in no powre earthly, but in yours;
To what end should I goe to bed my Lord,
That wholly mist the comfort of my bed?
Or how should sleepe possesse my faculties,
Wanting the proper closer of mine eyes?   15
MONTSURRY. Then will I never more sleepe night from
        thee :
All mine owne Businesse, all the Kings affaires,
Shall take the day to serve them : Every night
Ile ever dedicate to thy delight.   20
TAMYRA. Nay, good my Lord esteeme not my desires
Such doters on their humours, that my judgement
Cannot subdue them to your worthier pleasure :
A wives pleas'd husband must her object be
In all her acts, not her sooth'd fantasie.[5]   25
MONTSURRY. Then come my Love, Now pay those Rites
        to sleepe
Thy faire eyes owe him : shall we now to bed?
TAMYRA. O no my Lord, your holy Friar sayes,
All couplings in the day that touch the bed,   30
Adultrous are, even in the married;
Whose grave and worthy doctrine, well I know,
Your faith in him will liberally allow.
MONTSURRY. Hee's a most learned and Religious man :
Come to the Presence then, and see great D'Ambois 35

---

[4] *ready :* dressed.   [5] *fantasie :* imagination.

(Fortunes proud mushrome[3] shot up in a night)
Stand like an *Atlas* under our Kings arme;[10]
Which greatnesse with him Monsieur now envies
As bitterly and deadly as the Guise.

TAMYRA. What, he that was but yesterday his maker?   5
His raiser and preserver?

MONTSURRY.   Even the same.
Each naturall agent works but to this end,
To render that it works on, like itselfe;
Which since the Monsieur in his act on D'Ambois,   10
Cannot to his ambitious end effect,
But that (quite opposite) the King hath power
(In his love borne to D'Ambois) to convert
The point of Monsieurs aime on his owne breast,
He turnes his outward love to inward hate :   15
A Princes love is like the lightnings fume,
Which no man can embrace, but must consume.[4]

Exeunt.

20

[SCENA SECUNDA.]

[*Enter*] HENRY, D'AMBOIS, MONSIEUR, GUISE, ELENOR,
   ANNABELLE, CHARLOTTE, [*and*] *Attendants*.[1]

HENRY. Speak home Bussy,[2] thy impartiall words   25
Are like brave Faulcons that dare trusse[1] a Fowle
Much greater than themselves; Flatterers are Kites[2]
That check at[3] Sparrowes;[3] thou shalt be my
          Eagle,
And beare my thunder underneath thy wings :   30
Truths words like jewels hang in th'eares of Kings.

BUSSY. Would I might live to see no Jewes hang there
In steed of jewels; sycophants I meane,
Who use truth like the Devill, his true Foe,

ACT III. SCENE II.
[1] *trusse* : seize.   [3] *check at* : pursue wrongly and
[2] *Kites* : Carrion birds of prey.   ignobly.

Cast by the Angell to the pit of feares,
And bound in chaines; truth seldome decks Kings
          eares :
Slave flattery (like a Rippiers[4] legs rowl'd up
In boots of hay-ropes) with Kings soothed guts   5
Swadled and strappl'd now lives onely free.[(1)]
O tis a subtle knave; how like the plague
Unfelt, he strikes into the braine of man,[4]
And rageth in his entrailes when he can,
Worse than the poison of a red hair'd man?[(2)]   10
HENRY. Fly at him and his brood, I cast thee off,[5]
And once more give thee surname of mine Eagle.
BUSSY. Ile make you sport enough then, let me have
My lucerns[6] too, (or dogs inur'd to hunt
Beasts of most rapine) but to put them up,[7]   15
And if I trusse not,[(3)] let me not be trusted :
Shew me a great man (by the peoples voice,
Which is the voice of God) that by his greatnesse
Bumbasts[8] his private roofes, with publique riches;
That affects royaltie, rising from a clapdish;[9]   20
That rules so much more by[5] his suffering[(4)] King,
That he makes Kings of his subordinate slaves :
Himselfe and them graduate[(5)] like woodmongers
(Piling a stack of billets) from the earth,
Raising each other into steeples heights;   25
Let him convey this on the turning props
Of Protean Law, and (his owne counsell keeping[10])
Keepe all upright; let me but hawlk at him,
Ile play the Vulture, and so thump his liver,[(6)]
That (like a huge unlading Argosea)   30
He shall confesse all, and you then may hang him.
Shew me a Clergie man, that is in voice

---

[4] *Rippiers :* Fish peddler's.
[5] *cast thee off :* free for attack.
[6] *lucerns :* hounds.
[7] *put them up :* hunt them out.

[8] *Bumbasts :* Pads; stuffs (*a tailor's term*).
[9] *clapdish :* beggar's bowl.
[10] *his . . . keeping :* by retaining a special lawyer.

A Lark of Heaven, in heart a Mowle of earth;
That hath good living, and a wicked life;
A temperate look, and a luxurious gut;
Turning the rents of his superfluous Cures[11]
Into your Phesants and your Partriches;   5
Venting their Quintessence as men read Hebrew :[12]
Let me but hawlk at him, and, like the other,
He shall confesse all, and you then may hang him.
Shew me a Lawyer that turnes sacred law
(The equall rendrer of each man his owne,   10
The scourge of Rapine and Extortion,
The Sanctuary and impregnable defence
Of retir'd learning, and beseiged[6] vertue)
Into a Harpy, that eates all but's owne,
Into the damned sinnes it punisheth;   15
Into the Synagogue of theeves and Atheists;
Blood into gold, and justice into lust :
Let me but hawlk at him, as at the rest,[7]
He shall confesse all, and you then may hang him.
        Enter MONTSURRY, TAMYRA, *and* PERO.[8]   20
GUISE. Where will you find such game as you would
                        hawlk at?
BUSSY. Ile hawlk about your house for one of them.
GUISE. Come, y'are a glorious[13] Ruffin,[7] and runne
                        proud   25
Of the Kings headlong graces; hold your breath,
Or by that poyson'd vapour not the King
Shall back your murtherous valour against me.
BUSSY. I would the King would make his presence free
But for one bout[9] betwixt us : By the reverence   30
Due to the sacred space twixt kings and subjects,
Here would I make thee cast that popular purple,[14,(8)]
In which thy proud soule sits and braves[15] thy
                        soveraigne.

[11] *superfluous Cures :* more
   than one parish.
[12] *Hebrew;* i.e. backwards.
[13] *glorious :* bragging.
[14] *popular purple :* rabble-
   rousing royalty.
[15] *braves :* flaunts.

MONSIEUR. Peace, peace, I pray thee peace.

BUSSY.   Let him peace first
  That made the first warre.

MONSIEUR.   He's the better man.

BUSSY. And therefore may doe worst?   5

MONSIEUR.   He has more titles.

BUSSY. So *Hydra* had more heads.

MONSIEUR.   He's greater knowne.

BUSSY. His greatnesse is the peoples, mine's mine owne.

MONSIEUR. He's noblier[10] borne.   10

BUSSY.   He is not, I am noble.[10]
  And noblesse in his blood hath no gradation
  But in his merit.

GUISE.   Th'art not nobly borne,
  But bastard to the Cardinall of Ambois.(9)   15

BUSSY. Thou liest proud Guiserd; let me flie (my Lord).

HENRY. Not in my face; (my Eagle) violence flies
  The Sanctuaries of a Princes eyes.

BUSSY. Still shall we chide? and fome upon this bit?
  Is the Guise onely great in faction?   20
  Stands he not by himselfe? Proves he th'Opinion
  That mens soules are without them? Be a Duke,
  And lead me to the field.(10)

GUISE.   Come, follow me.

HENRY. Stay them, stay D'Ambois; Cosen Guise, I   25
                          wonder
  Your honour'd[11] disposition brooks so ill
  A man so good, that only would uphold
  Man in his native noblesse, from whose fall
  All our dissentions rise; that in himselfe   30
  (Without the outward patches of our frailty,
  Riches and honour) knowes he comprehends
  Worth with the greatest : Kings had never borne
  Such boundlesse Empire[12] over other men,
  Had all maintain'd the spirit and state of D'Ambois;   35
  Nor had the full impartiall hand of nature
  That all things gave in her originall,
  Without these definite terms of Mine and Thine,

Beene turn'd unjustly to the hand of Fortune,
Had all preserv'd her in her prime, like D'Ambois;
No envie, no disjunction had dissolv'd,
Or pluck'd one stick out[13] of the golden faggot,
In which the world of *Saturne* bound our lifes,[14]   5
Had all beene held together with the nerves,
The genius and th'ingenious[16], [15], (11) soule of
         D'Ambois.
Let my hand therefore be the Hermean rod[17]
To part and reconcile, and so conserve you,   10
As my combin'd embracers and supporters.
BUSSY. Tis our Kings motion, and we shall not seeme
(To worst eies) womanish, though we change thus
        soone
Never so great grudge for his greater pleasure.   15
GUISE. I seale to that, and so the manly freedome
That you so much professe, hereafter prove not
A bold and glorious licence to deprave :
To me his hand shall hold[16] the Hermean vertue
His grace affects, in which submissive signe   20
On this his sacred right hand, I lay mine.
BUSSY. Tis well my Lord, and so your worthy greatnesse
Decline not to[17] the greater insolence,
Nor make you think it a Prerogative,
To rack mens freedomes with the ruder wrongs;   25
My hand (stuck full of lawrell, in true signe
Tis wholly dedicate to righteous peace)
In all submission kisseth th'other side.
HENRY. Thanks to ye both : and kindly I invite ye
Both to a banquet where weele sacrifice   30
Full cups to confirmation of your loves;
At which (faire Ladies) I entreat your presence.
And[18] hope you Madam will take one carowse
For reconcilement of your Lord and servant.
ELENOR. If I should faile my Lord, some other Lady   35

---

[16] ingenuous (*spelled same as*   [17] *the Hermean rod :* the Cadu-
ingenious).   ceus, bearing two serpents.

Would be found there to doe that for my servant.

MONSIEUR. Any of these here?

ELENOR.   Nay, I know not that.

BUSSY. Think your thoughts, like my Mistresse, honour'd
                Lady.   5

TAMYRA. I think not on you Sir, y'are one I know not.

BUSSY. Cry you mercy Madam.

MONTSURRY.   Oh Sir, has she met you?[18]

      Exeunt HENRY, D'AMBOIS, [*and*] *Ladies.*[19]

MONSIEUR. What had my bounty drunk when it rais'd   10
    him?

GUISE. Y'ave stuck us up a very worthy[20] flag,

That takes more winde than we with all our sailes.

MONSIEUR. O so he spreds and flourishes.

GUISE.   He must downe,   15

Upstarts should never perch too neere a crowne.

MONSIEUR. Tis true my Lord; and as this doting hand,

Even out of earth, (like *Juno*) struck this Giant,

So *Joves* great ordinance(12) shall be here implide

To strike him under th'*Aetna* of his pride :   20

To which work lend your hands and let us cast

Where we may set snares for his ranging[21]
              greatnes :

I think it best, amongst our greatest women :

For there is no such trap to catch an upstart   25

As a loose downfall : for you know[22] their falls

Are th'ends of all mens rising : if great men

And wise make[23] scapes[18] to please advantage,

Tis with a woman : women that woorst may(13)

Still hold mens candels : they direct and know   30

All things amisse in all men; and their women

All things amisse in them : through whose charm'd
              mouthes

We may see all the close scapes of the Court :

When the most royall beast of chase, the Hart[24]   35

---

[18] *make scapes :* take chances.

(Being old, and cunning in his layres and
        haunts) [25]
Can never be discovered to the bow
The peece[19] or hound : yet where (behind some
        Queich[20]) [26]   5
He breaks his gall,[21] and rutteth with his hinde,[27]
The place is markt, and by his Venery
He still is taken. Shall we then attempt
The chiefest meane to that discovery here,
And court our greatest Ladies chiefest[28] women,   10
With shewes of love, and liberall promises?
Tis but our breath. If something given in hand,
Sharpen their hopes of more, 'twill be well ventur'd.
GUISE. No doubt of that : and 'tis the cunningst[29]
        point   15
Of our devis'd investigation.
MONSIEUR.   I[30] have broken
The yce to it already with the woman
Of your chast Lady, and conceive good hope,
I shall wade thorow to some wished shore[31]   20
At our next meeting.
MONTSURRY.   Nay, there's small hope there.[30]
GUISE. Take say[22, (14)] of her my Lord, she comes
        most fitly.

    Enter CHARLOTTE, ANNABELLE, [*and*] PERO.   25
MONSIEUR. Starting back?
GUISE. Y'are ingag'd indeed.[32]
CHARLOTTE. Nay, pray my Lord forbeare.
MONTSURRY. What skittish, servant?
ANNABELLE. No my Lord, I am not so fit for your   30
   service.
CHARLOTTE. Pray pardon me now my Lord, my Lady
   expects me.

[19] *peece :* gun.
[20] *Queich :* Grass.
[21] *breaks his gall :* releases his passion.
[22] *say :* assay.

GUISE. Ile satisfie her expectation, as far as an Uncle
may.[15]

MONSIEUR. Well said : a spirit of Courtship of all hands :
now mine owne Pero : hast thou remembred me for
the discovery I entreated thee to make of thy[33]   5
Mistresse? speak boldly, and be sure of all things I
have sworne to thee.[34]

PERO. Building on that assurance[35] (my Lord) I
may speak : and much the rather, because my Lady
hath not trusted me with that I can tell you; for now   10
I cannot be said to betray her.

MONSIEUR. That's all one, so wee reach our objects :[36]
forth I beseech thee.

PERO. To tell you truth, my Lord, I have made a strange
discovery.   15

MONSIEUR. Excellent![37] Pero thou reviv'st me : may
I sink quick to perdition,[38] if my tongue discover
it.

PERO. Tis thus then : This last night my Lord lay forth :
and I watching[39] my Ladies sitting up, stole up   20
at midnight from my pallat, and (having before made
a hole both through the wall and arras to her inmost
chamber) I saw D'Ambois and her selfe reading a
letter.[40]

MONSIEUR. D'Ambois?   25

PERO. Even he my Lord.

MONSIEUR. Do'st thou not dreame wench?

PERO. I sweare,[41] he is the man.

MONSIEUR. The devill he is, and thy Lady his dam :
[*Aside.*] Why this[42] was the happiest shot that   30
ever flewe, the just plague of hypocrisie level'd it.
Oh[42] the infinite regions betwixt a womans tongue
and her heart! Is this our Goddesse of chastity? I
thought I could not be so sleighted, if she had not
her fraught[43] besides : and therefore plotted this   35
with her woman : never dreaming of D'Amboys.[44]
Deare Pero I will advance thee for ever : but tell me

now : Gods pretious it transformes mee with admiration :[23] sweet Pero, whom should she trust with this conveyance? Or, all the dores being made sure, how should his[45] conveyance be made?

PERO. Nay my Lord, that amazes me : I cannot by any   5
study so much as guesse at it.

MONSIEUR. Well, let's favour our apprehensions(16)
with forbearing that a little : for if my heart were not
hoopt with adamant, the conceipt[24] of this would
have burst it : but heark thee.   *Whispers.*[46]   10

MONTSURRY. I pray thee resolve mee : the Duke will
never imagine that I am busie about's wife : hath
D'Ambois any privy accesse to her?

ANNABELLE. No my Lord, D'Ambois neglects her (as
shee takes it) and is therefore suspicious that either   15
your Lady, or the Lady[47] Beaupre hath closely[25]
entertain'd him.

MONTSURRY. By'r[48] lady a likely suspition; and very
neere the life;[49] especially of my wife.

MONSIEUR. Come, we'l disguise[50] all, with seeming   20
onely to have courted; away dry palm : sh'as a
liver(17) as dry[51] as a bisket :[26] a man may goe
a whole voyage with her, and get nothing but tempests from[52] her windpipe.

GUISE. Here's one, (I think) has swallowed a Porcupine,   25
shee casts pricks from her tongue so.

MONTSURRY. And here's a Peacock seemes to have devour'd one of the Alpes, she has so swelling a spirit,
and is so cold of her kindnes.

CHARLOTTE. We are[53] no windfalls my Lord; ye must   30
gather us with the ladder of matrimony, or we'l hang
till we be rotten.

MONSIEUR. Indeed that's the way to make ye right

---

[23] *admiration :* wonder.
[24] *conceipt :* conception.
[25] *closely :* secretly.

[26] *liver . . . bisket :* sign of indifference to love.

openarses.[27] But alas ye have no portions fit for such
husbands as we wish you.

PERO. Portions my Lord, yes and such portions as your
principality cannot purchase.

MONSIEUR. What woman? what are those portions?　　　　5

PERO. Riddle my riddle my lord.

MONSIEUR. I marry wench, I think thy portion is a right
riddle, a man shall never finde it out : but let's heare
it.

PERO. You shall my Lord.　　　　　　　　　　　　　　10
What's that, that being most rar's most cheap?
That when[54] you sow, you never reap?
That when it grows most, most you in it?
And still you lose it when you win it?
That when its commonest, tis dearest,　　　　　　　　15
And when tis farthest off, 'tis neerest?

MONSIEUR. Is this your great[55] portion?

PERO. Even this my Lord.

MONSIEUR. Beleeve me I cannot riddle it.

PERO. No my Lord, tis my chastity, which you shall　　20
neither riddle nor fiddle.

MONSIEUR. Your chastity? let me begin with the end of
it;[56] how is a womans chastity neerest a man,
when tis furthest off?

PERO. Why my Lord, when you cannot get it, it goes　　25
to th' heart on you; and that I think comes most neere
you : and I am sure it shall be farre enough off; and
so wee[57] leave you to our[58] mercies.

Exeunt women.

MONSIEUR. Farewell riddle.　　　　　　　　　　　　　30

GUISE. Farewell Medlar.

MONTSURRY. Farewell winter plum.

MONSIEUR. Now my Lords, what fruit of our inquisition?
feele you nothing budding yet? Speak good my Lord
Montsurry.　　　　　　　　　　　　　　　　　　　35

MONTSURRY. Nothing but this : D'Ambois is thought[59]
negligent in observing the Duchesse, and therefore

27 *openarses* : medlars.

she is suspicious that your Neece or my wife closely
entertaines him.

MONSIEUR. Your wife, my Lord? Think you that possible?

MONTSURRY. Alas, I know she flies him like her last   5
houre.

MONSIEUR. Her last houre? why that comes upon her
the more she flies it : Does D'Ambois so think you?

MONTSURRY. That's not worth the answering; Tis miraculous[60] to think with what monsters womens im-   10
aginations engrosse them when they are once en-
amour'd and what wonders they will work for their
satisfaction. They will make a sheepe valiant, a Lion
fearefull.

MONSIEUR. And an Asse confident, well my Lord,   15
more[61] will come forth shortly, get you to the
banquet.

GUISE. Come my Lord, I have the blinde side of one of
them.[62]   *Exit* GUISE *cum* MONTSURRY.

20

[SCENA TERTIA.][(1)]

MONSIEUR. O the unsounded Sea of womens bloods,
That when tis calmest, is most dangerous;
Not any wrinkle creaming in their faces,   25
When in their hearts are *Scylla* and *Caribdis*,[(2)]
Which still are hid in dark and standing foggs,[1]
Where never day shines, nothing ever growes,
But weeds and poysons, that no States-man knowes;
Not *Cerberus*[(3)] ever saw the damned nookes   30
Hid with the veiles of womens vertuous lookes.
But[2] what a cloud of sulphur have I drawne
Up to my bosome in this dangerous secret?
Which if my hast (with any spark) should light
Ere D'Ambois were engag'd[1] in some sure plot   35

ACT III. SCENE III.
[1] *engag'd :* trapped.

I were blowne up; He would be sure, my death.
Would I had never knowne it, for before
I shall perswade th'importance to Montsurry,
And make him with some studied stratagem,
Train D'Ambois to his wreak,[2] his maid may tell it,   5
Or I (out of my fiery thirst to play
With the fell[(4)] Tyger, up in darknesse tyed,
And give it some light) make it quite break loose.
I feare it afore heaven, and will not see
D'Ambois againe, till I have told Montsurry,   10
And set a snare with him to free my feares :
Whose there?

Enter MAFFE.

MAFFE.   My Lord?

MONSIEUR.   Goe call the Count Montsurry,   15
And make the dores fast, I will speak with none
Till he come to me.

MAFFE.   Well my Lord.   Exiturus.[3]

MONSIEUR.   Or else
Send you some other, and see all the dores   20
Made safe your selfe I pray, hast, flie about it.

MAFFE. You'l speak with none but with the Count
         Montsurry.

MONSIEUR. With none but he except it be the Guise.

MAFFE. See even by his, there's one exception more,   25
Your Grace must be more firme in the command,
Or else shall I as weakly execute.
The Guise shall speak with you?

MONSIEUR.   He shall I say.

MAFFE. And Count Montsurry?   30

MONSIEUR.   I, and Count Montsurry.

MAFFE. Your Grace must pardon me, that I am bold
To urge the cleare and full sence of your pleasure;
Which when so ever I have knowne, I hope
Your Grace will say, I hit it to a haire.   35

---

[2] *Train . . . wreak:* Lure Bussy   [3] *Exiturus:* He is about to go.
to his vengeance.

MONSIEUR. You have.

MAFFE.   I hope so, or I would be glad.—

MONSIEUR. I pray thee get thee gone, thou art so tedious
  In the strickt forme of all thy services,
  That I had better have one negligent.   5
  You hit my pleasure well, when D'Ambois hit you,
  Did you not, think you?

MAFFE.   D'Ambois? why my Lord?

MONSIEUR. I pray thee talk no more, but shut the dores.
  Doe what I charge thee.   10

MAFFE.   I will my Lord, and yet
  I would be glad the wrong I had of D'Ambois.—

MONSIEUR. [*Aside.*] Precious! then it is a Fate that
                    plagues me
  In this mans foolery, I may be murthered   15
  While he stands on protection of his folly.
  Avant about thy charge.

MAFFE.   I goe my Lord.
  [*Aside.*] I had my head broke in his faithfull service,
  I had no suit the more, nor any thanks,   20
  And yet my teeth must still be hit with D'Ambois.
  D'Ambois my Lord shall know.—

MONSIEUR.   The devil and D'Ambois.
                                   Exit MAFFE.

How am I tortur'd with this trusty foole?   25
Never was any curious in his place
To doe things justly, but he was an Asse :
We cannot find one trusty that is witty,[4]
And therefore beare their disproportion.
Grant thou great starre, and angell of my life,   30
A sure lease of it but for some few dayes,
That I may cleare my bosome of the Snake
I cherisht there, and I will then defie
All check to it but Natures, and her Altars
Shall crack with vessels crown'd with ev'ry liquor   35
Drawn from her highest, and most bloudy humors.

4 *witty* : intelligent.

I feare him strangely, his advanced valour
Is like a spirit rais'd without a circle,[5]
Endangering him that ignorantly rais'd him,
And for whose fury he hath lernt no limit.

         Enter MAFFE *hastily.*   5

MAFFE. I cannot help it, what should I do more?
  As I was gathering a fit Guard to make
  My passage to the dores, and the dores sure,
  The man of bloud[6] is enter'd.

MONSIEUR.   Rage of death.   10
  If I had told the secret, and he knew it,
  Thus had I bin endanger'd :—

         Enter D'AMBOIS.[3]

             My sweet heart![2]

How now? what leap'st thou at?   15
BUSSY.   O royall object.
MONSIEUR. Thou dream'st awake : Object in th'empty
               aire?
BUSSY. Worthy the browes[4] of *Titan,*[7] worth his
               chaire.   20
MONSIEUR. Pray thee what mean'st thou?
BUSSY.   See you not a Crowne
  Empale the forehead of the great King Monsieur?
MONSIEUR. O fie upon thee.
BUSSY.   Prince,[5] that is the Subject 25
  Of all these your retir'd and sole discourses.
MONSIEUR. Wilt thou not leave that wrongfull sup-
               position?
BUSSY. Why[6] wrongfull? to suppose the doubtlesse
               right   30
  To the succession worth the thinking on.
MONSIEUR. Well, leave these jests, how I am over-joyed
  With thy wish'd presence, and how fit thou com'st,
  For of mine honour I was sending for thee.
BUSSY. To what end?   35
MONSIEUR.   Onely for thy company,
  Which I have still in thought, but that's no payment
  On thy part made with personall appearance.[6]

Thy absence so long suffered oftentimes
Put me in some little[7] doubt thou do'st not love
    me.
Wilt thou doe one thing therefore now[8] sincerely?
BUSSY. I, any thing, but killing of the King.   5
MONSIEUR. Still in that discord, and ill taken note?
    How[9]   most   unseasonable   thou   playest   the
        Cucko, (8)
    In this thy fall of friendship?
BUSSY.   Then doe not doubt,   10
    That there is any act within my nerves,
    But killing of the King that is not yours.[9]
MONSIEUR. I will not then; to prove which by[10] my
        love
    Shewne to thy vertues, and by all fruits else   15
    Already sprung from that still flourishing tree,[11]
    With whatsoever may hereafter spring,[12]
    I charge thee utter (even with all the freedome
    Both of thy noble nature and thy friendship)
    The full and plaine state of me in thy thoughts.   20
BUSSY. What, utter plainly what I think of you?
MONSIEUR. Plaine as truth.[13]
BUSSY. Why this swims quite against the stream of
        greatnes.
    Great men would rather heare their flatteries,   25
    And if they be not made fooles, are not wise.
MONSIEUR. I am no such great foole, and therefore
        charge thee
    Even from the root of thy free heart, display[14]
        mee.   30
BUSSY. Since you affect[5] it in such serious termes,
    If your selfe first will tell me what you think
    As freely and as heartily of me,
    I'le be as open in my thoughts of you.
MONSIEUR. A bargain of mine honour; and make this,   35
    That prove we in our full dissection

[5] *affect :* wish.

Never so foule, live still the sounder friends.

BUSSY. What else Sir? come pay me home, ile bide it
                 bravely.[15]

MONSIEUR. I will I swear. I think thee then a man,
  That dares as much as a wilde horse or Tyger;   5
  As headstrong and as bloody; and to[16] feed
  The ravenous wolfe of thy most Caniball valour,
  (Rather than not employ it) thou would'st turne
  Hackster[6] to any whore, slave to a Jew,
  Or English usurer, to force possessions,   10
  And cut mens throats, of morgaged estates;
  Or   thou   would'st   tire   thee   like   a   Tinkers
                 strumpet,[17]
  And murther market folks, quarrel with sheepe,
  And runne as mad as *Ajax;*[9] serve a Butcher,   15
  Doe anything but killing of the King :
  That in thy valour th'art like other naturalls,[7]
  That have strange gifts in nature, but no soule
  Diffus'd quite through, to make them of a peece,
  But stop at humours, that are more absurd,   20
  Childish and villanous than that hackster, whore,
  Slave, cut-throat, Tinkers bitch, compar'd before :
  And in those humours would'st envie, betray,
  Slander, blaspheme, change each houre a religion;
  Doe any thing, but killing of the King;   25
  That in thy[18] valour (which is still the dunghill,
  To which hath reference[8, 19] all filth in thy house)
  Th'art more ridiculous and vaine-glorious
  Than any Mountibank; and impudent
  Than any painted Bawd; which, not to sooth   30
  And glorifie thee like a *Jupiter Hammon,*[10]
  Thou eat'st thy heart in vineger; and thy gall
  Turns all thy blood to poyson, which is cause
  Of that Toad-poole that stands in thy complexion;
  And makes thee (with a cold and earthy moisture, 35

---

[6] *Hackster :* Hired protector.   [8] *hath reference :* is brought.
[7] *naturalls :* idiots.

Which is the damme of putrifaction,
As plague to thy damn'd pride) rot as thou liv'st;
To study calumnies and treacheries;
To thy friends slaughters, like a Scrich-owle sing,
And to all mischiefes, but to kill the King.   5
BUSSY. So : Have you said?
MONSIEUR.   How thinkest thou? Doe I flatter?
Speak I not like a trusty friend to thee?
BUSSY. That ever any man was blest withall;
So here's for me. I think you are (at worst)   10
No devill, since y'are like to be no King;
Of which, with any friend of yours Ile lay
This poore Stillado⁹ here, gainst all the starres,
I, and 'gainst all your treacheries, which are more;
That you did never good, but to doe ill;   15
But ill of all sorts, free and for it selfe :
That (like a murthering peece,⁽¹¹⁾ making lanes in
                                  Armies
The first man of a rank, the whole rank falling)
If you have wrong'd[20] one man, you are so farre   20
From making him amends, that all his race,
Friends and associates fall into your chace :
That y'are for perjuries the very prince
Of all intelligencers;¹⁰ and your voice
Is like an Easterne winde, and[21] where it flies,   25
Knits nets of Catterpillars, with which you catch
The prime of all the fruits the Kingdome yeelds.
That your politicall head is the curst fount
Of all the violence, rapine, cruelty,
Tyrannie & Atheisme flowing through the realme.   30
That y'ave a tongue so scandalous, 'twill cut
The purest[22] Christall;¹¹ and a breath that will
Kill to¹² that wall a spider; you will jest
With God, and your soule to the devill tender¹³

⁹ *Stillado* : Dagger.   ¹² *to* : as far as.
¹⁰ *intelligencers* : spies.   ¹³ *tender* : offer.
¹¹ *Christall* : Diamond.

For lust; kisse horror, and with death engender.
That your foule body is a Lernean fenne[12]
Of all the maladies breeding in all men.
That you are utterly without a soule :
And (for your life) the thred of that was spunne,   5
When *Clotho* slept, and let her breathing rock[14]
Fall in the durt; and *Lachesis* still drawes it,
Dipping her twisting fingers in a boule
Defil'd, and crown'd with vertues forced soule.[13]
And lastly (which I must for Gratitude   10
Ever remember) That of all my height
And dearest life, you are the onely spring,
Onely in royall hope to kill the King.
MONSIEUR. Why now I see thou lov'st me, come to the
                 banquet.   *Exeunt.*   15
       Finis Actus Tertii.

      Actus quarti. Scena prima.

                      20

   [*Enter*] HENRY, MONSIEUR *with a Letter,* GUISE,
  MONTSURRY, BUSSY, ELENOR, TAMYRA, BEAUPRE,
     PERO, CHARLOTTE, ANNABELLE, PYRA,
        with foure Pages.[1]
HENRY. Ladies, ye have not done our banquet right,   25
Nor lookt upon it with those cheerefull rayes,
That lately turn'd your breaths to flouds of gold;
Your looks, me thinks, are not drawne out with
               thoughts,
So cleare and free as heretofore, but foule[2]   30
As if the thick complexions of men
Govern'd within them.
BUSSY.   'Tis not like, my Lord,[3]
That men in women rule, but contrary;
For as the Moone (of all things God created)   35

14 *breathing rock :* distaff of
life.

Not only is the most appropriate image
Or glasse to shew them how they wax and wane,
But in her height[4] and motion likewise beares
Imperiall influences that command
In all their powers, and make them wax and wane; 5
So women, that (of all things made of nothing)
Are the most perfect Idols[5] of the Moone,
(Or still-unwean'd sweet Moon-calves[1] with white
faces)
Not only are paterns of change to men : 10
But as the tender Moon-shine of their beauties
Cleares, or is cloudy, make men glad or sad,
So then they rule in men, not men in them.[6]
MONSIEUR. But here the Moons are chang'd (as the King
notes) 15
And either men rule in them, or some power
Beyond their voluntary faculty :[7]
For nothing can recover their lost faces.
MONTSURRY. None[8] can be alwayes one : our griefes
and joyes 20
Hold severall scepters in us, and have times
For their divided Empires :[9] which griefe now, in
them
Doth prove[10] as proper to his diadem.[8]
BUSSY. And griefe's a naturall sicknesse of the bloud, 25
That time to part asks, as his comming had;
Onely sleight fooles griev'd, suddenly are glad;
A man may say t'a dead man, "be reviv'd,"
As well as to one sorrowfull, "be not griev'd."
And therefore (Princely Mistresse) in all warres 30
Against these base foes that insult on weaknesse,
And still fight hous'd, behind the shield of Nature,
Of priviledge[11] law, treachery, or beastly need,
Your servant cannot help; authority here
Goes with corruption; something like some States, 35
That back woorst men; valour to them must creepe
That (to themselves left) would feare him asleepe.
ELENOR. Ye all take that for granted, that doth rest

Yet to be prov'd; we all are as we were,
As merry, and as free in thought as ever.
GUISE. And why then can ye not disclose your thoughts?
TAMYRA. Me thinks the man hath answer'd for us well.
MONSIEUR. The man? why Madam d'ee not know his   5
        name?
TAMYRA. Man is a name of honour for a King:
Additions[1] take away from each chiefe thing:
The Schoole of Modesty, not to learne, learnes
        Dames: 10
They sit in high formes[2] there, that know mens
        names.
MONSIEUR. Heark sweet heart, here's a bar[12] set to
        your valour:
It cannot enter here; no, not to notice   15
Of what your name is; your great Eagles beak
(Should you flie at her) had as good encounter
An Albion cliffe, as her more craggy liver.[2]
BUSSY. Ile not attempt her Sir, her sight and name
(By which I onely know her) doth deter me.   20
HENRY. So doe they all men else.
MONSIEUR.   You would say so
If you knew all.[3]
TAMYRA.   Knew all my Lord? What meane you?
MONSIEUR. All that I know Madam.   25
TAMYRA.   That you know? speak it.
MONSIEUR. No tis enough I feele it.
HENRY.   But me thinks
Her Courtship is more pure then heretofore:
True Courtiers should be modest, and[13] not nice:[3]   30
Bold, but not impudent: pleasure love, not vice.
MONSIEUR. Sweet heart, come hither: what if one
        should make

ACT IV. Scene i.   stools.
[1] *Additions:* Titles of honor.   [3] *nice:* fastidious.
[2] *in high formes:* on dunce

Horns at Montsurry? would it not[14] strike him
                                    jealous
Through all the proofes of his chaste Ladies vertues?
BUSSY. If[15] he be wise, not.
MONSIEUR. What? not if I should name the Gardener,   5
That I would have him think hath grafted him?
BUSSY. So the large licence that your greatnesse uses
    To jest at all men, may be taught indeed
    To make a difference of the grounds you play on,
    Both in the men you scandall, and the matter.   10
MONSIEUR. As[16] how? as how?
BUSSY.   Perhaps led with a traine,[4]
    Where you may have your nose made lesse, and
                                    slit,[15]
    Your eyes thrust out.   15
MONSIEUR.   Peace, peace, I pray thee peace.[16]
    Who dares doe that? the brother of his King?
BUSSY. Were your King brother in you, all your powers
    (Stretcht in the armes of great men and their Bawds)
    Set close downe by you, all your stormy lawes   20
    Spouted with Lawyers mouthes, and gushing bloud,
    Like to so many Torrents, all your glories,
    (Making you terrible, like enchanted flames,
    Fed with bare cockscombs, and with crooked
                                    hammes)   25
    All your prerogatives, your shames and tortures,
    All daring heaven, and opening hell about you,
    Were I the man ye wrong'd so, and provok'd,
    (Though ne're so much beneath you) like a box
                                    tree[4]   30
    I would (out of the roughnesse[17] of my root)
    Ramme hardnesse, in my lownesse, and like death
    Mounted on earthquakes, I would trot through all
    Honors and horrors, thorow foule and faire,

[4] *led with a traine* : deceived by
    a plot.

    And from your whole strength tosse you into the
               aire.[18]

MONSIEUR. Goe, th'art a devill; such another spirit
    Could not be still'd from all th'Armenian dragons,[5]
    O my Loves glory : heire to all I have :   5
    That's all I can say, and that all I sweare.
    If thou out-live me, as I know thou must,
    Or else hath nature no proportion'd end
    To her great labours : she hath breath'd a minde[19]
    Into thy entrails, of desert[20] to swell   10
    Into another great *Augustus Caesar :*
    Organs, and faculties fitted to her greatnesse :
    And should that perish like a common spirit,
    Nature's a Courtier and regards no merit.

HENRY. Here's nought but whispering with us : like a 15
              calme
    Before a tempest, when the silent ayre
    Layes her soft eare close to the earth to hearken
    For that she feares steales on to ravish[21] her;
    Some Fate doth joyne our eares to heare it comming. 20
    Come, my brave eagle, let's to Covert flie :
    I see Almighty Aether in the smoak
    Of all his clowds descending,[6] and the skie
    Hid in the dim ostents of Tragedy.

            Exit HENRY *with* D'AMBOIS *& Ladies.*[22] 25
GUISE. Now stirre the humour, and begin the brawle.
MONTSURRY. The King and D'Ambois now are growne
           all one.
MONSIEUR. Nay, they are two my Lord.

            [*He makes the sign of the* 30
            cuckold at MONTSURRY.]
MONTSURRY.   How's that?
MONSIEUR.   No more.
MONTSURRY. I must have more my Lord.
MONSIEUR.   What more than two? 35
MONTSURRY. How monstrous is this?
MONSIEUR.   Why?
MONTSURRY.   You make me Horns.

MONSIEUR. Not I, it is a work without my power,
    Married mens ensignes are not made with fingers?
    Of divine Fabrique they are, not mens hands;
    Your wife, you know, is a meere[5] *Cynthia*,[(7)]
    And she must fashion hornes out of her Nature.   5
MONTSURRY. But doth she? dare you charge her? speak
        false Prince.
MONSIEUR. I must not speak my Lord : but if you'l use
    The learning of a noble man, and read,
    Here's something[(8)] to those points : soft you must   10
        pawne
    Your honour having read it to return it.
        Enter TAMYRA *&* PERO.[23]
MONTSURRY. Not I, I pawne mine Honour for a paper?
MONSIEUR. You must not buy it under.   15
        Exeunt GUISE *and* MONSIEUR.
MONTSURRY.   Keepe it then,
    And keepe fire in your bosome.
TAMYRA.   What sayes he?
MONTSURRY. You must make good the rest.   20
TAMYRA.   How fares my Lord?
    Takes my Love any thing to heart he sayes?
MONTSURRY. Come, y'are a—
TAMYRA.   What my Lord?
MONTSURRY.   The plague of *Herod*[(9)]   25
    Feast in his rotten entrailes.
TAMYRA.   Will you wreak
    Your angers just cause given by him, on me?
MONTSURRY. By him?
TAMYRA.   By him my Lord, I have admir'd   30
    You could all this time be at concord with him,
    That still hath plaid such discords on your honour.
MONTSURRY. Perhaps tis with some proud[6] string[(10)] of
        my wives.
TAMYRA. How's that, my Lord?   35
MONTSURRY.   Your tongue will still admire,

---

[5] *meere :* pure.   [6] *proud :* lustfull.

Till my head be the miracle of the world.
TAMYRA. O woe is me.   *She seemes to swound.*[24]
PERO.   What does your Lordship meane?
Madam, be comforted; my Lord but tries you.
Madam? Help good my Lord, are you not mov'd?   5
Doe your set looks print in your words your thoughts?
Sweet[25] Lord, cleare up those eyes, [for shame of
                    Noblesse :]
Unbend that masking forehead, whence is it
You rush upon her with these Irish warres,   10
More   full   of   sound   then   hurt?(11)   But   it   is
                    enough,[25]
You have shot home, your words are in her heart;
She has not liv'd to beare a triall now.
MONTSURRY. Look up my Love, and by this kisse receive   15
My soule amongst thy spirits for supply
To thine, chac'd with my fury.
TAMYRA.   O my Lord,
I have too long liv'd to heare this from you.
MONTSURRY. 'Twas from my troubled bloud, and not   20
                    from me :
[*Aside.*] I know not how I fare; a sudden night
Flowes through my entrailes, and a headlong Chaos
Murmurs within me, which I must digest;
And not drowne her in my confusions,   25
That was my lives joy, being best inform'd : (12)
Sweet, you must needs forgive me, that my love
(Like to a fire disdaining his suppression)
Rag'd being discourag'd; my whole heart is wounded
When any least thought in you is but touch't,   30
And shall be till I know your former merits :
Your name and memory altogether crave
In just[26] oblivion their eternall grave;
And then you must heare from me, there's no meane
In any passion I shall feele for you :   35
Love is a rasor cleansing being well us'd,
But fetcheth blood still being the least abus'd :
To tell you briefly all; The man that left me

When you appear'd, did turne me worse than woman,
And stab'd me to the heart thus, with his fingers.[27]
TAMYRA. O happy woman! Comes my stain from
him?(13)
It is my beauty, and that innocence proves,　　　　　　5
That slew *Chymoera*, rescu'd *Peleus*
From all the savage beasts in Pelion;[28]
And rais'd the chaste Athenian Prince(14) from
hell :
All suffering with me; they for womens lusts,　　　　10
I for a mans; that the Augean[29] stable(15)
Of his foule sinne would empty in my lap :
How his guilt shunn'd me? sacred innocence
That where thou fear'st, art[30] dreadfull; and his
face　　　　　　　　　　　　　　　　　　　15
Turn'd in flight from thee, that had thee in chace :
Come, bring me to him : I will tell the serpent
Even to his venom'd teeth(16) (from whose curst
seed[31]
A pitcht field starts up 'twixt my Lord and me)　　20
That his throat lies, and he shall curse his fingers,
For being so govern'd by his filthy soule.
MONTSURRY. I know not, if himselfe will vaunt t'have
beene
The princely Author of the slavish sinne,　　　　　25
Or any other; he would have resolv'd me,
Had you not come; not by his word, but writing,
Would I have sworne to give it him againe,
And pawn'd mine honour to him for a paper.
TAMYRA. See how he flies me still : Tis a foule heart　30
That feares his owne hand : Good my Lord make
haste
To[32] see the dangerous paper : Papers hold
Oft-times the formes, and copies of our soules,
And (though the world despise them) are the prizes　35
Of all our honors, make your honour then
A hostage for it, and with it conferre[32]
My neerest woman here, in all shee knowes;

Who (if the sunne or *Cerberus*[17] could have seene
Any staine in me) might as well[33] as they :
And Pero, here I charge thee by my love,
And all proofes of it, (which I might call bounties)
By all that thou hast seene seeme good in mee,   5
And all the ill which thou shouldst spit from thee,
By pity of the wound this touch[34], [18] hath given
              me,
Not as thy Mistresse now, but a poore woman
(To death given over) rid me of my paines,   10
Powre on thy powder : cleare thy breast of me :
My Lord is only here : here speak thy worst,
Thy best will doe me mischiefe; If thou spar'st me,
Never shine good thought on thy memory :
Resolve my Lord, and leave me desperate.   15
PERO. My Lord? My Lord hath plaid a prodigals part,
To break his Stock for nothing; and an insolent,
To cut a Gordian when he could not loose it :[19]
What violence is this, to put true fire
To a false train? To blow up long crown'd peace   20
With sudden outrage? and beleeve a man
Sworne to the shame of women, 'gainst a woman,
Borne to their honours : but I will to him.[35]
TAMYRA. No, I will write (for I shall never more
Meet[36] with the fugitive) where I will defie him,   25
Were he ten times the brother of my King.
To him my Lord, and ile to cursing him.[37]

                               Exeunt.

                                    30

[SCENA SECUNDA.]

Enter D'AMBOIS *and* FRIAR.
BUSSY. I[1] am suspitious my most honour'd Father,
By some of Monsieurs cunning passages,   35
That his still ranging and contentious nosethrils,
To scent the haunts of mischiefe, have so us'd
The vicious vertue of his busie sence,

That he trails hotly of him, and will rowze him,
Driving him all enrag'd, and foming on us,
And therefore have entreated your deepe skill,
In the command of good aëriall spirits,
To assume these Magick rites, and call up one   5
To know if any have reveal'd unto him
Any thing touching my deare Love and me.

FRIAR. Good sonne you have amaz'd me but to make
The least doubt of it, it concernes so neerely
The faith and reverence of my name and order.   10
Yet I will justifie upon my soule
All I have done, if any spirit i'th earth or aire
Can give you the resolve,[1] doe not despaire.[1]

Musick: and TAMYRA *enters with* PERO[2] *bearing*
                                   a Letter.   15

TAMYRA. Away, deliver it : (*Exit* PERO.)[3] O may my
                lines
(Fill'd with the poyson of a womans hate
When he shall open them) shrink up his curst[4]
                eyes   20
With torturous darknesse, such as stands in hell,
Stuck full of inward horrors, never lighted;
With which are all things to be fear'd, affrighted.[5]

BUSSY. How is it with my honour'd Mistresse?

TAMYRA. O servant help, and save me from the gripes   25
Of shame and infamy. Our love[6] is knowne,
Your Monsieur hath a paper where is writ
Some secret tokens that decipher it.

BUSSY. What cold dull Northern brain, what foole but
                he,[6]   30
Durst take into his Epimethean[1] breast
A box of such plagues as the danger yeelds,
Incur'd in this discovery? He had better
Ventur'd his breast in the consuming reach
Of the hot surfets cast out of the clouds,   35

ACT IV. SCENE II.
[1] *resolve :* information.

402

Or stood the bullets that (to wreak the skie)
The Cyclops ramme in *Joves* artillerie.[2]

FRIAR. We soone will take the darknesse from his face
That did that deed of darknesse; we will know
What now the Monsieur and your husband doe;   5
What is contain'd within the secret paper
Offer'd by Monsieur, and your loves events :
To which ends (honour'd daughter) at your motion
I have put on these exorcising Rites,
And, by my power of learned holinesse   10
Vouchsaft me from above, I will command
Our resolution of a raised spirit.

TAMYRA. Good Father raise him in some beauteous
forme,
That with least terror I may brook his sight.   15

FRIAR. Stand sure together then what ere you[7] see,
And stir not, as ye tender all our lives.

                He puts on his robes.[8]

Occidentalium legionum spiritualium[9] imperator
(magnus ille Behemoth) veni, veni, comitatus cum   20
Astaroth[10] locotenente invicto. Adjuro te per
Stygis inscrutabilia arcana, per ipsos irremeabiles an-
fractus Averni : adesto ô Behemoth, tu cui pervia sunt
Magnatum scrinia; veni, per Noctis & tenebrarum
abdita profundissima; per labentia sydera; per ipsos   25
motus horarum furtivos, Hecatesque altum silentium :
Appare in forma spiritali, lucente splendida & ama-
bili.[2]

---

2 Emperor of the western legions of spirits, great Behemoth, come, come, with your
unconquered lieutenant Ash-
taroth. I adjure you by the
inscrutable secrets of Styx, by
the very irretraceable windings of Avernus : be present
O Behemoth, you for whom
the cabinets of the mighty are
open; come, by the hidden
depths of Night and darkness,
by the gliding stars, by the
secret motion of the hours,
and Hecate's deep silence.
Appear in the form of a spirit,
splendidly glowing and
lovely.

Thunder. Ascendit [BEHEMOTH, CARTOPHYLAX *and
spirits with torches.*]

BEHEMOTH. (3) What would the holy Friar?

FRIAR.   I would see
What now the Monsieur and Montsurry doe;   5
And see the secret paper that the Monsieur
Offer'd to Count Montsurry, longing much
To know on what events the secret loves
Of these two honour'd persons shall arrive.

BEHEMOTH. Why call'dst[11] thou me to this accursed   10
          light,
To these light purposes? I am Emperor
Of that inscrutable darknesse, where are hid
All deepest truths, and secrets never seene,
All which I know, and command Legions   15
Of knowing spirits that can doe more than these.
Any of this my Guard that circle me
In these blew fires, and out of whose dim fumes
Vast murmurs use to break, and from their sounds
Articulat[12] voyces, can doe ten parts more   20
Than open such sleight truths, as you require.

FRIAR. From the last nights black depth, I call'd up one
Of the inferiour ablest Ministers,
And he could not resolve me; send one then
Out of thine owne command, to fetch the paper   25
That Monsieur hath to shew to Count Montsurry.

BEHEMOTH. I will : Cartophylax : (4) thou that properly
Hast in thy power all papers so inscrib'd.
Glide through all barres to it, and fetch that paper.

CARTOPHYLAX. I will.   *A Torch removes.*
                                                              30
FRIAR.   Till he returnes (great prince of
          darknesse)
Tell me, if Monsieur and the Count Montsurry
Are yet encounter'd.

BEHEMOTH.   Both them and the Guise
Are now together.   35

FRIAR.   Shew us all their persons,
And represent the place, with all their actions.

BEHEMOTH. The spirit will strait return, and then Ile
                    shew thee :   [*A Torch returns.*]
    See he is come; why brought'st thou not the paper?
CARTOPHYLAX. He hath prevented me, and got a spirit
    Rais'd by another, great in our command, [5]   5
    To take the guard of it before I came.
BEHEMOTH. This is your slacknesse, not t'invoke our
                    powers
    When first your acts set forth to their effects;
    Yet shall you see it, and themselves : behold   10
    They come here & the Earle now holds the paper.
    Enter MONSIEUR, GUISE, MONTSURRY *with a paper.*[13]
BUSSY. May we not heare them?
[FRIAR.][14]   No, be still and see.
BUSSY. I will goe fetch the paper.   15
FRIAR.   Do not stirre.
    There's too much distance, and too many locks
    Twixt you and them : (how neere so e're they seeme)
    For any man to interrupt their secrets.
TAMYRA. O honour'd spirit, flie into the fancie   20
    Of my offended Lord : and doe not let him
    Beleeve what there the wicked man hath written.
BEHEMOTH.[15] Perswasion hath already enter'd him
    Beyond reflection; peace till their departure.
MONSIEUR. There is a glasse of Ink where you may[16]   25
                    see [6]
    How to make ready black fac'd Tragedy :
    You now discerne, I hope through all her paintings,
    Her gasping wrinkles, and fames sepulchres.
GUISE. Think you he faines my Lord? what hold you   30
                    now?
    Doe we maligne your wife : or honour you?
MONSIEUR. What stricken dumb? nay fie, Lord be not
                    danted :
    Your case is common : were it ne're so rare   35
    Beare it as rarely : now to laugh were manly :
    A worthy man should imitate the weather
    That sings in tempests : and being cleare is silent.

GUISE. Goe home my Lord and force your wife to write
    Such loving lines[17] to D'Ambois as she us'd
    When she desir'd his presence.

MONSIEUR.   Doe my Lord,
    And make her name her conceal'd messenger :   5
    That close and most inennerable[3] Pander
    That passeth all our studies to exquire[18]
    By whom convay the letter to her love :
    And so you shall be sure to have him come
    Within the thirsty reach of your revenge;   10
    Before which, lodge an ambush in her chamber
    Behind the arras of your stoutest men
    All close and soundly arm'd : and let them share
    A spirit amongst them, that would serve a thousand.

                Enter PERO *with a Letter.*[19]   15

GUISE. Yet stay a little : see she sends for you.

MONSIEUR. Poore, loving Lady, she'l make all good yet,
    Think you not so my Lord?

              MONTSURRY *stabs* PERO.[20]   *Exit.*

GUISE.   Alas poore soule.   20

MONSIEUR. This was cruelly done y'faith.[21]

PERO.   T'was nobly done.
    And I forgive his Lordship from my soule.

MONSIEUR. Then much good doo't thee Pero : hast a
           letter?   25

PERO. I hope it rather be a bitter[22] volume
    Of worthy curses for your perjury.

GUISE. To you my Lord.[23]

MONSIEUR.   To me? Now out upon her.

GUISE. Let me see my Lord.   30

MONSIEUR. You shall presently : how fares my Pero?
    Who's there?

                Enter servant.[24]
    Take in this Maid, sh'as caught a clap,[4]

---

[3] *inennerable :* unspeakable.   [4] *caught a clap :* been struck a
                                              blow.

And fetch my Surgeon to her; Come my Lord,
We'l now peruse our letter.
    Exeunt MONSIEUR [*and*] GUISE. *Lead her out.*
PERO.   Furies rise
Out of the black lines, and torment his soule.   5
TAMYRA. Hath my Lord slaine my woman?
BEHEMOTH.   No, she lives.
FRIAR.[25] What shall become of us?
BEHEMOTH.   All I can say
 Being call'd thus late, is briefe, and darkly this: 10
 If D'Ambois Mistresse die[26] not her white hand
 In her[27] forc'd bloud, he shall remaine untoucht:
 So Father, shall your selfe, but by your selfe:
 To make this Augurie plainer: when the voyce
 Of D'Ambois shall invoke me, I will rise, 15
 Shining in greater light, and shew him all
 That will betide ye all; meane time be wise
 And curb his valour, with your policies.[28]
        Descendit cum suis.
BUSSY. Will he appeare to me, when I invoke him? 20
FRIAR. He will: be sure.
BUSSY.   It must be shortly then:
 For his dark words have tyed my thoughts on knots
 Till he dissolve, and free them.
TAMYRA.   In meane time 25
 Deare servant, till your powerful voice revoke him,
 Be sure to use the policy he advis'd:
 Lest fury in your too quick knowledge taken
 Of our abuse, and your defence of me,
 Accuse me more than any enemy: 30
 And Father, you must on my Lord impose
 Your holiest charges, and the Churches power,
 To temper his hot spirit: and disperse
 The cruelty and the bloud, I know his hand
 Will showre upon our heads, if you put not 35
 Your finger to the storme, and hold it up,
 As my deare servant here must doe with Monsieur.
BUSSY. Ile sooth his plots, and strow my hate with smiles,

Till all at once the close mines of my heart
Rise at full date, and rush into his bloud :
Ile bind his arme in silk, and rub his flesh,
To make the veine swell, that his soule may gush
Into some kennell,[5] where it longs[6] to lie,   5
And policy shall be flanckt with policy.
Yet shall the feeling center[7] where we meet
Groane with the wait of my approaching feet :
Ile make th'inspired threshals of his Court
Sweat with the weather of my horrid steps   10
Before I enter : yet will I appeare
Like calme security, before a ruine :
A Politician, must like lightning melt
The very marrow, and not taint[29] the skin :
His wayes must not be seene, the superficies   15
Of the greene center must not taste his feet,
When hell is plow'd up with his wounding tracts,
And all his harvest reap't by[30] hellish facts.

                                                         Exeunt.
                    Finis Actus Quarti.   20

Actus quinti.[1] Scena prima.

[*Enter*] montsurry *bare, unbrac't, pulling* tamyra *in*   25
    by the haire,[2] friar, [*and*] *One bearing light,*
        a standish[1] *and paper, which sets a Table.*

tamyra. O[3] Help me Father.

friar.   Impious Earle forbeare.
    Take violent hand from her, or by mine order   30
    The King shall force thee.

montsurry.   Tis not violent;
    Come you not willingly?

tamyra.   Yes good my Lord.[3]

---

5 *kennell :* gutter.   Act V. Scene i.
6 *longs :* deserves.   1 *standish :* stand for pen and
7 *feeling center :* sensitive earth.   ink.

FRIAR. My Lord remember that your soule must seek
    Her peace, as well as your revengefull bloud :
    You ever to this houre have prov'd your selfe
    A noble, zealous, and obedient sonne,
    T'our holy mother : be not an Apostate :   5
    Your wives offence serves not, (were it the worst
    You can imagine, without greater proofes)
    To sever your eternal bonds, and hearts;
    Much lesse to touch her with a bloudy hand :
    Nor is it manly (much lesse husbandly)   10
    To expiate any frailty in your wife,
    With churlish strokes, or beastly ods of strength :
    The stony birth of clowds,[2] will touch no lawrell,[1]
    Nor any sleeper; your wife is your lawrell,
    And sweetest sleeper; doe not touch her then   15
    Be not more rude than the wild seed of vapour,
    To her that is more gentle than that[4] rude;
    In whom kind nature suffer'd one offence
    But to set off her other excellence.
MONTSURRY. Good Father leave us : interrupt no more   20
    The course I must runne for mine honour sake.
    Rely on my love to her, which her fault
    Cannot extinguish : will she but disclose
    Who was the secret[5] minister of her love,
    And through what maze he serv'd it, we are friends.   25
FRIAR. It is damn'd work to pursue those secrets,
    That would ope more sinne, and prove springs of
                slaughter;
    Nor is't a path for Christian feet to tread;[6]
    But out of all way to the health of soules;   30
    A sinne impossible to be forgiven :
    Which he that dares commit—
MONTSURRY.   Good Father cease your terrors :[7]
    Tempt not a man distracted; I am apt
    To outrages that I shall ever rue :   35

[2] *stony birth of clowds :* thun-
    derstones; thunderbolts.

I will not passe the verge that bounds a Christian,
Nor break the limits of a man nor husband.

FRIAR. Then heaven inspire you[8] both with thoughts
                    and deeds
Worthy his high respect, and your owne soules.   5

TAMYRA. Father.[9]

FRIAR.   I warrant thee my dearest daughter
He will not touch thee, think'st thou him a Pagan;
His honor and his soule lies for thy safety.[9] *Exit.*

MONTSURRY. Who shall remove the mountaine from my   10
                    brest,[10]
Stand the opening[11] furnace of my thoughts,
And set fit out-cries for a soule in hell?

                    MONTSURRY *turnes a key.*

For[12] now it nothing fits my woes to speak,   15
But thunder, or to take into my throat
The trump of Heaven; with whose determinate³ blasts
The windes shall burst, and the devouring[13] seas
Be drunk up in his sounds; that my hot woes
(Vented enough) I might convert to vapour,   20
Ascending from my infamie unseene;
Shorten the world, preventing the last breath⁴
That kils the living, and regenerates death.

TAMYRA. My Lord, my fault (as you may censure it
With too strong arguments) is past your pardon: 25
But how the circumstances may excuse mee
Heaven[14] knowes, and your more temperate minde
                    hereafter
May let my penitent miseries make you know.

MONTSURRY. Hereafter? Tis a suppos'd infinite,   30
That from this point will rise eternally:
Fame grows in going;(2) in the scapes of vertue
Excuses damne her: They be fires in Cities
Enrag'd with those winds that lesse lights extinguish.
Come Syren, sing, and dash against my rocks   35

---

³ *determinate :* final.
⁴ *preventing the last breath :*

anticipating Gabriel's trumpet
blast.

Thy ruffin Gally,[5, (3)] rig'd[15] with quench for lust :
Sing, and put all the nets into thy voice,[(4)]
With which thou drew'st into thy strumpets lap
The spawne of *Venus;* and in which ye danc'd;
That, in thy laps steed, I may digge his tombe,   5
And quit his manhood with a womans sleight,
Who never is deceiv'd in her deceit.
Sing, (that is, write) and then take from mine eyes
The mists that hide the most inscrutable Pandar
That ever lapt up an adulterous vomit :   10
That I may see the devill, and survive
To be a devill, and then learne to wive :
That I may hang him, and then cut him downe,
Then cut him up, and with my soules beams search
The cranks and cavernes of his braine, and study   15
The errant wildernesse of a womans face;
Where men cannot get out, for[6] all the Comets
That have beene lighted at it; though they know
That Adders lie a sunning in their smiles,
That Basilisks drink their poyson from their eyes,   20
And no way there to coast out to their hearts;
Yet still they wander there, and are not stay'd
Till they be fetter'd, nor secure before
All cares devoure[16] them, nor in humane Consort
Till they embrace within their wives two breasts   25
All Pelion and Cythaeron[(5)] with their beasts.
Why write you not?
TAMYRA.   O, good my Lord forbeare
In wreak of great faults[17] to engender greater,
And make my Loves corruption generate murther.   30
MONTSURRY. It followes needfully as childe and parent;
The chaine-shot[(6)] of thy lust is yet aloft,
And it must murther; tis thine owne deare twinne :
No man can add height to a womans sinne.
Vice never doth her just hate so provoke,   35
As when she rageth under vertues cloake.

---

[5] *Gally :* Bussy.   [6] *for :* in spite of.

411

Write; For it must be : by this ruthlesse steele,
By this impartiall torture, and the death
Thy tyrannies have invented in my entrails,
To quicken life in dying, and hold up
The spirits in fainting, teaching to preserve   5
Torments in ashes, that will ever last.
Speak : Will you write?

TAMYRA.   Sweet Lord enjoyne my sinne
Some other penance than what makes it worse :
Hide in some gloomie dungeon my loth'd face,   10
And let condemned murtherers let me downe
(Stopping their noses) my abhorred food.
Hang me in chaines, and let me eat these armes
That have offended : Binde me face to face
To some dead woman, taken from the Cart   15
Of Execution, till death and time
In graines of dust dissolve me; Ile endure :
Or any torture that your wraths invention
Can fright all pitie from the world withall :
But to betray a friend with shew of friendship   20
That is too common for the rare revenge
Your rage affecteth; here then are my breasts,
Last night your pillowes; here my wretched armes,
As late the wished confines of your life :
Now break them as you please, and all the bounds   25
Of manhood, noblesse, and religion.

MONTSURRY. Where all these have bin broken, they are
                              kept,
In doing their justice there with any shew[18]
Of the like cruelty : Thine armes have lost   30
Their priviledge in lust, and in their torture
Thus they must pay it.   *Stabs her.*[19]

TAMYRA.   O Lord.

MONTSURRY.   Till thou writ'st
Ile write in wounds (my wrongs fit characters)   35
Thy right of sufferance. Write.

TAMYRA.   O kill me, kill me,
Deare husband be not crueller than death;

You have beheld some Gorgon : Feele, O feele
How you are turn'd to stone; with my heart blood
Dissolve your selfe againe, or you will grow
Into the image of all Tyrannie.

MONTSURRY. As thou art of adultry, I will ever[20]   5
  Prove thee my parallel,[21] being most a monster :
  Thus I expresse thee yet.   *Stabs her againe.*[22]

TAMYRA.   And yet I live.

MONTSURRY. I, for thy monstrous idoll is not done yet,
  This toole hath wrought enough : now, Torture,   10
         use[23]
   Enter servants[24] [*who put her on a rack.*]
  This other engine on th'habituate powers
  Of her thrice damn'd and whorish fortitude.
  Use the most madding paines in her that ever   15
  Thy venoms sok'd through, making most of death;
  That she may weigh her wrongs with them, and then
  Stand vengeance on thy steepest rock a victor.

TAMYRA. O who is turn'd into my Lord and husband?
  Husband? My Lord? None but my Lord and hus- 20
        band?[25]
  Heaven, I ask thee remission of my sinnes,
  Not of my paines : husband, O help me husband.
    Ascendit FRIAR *with a sword drawne.*[26]

FRIAR. What rape[(7)] of honour and religion?   25
  O wrack of nature!   *Falls and dies.*[27]

TAMYRA.   Poore man : O my Father.
  Father, look up; O let me downe my Lord,
  And I will write.

MONTSURRY.   Author of prodigies!   30
  What new flame breakes out of the firmament,
  That turnes up counsels never knowne before?
  Now is it true, earth moves, and heaven stands still :
  Even Heaven it selfe must see and suffer ill :
  The too huge bias of the world hath sway'd   35
  Her back-part upwards, and with that she braves
  This Hemisphere, that long her mouth hath mockt :
  The gravity of her religious face,

(Now growne too waighty with her sacriledge,
And here discern'd sophisticate enough)
Turnes to th'Antipodes : and all the formes
That her illusions have imprest in her,
Have eaten through her back : and now all see,　　　5
How she is riveted with hypocrisie :
Was this the way? was he the mean betwixt you?
TAMYRA. He was, he was, kind worthy[28] man he was.
MONTSURRY. Write, write a word or two.
TAMYRA.　　　　　　　　　I will, I will.　　　10
Ile write but with[29] my bloud that he may see,
These lines come from my wounds & not from me.
　　　　　　　　　　　　Writes.[30]
MONTSURRY. Well might he die for thought : me thinks
　　　　　the frame[8]　　　15
And shaken joynts of the whole world should crack
To see her parts so disproportionate;
And that his generall beauty cannot stand
Without these staines in the particular man.
Why wander I so farre? here, here was she　　　20
That was a whole world without spot to me,
Though now a world of spots; oh what a lightning
Is mans delight in women? what a bubble
He builds his state, fame, life on, when he marries?
Since all earths pleasures are so short and small,　　　25
The way t'enjoy it, is t'abjure it all.
Enough : I must be messenger my selfe,
Disguis'd like this strange creature : in, Ile after,
To see what guilty light gives this Cave eyes,
And to the world sing new impieties.　　　30
　　　　　　　　　　Exeunt [*servants.*]
He puts the FRIAR *in the vault and follows, She*
　　raps her self in the Arras.[31]

[Scena secunda.]

Enter monsieur *and* guise.   5
monsieur. Now shall we see that nature hath no end
  In her great works, responsive to their worths,
  That she that[1] makes so many eyes and soules
  To see, and fore-see, is stark blind her selfe,
  And as illiterate men say Latine prayers   10
  By rote of heart, and dayly iteration,[2]
  Not knowing what they say;[3] so Nature layes
  A deale[4] of stuffe together, and by use
  Or by the meere necessity of matter
  Ends such a work, fills it, or leaves it empty   15
  Of strength, or vertue, error, or cleare truth,
  Not knowing what she does, but usually
  Gives that which [we call][5] merit to a man,
  And [beleeve should][6] arrive him on huge riches,
  Honour and happinesse, that effects his ruine.   20
  [Right] as[7] in ships of warre whole lasts[1] of powder
  Are laid [(men thinke)][8] to make them last and
                         guard [them];
  When a disorder'd spark that powder taking,
  Blowes up with sodaine violence and horror   25
  Ships that (kept empty) had sayl'd long with terror.
guise. He that observes but like a worldly man
  That which doth oft succeed, and by th'events
  Values the worth of things, will think it true
  That Nature works at random, just with you :   30
  But with as much proportion[9] she may make
  A thing that from the feet up to the throat
  Hath all the wondrous fabrique man should have,
  And leave it headlesse for a perfect[10] man;
  As give a full[11] man valour, vertue, learning,   35

Act V. Scene ii.
[1] One "last" is 24 barrels.

Without an end more excellent then those
On whom she no such worthy part bestowes.

MONSIEUR. Yet shall you[12] see it here, here will be
             one
Young, learned, valiant, vertuous, and full mann'd,   5
One on whom nature spent so rich a hand,
That with an ominous eye she wept to see
So much consum'd her vertuous treasurie.
Yet as the winds sing through a hollow tree,
And (since it lets them passe through) let it[13]   10
             stand;
But a tree solid (since it gives no way
To their wild rage)[14] they rend up by the root :
So[15] this whole man
(That will not wind with every crooked way,   15
Trod by the servile world) shall reele and fall[15]
Before the frantic puffes of blind borne[16] chance,
That pipes through empty men, and makes them
             dance.
Not[1] so the Sea raves on the Libian sands,   20
Tumbling her billowes in each others neck :
Not so the surges of the Euxian[17] Sea
(Neere to the frosty pole, where free *Boötes*
From those dark deep waves turnes his radiant
             teame,)   25
Swell (being enrag'd even from their inmost drop)
As fortune swings about the restlesse state
Of vertue, now throwne into all mens hate.[1]
    Enter MONTSURRY *disguis'd, with*
        the murtherers.[18]   30
Away my Lord, you are perfectly disguis'd,
Leave us to lodge your ambush.

MONTSURRY.   Speed me vengeance.
                                Exit.

MONSIEUR. Resolve my Masters, you shall meet with one   35
    Will try what proofes your privy coats[2] are made on :

―――――――――

[2] *privy coats :* of chain mail.

When he is entred, and you heare us stamp,
Approach, and make all sure.
MURTHERERS.   We will my Lord.
                                          Exeunt.

5

[SCENA TERTIA.]

[*Enter*] D'AMBOIS *with two Pages with Tapers.*
BUSSY. Sit up to night, and watch, Ile speak with none   10
But the old Friar, who bring to me.
PAGES.   We will Sir.
                                          Exeunt.
BUSSY. What violent heat is this? me thinks the fire
Of twenty lives doth on a suddaine flash   15
Through all my faculties : the ayre goes high
In this close chamber, and the frighted earth
                                    Thunder.[1]
Trembles, and shrinks beneath me : the whole house
Nods[2] with his shaken burthen : blesse me, heaven.   20
              Enter UMBRA FRIAR.
UMBRA FRIAR. Note what I want[1] deare[3] sonne, and
              be fore-warn'd.
O there are bloudy deeds past and to come :
I cannot stay, a fate doth ravish me :   25
Ile meet thee in the chamber of thy love.   *Exit.*
BUSSY. What dismall change is here? the good old Friar
Is murther'd; being made knowne to serve my love;
And[4] now his restlesse spirit would fore-warne me
Of some plot dangerous, and imminent.[4]   30
Note what he wants? he wants his upper[5] weed,[2]
He wants his life, and body : which of these
Should be the want he meanes, and may supply me
With any fit fore-warning? this strange vision,
(Together with the dark prediction   35

ACT V. SCENE III.
[1] *want :* lack.   [2] *weed :* gown.

417

Us'd by the Prince of darknesse that was rais'd
By this embodied shadow) stirre my thoughts
With reminiscion of the Spirits promise,
Who told me, that by any invocation
I should have power to raise him; though it wanted   5
The powerfull words, and decent rites of Art;
Never had my set braine such need of spirit,
T'instruct and cheere it; now then I will claime
Performance of his free and gentle vow,
T'appeare in greater light; and make more plain   10
His rugged Oracle : I long to know
How my deare Mistresse fares; and be inform'd
What hand she now holds on the troubled bloud
Of her incensed Lord : me thought the Spirit
(When he had utter'd his perplext presage)   15
Threw his chang'd countenance headlong into clouds;
His forehead bent, as it would hide his face;
He knockt his chin against his darkned breast,
And struck a churlish silence through his pow'rs.
Terror of darknesse, O thou King of flames,   20
That with thy Musique-footed horse dost strike
The cleare light out of chrystall, on dark earth,
And hurlst instructive fire about the world,
Wake, wake, the drowsie and enchanted night,
That sleepes with dead eyes in this heavy riddle;   25
Or thou great Prince of shades where never sunne
Stickes his far-darted beames, whose eyes are made
To shine[6] in darknesse, and see ever best
Where men are[7] blindest, open now the heart
Of thy abashed oracle, that for feare   30
Of some ill it includes would faine lie hid,
And rise thou with it in thy greater light.
     Thunders.[8] *Surgit spiritus cum suis.*
BEHEMOTH.[9] Thus to observe my vow of apparition
  In greater light, and explicate thy fate,   35
  I come; and tell thee that if thou obey
The summons that thy mistresse next will send thee,
Her hand shall be thy death.

BUSSY.   When will she send?

BEHEMOTH. Soone as I set againe, where late I rose.

BUSSY. Is the old Friar slaine?

BEHEMOTH.   No, and yet lives not.

BUSSY. Died he a naturall death?   5

BEHEMOTH.   He did.

BUSSY.   Who then

  Will my deare mistresse send?

BEHEMOTH.   I must not tell thee.

BUSSY. Who lets[3] thee?   10

BEHEMOTH.   Fate.

BUSSY.   Who are fates ministers?

BEHEMOTH. The Guise and Monsieur.

BUSSY.   A fit paire of sheeres

  To cut the threds of Kings, and kingly spirits,   15

  And consorts fit to sound forth harmony,

  Set to the fals of Kingdomes : shall the hand

  Of my kind Mistresse kill me?

BEHEMOTH.   If thou yeeld, *Thunders.*[10]

  To her next summons; y'are faire warn'd : farewell.   20

                Exit [with attendant spirits.]

BUSSY. I must fare well, how ever : though I die

  My death consenting with his augurie;

  Should not my powers obay when she commands,

  My motion must be rebell to my will :   25

  My will to life,[11] if when I have obay'd,

  Her hand should so reward me : they must arme it,

  Binde me or force[12] it : or I lay my life

  She rather would convert it many times

  On her owne bosome, even to many deaths :   30

  But were there danger of such violence,

  I know 'tis far from her intent to send :

  And who she should send is as farre from thought,

  Since he is dead, whose only mean she us'd.

                    Knocks.[13]   35

  Whose there? look to the dore : and let him in,

---

[3] *lets :* stops.

Though politick Monsieur, or the violent Guise.
Enter MONTSURRY *like the Friar, with a Letter
written in bloud.*[14]

MONTSURRY. Haile[15] to my worthy sonne.

BUSSY.   O lying Spirit!   5
To say the Friar was dead; Ile now beleeve
Nothing of all his forg'd predictions.
My kinde and honour'd Father, well reviv'd,
I have beene frighted with your death, and mine,
And told my Mistresse hand should be my death   10
If I obeyed this summons.

MONTSURRY.   I beleev'd
Your love had bin much clearer, then to give
Any such doubt a thought, for she is cleare.
And having freed her husbands jealousie,   15
(Of which her much abus'd hand here is witnesse)
She prayes for urgent cause your instant presence.[15]

BUSSY. Why[16] then your prince of spirits may be
                          call'd
The prince of lyers.   20

MONTSURRY.   Holy writ so calls him.[16]

BUSSY. What? writ in bloud?

MONTSURRY.   I, 'tis the ink of lovers.

BUSSY. O, 'tis a sacred witnesse of her love,
So much elixer of her bloud as this   25
Dropt in the lightest dame, would make her firme
As heat to fire : and like to all the signes,[4]
Commands the life confinde in all my veines;
O how it multiplies my bloud with spirit,
And makes me apt t'encounter death and hell :   30
But, come kinde Father; you fetch me to heaven,
And to that end your holy weed was given.
                          Exeunt.[17]

[4] *signes :* of the heavens.

[Scena quarta.]

Thunder. Intrat umbra friar, *and discovers*   5
          tamyra.

umbra friar. Up[1] with these stupid thoughts, still
          loved daughter.
And strike away this heartlesse trance of anguish,
Be like the Sunne, and labour in eclipses,   10
Look to the end of woes : oh can you sit
Mustering the horrors of your servants slaughter
Before your contemplation, and not study[1]
How to prevent it? watch when he shall rise,
And with a suddaine out-crie of his murther,   15
Blow his retreat before he be revenged.[2], (1)
tamyra. O Father. Have my dumb woes wak'd your
          death.
When will our humane griefes be at their height?
Man is a tree, that hath no top in cares;   20
No root in comforts; all his power to live
Is given to no end, but have [3] power to grieve.
umbra friar. It[4] is the misery of our creation.
Your true friend,
Led by your husband, shadowed in my weed,   25
Now enters the dark vault.
tamyra.   But my dearest Father,
Why will not you appeare to him your selfe,
And see that none of these deceits annoy him.
umbra friar. My power is limited, alas I cannot,   30
All that I can doe—See the Cave opens.[4]   *Exit.*
      d'ambois *at the gulfe.*
tamyra. Away (my Love) away, thou wilt be
          murther'd.
     Enter monsieur *and* guise *above.*[5]
                               35
bussy. Murther'd? I know not what that Hebrew means :
That word had ne're bin nam'd had all bin D'Ambois.
Murther'd? By heaven he is my murtherer

That shewes me not a murtherer : what such bugge[1]
Abhorreth not the very sleepe of D'Ambois?
Murther'd? Who dares give all the room I see
To[6] D'Ambois reach? or look with any odds
His fight i'th face, upon whose hand sits death;   5
Whose sword hath wings, and every feather pierceth?
If[7] I scape Monsieurs Pothecarie Shops,
Fouter for Guises Shambles! 'Twas ill plotted;[8]
They should have mall'd me here,
When I was rising, I am up and ready.[7]   10
Let in my politick visitants, let them in,
Though entring like so many moving armours,
Fate is more strong than arms, and slie than treason,
And I at all parts buckl'd in my Fate.

MONSIEUR. ⎫
            ⎬ Why enter not the coward villains?[9]   15
GUISE.   ⎭

BUSSY. Dare they not come?

Enter murtherers with [UMBRA] FRIAR *at the other
                    dore.*[10]

TAMYRA.   They come.   20
MURDERER I.   Come all at once.
UMBRA FRIAR. Back coward murtherers, back.
OMNES.   Defend us heaven.
            Exeunt all [Murderers] *but the first.*
[MURDERER] I. Come ye not on?   25
BUSSY.   No, slave, nor goest thou off.
                                    [*They fight.*]
Stand you so firme? Will it not enter here?
You have a face yet :
                    [*He thrusts him in the head.*]   30
                    so in thy lifes flame
I burne the first rites to my Mistresse fame.

UMBRA FRIAR. Breath thee[2] brave sonne against the
                    other charge.
BUSSY. O is it true then that my sense first told me?   35

ACT V. SCENE IV.
[1] *bugge* : bugbear; goblin.

Is my kind Father dead?

TAMYRA.   He is my Love

'Twas the Earle my husband in his weed that brought
        thee.

BUSSY. That was a speeding sleight,[3] and well re-   5
        sembled.

Where is that angry Earle? My Lord,[11] come
        forth

And shew your owne face in your owne affaire;

Take not into your noble veines the blood   10

Of these base villaines, nor the light reports

Of blister'd tongues, for clear and weighty truth:

But me against the world, in pure defence

Of your rare Lady, to whose spotlesse name

I stand here as a bulwark, and project   15

A life to her renowne, that ever yet

Hath beene untainted even in envies eye,

And where it would protect a Sanctuarie.

Brave Earle come forth, and keep your scandall in:

'Tis not our fault if you enforce the spot,[4]   20

Nor the wreak yours if you performe it not.

     Enter MONTSURRY *with all the murtherers.*[12]

MONTSURRY. Cowards, a fiend or spirit beat ye off?

They are your owne faint spirits that have forg'd

The fearefull shadowes that your eyes deluded: 25

The fiend was in you; cast him out then thus.

    [*They fight.*] D'AMBOIS *hath* MONTSURRY *downe.*[13]

TAMYRA. Favour my Lord, my Love,[14] O favour
        him.

BUSSY. I will not touch him: Take your life, my Lord, 30

And be appeas'd: *Pistolls shot within.*[15]

        O then the coward Fates

Have maim'd themselves, and ever lost their honour.

UMBRA FRIAR. What have ye done slaves? irreligious
        Lord?   35

BUSSY. Forbeare them, Father; 'tis enough for me

That Guise and Monsieur, death and destinie

Come behind D'Ambois: is my body then

But penetrable flesh? And must my mind
Follow my blood? Can my divine part adde
No ayd to th'earthly in extremity?
Then these divines are but for forme, not fact :
Man is of two sweet Courtly friends compact;   5
A Mistresse and a servant : let my death
Define life nothing but a Courtiers breath.
Nothing is made of nought, of all things made,
Their abstract being a dreame but of a shade,
Ile not complaine to earth yet, but to heaven,   10
And (like a man) look upwards even in death.
And if *Vespasian* thought in majestie
An Emperour might die standing,(5) why not I?
                             She offers to help him.[16]
Nay without help, in which I will exceed him;   15
For he died splinted with his chamber Groomes.[16]
Prop me, true sword, as thou hast ever done :
The equall thought I beare of life and death,
Shall make me faint on no side; I am up
Here like a Roman Statue; I will stand   20
Till death hath made me Marble : O(6) my fame
Live in despight of murther; take thy wings
And haste thee where the gray-ey'd morne per-
                             fumes[17]
Her Rosie chariot with Sabaean spices,   25
Fly, where the evening from th'Iberean vales,
Takes on her swarthy shoulders, *Heccate*
Crown'd with a Grove of Oakes : flie where men
                             feele
The burning axeltree[2] : and those that suffer   30
Beneath the chariot of the Snowy Beare :
And tell them all that D'Ambois now is hasting
To the eternall dwellers; that a thunder
Of all their sighes together (for their frailties

[2] *The burning axeltree : The
"feruenti axe" of Seneca, the
sun's path.*

Beheld in me) may quit my worthlesse fall[3]
With a fit volley for my funerall.[(6)]
UMBRA FRIAR. Forgive thy murtherers.
BUSSY.   I forgive them all :
  And you my Lord, their fautor[4]; for true signe   5
  Of which unfain'd remission, take my sword;
  Take it, and onely give it motion,
  And it shall finde the way to victory
  By his owne brightnesse, and th'inherent valour
  My fight hath still'd into't, with charmes of spirit.   10
  Now[18] let me pray you, that my weighty bloud
  Laid in one scale of your impertiall spleene,
  May sway the forfeit of my worthy love
  Waid in the other : and be reconcil'd
  With all forgivenesse to your matchlesse wife.   15
TAMYRA. Forgive thou me deare servant, and this hand
  That lead thy life to this unworthy end.
  Forgive it, for the bloud with which 'tis stain'd,
  In which I writ the summons of thy death :
  The forced summons, by this bleeding wound,   20
  By this here in my bosome : and by this
  That makes me hold up both my hands embrew'd
  For thy deare pardon.
BUSSY.   O, my heart is broken
  Fate, not[19] these murtherers, Monsieur, nor the   25
                 Guise,
  Have any glory in my death, but this :
  This killing spectacle : this prodigie :
  My sunne is turn'd to blood in[20] whose red beams
  Pindus and *Ossa* (hid in drifts of[21] snow,   30
  Laid on my heart and liver) from their veines[22]
  Melt like two hungry torrents : eating rocks
  Into the Ocean of all humane life,
  And make it bitter,[(7)] only with my bloud :
  O fraile condition of strength, valour, vertue   35

---

[3] *quit . . . fall :* repay my dis-   [4] *fautor :* protector.
honorable assassination.

In me (like warning fire upon the top
Of some steepe Beacon, on a steeper hill)
Made to expresse it : like a falling starre
Silently glanc't, that like a thunderbolt,
Look't to have stuck and shook the firmament.   5

         Moritur.[23]

UMBRA FRIAR. Farewell[24] brave reliques[25] of a
      compleat man.
Look up and see thy spirit made a starre,
[Join] flames [with Hercules,][26] and when thou   10
      set'st[8]
Thy radiant forehead in the firmament,
Make the vast chrystall[27] crack with thy receipt :
Spread to a world of fire, and the aged skie
Cheere with new sparks of old humanity.[24]   15
[*To* MONTSURRY.] Son of the earth, whom my un-
      rested soule
Rues t'have begotten in the faith of heaven;[28]
Assay to gratulate⁵ and pacifie,
The soule fled from this worthy by performing   20
The Christian reconcilement he besought
Betwixt thee and thy Lady, let her wounds
Manlesly[9] digg'd in her, be eas'd and cur'd
With balme of thine owne teares : or be assur'd
Never to rest free from my haunt and horror.   25
MONTSURRY. See how she merits this : still kneeling[29]
      by
And mourning his fall, more than her own fault.
UMBRA FRIAR. Remove, deare daughter, and content thy
      husband :   30
So piety wills thee, and thy servants peace.
TAMYRA. O wretched piety, that are so distract
In thine owne constancie; and in thy right
Must be unrighteous : if I right my friend
I wrong my husband : if his wrong I shunne,   35
The duty of my friend I leave undone;

⁵ *gratulate :* gratify.

Ill playes on both sides; here and there, it riseth;
No place : no good so good, but ill compriseth;[30]
O had I never married but for forme,
Never vow'd faith but purpos'd to deceive :
Never made conscience of any sinne,   5
But clok't it privately, and made it common :
Nor never honour'd beene, in blood, or mind,
Happy had I beene then, as others are
Of the like licence; I had then beene honour'd :
Liv'd without envie : custome had benumb'd   10
All sense of scruple, and all note of frailty :
My fame had beene untouch'd, my heart unbroken :
But (shunning all) I strike on all offence,
O husband? deare friend? O my conscience!
MONSIEUR. Come let's away, my sences are not proofe   15
　　Against those plaints.
　　Exeunt GUISE [*and*] MONSIEUR. D'AMBOIS *is borne off.*
MONTSURRY. I must not yeeld to pity nor to love
　　So servile and so trayterous : cease my bloud
　　To wrastle with my honour, fame, and judgement :   20
　　Away, forsake my house, forbeare complaints
　　Where thou hast bred them : here [are] all things
　　　　　　　　full,[31]
　　Of their owne shame and sorrow, leave my house.
TAMYRA. Sweet Lord forgive me, and I will be gone,   25
　　And till these wounds, that never balme shall close
　　Till death hath enterr'd at them, so I love them
　　(Being opened by your hands) by death be cur'd
　　I never more will grieve you with my sight :
　　Never endure that any roofe shall part   30
　　Mine eyes and heaven : but to the open Deserts
　　(Like to a hunted[32] Tygres) I will flie :
　　Eating my heart, shunning the steps of men,
　　And look on no side till I be arriv'd.
MONTSURRY. I doe forgive thee, and upon my knees   35
　　With hands (held up to heaven) wish that mine
　　　　　　　　honour
　　Would suffer reconcilement to my Love :

But since it will not, honour, never serve
My love with flourishing object till it sterve[6] :
And as this Taper, though it upwards look,
Downwards must needs consume,[(10)] so let our
          love;   5
As having lost his hony, the sweet taste
Runnes into savour, and will needs retaine
A spice of his first parents, till (like life)
It [seres][33] and dies; so let our love : And lastly,
As when the flame is suffer'd to look up,   10
It keepes his luster : but, being thus turn'd downe
(His naturall course of usefull light inverted)
His owne stuffe puts it out : so let our love.
Now turne from me, as here I turn from thee,
And may both points of heavens strait axeltree[(11)] 15
Conjoyne in one, before thy selfe and me.
                Exeunt severally.[34]
   Finis Actus Quinti & ultimi.

                    20

        Epilogue[35]

With many hands you have seene D'Ambois slaine,
Yet by your grace he may revive againe,
And every day grow stronger in his skill   25
To please, as we presume he is in will.
The best deserving Actors of the time
Had their ascents; and by degrees did clime
To their full height, a place to studie due
To make him tread in their path lies in you;   30
Hee'le not forget his Makers; but still prove
His thankfulnesse as you encrease your love.

[6] *sterve :* die.

VARIANTS

VARIANTS

In order to simplify notation, brackets inserted in the text have not been repeated in the variants. Punctuation is repeated only where significant. Variations of spelling in titles and speech headings are not recorded. The frequent errors in placement and names of characters in stage directions are not recorded unless (as in the case of *Bussy D'Ambois*) they are of special interest.

EVERY MAN IN HIS HUMOUR

The text of this edition is that of the 1616 Folio. The copies used were the Houghton Library copies. Variants are selected.

    Q   Quarto 1601.
    F   Folio 1616.
    HS   Edition of Herford and Simpson.

DEDICATION *and* PROLOGUE *in* F *only*. CLARENTIAUX *HS*.

DRAMATIS PERSONAE :

KNO'WELL] Lorenzo senior *Q*.
EDWARD KNO'WELL] Lorenzo junior *Q*.
BRAYNE-WORME] Musco *Q*.
MASTER STEPHEN] Stephano *Q*.
DOWNE-RIGHT] Giulliano *Q*.
WELL-BRED] Prospero *Q*.
JUSTICE CLEMENT] Doctor Clement *Q*.
ROGER FORMALL] Peto *Q*.
KITELY] Thorello *Q*.
DAME KITELY] Biancha *Q*.
MISTRESS BRIDGET] Hesperida *Q*.
MASTER MATTHEW] Matheo *Q*.
CASH] Pizo *Q*.
CAPTAIN BOBADILL] Bobadilla *Q*.

431

SCENE :

LONDON] [Florence] *Q.*

ACT I. SCENE I.

[1] both our *universities*] all our *Academies Q.*

[2] *F only.*

[3] *F only.*

[4] prodigall absurd cocks-combe] prodigal, and selfe-wild foole *Q.*

[5] *F only.*

ACT I. SCENE II. *See explanatory note on scene headings.*

[1] *F only.*

[2] *F only.*

[3] *F expansion of*] Therefore ile studie (by some milder drift)/To call my sonne unto a happier shrift. *Q.*

ACT I. SCENE III.

[1] well I thanke thee, Brayne-Worme] well *Musco* hie thee in againe, Least thy protracted absence do lend light, / To darke suspition : *Musco* be assurde / Ile not forget this thy respective love. *Q.*

[2] be gelt] be-gelt *F*] be made an *Eunuch Q.*

[3] How now, coussen Stephen, melancholy'?] Cousin Stephano : good morrow, good cousin, how fare you? *Q.*

[4] *F only.*

[5] *Cf. the earlier version*] Your turne? why cousin, a gentleman of so faire sort as you are, of so true cariage, so speciall good parts; of so deare and choice estimation; one whose lowest condition beares the stampe of a great spirit; nay more, a man so grac'd, guilded, or rather (to use a more fit *Metaphor*) tinfoyld by nature, (not that you have a leaden constitution, couze, although perhaps a little inclining to that temper, & so the more apt to melt with pittie, when you fall into the fire of rage) but for your lustre onely, which reflects as bright to the world as an old Ale-wives pewter againe a good time; and will you now (with nice modestie) hide such reall ornaments as these, and shadow their glorie as a Millaners wife doth her wrought stomacher, with a smoakie lawne or a blacke cipresse? Come, come, for shame doe not wrong the qualitie of your desert in so poore a kind : but let the *Idea* of what you are, be portraied in your aspect, that men may reade in your

432

lookes; *Here within this place is to be seene, the most admirable rare & accomplisht worke of nature;* Cousin what think you of this? *Q.*

ACT I. SCENE V.

[1] peremptory-beautifull] beautifull *Q.*

[2] peremptory absurd clowne of *christendome*] peremptorie absurd clowne (one a them) in *Christendome Q.*

[3] *Cf. the earlier version*] By the life of Pharaoh, and't were my case nowe, I should send him a challenge presently : the bastinado? come hither, you shall challenge him; ile shew you a tricke or two, you shall kill him at pleasure, the first *stockado* if you will, by this ayre. *Q.*

[4] *F only.*

ACT II. SCENE I.

[1] *Prose variation in Q.*

[2] *F only.*

[3] *F only.*

[4] *Cf. the earlier version*] Faith I know not what I should say to him : so God save mee, I am eene at my wits end, I have tolde him inough, one would thinke, if that would serve : well, he knowes what to trust to for me : let him spend, and spend, and domineere till his hart ake : & he get a peny more of me, Ile give him this eare.

[5] heate of humour] heate of passion *Q.*

[6] *F only.*

[7] *F only.*

ACT II. SCENE II. *Not a separate scene in Q, which may account for the omission of* To them *as a heading in F.*

[1] Gentleman o' the house] Gentleman *Q.*

[2] cow] ——— *Q.*

ACT II. SCENE III. To them *F erroneous marginal heading.*

[1] *F only.*

[2] harme, in troth] harme in, troth *F.*

[3] Or, knowing it, to want the mindes erection] And want the free election of the soul *Q.*

ACT II. SCENE IV.

[1] *F only.*

[2] *F only.*

[3] fellow] friend Q.

[4] *F expansion of*] Tut, ile buy this, so I will; tell me your lowest price. Q.

ACT II. SCENE V.

[1] *Cf. the earlier version*]
My labouring spirit being late opprest
With my sonnes follie, can embrace no rest,
Till it hath plotted by advise and skill,
How to reduce him from affected will
To reasons manage; which while I intend,
My troubled soule beginnes to apprehend
A farther secret, and to meditate
Upon the difference of mans estate :
Where is deciphered to true judgements eye
A deep, conceald, and precious misterie.
Yet can I not but worthily admire
At natures art : who (when she did inspire
This heat of life) plac'd Reason (as a king)
Here in the head, to have the marshalling
Of our affections : and with soveraigntie
To sway the state of our weake emperie.
But as in divers commonwealthes we see,
The forme of government to disagree :
Even so in man who searcheth soone shal find
As much or more varietie of mind.
Some mens affections like a sullen wife,
Is with her husband reason still at strife.
Others (like proud Arch-traitors that rebell
Against their soveraigne) practise to expell
Their liege Lord Reason, and not shame to tread
Upon his holy and annointed head.
But as that land or nation best doth thrive,
Which to smooth-fronted peace is most proclive,
So doth that mind, whose faire affections rang'd
By reasons rules, stand constant and unchang'd,
Els, if the power of reason be not such,
Why do we attribute to him so much?
Or why are we obsequious to his law,
If we want spirit our affects to awe?
Oh no, I argue weakly, he is strong,

434

Albeit my sonne have done him too much wrong. *Q.*

[2] Fitz-Sword] *Portensio Q.*

[3] never was bottle, or bag-pipe fuller *F only.*

[4] *F only.*

Act III. Scene i.

[1] Plinie, or Symmachus epistles] *Plinies* familiar Epistles *Q.*

[2] full view o' your flourishing stile] the proving of your copy *Q.*

[3] some strange dissolute yong fellow] a damn'd dissolute villain *Q.*

[4] hang-by's] *Zanies Q.*

[5] *F only.*

[6] of—what doe you call it] of *Tortosa Q.*

[7] and what doe you call't *F only.*

Act III. Scene ii.

[1] a drumme] a Barbers virginals *Q.*

[2] *F only.*

Act III. Scene iii.

[1] *Cf. the earlier version*]
Oh beauty is a *Proiect* of some power,
Chiefely when oportunitie attends her :
She will infuse true motion in a stone,
Put glowing fire in an Icie soule,
Stuffe peasants bosoms with proud *Caesars* spleene,
Powre rich device into an empty braine :
Bring youth to follies gate : there traine him in,
And after all, extenuate his sinne.
Well, I will not go, I am resolv'd for that.
Goe cary it againe, yet stay : yet do too,
I will deferre it till some other time. *Q.*

Act III. Scene iv.

[1] a gentleman-like monster, bred, in the speciall gallantrie of our time] a monster bred in a man by selfe love *Q.*

[2] 'hem] hem *F.*

Act III. Scene v.

[1] artificer] gallant *Q.*

[2] An artificer! An architect! *F only.*

ACT III. SCENE VI.

[1] head] heart Q.
[2] *F only.*
[3] mustard revenge] russet revenge Q.

ACT III. SCENE VII.

[1] A gentleman, and a souldier, he saies he is, o' the citie here.] A gentleman in the citie sir. Q.
[2] *F only.*
[3] *Reduced from the earlier lines*]
Troth would I could sir : but enforced mirth
(In my weake judgement) ha's no happy birth.
The minde, being once a prisoner unto cares,
The more it dreames on joy, the worse it fares.
A smyling looke is to a heavie soule,
As a guilt bias, to a leaden bowle,
Which (in it selfe) appeares most vile, being spent
To no true use; but onely for ostent. Q.

ACT IV. SCENE II.

[1] *Incipere*] *Insipere F*] Incipere Q.
[2] O, forgive it him.] Nay good *Critique* forbeare. Q.

ACT IV. SCENE VIII.

[1] *In Q* Clement *enters with* Thorello *here to ask after his man as* Thorello *does after his wife.*

ACT IV. SCENE X.

[1] *Marginal note Of*] *By F.*

ACT V. SCENE V.

[1] *Q adds*]
PROSPERO. Oh he writes not in that height of stile.
CLEMENT. No : weele come a steppe or two lower then.
    From Catadupa and the bankes of Nile,
        Where onely breedes your monstrous Crocodile :
            Now are we purposd for to fetch our stile.
[2] *Q reads*]
Unto the boundlesse ocean of thy bewtie,
    Runnes this poor river, chargd with streames of zeale,
    Returning thee the tribute of my dutie :

436

    Which here my youth, my plaints, my love reveale.
    Good! is this your owne invention?
MATHEO. No sir, I translated that out of a booke, called *Delia*.
    [3] *Q reads and adds*]
LORENZO JUNIOR. Poetry? nay then call blasphemie, religion;
    Call Divels, Angels; and Sinne, pietie :
    Let all things be preposterously transchangd.
LORENZO SENIOR. Why how now sonne? what? are you startled now?
    Hath the brize prickt you? ha? go to; you see,
    How abjectly your Poetry is ranckt,
    In generall opinion.
LORENZO JUNIOR. Opinion, O God let grosse opinion
    Sinck & be damnd as deepe as *Barathrum*.
    If it may stand with your most wisht content,
    I can refell opinion, and approve
    The state of poesie, such as it is,
    Blessed, aeternall, and most true devine :
    Indeede if you will looke on Poesie,
    As she appeares in many, poore and lame,
    Patcht up in remnants and olde worne ragges,
    Halfe starvd for want of her peculiar foode,
    Sacred invention, then I must conferme,
    Both your conceite and censure of her merrite.
    But view her in her glorious ornaments,
    Attired in the majestie of arte,
    Set high in spirite with the precious taste
    Of sweete philosophie, and which is most,
    Crownd with the rich traditions of a soule,
    That hates to have her dignitie prophand,
    With any relish of an earthly thought :
    Oh then how proud a presence doth she beare.
    Then is she like her selfe, fit to be seene
    Of none but grave and consecrated eyes:
    Nor is it any blemish to her fame,
    That such leane, ignorant, and blasted wits,
    Such brainlesse guls, should utter their stolne wares
    With such aplauses in our vulgar eares :
    Or that their slubberd lines have currant passe,
    From the fat judgements of the multitude,
    But that this barren and infected age,
    Should set no difference twixt these empty spirits,

And a true Poet : then which reverend name,
Nothing can more adorne humanitie.   *Enter with torches.*
CLEMENT. I Lorenzo, but election is now governd altogether by the
influence of humor, which insteed of those holy flames that
should direct and light the soule to eternitie, hurles foorth nothing but smooke and congested vapours, that stifle her up, & be-
reave her of al sight & motion. But she must have store of *Elle-
bore* given her to purge these grosse obstructions : oh thats well
sayd, give me thy torch, come lay this stuffe together.

THE MALCONTENT

The copy used was the Houghton Library copy. The editions of Hazelton Spencer and H. Harvey Wood were occasionally useful, as is credited below.

Q   Quarto 1604.

INDUCTION

[1] Condell] Cundale Q. Burbage] Burbidge Q.

[2] *Stage direction:* SINKLO] Sinkclow Q.

[3] *Stage direction:* Enter D: Burbidge, H: Cundale, I: Lewin. Q.

[4] feather] father Q.

[5] Herald] Harralde Q.

[6] marmoset] marmasite Q.

[7] *Stage direction: Exit Burbidge* Q.

[8] they] he Q.

ACT I. SCENE II.

[1] Ganymede] Ganimed Q.

[2] ah] a Q.

[3] goatish] gotish Q.

ACT I. SCENE III.

[1] Malcontent] Malecontent Q.

[2] ah] a Q.

[3] make-place] make-pleece Q.

[4] world, even] world even Q.

[5] should show] shue, should Q.

[6] state's] stat's Q.

ACT I. SCENE IV.

[1] *Prose in* Q.

[2] *Prose in* Q.

[3] Lord] Lerd Q.

ACT I. SCENE V.

[1] ah] a Q. hot reinde] hot rainde Q.

[2] languishing] langushing Q.

439

ACT I. SCENE VI.

[1] jawde] jade Q.
[2] Emilia] AEmilia Q.
[3] *Prose in* Q.

ACT I. SCENE VII.

[1] sir] sit Q.
[2] Lose] Loose Q.
[3] Princess] Princes Q.

ACT I. SCENE VIII.

[1] gilt] guilt Q.

ACT II. SCENE III.

[1] slaves I' favour] slaves I favour Q.
[2] PIETRO] *Mend.* Q.

ACT II. SCENE IV.

[1] candied] candide Q.
[2] sentinell] centinell Q.

ACT II. SCENE V.

[1] spirits pent] spirits spent Q. *Dodsley suggested* spirits speed. *His reading is adopted by Spencer and Wood.*

ACT III. SCENE I.

[1] Lucius Anaeus] Lucius Anneus Q.
[2] *Stage direction : Enter Bilioso and Bianca.* Q.
[3] Harlequin] Herlakeene Q.

ACT III. SCENE II.

[1] hart a'] hart a Q.
[2] *Prose in* Q.

ACT III. SCENE III.

[1] *Prose in* Q.
[2] *Prose in* Q.
[3] *Prose in* Q.
[4] *Prose in* Q.

ACT III. SCENE V.

[1] PIETRO] *Cel.* Q.

Act IV. Scene i.

[1] Sentinell] Centinell Q.
[2] sencelesse] fenceless Q.
[3] *These lines are spoken by* Emilia *in* Q.

Act IV. Scene iii.

[1] Like lightning *added to the foregoing speech of* Mendoza
in Q.
[2] *Marginal gloss :* (shootes under his belly.) Q.

Act IV. Scene iv.

[1] rant] rand Q.

Act IV. Scene v.

[1] *Stage direction :* Halberds] Holberts Q.
[2] a'] a Q.
[3] for publishing] for banishing Q. *The emendation was first
suggested by K. Deighton.*

Act V. Scene i.

[1] th'se'ves] thieves Q] them *Spencer.*
[2] *Stage direction : Exeunt severally*] *Exit.* Q.

Act V. Scene ii.

[1] (pox)] (   ) Q.
[2] a'] a Q.

Act V. Scene iii.

[1] *Heading :* Scena tertia] Scena secunda Q.
[2] sex] fex Q.

Act V. Scene iv.

[1] *Heading :* Scena quarta] Scena tertia Q.
[2] Q *adds here :*
                    Enter Malevole and Mendoza :
Mend. Hast bin with *Maria.*
Male. As your scrivener to your usurer
I have delt about taking of this commoditie, but shes could
frosty.
[3] here's] her's Q.

[4] conduits] comodites Q. *The emendation is suggested by Spencer.*
[5] *Prose in Q.*
[6] What shape?] Why shape? Q.
[7] *Prose in Q.*
[8] *Prose in Q.*

ACT V. SCENE V.

[1] warpt] wrapt Q.

ACT V. SCENE VI.

[1] *Heading :* SCENA SEXTA] SCENA QUARTA Q.
[2] forfeited] forteified Q. examined] axamined Q.
[3] court] count Q.
[4] MALEVOLE] *Pietro.* Q.

THE WHITE DEVIL

The copy used was the Houghton Library copy. The editions of Brown and Lucas were consulted.

Q   Quarto of 1612.
B   Edition of John Brown.
L   Editions of Lucas (1927, 1958).

To the Reader:

[1] blacke] bleak *suggested by Malone, according to Dyce in his edition of 1830.*

Act I. Scene i.

[1] have you] have you, you Q.
[2] *Stage direction: Enter Senate Q.*

Act I. Scene ii.

[1] whereas] where a Q.
[2] your] you Q.
[3] leave] leaves Q.
[4] his] this Q.
[5] pitifull] pittful Q.

Act II. Scene i.

[1] That you that have] That you have Q. *The emendation is suggested by L and adopted by B.*
[2] *repostum] repositum Q.*
[3] another's] another Q.

Act II. Scene ii.

[1] brachiano] mar. Q.

Act III. Scene i.

[1] *Stage direction: Embassadour] Embassadours Q.*

Act III. Scene ii.

[1] assign'd] assing'd Q.
[2] gentlewoman] gentlewomen Q.
[3] language] languag Q.
[4] emptied] empted Q.
[5] brings] bring Q.

443

[6] ones] on's *Q.*

[7] mouths] mouth's *Q.*

[8] he] her *Q.*

[9] repetition] repetion *Q.*

[10] VIT. *erroneous heading in Q.*

[11] mawe] mawes *Q.*

[12] on] one *Q.*

[13] *This line is given to* FRANCISCO *in Q.*

ACT III. SCENE III.

[1] Cannon] Canon *Q.*

[2] girne, rogue] grine rouge *Q.*

ACT IV. SCENE I.

[1] bride's] brid's *Q.*

[2] Cannon] Canon *Q.*

[3] heats] heat's *Q.*
The stage direction is in a corrected copy of Q noted by B.

[4] list] life *Q.*

[5] in so] so *Q.*

[6] Now I—ha't] Now I—d' foot *Q. The emendation is from a corrected copy of Q noted by B.*

ACT IV. SCENE II.

[1] That?] What? *Q. The emendation is from a corrected copy of Q noted by B.*

[2] In] No *Q. The emendation is from a corrected copy of Q noted by B.*

[3] Yee'ld] ee'ld *Q.*

[4] two] ten *Q. The emendation is from a corrected copy of Q noted by B.*

[5] lends] lend's *Q.*

ACT IV. SCENE III.

[1] A CONCLAVIST] A CAR. *Q. The emendation is suggested by B.*

[2] *Stage direction : A Cardinal on the Tarras Q.*

[3] *This speech is given to* LODOVICO *in Q.*

[4] looks] look's *Q.*

ACT V. SCENE I.

[1] *Stage direction :* HORTENSIO] MARCELLO *Q.*

[2] *Stage direction : Exeunt* LODAVICO ANTONELLI *Q.*

[3] too much] to much *Q*.
[4] morality] mortality *Q*.
[5] two] 10 *Q*. *The emendation is from a corrected copy of Q noted by B.*
[6] FRANCISCO] FLA. *Q*.

ACT V. SCENE III.

[1] *The stage direction is suggested by B.*
[2] FRANCISCO] FLA. *Q*.

ACT V. SCENE IV.

[1] *decimo*] *dicimo Q*.
[2] art] hart *Q*.
[3] LADY] WOM. *Q*.

ACT V. SCENE VI.

[1] CARLO] CON. *Q*.
[2] too] to *Q*.

BUSSY D'AMBOIS

The text of this edition is that of the 1641 Quarto. The copy used was the Houghton Library copy. Complete variants from the first quarto are here presented from the Morgan Library copy.

A   Quarto 1607.
B   Quarto 1641.
J   Edition of Jean Jacquot.
P   Edition of T. M. Parrott.
Pa   Edition of Marcello Pagnini.

PROLOGUE *B only.*

ACT I. SCENE I.

[1] continuall] incessant *A.*
[2] forming] forging *A.*
[3] men meerely great] our Tympanouse statists *A.*
[4] wealth] powers *A.*
[5] faine] glad *A.*
[6] earth] world *A.*
[7] meane] poore *A.*
[8] possible] likely *A.*
[9] good to] fit I *A.*
[10] Callest] Think'st *A.*
[11] doe] doth *A.*
[12] wish me?] wish me doe? *A.*
[13] where] as *A.*
[14] humorous] portly *A.*
[15] And (hearing villaines preacht) t'unfold their Art *B A.*
[16] Loves] eies *A.*
[17] old] rude *A. Not noted in J.*
[18] wise] rul'd *A. Not noted in J.*
[19] *B only.*
[20] To fit his seed-land soyl] But hee's no husband heere *A. The A variant suggests that* his *in B may be a compositor's error for "this."*
[21] for] with *A.*
[22] wretch] man *A. Not noted in J, Pa, P.*
[23] doe serve] serve *A. Not noted in Pa, P.*
[24] *Marginal note in B :* Table Chesbord & Tapers behind the

Arras. *These stage props were used in the following scene. The printer's copy for B was probably a prompt book.*

[25] His Passe] A Passe A.

[26] respect] good fashion A.

[27] some] a A. *Not noted in J, Pa, P.*

[28] your great Masters goodnesse] his wise excellencie A.

[29] rude] bad A.

[30] Graces] highnes A.

[31] Poet] scholar A.

[32] bounteous Grace] excellence A. *J notes* excellencie.

[33] And to you of long ones.] And to your Deserts / The reverend vertues of a faithfull Steward; A.

[34] pleasant] merrie A.

[35] by'r lady] berlady B] beleeve it A.

[36] his Grace] my Lord A.

[37] Is] I is B.

[38] *B only.*

[39] If you be thriftie and] Serve God A.

[40] set] sown A.   their] the B.

ACT I. SCENE II.

[1] that] this A.

[2] under the hand] under hand A.

[3] Court-fashion] Court forme A.

[4] Demi-gods] Demi gods B] Semi-gods A.

[5] *B only.*

[6] vaunt] boast A.

[7] Clowneries] Rudenesse A.

[8] confusion] deformitie A.   eyes] sight A.

[9] sole heire] first borne A.

[10] and we more] and wee A.

[11] To be the Pictures of our vanitie; A.

[12] *B only.*

[13] a Gentleman to court] this Gentleman t'attend you A.

[14] *Prose in A and B.*

[15] We] I A. *Not noted in J.*

[16] We] I A. *Not noted in J.*

[17] He that will winne, must wooe her; shee's not shamelesse A.

[18] *Prose in A and B. The stage direction after line 20, p. 351 is suggested by J.*

[19] sweet heart] my love A.

[20] Montsurry] Mountsurreaue *B A.*

[21] *B only.*

[22] my Lord *B only. Not noted in Pa, P.*

[23] *B only.*

[24] *The stage direction following this line occurs in A after line 27, p. 353.*

[25] *B only.*

[26] Duke] Sir *A.*

[27] princely Mistresse] Madam *A.*

[28] *B only.*

[29] young] good *A.*

[30] *In A this passage follows the variant of line 27, p. 353.*

[31] Ile doe't by this hand] So Sir, so *A.*

[32] *Versification adopted from J and P.*

[33] Another riddle] more Courtship, as you love it *A.*

[34] Courting] Courtship *A. Not noted in Pa, P.*

[35] Their heat] Ardor *A.*

[36] but] And *A. Not noted in Pa, P.*

[37] *Flourish short B only. Not noted in Pa, P.*

[38] newly drawne] come new *A. Not noted in Pa, P.*

[39] braying] roaring *A.*

[40] sake *B only. Not noted in Pa, P.*

[41] *Exeunt Ladies B only.*

[42] *Verse in A and B. Prose adopted from J and P.*

[43] O miraculous jealousie] O strange credulitie *A. This speech is given to* Pyrhot *in A.*

[44] the matter of *B only.*

[45] *This speech is given to* BARRISOR *in A.*

[46] *This speech is given to* L'ANOU *in A.*

[47] in] with *A.*

[48] else *B only.*

[49] Follow us] Come follow us *A.* Not noted in *Pa, P.*

ACT II. SCENE I.

[1] *Stage direction :* MONTSURRY, *and Attendants*] BEAUMOND, NUNCIUS *A.*

[2] Where] When *A.*

[3] their] his *A.*

[4] Sparkl'd] Spakl'd *B*] Sparkl'd *A.*

[5] MONTSURRY *In B this speech is given to* BEAUMOND *by mistake.*

448

[6] swift a foot] quicke an eie *A*.
[7] the tw'other] th'tw'other *B*] the tw'other *A*.
[8] spirit] spirits *A*.
[9] but hee? *B only.*
[10] freckled] feebled *A*.
[11] lips] cheekes *A*.
[12] true] full *A*.
[13] daring] violent *A*.
[14] law] God *A*.
[15] Law] King *A*.
[16] *In the outer margin A and B have* Exit REX cum BEAU.
[17] Who would] Mort dieu, who would *A*.
[18] *B only. A has:*

BUSS. How shall I quite your love?
MONS. Be true to the end:
  I have obtain'd a Kingdome with my friend.   *Exit.*

ACT II. SCENE II.

[1] *The following fifty lines are in A only, opening the scene.*
    Enter MONTSURRY, TAMYRA, BEAUPRE, PERO, CHARLOTTE,
                  and PYRA.

MONTSURRY. He will have pardon sure.
TAMYRA.   'Twere pittie else:
  For though his great spirit something overflow.
  All faults are still borne, that from greatnesse grow:
  But such a sudden Courtier saw I never.
BEAUPRE. He was too sudden, which indeede was rudenesse.
TAMYRA. True, for it argued his no due conceit
  Both of the place, and greatnesse of the persons:
  Nor of our sex: all which (we all being strangers
  To his encounter) should have made more maners
  Deserve more welcome.
MONTSURRY.   All this fault is found
  Because he lov'd the Duchesse and left you.
TAMYRA. Ahlas, love give her joy; I am so farre
  From Envie of her honour, that I sweare,
  Had he encounterd me with such proud sleight:
  I would have put that project face of his
  To a more test, than did her Dutchesship.
BEAUPRE. Why (by your leave my Lord) Ile speake it heere,
  (Although she be my ante) she scarce was modest,

449

When she perceived the Duke her husband take
Those late exceptions to her servants Courtship,
To entertaine him.

TAMYRA.   I, and stand him still.
Letting her husband give her servant place :
Though he did manly, she should be a woman.

Enter GUISE.

GUISE. D'Ambois is pardond: wher's a king? where law?
See how it runnes, much like a turbulent sea;
Heere high, and glorious, as it did contend
To wash the heavens, and make the stars more pure :
And heere so low, it leaves the mud of hell
To every common view : come count Montsurry
We must consult of this.

TAMYRA.   Stay not, sweet Lord.

MONTSURRY. Be pleased, Ile strait returne.   *Exit cum* GUISE.

TAMYRA.   Would that would please me.

BEAUPRE. Ile leave you Madam to your passions.
I see, ther's change of weather in your lookes.   *Exit cum suis.*

TAMYRA. I cannot cloake it : but, as when a fume,
Hot, drie and grosse : within the wombe of earth
Or in her superficies begot :
When extreame cold hath stroke it to her heart,
The more it is comprest, the more it rageth;
Exceeds his prisons strength that should containe it,
And then it tosseth Temples in the aire;
All barres made engines, to his insolent fury :
So, of a sudden, my licentious fancy
Riots within me : not my name and house
Nor my religion to this houre observ'd
Can stand above it : I must utter that
That will in parting breake more strings in me,
Than death when life parts : and that holy man
That, from my cradle, counseld for my soule :
I now must make an agent for my bloud.

Enter MONSIEUR.

MONSIEUR. Yet, is my Mistresse gratious?

TAMYRA.   Yet unanswered?

[2] joyning a lose] weighing a dissolute *A.*
[3] common] solemn *A.*
[4] you *B only. Not noted in J.*

450

[5] honour] profit A.

[6] B only.

[7] wave] wane J P.

[8] yee] the A. Not noted in J.

[9] that which] that that A.

[10] For love is hatefull without love againe A.

[11] The stage direction is in B only and in the margin of line 9, p. 368.

[12] B only. A has:

See, see the gulfe is opening, that will swallow
Me, and my fame for ever; I will in,

[13] The stage direction is in B only.

[14] The FRIAR is designated as COMOLET throughout A.

[15] know worths] know her worths A. Not noted in Pa, P.

[16] Orbe move] Orbe Move B.

[17] with a Book. B only.

[18] suspicious B A P] suspicions J.

[19] wakes] sits A.

[20] Made some deepe scruple] Was something troubled A.

[21] honour] hand A.

[22] B only. A has: (And therefore made his quarrell; which my presence

[23] good] comfort A.

[24] The concluding stage directions are in B only.

ACT III. SCENE I.

[1] B only.

[2] Servile] Goddesse A.

[3] him in] him : in A.

[4] in one soule] in our one soule A.

[5] my selfe] my truth A.

[6] one] men A.

[7] B only. After 19, p. 373 A has : Exit D'Amb. Manet Tamy.

[8] appos'd J] oppos'd B A.

[9] thine eyes] thy beauties A.

[10] under our Kings arme] underneath the King A.

ACT III. SCENE II.

[1] In A the opening stage direction includes MONTSURRY, TAMYRA, and PERO.

[2] Bussy] my Bussy A.

451

[3] Sparrowes] nothing A.

[4] man] truth A.

[5] by] than A.

[6] beseiged] oppressed A.

[7] rest] tother A.

[8] *The stage direction is in B only. Not noted in Pa, P.*

[9] bout] charge A.

[10] noblier *first proposed by F. S. Boas, accepted by P and J].* nobly B] noblie A.

[11] honour'd] equall A.

[12] Empire] eminence A.

[13] one stick out] out one sticke A.

[14] bound our lifes] was compris'd A.

[15] ingenious] ingenuous A.

[16] hold] proove A.   vertue] rodde A.

[17] Decline not to] Engender not A.

[18] *B only.*

[19] Monts.] Mons. J. Ladies] Ely., Ta. A.

[20] worthy] proper A.

[21] ranging] gadding A.

[22] for you know] and indeed A.

[23] wise make] wise; make A.

[24] the Hart] (being old A.

[25] And cunning in his choice of layres and haunts) A.

[26] (behind some Queich)] his custom is A.

[27] To beat his vault, and he ruts with his hinde A.

[28] chiefest] greatest A.

[29] the cunningst] an excellent A.

[30] *B only. A has:*

I have already broke the ice, my Lord,

With the most trusted woman of your Countesse,

And hope I shall wade through to our discovery.

MONTSURRY. Take say of her my Lord, she comes most fitly

And we will to the other.

[31] *J omits this line.*

[32] indeed *B only.*

[33] of thy] concerning thy A.

[34] sworne to thee] promised A.

[35] assurance] you have sworne A.

[36] so wee reach our objects] so it bee not to one that will betray thee A.

[37] Excellent! Pero] Excellent Pero A.

[38] to perdition] into earth heere A.

[39] watching] wondring A.   stole up] stole A.

[40] her selfe reading a letter] she set close at a banquet A.

[41] I sweare] No my Lord A.

[42] *From* Why this *to* Oh the B *only.*

[43] fraught] freight A. *Not noted in Pa, P.*

[44] never dreaming of D'Amboys B *only.*

[45] should his] could his A.   made] performed A.

[46] Whispers B *only. After this line A has :*

CHARLOTTE. I sweare to your Grace, all that I can conjecture touching my Lady your Neece, is a strong affection she beares to the English Mylor.

GUISE. All quod you? tis enough I assure you, but tell me.

[47] Lady] Countesse A. *Not noted in Pa, P.*

[48] By'r] Ber B.

[49] the life] the life, if she marks it A.

[50] disguise] put off A.

[51] as dry] as hard A. *Not noted in Pa, P.*

[52] from] at A.

[53] are] be A.

[54] when] if A. *Not noted in Pa, P.*

[55] great B *only.*

[56] it] you A.

[57] wee] I A.

[58] our] my A.   Exeunt] Exit A.

[59] thought B *only.*

[60] miraculous] horrible A.

[61] well my Lord, more] my Lord, tis true, and A.

[62] B *only.*

ACT III. SCENE III.

[1] dark and standing foggs] monster-formed cloudes A.

[2] B *only. A has :*

I will conceale all yet, and give more time
To D'Ambois triall, now upon my hooke;
He awes my throat; else like Sybillas Cave
It should breath oracles; I feare him strangely,
And may resemble his advanced valour
Unto a spirit rais'd without a circle,
Endangering him that ignorantly rais'd him,

And for whose furie he hath learn'd no limit.
The last four and a half lines of this passage are paralleled in B
1–4, p. 389.

   [3] *The stage direction follows line 15, p. 389 in B.*

   [4] browes] head A.

   [5] Prince] Sir A.

   [6] *B only.*

   [7] Put me in some little] This still hath made me A.

   [8] therefore now] for me then A. *Not noted in J.*

   [9] *B only. A has:*

D'AMBOIS. Come, doe not doubt me, and command mee all things.

   [10] to prove which by] and now by all A.

   [11] still flourishing tree] affection A.

   [12] *B only.*

   [13] *B only.*

   [14] heart, display] heart display A.

   [15] pay me home, ile bide it bravely] begin, and speak me
simply A.

   [16] to] so B] to A.

   [17] strumpet] wife A. *Not noted in J.*

   [18] thy] that A. the] my A.

   [19] hath reference] I carrie A.

   [20] wrong'd] once wrong'd A. *Not noted in J, Pa, P.*

   [21] and] that A. *Not noted in J.*

   [22] The purest] A perfect A.

ACT IV. SCENE 1.

   [1] *Stage direction :* with a letter *B only.*

   [2] foule] fare A.

   [3] Tis not like my Lord *B* A.

   [4] height] light A. *Not noted in J, Pa, P.*

   [5] Idols] images A.

   [6] *B only.*

   [7] faculty] motions A.

   [8] *These lines are given to* BUSSY *in A.*

   [9] divided Empires] predominance A.

   [10] prove] claim A.

   [11] priviledge] tyrannous A.

   [12] bar] bound A. *Not noted in Pa, P.*

   [13] and] but A.

   [14] not *B only. Not noted in Pa, P.*

[15] *B only. A has :*

BUSSY. No I thinke not.

MONSIEUR. Not if I nam'd the man
With whom I would make him suspicious
His wife hath arm'd his forehead?

BUSSY. So, you might
Have your great nose made lesse indeed : and slit :

[16] *Versification arranged according to A.*

[17] roughnesse] toughnesse *A.*

[18] into the aire] into aire *A.*

[19] minde] spirit *A.*

[20] desert] effect *A.*

[21] steales on to ravish] is comming to afflict *A.*

[22] & Ladies *B only.*

[23] *The stage direction occurs after line 17, p. 398 in A, with
the other one.*

[24] *Stage direction in B only.*   swound] sound *B.*

[25] *Revised with the aid of A, which has :*

Sweete Lord, cleere up those eies, for shame of Noblesse :
Mercilesse creature; but it is enough,

[26] just] loth'd *A. Not noted in Pa, P.*

[27] fingers] hand *A.*

[28] Pelion] Peleon *B.*

[29] Augean] Egean *B A.*

[30] art] are *A.*

[31] Even to his teeth (whence, in my honors soile, *A.*

[32] *B only. A has :*

To see the dangerous paper : Be not nice
For any trifle, jeweld with your honour
To pawne your honor; and with it conferre

[33] well] much *A.*

[34] this touch] my Lord *A.*

[35] but I will to him] Ile attend your Lordship *A.*

[36] Meet] Speake *A.*

[37] *B only.*

Act IV. Scene ii.

[1] *B only.*

[2] with PERO] with PERO and her maid *B.*

[3] Exit PERO *B only.*

[4] curst *B only.*

[5] *After this line A adds:*
Father?

     Ascendit BUSSY *with* COMOLET.

[6] *From* Our love *to* but he B *only. A has:*
D'AMBOIS. What insensate stocke,
 Or rude inanimate vapour without fashion,
[7] you] ye A.
[8] *Stage direction in B only.*
[9] spiritualium] spiritalium A.
[10] Astaroth] Asaroth A.
[11] call'dst] calledst A.
[12] Articulat] Articular B] Articulat A.
[13] with a paper B *only.*
[14] FRIAR] Mons. B A.
[15] BEHEMOTH] Pre. B A.
[16] where you may] wherein you A.
[17] lines] stuffe A. *Not noted in J, Pa, P.*
[18] exquire] exquire : B.
[19] *Stage direction in B only.*
[20] *Stage direction in B only.*
[21] This was ill done y'faith. *Exit Mont.* A.
[22] rather be a bitter] be, at least, if not a A.
[23] To you my Lord. / To me? B *only.*
[24] *Stage direction in B only.*
[25] FRIAR] Com. B.
[26] die] stay A. *Perhaps an error for* "stayne."
[27] In her] With his A.
[28] And let him curb his rage, with policy. A.
[29] taint] print A.
[30] by] from A.

ACT V. SCENE I.

[1] *The order of B scenes in A is:* i. iii. ii. iv.
[2] *Stage direction:* by the haire B *only.*
[3] B *only.*
[4] than that] than it A.
[5] secret] hateful A.
[6] tread] touch A.
[7] your terrors B *only.*
[8] FRIAR] Com. B. heaven] God A. you] ye A.
[9] B *only.*

[10] brest] heart A.
[11] Stand the opening] Ope the seventimes-heat A.
[12] For] O A. *Not noted in J, Pa, P.*   woes] cares A.
[13] devouring] enraged A.
[14] Heaven] God A.
[15] rig'd with quench for] laden for thy A.
[16] devoure] distract A.   Consort] state A.
[17] faults] sins A.
[18] with any shew / Of the like cruell cruelty *B only. P and J also omit the adjective* cruell.
[19] *Stage direction in B only.*
[20] ever] still A.
[21] parallel] like in ill A.
[22] *Stage direction in B only.*
[23] now, Torture, use] now Torture use *B* A.
[24] servants] servant *B. Stage direction in B only.*
[25] and husband?] and husband A.
[26] *As stage direction A has:* Ascendit COMOLET.
[27] *Stage direction in B only.*
[28] worthy] innocent A.
[29] with] in A. *Not noted in Pa, P.*
[30] *Stage direction in B only.*
[31] *Stage directions in B only.*

ACT V. SCENE II.

[1] that] who A.
[2] *After this line A has:*
In whose hot zeale, a man would thinke they knew
What they ranne so away with, and were sure
To have rewards proportion'd to their labours;
Yet may implore their owne confusions
For any thing they know, which oftentimes
It fals out they incurre : so Nature laies
[3] Not knowing what they say *B only.*
[4] deale] masse A.
[5] she calls] we call A.
[6] beliefe must] beleeve should A.
[7] Even as] Right as A.
[8] (me thinks)] (men thinke) A.   guard] guard them A.
[9] proportion] decorum A.
[10] a perfect] an absolute A.

[11] full] whole *A*.
[12] Yet shall you] Why you shall *A*.
[13] let it] let's it *B*] let it *A*.
[14] rage] rages *A*.
[15] *A has :* So this full creature now shall reele and fall,
[16] blind borne] purblinde *A*.
[17] Euxian] euxine *A*.
[18] *From the stage direction to end of scene in B only.*

ACT V. SCENE III.

Stage direction : with tapers *B only.*
[1] *Stage direction in B only.*
[2] Nods] Crackes *A*.
[3] deare] my *A*.
[4] *B only.*
[5] upper] utmost *A*.
[6] shine] see *A*.
[7] men are] sense is *A*.
[8] Thunders *B only.*
[9] BEHEMOTH] SPIRITUS *B. Thus in the following speeches.*
[10] Thunders *B only.*
[11] My will to life] My will : to life *A*.
[12] or force] and force *A*. life] soule *A*. *Latter not noted in Pa, P.*
[13] *Stage direction in B only.*
[14] with a letter written in bloud *B only.*
[15] *B only. A has :*

D'AMBOIS. O lying Spirit : welcome loved father
How fares my dearest mistresse?
MONTSURRY. Well, as ever
Being well as ever thought on by her Lord :
Whereof she sends this witnesse in her hand
And praies, for urgent cause, your speediest presence.
[16] *B only.*
[17] Exeunt] Exit *A*.

ACT V. SCENE IV.

A has as a stage direction : Intrat umbra COMOLET to the COUNTESSE, wrapt in a Canopie.
[1] *B only. A has :*
Revive those stupid thoughts, and sit not thus,

458

Gathering the horrors of your servants slaughter
(So urged by your hand, and so imminent)
Into an idle fancie, but devise
    [2] revenged] engag'd A.
    [3] have] t'have A.
    [4] B only. A has:
Tis the just curse of our abus'd creation,
Which we must suffer heere, and scape heereafter:
He hath the great mind that submits to all,
He sees inevitable; he the small
That carps at earth, and her foundation shaker
And rather than himselfe, will mend his maker.
J notes shakes *in the second to last line. The Morgan*
Library copy, however, has the rime with maker.
    [5] *Stage direction in B only.*
    [6] To] T B] To A.
    [7] B only.
    [8] Fouter, for Guises Shambles, 'twas ill plotted B.
    [9] B only.
    [10] *Stage directions in B only, except for* Exeunt *in A.*
    [11] Where is that angrie Earle my Lord? Come forth B A.
    [12] all the murtherers] others A.
    [13] *Stage direction in B only.*
    [14] Favour (my Lord) my Love B A.
    [15] *Stage direction in B only.*
    [16] *From stage direction through 16, p. 424 in B only.*
    [17] perfumes] perfines A.
    [18] Now] And A.
    [19] Fate, not] Fate, nor A.
    [20] in] gainst A.
    [21] drifts of] endlesse A.
    [22] Laid on my heart and liver; from their veines) B.
    [23] *Stage direction in B only.*
    [24] *In A these lines occur at the very end of the play and are*
preceded by:
My terrors are strook inward, and no more
My pennance will allow they shall enforce
Earthly afflictions but upon my selfe:
    [25] reliques] relicts A.
    [26] Jove flames with her rules] Join flames with Hercules A.
    [27] chrystall] continent A.

[28] *After this line A adds:*
(Since thy revengefull Spirit hath rejected
The charitie it commands, and the remission
To serve and worship, the blind rage of bloud)
    [29] kneeling] sitting *A.*
    [30] *After this line A adds:*
My soule more scruple breeds, than my bloud, sinne,
Vertue imposeth more than any stepdame:
    [31] here all things full *B. P and J add* are.
    [32] to a hunted] to hunted *A.*
    [33] seres] sees *B A. Emendation proposed by A. S. Ferguson and adopted by J.*
    [34] *Stage direction in B only.*
    [35] Epilogue *B only.*

NOTES

NOTES

EVERY MAN IN HIS HUMOUR

TITLE-PAGE MOTTO. From Juvenal, Satires, VII, 93 : "Yet you need not envy the poet, who gets his living from the theatre."

DEDICATION. To William Camden, Jonson's master at Westminster School, at whose expense he was educated.

Clarentiaux. The Clarenceau King-at-arms of the College of Heralds.

Professors. Those who "profess" poetry as a livelihood.

PERSONS OF THE PLAY :

GULL. A natural victim of knavery.

WELL-BRED. The English equivalent of "Euphues."

KITELY. A *kite* was a carrion bird of prey.

COB; TIB. Both names are sexually significant.

BOBADILL. The name is a corruption of Boadbil, a Moorish king who was slain at the Battle of Granada in 1492.

PAULES-MAN. A frequenter of the middle aisle of St. Paul's Cathedral, a business and social center.

THE SCENE. In the version produced in 1598 and printed in 1601 the scene is Italy. Jonson first used an English setting in *Epicoene* (1609), continuing in *The Alchemist* (1610) and the revision of this play.

PROLOGUE :

(1) An attack on Shakespeare's early history plays and their kind. A similar attack is made in *Every Man Out of His Humour*, Induction, 281–283.

(2) The common Elizabethan Chorus is most familiar in Shakespeare's *Henry V.*

(3) Such a descending throne is used in the last act of *Cymbeline.*

(4) *squibbe.* A fire-cracker, which was the standard prop of the devilish Vice in morality plays.

(5) Cannon balls were rolled on the floor to simulate thunder.

(6) *monsters.* Jonson is thinking less of spectacular figures like Caliban in *The Tempest* than he is of most Elizabethan dramatic heroes.

ACT I. SCENE I.

(1) Jonson was an honorary M.A. of both Oxford and Cambridge.

(2) *Cossin.* A general term of relationship.

(3) *booke.* Popular manuals of hunting were written by George Turberville (1575), Gervase Markham (1595), and William Grindall (1596).

(4) *Hogsden.* Hoxton, a London suburb. Jonson killed Gabriel Spencer in a duel in Hoxton Fields, 20 September 1598.

(5) *Islington.* See the note on the new river, *The White Devil*, V. iii. 12, p. 312.

ACT I. SCENE II.

(1) Jonson's usual method of heading a scene is to give the full list of characters appearing in it, even when some enter later. For scenes beginning with the entry of a new character or group, he apparently wished to give only the names of those entering, adding *To them* in the margin. This form is correctly used the first time in IV. iii, where Kitely enters. At II. iii, he used a mixed form, combining the entering character, Cob, with Kitely (on stage) and Dame Kitely, who enters later. He also adds *To them* in the margin, forgetting that at the end of the previous scene Downe-Right made his exit, leaving Kitely to receive Cob alone. The marginal *To them* also occurs wrongly at IV. vii, and ix. It should occur at V. ii, and iii but is omitted, although it occurs elsewhere in Act V correctly. Since I have altered Jonson's method of listing characters for each scene I have kept the marginal *To them* only where it actually occurs and correctly, listing the erroneous occurrences in the variants.

(2) *Jewrie.* The name was a medieval survival.

(3) The *olde shirte* is old Kno'well and the *whole smocke* an undiseased prostitute.

(4) *Turkie companie.* Chartered in 1587 for trade in the Levant.

(5) *batch.* All the bread baked from one preparation.

(6) *Wind-Mill.* A tavern which was earlier a Jewish synagogue.

(7) *Spittle*. In this instance, a hospital particularly for venereal disease. *Pict-hatch*. A notorious haunt of prostitutes.

ACT I. SCENE III.

(1) *scander-bag*. From Iskanderbeg, the Turkish name of George Castriot (1414–1467), who won Albania from the Turks. The epithet seems to mean something like "upstart Tamberlaine."

(2) *Costar'-monger*. One who sold fruit in the open street.

(3) *familiar Epistles*. Alluding to those of Cicero or Pliny. See also the note on III. i. 33, p. 46.

(4) *John Trundle*. Bookseller and publisher of light literature. He published, with Nicholas Ling, the "bad" first quarto *Hamlet* (1603).

(5) *melancholy'*. The fashionable affliction of poets and creative geniuses. Jonson added an ' to indicate the abbreviation of "melancholic."

(6) *Drakes old ship*. The *Golden Hind*, at Deptford, on which Queen Elizabeth knighted Drake, 4 April 1581, after his circumnavigation of the earth.

ACT I. SCENE IV.

(1) *Roger Bacon*. The great Franciscan friar (1214?–1294). Perhaps Cob is invoking a popular belief that Bacon was burned at the stake for heresy or black magic.

(2) *taverne-token*. The half-penny farthing issued by London tradesmen.

(3) *Brasen-head*. Roger Bacon was reputed to have made a brazen head speak (as dramatized in Robert Greene's *Friar Bacon and Friar Bungay*). The brazen head said : "Time is, time was, time will be"; or in another version : "There are more fools to be met with."

(4) *worshipfull*. A title of respect for a full member of the London company.

ACT I. SCENE V.

(1) Stage direction. *discovered*. "Revealed" by drawing back the curtain of the rear stage area.

(2) *'ods so*. A corruption of *Cazzo* (Italian for the male sexual member) by attraction to "By God's soul." Cf. *The Malcontent*, Induction, 19, p. 123.

(3) *Goe by, Hieronymo*. Thomas Kyd's *The Spanish Tragedy*.

The phrase is a quotation from III. xii. 31. See the edition of Philip Edwards (London, 1959).

(4) *O eyes.* From *The Spanish Tragedy*, III. ii. 1–4.

(5) The source of this parody has not been found.

(6) *holden.* For Jonson's use of this and similar forms see A. C. Partridge, *Accidence*, pp. 202, 233.

(7) *Caranza.* Jeronimo de Carranza, who wrote *De la Filosofia de las Armas* (1569), manual of fencing and knightly honor.

(8) *accommodate.* Jonson considered the word affected. See *Timber*, Herford and Simpson, VIII, 632.

(9) *passada.* A thrust executed by striding forward with one foot.

(10) *stoccata.* Italian terms were preferred because of the influential fencing manual by Vincentio Saviolo (1595).

(11) *close the orifice of the stomach.* A phrase used by Aeneas Silvius, Pope Pius II (1458–1464) in his *De curialium miseriis*. See Herford and Simpson, IX, 358, 359.

Act II. Scene i.

(1) *Hospitall.* Probably Christ's Hospital, school for foundlings as well as London citizens' sons.

(2) *three-farthings.* Silver coins with the head of Elizabeth over a rose.

(3) *Counters.* There were two Counter prisons, one in Wood Street, Cheapside, the other in the Poultry, near St. Mildred's Church.

(4) Note the Alexandrine.

(5) *flat cap.* A black woolen cap worn by citizens from the reign of Henry VIII on but now out of fashion. Shined or blackened shoes also marked the citizen.

(6) *quarrell'd.* Transitive use occurs in Jonson's *Grammar*, I. iv. 8. See Herford and Simpson, VIII, 480.

Act II. Scene ii.

(1) *to night.* Last night.

(2) *Garagantua.* Probably not an allusion to Rabelais' work but to its older mythical sources in contemporary form. A *Gargantua his prophesie* was entered into the Stationers' Register in 1592, and *The historie of Gargantua* in 1594. See Huntington Brown, *Rabelais in English Literature* (Cambridge, Mass., 1933). Cf. *As You Like It*, III. ii. 210.

ACT II. SCENE III.

(1) *pride of bloud.* Willful passion. "Blood" is commonly the word for sinful passion.

(2) *rose-water.* Fruit was eaten with rose-water.

(3) *angells.* Coins worth ten shillings.

(4) *new disease.* Probably some form of typhoid, of which Prince Henry died.

(5) Fresh air was thought bad for sick people.

(6) *houses.* The brain had three houses or ventricles. In front was the house of imagination (sensory report), next came that of reason, and in back that of memory.

ACT II. SCENE IV.

(1) *Fico.* The insult was offered by thrusting a thumb through the fingers or by inserting a thumb inside a cheek and stretching it.

(2) Cf. Rosalind's words, "Caesar's thrasonical brag of 'I came, saw, and overcame'," in *As You Like It*, V. ii. 34.

(3) *true garb.* Referring to the common begging apparel of soldiers in Moorfields. *lance-knights.* From the German *Lanzknecht.*

(4) *jet.* A popular substance for rings because of its electrical-magnetic quality. The inscription or posie was probably on a silver lining.

(5) This antithetical construction was common in Euphuism as popularized by John Lyly. It indicates an affectation of refinement. Cf. Shift in *Every Man Out of His Humour*, III. vi. 48–68; and V. x. 34–36, where *Euphues* is quoted.

(6) The battles here referred to are largely those of Ferdinand I, King of Hungary (1527–1541), against the Turkish rulers and their vassals. Alepo, in Syria, was captured by the Turk in 1516. Vienna was saved in 1529. The *Adriatique* would suggest the Battle of Lepanto, 1571. All in all, the collection makes an incredible career.

(7) *Higgin-Bottom.* Used here as a mythical name for a country bumpkin. See Herford and Simpson, IX, 366.

ACT II. SCENE V.

(1) Perhaps an echo of Ovid, *Fasti*, V, 57, 69, 70.

(2) Cf. Quintilian, *Institutionis Oratoriae*, I. ii. 6 ff : "Would that we did not too often ruin our children's character ourselves! We spoil them from the cradle. That soft upbringing, which we call kindness, saps all the sinews both of mind and body. If the child crawls on purple, what will he not desire when he comes to man-

hood? Before he can talk he can distinguish scarlet and cries for the very best brand of purple. We train their palates before we teach their lips to speak. They grow up in litters : if they set foot to earth, they are supported by the hands of attendants on either side. We rejoice if they say something over-free, and words which we should not tolerate from the lips even of an Alexandrian page are greeted with laughter and a kiss. We have no right to be surprised. It was we that taught them : they hear us use such words, they see our mistresses and minions; every dinner party is loud with foul songs, and things are presented to their eyes of which we should blush to speak. Hence springs habit, and habit in time becomes second nature." Translation of H. E. Butler (London, 1921).

(3) *liver.* Seat of the passions.

(4) *heart.* Seat of the intelligence or reason.

(5) Similar examples are used by Horace, *Epistles,* I, and Juvenal, *Satires,* XIV.

(6) The price would be twopence.

(7) *mettall.* "Mettle" and "metal" were interchangeable spellings and metaphorical senses.

(8) Musket-rests were used until the middle of the seventeenth century.

(9) *Mile-end.* Just east of London wall, a training ground for the militia.

Act III. Scene i.

(1) *quos.* . . . "Whom gracious Jove has loved." *Aeneid,* VI, 129.

(2) Note the use of parentheses here to indicate an *aside.* See also line 30 p. 48, 3, 4 p. 50, and, for a different purpose, line 5 ff.

(3) *Symmachus.* A statesman (consul in 391 A.D.) who modelled his letters on the style of Pliny the Younger (61–115? A.D.), nephew of the Pliny who wrote the *Natural History.*

(4) Note the use of parentheses here to mark an aside.

(5) *I faith.* Probably "Ay, faith," rather than "In faith," considering the care with which Jonson used the apostrophe for dropped letters.

(6) *Strigonium.* Graan in Hungary, won from the Turks in 1595.

(7) *demi-culverings.* Cannon of about a four-inch barrel.

(8) Morglay was the sword of Bevis of Southampton, Excalibur of King Arthur, and Durindara of Orlando.

(9) *guilder*. Dutch silver coin worth about one shilling eight pence.

Act III. Scene ii.

(1) *Colman-street*. Then a street of high-class shops and houses.
(2) *car-men*. Users of carts for transport.

Act III. Scene iii.

(1) It seems better theatre to have Cash remain on stage throughout Kitely's fit of crafty madness. *Q* does mark an exit for *Piso* (Cash) at the beginning of Thorello's (Kitely's) speech and an entrance at its end.
(2) Note the observation on jet's magnetic power.
(3) *leape*. Here the sexual act is clearly implied. Cf. II. i. 9, p. 31.
(4) *caps*. They were usually of velvet. The best velvet was three-pile. There is also an allusion to the velvet horns of a hart, hence cuckoldry.
(5) Exchange time was about eleven o'clock. Here *Q* 1601 reads "Past ten."

Act III. Scene iv.

(1) By an Act of 1548, Fridays, Saturdays, Ember days (the four seasonal religious fasts), vigils (eves of holy days), and Lent were meatless days, to promote the fishing industry. In 1562 all Wednesdays were added, but removed in 1585.
(2) Cf. Lyly's *Midas*, III. ii. 56–58 (ed. R. W. Bond, Oxford, 1902). "Rheum" was a courtly term about 1590, when "Catarre" or "Pose" was common.
(3) The Flemings were known all over Europe as great butter eaters. Flemish refugees in England were very unpopular.
(4) "King Cophetua and the Beggar Maid" was a popular ballad. He was the fabulously wealthy King of Africa.
(5) *stock-fish*. Cod dried and flattened. *conger*. Eels.

Act III. Scene v.

(1) The seven wise masters. Bias, Pittacus, Cleobulus, Periander, Solon, Chilon and Thales.
(2) *shove-groat shilling*. A smooth shilling used in the game of shovel-board.
(3) *Reformado's*. Officers of disbanded companies.
(4) *Serjeant-Major*. Officer next in rank to a lieutenant-colonel.

(5) *Hounds-ditch man.* Dealer in second-hand goods named for the common place of activity. "Broker" came to mean any knavish middle-man.

(6) *shifts.* A pun on "tricks" and "changes of clothing."

(7) *Nicotian.* From Jaques Nicot, French ambassador at Lisbon, who brought tobacco to France in 1560.

(8) Note Bobadill's use of *rhewmes.* Cf. III. iv. (2).

(9) *tabacco-traders mouth.* Q 1601 has *pothecaries.* In *The Alchemist,* Abel Drugger sells tobacco.

(10) *cullion.* The male testicle.

(11) Finsbury Fields had posts as markers.

(12) *artillerie garden.* The Honourable Artillery Company had its headquarters outside Bishopsgate in Tassell Close. "Artillery" meant small arms, including bows.

(13) *french dressing.* The French were proverbial swearers.

ACT III. SCENE VI.

(1) *Bride-well.* Once a palace of Henry VIII, it became a city workhouse after 1553.

(2) *what.* Common for "why."

(3) *egges on the spit.* I.e., "I am very busy."

(4) *bands.* Neck-bands or collars.

ACT III. SCENE VII.

(1) *Greene Lattice.* Lattice work was the usual sign of a tavern, usually painted red.

(2) *twelve-moneth and a day.* The legal limit for establishing death from injury.

(3) *Sweet Oliver.* According to Simpson, the popular name for the rival of Orlando in *Orlando Furioso.*

(4) *pisse-pot mettle.* Pewter.

(5) *sacke.* Sherry or Spanish wine.

ACT IV. SCENE I.

(1) *S'lud.* Like S'*lid,* "By God's lid."

ACT IV. SCENE II.

(1) *Servant.* The courtly term for an acknowledged admirer.

(2) According to Herford and Simpson, the aposiopesis, or breaking off in the middle of a phrase, was for Jonson a sign of af-

fectation and "vacuity." Later Matthew affects having forgotten the name of the tavern they went to that morning.

(3) A quotation of Marlowe's *Hero and Leander*, printed in 1590, with a number of changes.

(4) *tricks.* The word had a licentious connotation from the Latin pun *meretrix* (merry tricks), a prostitute.

(5) *take it in snuffe.* To disapprove, from the unpleasant odor of a candle-end.

(6) Royal commissions were allowed to search out property which should have passed into royal control with the dissolution of the monasteries. The abuse of these search-grants by courtiers was notorious, and Elizabeth revoked them in 1572 and 1579.

(7) *companions.* Like "consort," usually a term of abuse.

(8) *cut a whetstone.* Cf. *Bussy D'Ambois*, I. ii. 9–10, p. 353. In Livy's history, Accius Naevius cut a whetstone with a razor at the command of Tarquinius Priscus.

(9) *Holofernes.* A term used by Captain Tucca in *Satiromastix*.

(10) *coystrill.* Originally a knight's attendant, *custrel*, but perhaps associated with *custron*, a scullion.

ACT IV. SCENE III.

(1) *Songs, and sonnets. Tottel's Miscellany* of 1557 and many later editions. Cf. Slender in *Merry Wives of Windsor*, I. i. 179–180.

(2) The suggestion is : a good master, who rewards.

ACT IV. SCENE IV.

(1) *Burgullian.* Burgundians seem to be noted fencers and quarrelers at this time. Herford and Simpson note allusions in Marston's *Scourge of Villainy*, IX, and Dekker's preface to *Satiromastix*. Stow records the execution of a "Burgonian" fencer for killing an officer.

(2) Because of the mythological founding of Britain by Brutus, grandson of Aeneas, the English favored the Trojans rather than the Greeks. Cf. the Induction to *The Malcontent*.

ACT IV. SCENE V.

(1) *pretend'st.* Used in the sense of "apparent seriousness" rather than the modern sense. "Pretend" commonly means "Intend."

ACT IV. SCENE VI.

(1) *seem'd.* In the sense of "were seen as." Cf. *The Alchemist*, I. iii. 70–71.

(2) *Anatomie.* Specifically, a skeleton.

ACT IV. SCENE VII.

(1) *hay.* From Italian, *hai* : "you have it (in the body)."

(2) These were all disreputable parts of London.

(3) The *Reverso* was properly a back-stroke; the *Imbroccata* was delivered over the dagger used as a ward; the *Passada* was delivered with a stride; and the *Montanto* from an upright position.

(4) The influence of the heavenly bodies was still common belief. In Shakespeare, villains like Edmund deny it.

ACT IV. SCENE VIII.

(1) The poisoning of Queen Elizabeth's stirrup or shoe was considered a possible means of assassinating her.

(2) Since the Tower was outside parochial controls, immediate marriage was possible there.

ACT IV. SCENE IX.

(1) The heading of the scene incorrectly includes Downe-Right. Herford and Simpson suggest that Jonson was considering an appearance by Downe-Right, as the incorrect *To them* in the margin also suggests.

(2) *retricato.* An unexplainable term, unless Bobadill is confusing some form of *rintricato* ("entangled"). See Herford and Simpson, III, 387.

(3) *crosse.* A silver penny or half-penny.

(4) *jewell in my eare.* A fashionable practice of men rather than women.

ACT IV. SCENE X.

(1) *Of Thomas.* The marginal note is printed as *By Thomas,* with *By* meaning "Of" or "Concerning."

(2) *hoddie-doddie.* A snail shell; with an allusion to horns.

ACT IV. SCENE XI.

(1) *mace.* The badge of a city sergeant. Cf. "mase of conscience," *The White Devil,* V, iv. 1, p. 320. The following lines pun on "mace," the spice of dried nutmeg.

ACT V. SCENE III.

(1) *reform'd.* Disbanded or demobilized. Cf. III. v. 2, p. 62, *Reformado's.*

Act V. Scene iv.

(1) Herford and Simpson note that the episode of a walk through London in armor occurs in *The Jests of George Peele*. See Peele's *Works*, ed. A. H. Bullen (London, 1888) II, 400.

(2) "Give you joy" was the usual greeting to a newly married couple.

Act V. Scene v.

(1) Perhaps borrowed from Robert Greene's *Orlando Furioso*. See the note in Herford and Simpson, III, 389.

(2) *realme*. Commonly pronounced "ream," making the pun inevitable.

(3) A parody of the first sonnet in Daniel's *Delia*, 1592.

(4) *embleme*. An "emblem" was a symbolic picture with a motto in a foreign language and explanatory verses in the language of the maker.

(5) *They have it with the fact.* The deed is its own punishment, a Senecan tag.

(6) If such a part in a play existed, it has not been traced. Similar verses have been found by Herford and Simpson. The play is probably this one.

(1) DEDICATION. To Benjamin Jonson, poet most refined and grave, his candid and prudent friend—John Marston, child of the Muses, dedicates this his rough comedy. There is a play in *ASPERAM* on "unpolished" and "bitter" or "severe." Cf. Asper in Jonson's *Every Man Out of His Humour*: "of an ingenious and free spirit, eager and constant in reproofe, without feare controuling the world's abuses;" and Cordatus : "the Authors friend; A man inly acquainted with the scope and drift of his Plot : Of a discreet, and understanding judgement."

(2) TO THE READER. Probably Marston's way of smoothing over his recent exchange of satire (aided by Dekker) with Jonson. He is also conscious of the recent chorus of moral indignation raised by his *Scourge of Villainy*.

(3) *Sine aliqua*. . . . There is no truth (or poetry) without a bit of madness.

(1) INDUCTION. All the persons in the Induction are members of Shakespeare's company, The King's Men : William Sly, Henry Condell, Richard Burbage, John Sinklo (Sincklo, Sincler), and John Lowin. John Sinklo was extremely tall and thin, being used in such parts as Robert Faulconbridge, half-brother of the Bastard in *King John*, and Sir Andrew Aguecheek. William Sly, one of the major actors who made the transition from the Chamberlain's to the King's Men, became a sharer about 1605 and died in 1608. Condell's name is familiar with that of John Heminge in the address "To the great Variety of Readers" in the Shakespeare First Folio (1623). Lowin was usually cast as the bluff and honest man, friend or villain. After the retirement of Condell (c. 1620) and of Heminge (c. 1628), Lowin became a leading figure and manager of the King's Men. Richard Burbage (c. 1573–1619) was the foremost actor of the age. He played Malevole, Ferdinand in *The Duchess of Malfi*, Richard in *Richard III*, Hamlet, Lear, and Othello, among other major roles.

(2) *sixpence*. The minimum fee for a stool.
stale suits. Unsuccessful suits at court or at law, causing financial embarrassment.

(3) *Gods so*. A corruption of *Cazzo* (Italian for the male sexual member) by attraction to "By God's soul." Cf. *Every Man in His Humour*, I. v. 28, p. 23.

(4) *for feathers.* The Blackfriars district was the center of the feather trade. Sly refers to a performance at the Blackfriars Theatre, and the line : "no Cuckold but haz his hornes, & no foole but haz his feather" (V. iii. 6–7, p. 196).

(5) As Wood notes, this superstition is usually applied to the beaver. From Pliny, *Natural History*, XXXII, 3.

(6) *Jeronimo. The Spanish Tragedy.* See Philip Edwards, ed., *The Spanish Tragedy* (London, 1959), pp. xxi, 137, 138.

(7) *Decimo sexto.* A very small book size. Cf. *The White Devil*, V. iv. 27–28, p. 316, where Flamineo refers to the young Giovanni.

(8) *One for another.* Alluding to the retaliatory action.

(9) *custome.* Long musical interludes were more common in the "private" theatres.

(10) *Ad Parminonis suem.* According to Plutarch's *Quaestiones Convivialum* (V. i.), Parmeno was so famed for imitating the grunting of a pig that when a real pig was secretly put into a competition his admirers cried, "Nothing to Parmeno's pig!"

(11) *lost your eares.* A common punishment for felonies.

(12) *five and fiftie.* According to Dyce, an exaggeration.

(13) *Hector.* The English favored the Trojans rather than the Greeks, since Britain was thought to have been founded by Brutus, grandson of Aeneas.

(14) From Petrarch's sonnet *Giunto Alessandro ala famosa tomba*, roughly as translated by John Harvey, younger brother of Gabriel. The exact wording is : "Noble Alexander, when he came to the tombe of Achilles, / Sighing spake with a bigge voyce : O thrice blessed Achilles, / That such a Trump, so great, so loude, so glorious hast found, / As the renowned, and surprizing Archpoet Homer." The meter is hexametric. See Alexander B. Grosart, ed., *The Works of Gabriel Harvey, D.C.L.* (3 vols., privately printed, [London], 1884, 1885), I, 89, 90.

ACT I. SCENE I.

(1) *Vexat censura columbas.* This represents Marston's apology to women. It is from Juvenal, *Satires* (II. 63). The context is Laronia's defence of women by citing male offences : "de nobis post haec tristis sententia fertur? dat veniam corvis, vexat censura columbas." "After these things what evil judgment can be put on us women. [The criticizing male] absolves the crows and passes judgment on the doves."

ACT I. SCENE II.

(1) *Ganymede*. Jupiter's cup-bearer and paramour.

(2) *Toderers*. A "tod" was a fox. A "tetter" was a scab. Perhaps Marston is combining the two.

ACT I. SCENE III.

(1) *Sir Patrick Penlolians*. Probably a mythical type.

(2) *come . . . wham*. The ape-ward's call when he wants his monkey to perform.

(3) *Catito*. Alluding to the boys' games of "cat" and "trap" in which a ball was struck and caught with a wooden stick.

(4) *at the Ring*. The object was to pierce the circle of a ring with a lance.

(5) *Pompey the huge*. Caesar's rival, Pompey the Great, also so-called in *Love's Labour's Lost*, V. ii. 692.

(6) *Catzo*. From the Italian *Cazzo*. Frequently it occurs in the corruption "God so." See the note for "Induction," (3).

ACT I. SCENE IV.

(1) *servant*. Courtly lover, as Matthew of Bridget in *Every Man in His Humour*.

(2) *Castilio*. Courtier; an allusion to Baldassare Castiglione, author of *The Book of the Courtier*.

ACT I. SCENE V.

(1) *Egistus*. Aegisthus, the son of Thyestes and lover of Clytemnestra who murdered Agamemnon on his return from Troy.

(2) *Orestes*. Son of Agamemnon, who avenged his father's murder.

(3) *Phaeton*. Son of the sun-god Helios, who persuaded his father to let him drive the sun-chariot. Unable to control the sun-steeds, he endangered the world and was destroyed by a thunderbolt from Jove.

(4) *in despight of Phoebus*. Probably alluding to the habit of poets of writing that their mistresses were brighter than the sun.

ACT I. SCENE VI.

(1) *dog*. The dog-star Sirius, whose influence in August and September was considered malignant.

ACT I. SCENE VIII.

(1) A pamphlet of 1588 describes this phenomenon. The woman was Margaret Griffith, wife of David Owen of Llan Gaduain, Montgomeryshire. See Bullen's edition, I, 233, note.

(2) *Flushing*. The English had permanent garrisons at Brill and Flushing to aid the Dutch against the Spanish.

(3) *peeleth*. This occurred because cosmetics contained corrosives like vitriol and white lead.

(4) *Switzer*. The reputation for lying probably arose from the Swiss occupation of supplying mercenary troops to anyone who would pay.

(5) *petti-fogger*. A lawyer of low status who handled small cases. The term was usually applied in the sense of "crook."

ACT II. SCENE I.

(1) *clouds*. According to one version of their origin, the centaurs were created when Ixion, thinking to embrace Juno, mated with Nephele (rain-cloud). See also Davenport, *Poems*, pp. 68, 220, 221.

(2) From Seneca, *Thyestes*, 925.

ACT II. SCENE II.

(1) *Dipsas*. An old bawd mentioned by Ovid in *Amores*, I. viii. 2. Also a serpent whose bite caused intense thirst.

(2) *olde Cole*. Old or nearly burnt-out coal. A "cole" was also a "cheater." Overbury's *Characters* included : "A Maquerela, in plaine English a Bawde, Is an old char-cole, that had been burnt her selfe, and therefore is able to kindle a whole greene coppice." See Edward F. Rimbault, ed., *The Miscellaneous Works in Prose and Verse of Sir Thomas Overbury, Knt.* (London, 1856), pp. 99–100. Cited by Bullen, I, 238.

(3) *Janivere*. An old man. Cf. Chaucer's tale of the marriage of January and May.

(4) Shell-fish were commonly thought of as aphrodisiacs. Marston also uses the illustration in Satire III of *The Scourge of Villainy*.

(5) *posset*. A drink of milk curdled with wine or liquor.

ACT II. SCENE III.

(1) Three famous dukes (or kings) who were cuckolds. "When Arthur first in Court" was a popular ballad. Falstaff begins to sing it in *Henry IV Part Two*, II. ii. 36. See Matthias A. Shaaber, ed.,

The Second Part of Henry the Fourth: New Variorum (Philadelphia and London, 1940), p. 167.

(2) The fable of the eagle and the tortoise is in Aesop. See Jacobs, II, 217.

(3) *Priapisme.* Priapus was a Greek fertility deity represented by an immense phallus.

(4) The sense is : whatever abilities (*partes*) in a man the king allows to grow near him must also be watched by a royal spy.

ACT II. SCENE IV.

(1) *Eringos.* Candied sea-holly root. Marston also uses it in Satire III of *The Scourge of Villainy.* In *The Merry Wives of Windsor,* V. v. 23, Falstaff uses the term in an amorous context.

(2) *Lambe stones.* Testicles of a lamb.

ACT II. SCENE V.

(1) *Argos eyes.* In differing versions, Argos had a third eye in the back of his head, two before and behind, or very many.

(2) *pent.* The sense is that aspiring spirits, feeling themselves restricted or confined, rise by treachery. Cf. *Antonio's Revenge,* V. iii. 12–13 : "Like high-swoln floods, drive down the muddie damnes / Of pent allegeance."

(3) From Ovid, *Heroides,* I. 53 : "iam seges est, ubi Troia fuit, resecandaque falce / luxuriat Phrygis sanguine pinguis humus." "Now there are corn fields where Troy was, and soil rich with Phrygian blood blooms for the harvesting sickle."

(4) From *Aeneid,* II, 554 : "haec finis Priami fatorum." "Such was the end of Priam's fortunes."

ACT III. SCENE I.

(1) Bullen and Reed cite *Physic against Fortune* (1579), Thomas Twyne's version of Petrarch's work on remedies for misfortune.

(2) *Barnacle.* According to common belief, the tree barnacle became a Solan goose (fish or bird). See the note in Frank Kermode, ed., *The Tempest* (London, 1954), IV. 248.

(3) *gentlemen.* In Middleton's *The Family of Love,* I. iii, there is a similar joke. Bullen, in his edition of Middleton (8 vols., London, 1885–1886), III, 23, notes an Overbury "character" on "A Braggadochio Welshman."

Act III. Scene ii.

(1) *Elder of Israell.* Probably an old, wicked Judge, as characterized by Thomas Nashe in *Pierce Penilesse,* "these wicked Elders of Israel." See R. B. McKerrow and F. P. Wilson, edd., *Works of Thomas Nashe* (5 vols., Oxford, 1958), I, 188.

(2) In masques Hymen usually wore a saffron robe.

Act III. Scene iii.

(1) *Illo, ho, ho, ho.* The falconer's cry to his bird. Cf. *Hamlet,* I. v. 115 ff. *true penny.* An epithet for the Devil's Vice in earlier plays.

(2) Cf. Thomas Nashe, *Pierce Penilesse:* "The Irishman will draw his dagger, and bee ready to kill and slay, if one breake winde in his company." See the same page noted for III. ii. (1).

(3) From Seneca, *Epistle XLIV.* Also in Plato, *Theaetetus* (Loeb Classics), p. 123 (174 : E).

(4) *Lacedemonian.* The Spartans were typically tenacious and shrewd.

(5) *Carowse.* Drink down.

Act IV. Scene i.

(1) *cunny.* I take this to be a variant of "cony" (rabbit) for "woman." But it may be the similarly spelled word "cuny" for "corner."

Act IV. Scene ii.

(1) *galliard tricke.* A dance in triple time. Phrases with "twenty" were intensive expressions for "very much." *curranto pace.* Lively.

(2) *maze.* The Cretan labyrinth of the Minotaur. Aurelia is unconsciously associating herself with Pasiphaë and her unnatural lust.

Act IV. Scene iii.

(1) *sowse.* A technical term for the dive of a hawk on its prey.

(2) *Slatted.* A northern word for "dashed" or "knocked."

(3) *kennell.* Gutter.

(4) From Seneca, *Phoenissae,* 632–633, where it is in the second person singular.

(5) *stawking horse.* In the quarto there is a marginal gloss here: *Shootes under his belly.* As Wood suggests, this may be a stage direction for Mendoza. A stalking-horse was trained to precede the hunter and deceive the game.

ACT IV. SCENE V.

(1) The sense is : My condemnation is just even if it comes from Mendoza.

(2) *Amphitrio.* Amphitryon was cuckolded by Zeus. His wife Alcmene bore twins, Heracles of Zeus and Iphicles of Amphitryon. Plautus dramatized the story.

(3) *but a paire.* That is, they were cut from the same cloth.

ACT V. SCENE I.

(1) *coisterd.* A nonce word explained by Nares as "coiled up into small compass." I take it to be a variant of "coistrel." Perhaps an *l* has been lost in the form "coisterld." The idea seems to be that gentlemen forgot social differences to prove their strength and were made ridiculous. Halliwell's equivalent of "inconvenienced" seems to imply something similar. See *NED.*

ACT V. SCENE III.

(1) *no foole but haz his feather.* Cf. the "Induction," 19 ff., p. 123.

(2) From Cicero's *Epistolae ad Familiares,* IX, 22, in which he discusses obscene language.

(3) From Ovid's *Tristia,* II, 33–34 : "si, quotiens peccant homines, sua fulmina mittat / Iuppiter, exiguo tempore inermis erit." "If, as often as humans sin Jupiter would send his thunderbolts, he would be weaponless in short time."

(4) The Latin is immediately translated by Marston.

ACT V. SCENE IV.

(1) From Seneca's *Agamemnon,* 115, where it is spoken by Clytemnestra.

ACT V. SCENE V.

(1) *Count . . .* "Count Anyone of Whatever You Wish."

(2) *unydle.* Because some copies of the quarto read *wimdle* here, Bullen suggests that the correct meaning may be "wimble" for "nimble." Marston uses "wimble" in *I Antonio and Mellida,* III. ii. 198.

ACT V. SCENE VI.

(1) Bullen cites Thomas Bastard's *Chrestoleros* (1598), IV, 32, as the source.

(2) *suburbs.* Where the brothels were.

For the historical background of the play see the general introduction. General acknowledgement is here made of a debt to the
editions of Brown and Lucas, and the collection of Webster's borrowings by Robert W. Dent. Earlier scholars who traced Webster's
borrowings are credited indirectly through these works.

THE TITLE. A White Devil was a devil in attractive disguise.
Lucas notes a sermon preached at Paul's Cross, March 1613, by
T. Adams, *The white divell, or the Hypocrite uncased.* Judas is
the prototype of the hypocrite or Whited Sepulchre. The phrase
was proverbial and widely used.

Ursini. The spellings *Ursini* and *Orsini* were interchangeable. The
more Latinate would remind us of the emblem of a bear.

Venetian Curtizan. Lucas suggests a confusion in Webster's mind
between the play's Umbrian Vittoria and the Venetian Bianca
Capello, who was married to the Duke of Florence. Bianca
Capello would also suggest a fair-haired devil.

Queenes Majesties Servants. Queen Anne's Men, formerly the Earl
of Worcester's Men, active 1604–1619.

Non inferiora secutus. From *Aeneid*, VI, 170, where Misenus, having left the service of Hector for that of Aeneas, is described as
now "following no less noble lord." Webster's application of the
phrase is not apparent.

ACT I. SCENE I.

(1) Lodovico seems to be invoking Democritus as the master of
Epicurus, whose teaching—popularly conceived—was that human
conduct is determined by the search for pleasure and avoidance of
pain.

(2) *Caviare.* The earliest recorded use of the term is for 1591.

(3) *Meteor.* A general term for atmospheric illumination thought
to be drawn from the earth by the sun.

(4) Typical of Webster's style in dialogue. Cf. *The Duchess of
Malfi,* I. i. 318 ff.; *The Devil's Law Case,* II. i. 176 ff.; and *Appius
and Virginia,* IV. i. 216 ff.

(5) *mediate.* That is, take a merciful, moderate course.

(6) Although we learn later that Lodovico lusts after Brachiano's
Duchess Isabella (II. ii. 30–32, p. 249; IV. iii. 26–29, p. 291),
there is no reason to infer here that Brachiano has had him banished.

(7) Perhaps indebted to Florio's Montaigne, III. v : "as hearbes and trees are bettered and fortified by being transplanted." See also Dent, pp. 76–77.

ACT I. SCENE II.

(1) Cf. Florio's Montaigne II, xvii : "Wee have taught ladies to blush, onely by hearing that named which they nothing feare to doe." Brown notes Webster's inventive word play in "handle," which can also mean "to talk of."

(2) Cf. Florio's Montaigne II, xv : "discontent and vexation . . . sharpen love and set it afire. Whereas satiety begets distaste : it is a dull, blunt, weary, and drouzy passion."

(3) *buttery.* Primarily a store-room for drinks. Derived from *boterie* (modern *bouteillerie*).

(4) In gilding mercury was used initially and then eliminated as a vapor which caused severe damage to the brain when inhaled.

(5) The feathers would be from the combatants' helmets. The loss of hair was a sign of venereal disease or weakened masculinity.

(6) This trait of Irish gamblers is recorded in Richard Stanyhurst's "Description of Ireland," Holinshed's *Chronicles* (1577). Camillo, having no virility, would risk his testicles.

(7) Cf. Florio's Montaigne III, v : "[Marriage] may be compared to a cage, the birds without dispaire to get in, and those within dispaire to get out."

(8) The pun "travail - travel" was common.

(9) *Jumpe.* Continuing the sequence of bawdy puns. The "mistress" in bowling was the small white ball towards which the bowls were aimed. Note the continued association of white with Vittoria.

(10) Flamineo creates a picture of Camillo trying to shave away his cuckold's horns and hiding them in his pillow.

(11) Camillo refers to horns and Flamineo to ass's ears.

(12) Cf. Florio's Montaigne II, viii : "[Women are] more willingly and gloriously chaste, by how much fairer they are."

(13) *capricious.* An ironic pun on Latin *caper,* "goat." Camillo will be horned but not goatish (lustful).
Mathematically. Scientifically exact.

(14) Flamineo is combining an allusion to loose women (*mutton*) and the contemporary abuse of enclosing common land for sheep pasturage.

(15) The last Jubilee was in 1600. Jubilee was instituted in

1300 by Pope Boniface VIII as a time within which plenary indulgence could be won by acts of piety.

(16) Cf. Florio's Montaigne II, xii : "Such as are troubled with the yellow jandise deeme all things they looke upon to be yellowish."

(17) *Ida*. The sacred mountain over the Trojan plains. Brown suggests also the Mount Ida of Crete.

(18) Black or brunette complexion was conventionally ugly.

(19) *carved*. Here used in the sense of "castrated," as a capon is.

(20) *blacke guard*. In its original sense of a menial servant.

(21) Lucas notes that there was a glass factory near Blackfriars Theatre. It is also alluded to in *The Duchess of Malfi*, II. ii. 6.

(22) *philosophers stone*. The mythical stone sought by the alchemists which might turn the lower metals into gold, perform cures and prolong life. Lucas cites Lyly's *Gallathea*, V. i. 24–26, for a similar bawdy joke.

(23) *smothered in roses*. Lucas cites Goulart's *Histoires Admirables* in Grimeston's translation (1607) for the story of a Bishop of Breslau who was so smothered; and a similar general use of the idea in Nashe's *Unfortunate Traveller*.

(24) Cf. Florio's Montaigne, II. xiii : "As they who travell by sea, to whom mountaines, fields, townes, heaven and earth, seeme to goe the same motion, and keepe the same course they doe."

(25) Lucase cites a similar image in Horace, *Odes*, III. xxiv. 5–8.

(26) *brees*. The plural form was the same as the singular.

(27) "Adamant" was sometimes identified with the loadstone, but it is usually cited for its hardness.

(28) Cf. Florio's Montaigne, III. xiii : "[The mind] incessantly goeth turning, winding, building, and entangling her selfe in hir owne worke, as doe our silke-wormes, and therein stifle hir selfe."

(29) Cf. Florio's Montaigne, III. v : "[Women] will have fire. . . . Luxurie is like a wild beast, first made fiercer with tying, and then let loose." A "curst" dog is a vicious one.

(30) "Loose" and "lose" were spelled the same; hence the pun was inevitable.

(31) Lucas notes that the same pun *Eu* (Yew) "you" occurs in Lyly's *Sapho and Phao*, III. iv. 75–79, followed by a dream about a tall cedar tree.

(32) The *crosse-sticks* have been variously explained. Lucas thinks they may be osiers woven so as to protect and bind the

grave. Brown suggests a pattern on the grave due to the light falling through the trees. Harrison thinks them to be the supports laid across the grave on which the coffin is set.

(33) The *withered blacke-thorne* is unexplainable. But then Vittoria's whole dream is ambiguous. Perhaps first the *goodly Eu* is marriage and the blackthorn is scandalous vice. But the *Eu* should also be Camillo, and it soon becomes Brachiano.

(34) Lucas notes that *envy* here retains some of its Latin sense of "looking evilly upon" (*invidia*).

(35) Thessaly, in Greece, was renowned for witches and poisons.

(36) *frequently*. In the sense of "incessantly."

(37) Lucas suggests an allusion to Antonio Guevara's *Dial of Princes*, translated in 1557 by Sir Thomas North.

(38) Cornelia's *joyne* may suggest that Vittoria has kneeled and that she now kneels also.

(39) *prodigious*. Like a "prodigy," portending disaster.

(40) Lucas notes that it was common for students at Oxford to earn a living by doing menial tasks for richer students. Brown cites similar cases at Cambridge. Flamineo probably means that he was graduated through bribery.

(41) *crooke*. An unusual form for "crooked" but more common in compounds. *forced bankes*. Lucas suggests banks "imposed upon" their waters. Brown prefers "fabricated" or "artificial" banks. The idea of "pressured" banks seems best.

(42) Brown notes that Webster may be alluding to the "mythical amphisbaena," an adder with two heads, "the only snake which putteth out himselfe in cold."

Act II. Scene i.

(1) *Pole-cats*. A predator of poultry (whence the name) rather like a ferret or weasel.

(2) The horn of the unicorn both revealed the presence of any poison nearby and was an antidote. They were sold at fabulous prices. Brown notes that what Isabella describes was actually performed as a test by the Royal Society in 1661.

(3) Lucas cites J. Maplet's *Green Forest* (1567) for an example of this belief.

(4) *Happely*. Often used for "haply," in the sense of "usually."

(5) *cloth of Tissue*. Cloth interwoven with gold or silver.

(6) Swiss mercenary troops were common in Italian wars.

(7) Brachiano's line may be a sneer at Isabella's piety, accord-

ing to Lucas, comparing *Richard III*, I. ii. 104–105 : "anne [of Henry VI]. O he was gentle, mild, and virtuous. / gloucester. The fitter for the King of heaven, that hath him."

(8) *crackers.* An empty threat, like a fire-cracker.

(9) *new plow'd.* Furrowed with anger.

(10) *proling.* For "prowling." This passage on hunting alludes to Brachiano's lecherous life.

(11) *wild-duckes.* Prostitutes.

(12) *moulting.* Probably another allusion to the loss of hair due to venereal disease.

(13) *tale of a tub.* A cock-and-bull story. Lucas notes the origin of the phrase in an episode of Apuleius copied by Boccaccio. A wife hides her lover in a large jar. When discovered by the husband, the lover pretends that he got inside the jar to examine it for purchase. Brown notes the allusion to the sweating-tub used as a cure for venereal disease.

(14) Stags separate after rutting and become placid. Spencer notes another allusion to the tub used as a cure for venereal disease in *season*, for "salt and pickle."

(15) *Champion.* Giovanni is wearing the armor he mentions in lines 24–25, p. 233 as promised him.

(16) Brown cites G. Pettie's translation of Guazza's *Civil Conversation* (1581) as the source for this precept.

(17) From *The Battle of Frogs and Mice*, a burlesque epic attributed to Homer.

(18) Lucas notes a similar discussion in Florio's Montaigne, II. xxi.

(19) *danske.* The Danish were noted drummers.

(20) The lapwing is a favorite Elizabethan example of natural precocity. But *flies* here probably means "runs."

(21) According to G. Boklund, in some versions of the background Lodovico became a bandit, but he was never accused of piracy.

(22) Isabella means devotion to Brachiano. He deliberately misinterprets her words.

(23) *am to learne.* Common for "am ignorant of." Jealousy was considered the predominant Italian trait.

(24) *corpulent.* Lucas suggests a pun on Francisco's title "Grand Duke." In history it was Brachiano himself who was extremely corpulent. Nowhere in the play does Francisco seem to be fat.

(25) *shav'd.* The Poles shaved their heads except at the forehead.

(26) *apprehended.* That is, "conscious." "Apprehension" is the word for "intelligence" or "sense."

(27) From *I Kings,* XII. 11 : "My father hath chastised you with whips, but I will chastise you with scorpions." Some commentators thought "scorpions" a metaphor for barbed whips.

(28) From *Aeneid,* I, 26.

(29) Lucas compares Seneca's *Phaedra,* 607 : Curae leves loquuntur, ingentes stupent." "Light cares speak, deep ones are silent."

(30) Lucas cites Nashe's *Unfortunate Traveller* for the belief that the Cretans lived on serpents and poisonous foods.

(31) The story of St. Patrick's clearing the snakes from Ireland was found by Webster in Richard Stanyhurst's *Description of Ireland.*

(32) A Spaniard, Don Diego, was famous for offending worshippers in St. Paul's in this way.

(33) *Saint Anthony fire.* Erysipelas, a disease causing inflammation of the skin. Prayers to St. Anthony were said to have saved many lives in an epidemic of 1089.

(34) *gallouses.* Men condemned to the gallows. Sampson explains : a method of hanging in which one condemned man stands on the shoulders of another, who then steps aside, leaving the other suspended.

(35) From Ovid's *Metamorphosis,* III. 466 : Narcissus to his reflection. The general sense seems to be that the plenty of satisfaction Vittoria has given others has left Camillo with none. And Vittoria's unfaithfulness is metaphorically the plenty of horns Camillo has.

(36) *old tale.* Lucas cites the source as Aesop's *Fables* or *Phaedrus,* I. 6.

ACT II. SCENE II.

(1) An allusion to John Banks' performing horses, one of which was named Morocco.

(2) The pun "ream - realm" was inevitable, due to like pronunciation.

(3) *Dumbe Shew.* Lucas traces the development of the dumb show from a brief allegorical presentation of later action (*Gorboduc, Gismond of Salerne*) to a more integrated function of the action, achieving compression (as here) or variety (*Henry VIII*).

Pictures were usually covered with curtains to protect them from dust.

(4) *Second Dumbe Shew.* In actual fact, Peretti (Camillo) was shot on Monte Cavallo, which may have suggested the bizarre object (mounting horse) used to conceal the murder.

(5) *boone voyage.* Elizabethan form of *bon voyage.*

Act III. Scene i.

(1) *Leiger Embassadours.* Those resident in a country rather than on special envoy.

(2) Brown notes that this lawyer seems so different from the one in Scene ii that they may be different characters. Brown also suggests a possible error from copy for "Courtier."

(3) Brown cites G. Gifford's, *Witches and Witchcrafts* (1593) for the practice of witches feeding their familiar spirits with blood.

(4) Cf. Florio's Montaigne, II. xii : "It would be even as if one should go about to graspe the water : for, how much the more he shal close and presse that which by its owne nature is ever gliding, so much the more he shall loose what he would hold and fasten."

(5) Chamois was worn under armor. Also mentioned in Florio's Montaigne, I. xliii.

(6) Examples of inevitable disadvantage in every context of action or nature exploited by great men against the lesser. A "builder oak" was one useful for building. The mandrake was poisonous but also useful in medical treatment. When pulled from the ground it was reputed to shriek. Since it had a forked root it was emblematic of human form. The mistletoe was useful in reducing swellings and the Druids considered it a panacea. Lucas cites evidence for the belief that mistletoe-bearing oaks usually had mandrakes growing nearby.

(7) *Tilter.* The word easily lent itself to bawdy interpretation.

(8) *lofty trickes.* Alluding to acrobatics or tumbling.

Act III. Scene ii.

(1) This lawyer's remarks are not supposed to be lucid or logical. "Connive" should mean "to overlook."

(2) *exulceration.* Probably used in the sense of cure or removal, as of a sore.

(3) *buckeram.* Stiff linen used for attorney's bags, similar to the Harvard bag.

(4) *graduatically.* The lawyer probably means "in deliberate

good form" but he would suggest to hearers "like a graduate of the schools."

(5) *effected*. In the sense of "developed" or "perfected." But *affected* may well be the correct reading, in the sense of "self-indulged" or "cherished." Brown notes a possible confusion by Webster or one of general usage.

(6) The source of this legend is *Deuteronomy* XXXII. 32: "For their vine is of the vine of Sodom, and of the fields of Gomorrah : their grapes are grapes of gall, their clusters are bitter."

(7) Sampson noted that scarlet was the color of the legal faculty as well as of a cardinal's rank.

(8) Monticelso deliberately misinterprets Vittoria's "What's that you say?"

(9) *character*. The literary variety of the sort Webster contributed to the 1615 edition of Overbury's collection.

(10) Fynes Moryson, in his *Itinerary* described taxes almost equal to the price of the commodity.

(11) The most notable case was Sir Walter Raleigh's loss of his Sherborne estate because of a clerk's earlier omission of ten words in a transfer to his wife.

(12) *uncivil*. Uncivilized, in contrast to "Christian," used both religiously and culturally.

(13) Percy Simpson [in *MLR*, II (1907), 162, 163] pointed out that Webster was indebted here to Jonson's *Masque of Queens* (1609) for Perseus as a type of masculine virtue. See Allan Gilbert, *Symbolic Persons*, p. 252.

(14) Editors since Lucas have based the punctuation of this line on parallel passages : *Devil's Law Case*, IV. ii. 126, 163, and 370; *Appius and Virginia*, IV. i. 213. But "to the point" can mean simply "in every detail."

(15) *strikt combined*. Closely and secretly in league. Brown suggests a play on "military heads" and "hammer heads."

(16) Two tales have been noted by Lucas in which a hero unprovided with a seat leaves behind his cloak, saying that he would not carry away his stool. The first is of Robert of Normandy, father of William the Conqueror, the second of Horacio in Lope de Vega's *El honrado hermano,* published 1623 but perhaps written before 1604.

(17) Lucas notes that this motto first appeared on the "Thistle-mark," a coin issued by James VI in 1578.

(18) The reference is probably to a suburban garden-house, commonly of evil reputation in Elizabethan England.

(19) *dog-daies*. Days under the influence of the star Sirius, in Canis Major and brightest of the fixed stars; usually the second half of August and first half of September. They were thought to incite lust, being very hot.

(20) Brown cites the same example in Nicholas de Montreux, *Honour's Academy*, translated by Robert Tofte (1610).

(21) *Crusado's*. Portuguese coins of gold or silver.

(22) *choake-peare*. Inedible kind of pear used figuratively for "stopper."

(23) Historically inaccurate. Vittoria was born at Gubbio, Umbria, of the Accoramboni. The Vitelli were a noted Roman family. Lodovico Orsini was banished for the murder of Vincenzo Vitelli.

(24) The coin *Julio* was minted by Pope Julius II (1503–1513).

(25) *Ryalto talke*. Talk of the town. Brown cites Thomas Coryat, *Crudities* (1611) for the Rialto as "the Exchange of Venice." It was completed in 1591.

(26) *ballated*. The contemporary ballad writer was a kind of journalist.

(27) *patent*. Vittoria may be alluding to contemporary patents of monopoly as well as of nobility.

(28) *A rape*. Lucas cites parallels in *The Tragedy of Chabot*, V. ii. 122, and *The Atheist's Tragedy*, I. iv.

(29) *horse-lech*. Bloodsucker. Also used at V. vi. 3, p. 328.

(30) *t'attone*. To reconcile or "make at one."

(31) Brachiano is ironically alluding to the death of Isabella, as Flamineo explains.

(32) *palsy*. Alluding to uncontrolled wagging and movement.

Act III. Scene iii.

(1) Lucas notes that Poland was overrun with Scotch and Irish pedlars.

(2) *piles*. The one sense, of disease, goes along with *pox*, venereal disease.

(3) Lucas explains : up to 1772, those refusing to plead guilty or innocent for felonies other than treason were tortured with weights of iron. But if the victim died under torture his goods could not be confiscated.

(4) *pitch*. Full height.

(5) Alluding to Cain's dispute with Abel, *Genesis*, IV. 3–8.

(6) *mushromes.* Upstarts. An earlier use of the metaphor is in Marlowe's *Edward II*, I. iv. 283.

(7) The career of Richard Wolner is described in Moffet's *Health's Improvement* (1655). He ate iron, glass, and other objects but died of eating a raw eel. Cited by Lucas.

(8) *purchast.* Meaning "obtained" but not necessarily with money.

(9) *stigmaticke.* Stigmatized or marked with a deformity.

(10) *ingeniously.* The words "ingenuous" and "ingenious" were used interchangeably.

(11) *gentile.* The words "genteel" and "gentle" were used interchangeably.

(12) The hare was considered melancholic and the eating of its flesh caused melancholy.

(13) The receptacle used to catch the blood in blood-letting was called a "saucer."

(14) *breake.* The object of the verb understood is "faith."

ACT IV. SCENE I.

(1) Virgin brides wore their hair loose. Notable examples were Anne Boleyn and the daughter of King James, Elizabeth.

(2) Lucas notes that the "black book" was originally any official register. The term became sinister after its use for the record of monastic abuses under Henry VIII.

(3) *taking up.* A form of swindling in which the commodity was loaned out and payment demanded in cash at an inflated evaluation. Lucas cites the example dramatized in Middleton's *Michaelmas Term*, II. iii. *bankroupts.* Lucas cites the record in Dekker's *Seven Deadly Sins.* After borrowing heavily the swindler declared himself bankrupt and hid until his creditors made a bargain.

(4) Apparently, scriveners were often asked to recommend usurers and received a percentage.

(5) King Edgar, great-grandson of Alfred, ordered the Welsh to pay a tribute of three hundred wolf heads a year instead of money.

(6) Lucas cites a letter from Mountjoy to Cecil (9 April 1600), assuring him that the gutters are now running full of Irish heads.

(7) *leash.* A sporting term for a set of three.

(8) The falconers' lure was a feathered object resembling its prey swung on a long cord. The falcon was fed by placing food in the interstices of the structure.

(9) From *Aeneid*, VII, 312. The river Acheron and the lower world were symbolic of hell.

ACT IV. SCENE II.

(1) Pope Gregory XIII died on 10 April 1585.

(2) *coffind*. The common word for a pie crust was "coffin." The macabre connotation thus was partly fortuitous.

(3) *conveyance*. Means, in the sense of "trickery." A "conveyer" was also a "thief."

(4) Rejected lovers wore willow.

(5) Brown notes that fruit was ripened in straw.

(6) A play on lines as "recorded wisdom" and "wrinkles," while *convinces* means "overcomes."

(7) *Atheists*. The term was used loosely to refer to blasphemous or impious states of mind.

(8) *irregular*. Wild and uncivilized. Lucas cites "the irregular and wild Glendower" (*I Henry IV*, I. i. 40).

(9) Flamineo alludes to the gloss of watered silk, interpreting Brachiano's image of fickle woman ("changeable stuff") as clothing.

(10) *stand*. Withstand or defy.

(11) According to Dekker, *Seven Deadly Sins* (1606), the Russians beat debtors on the shins. Cited by Lucas.

(12) *methodically*. Completely and in detail.

(13) From *Odyssey*, IX, 369–370.

(14) *receiver*. The pander who receives love letters for the prostitute.

(15) *pretious*. The noun understood is "blood" or "body."

(16) A *reclaimed* hawk was a tamed one. Bells were tied to the hawk's legs to make it easy to find and to frighten its prey. An untameable hawk would usually be freed without its bells. But freeing it "bells and all" adds emphasis. Lucas cites the parallel in *Othello*, III. iii. 260–263. The phrase *ware hawke* is commonly misunderstood (as in Lucas). The term "ware" is not for "beware."

(17) A variation on the play's title. According to Robert Scot, *Discovery of Witchcraft* (1584), there were charms capable of confining spirits in crystals, and others capable of making spirits appear as white, green, or black angels, and in human form. Cited by Lucas and Brown.

(18) Found in Florio's Montaigne, III. v. in its more usual form of "man unto man." Tilley M 247.

(19) *Adamants.* Magnets.

(20) Another item Webster probably read in Stanyhurst's "Description of Ireland." Cf. I. ii. (6).

(21) Foxes were handled by those suffering paralysis to effect a cure. Ben Jonson tried it. See Herford and Simpson, I, 213.

(22) Alluding to *Mark*, IX. 45 : "And if thy foot offend thee, cut it off."

(23) The sense is that "young rabbits do not resist long."

(24) *forgetfull wine.* Wine inducing forgetfulness.

(25) These observations on wine and the sea are from Nicholas de Montreux, *Honour's Academy* (1610). Cited by Brown. The experience of shooting London Bridge would supply the culminating image.

(26) *still.* In its usual sense of "always" or "consistently."

(27) This Elizabethan exemplum was derived from Pliny, *Natural History*, VIII. 25. In Lyly's *Euphues* it is limited to illustrate gratitude.

(28) Despite his denial, Flamineo is of course thinking of his own gain. He may also be adding a bawdy pun.

Act IV. Scene iii.

(1) Webster's source for the details of this scene was Hierome Bignon, *A Briefe . . . Treatise of the Election of Popes,* translated and published in 1605.

(2) *Rhodes.* The Order of the Knights of St. John of Jerusalem, founded during the First Crusade (1096–1099). The order moved from there to Rhodes, Crete, and finally Malta. Their purpose was to fight the Mohammedans. They dressed in black robes with the eight-pointed silver (Maltese) cross. *St. Michael.* Order founded by Louis XI in 1469.

(3) *golden fleece.* Order founded by Philip the Good, Duke of Burgundy, in 1430.

(4) *Holy-Ghost.* Order of *Saint Esprit* founded by Henry III in 1578 to rank above the Order of St. Michael.

(5) *Annuntiation.* The highest order of Italian knighthood, founded by Amadeus VI of Savoy in 1362. Their dress was white satin with purple velvet cloak.

(6) *Garter.* The foundation of this order is variously dated (1346–1348) and accounted for.

(7) *window.* The Red Bull stage had a rear balcony (the terrace—battlements below) with windows.

(8) The speech heading is convincingly represented by Brown in his note on this passage.

(9) The historical Felice Peretti, Cardinal Montalto, became Sixtus V.

ACT V. SCENE I.

(1) *Stage Directions.* Brown notes that the *others* are probably the Ambassadors in their robes, underlining the hypocrisy of court life.

(2) *Candy.* Crete.

(3) *Two Noblemen.* Probably Lodovico and Gasparo, who enter disguised below.

(4) The Capuchins were an austerely pious order that branched off from the Franciscans in 1528. They became independent in 1619.

(5) *presence.* The presence-chamber.

(6) *paire.* A set of beads. Lucas cites also "a pair of stairs."

(7) To strike the ball into the hazzard was a winning stroke. The metaphor is one of self-damnation in apparent victory.

(8) The *Arras* would indicate luxury and be convenient to hide behind.

(9) More exactly, a *haggard* was an untameable or wild female hawk. Othello uses the term of Desdemona in III. iii. 260–263.

(10) Violence in the court was severely punished.

(11) In *Every Man in His Humour* Bobadill uses a bed-staff as a sword. It was used to beat and smooth the bed. Cornelia apparently beat the maids with one, but her reason may have been finding the maids in bed with a man.

(12) Eteocles and Polynices slew each other in fighting for possession of their father's throne. Put on one funeral pyre, the flames of the two bodies refused to burn together. From Statius, *Thebais,* XII. 431. Brown cites the occurrence of the episode in Pettie's translation of Guazza's *Civil Conversation,* III. 84.

(13) *And thou.* If thou. A common usage of "and." The more familiar usage follows.

(14) Michaelmas is the 29th of September. Francisco refers to the English St. Martin's Summer or the American Indian Summer.

ACT V. SCENE II.

(1) Cornelia is wearing the crucifix.

(2) *graz'd.* A spelling of "grassed," for "lost in the grass."

(3) *Stage Direction.* The "beaver" was the face-piece of a helmet.

ACT V. SCENE III.

(1) *barre.* The barrier across which the swordsmen duelled.

(2) Lucas cites these words from *Arcadia*, III : "I sweare, that Death bringes nothing with it to grieve me, but that I must leave thee, and cannot remaine to answere part of thy infinit deserts." But the comparison supports the argument that Webster did not use Sidney's *Arcadia* before writing *The Duchess of Malfi.*

(3) Owls portended death.

(4) Lucas cites W. Minto for the observation that Webster here draws an ironic parallel with the way in which Isabella died.

(5) *Franciscans.* More exactly, Lodovico and Gasparo are in the habit of Capuchins. Brown notes the ironic use of Francisco's name here.

(6) Explained by Lucas. The *verge* (*virga*) was the rod of the Lord High Steward, who had jurisdiction over all matters within twelve miles of the court.

(7) *wolfe.* The popular name for an ulcer.

(8) *poultry.* Ulcers were "fed" with raw meat to prevent their preying on the body. The historical Bracciano had an ulcer treated with raw meat. Brown suggests a pun on "paultry" for "trash."

(9) *quailes.* No doubt a confession of lechery. A "quail" was a "whore" as well as a delicacy contrasting the common *dog-fish.*

(10) The codpiece accentuated the male sexual organ. Shakespeare mentions the fashion in *Two Gentlemen*, II. vii. 53–56.

(11) *rose.* A rosette of ribbons.

(12) *linguist.* In two senses, of speaking all languages and any language well.

(13) *Arras powder.* Powder of orris or iris root, used to whiten hair. The gray in Vittoria's hair is a delusion of Bracciano's. The *Pastrie* was the place where pastry was made.

(14) A rat without a tail is probably a witch in rat form. Cf. *Macbeth*, I. iii. 8–9.

(15) In *TLS* (14 June 1947), A. W. Reed showed the source of this Latin sequence to be Erasmus' *Colloquia*, "Funus." Lucas cites the death of Queen Elizabeth as an example of the use of signs to indicate faith.

(16) *conscience.* Combining both "consciousness" and "moral reason."

(17) An allusion to the death of Amy Robsart, the Earl of Leicester's wife. She was found at the foot of the staircase at Cumnor Place, 8 September 1560. In a pamphlet of 1584, *Leicester's Commonwealth*, the Earl was accused of trying to poison her before throwing her down the stairs to her death. The pamphlet also accuses Leicester of employing a poisoner named Giulo (Julio) Borgarucci. For more details see Lucas' note.

(18) The distinction between *Mercarie* and *quick-silver* is suggested by Brown. Lucas suggests "mercuric chloride" for *Mercarie*.

(19) *snuffe*. End of a candle. Nurses or "woman-keepers" were suspected of hastening the deaths of patients.

(20) *Pest-house*. For those infected with the plague, erected in London in 1594.

(21) *more rivers*. An allusion to the project of Sir Hugh Middleton, which ran from Ware to Islington, about thirty-nine miles. It was constructed from 1609 to 1613.

(22) *good cheape*. At a bargain; *cheepe* is a noun.

(23) *Machivillian*. With a pun on "villain."

(24) *jumpes*. An allusion to the slippery top of court favor. Lucas parallels *Duchess of Malfi*, V. ii. 367–369 : "I must looke to my footing; / In such slippery yce-pauements. . . .

(25) *descant*. Sing variations on a theme.

(26) *Irish mantle*. The Irish reputedly wore nothing under their mantles, which served for all weathers and situations.

(27) *'fum'd*. For "perfumed."

(28) From *Jeremiah*, XIII. 23 : "Can the Ethiopian change his skin, or the leopard his spots?"

(29) Laurel was used medicinally, as well as serving as the emblem of fame.

ACT V. SCENE IV.

(1) This comment by the peacock is from Pettie's translation of Guazza's *Civil Conversation*. Cited by Brown.

(2) *Anacharsis*. An error for Anaxarchus which Webster found in Nicholas de Montreux, *Honour's Academy*. See Lucas and Brown.

(3) *decimo sexto*. A very small book size, each page being one-sixteenth of a full sheet. Compare Webster's "Induction" to *The Màlcontent*.

(4) In history, Vittoria was imprisoned for a while in the Castle San Angelo in Rome. Here it is equated with the Tower of London.

495

(5) *flaming firebrand.* Lucas suggests that Flamineo is playing on his own name.

(6) *Traverse.* The curtain across the recessed area at the rear of the stage.

(7) An echo of Ophelia in IV. v. of *Hamlet.* Rosemary was an evergreen emblematic of remembrance. Pliny noted that bays protected the wearer from lightning.

(8) *Rue.* A bitter herb.

(9) *Hearts-ease.* Pansies.

(10) The toad was thought a venemous creature.

(11) *Couslep-water.* A general cordial.

(12) Lucas cites the wide belief that the robin tended the dead. The wren was considered the robin's wife.

(13) The superstition was that the wolf dug up the bodies of murdered men.

(14) A proverb (Tilley, W 68) which Camden said was used by St. Thomas More in prison when deprived of books and paper. Cited by Lucas. Brown suggests that at this point the *traverse* was again drawn across.

(15) *mase.* Bewilderment and perhaps like "maze," puzzled windings.

(16) *Stage Direction.* The leather cassock was primarily the garment of soldiers. The lilies and the skull were emblematic of vice leading to death. Brown cites George Wither's *Emblems* (1635).

(17) *mockery.* Illusion or shadow. *sad.* Grave or serious rather than melancholy.

ACT V. SCENE v.

(1) *cariere.* Lucas explains : a full gallop with a sudden stop. But in this instance the rider seems unwilling to follow the recognized pattern.

ACT V. SCENE vi.

(1) *Stage Direction.* Carrying a book was a sign of melancholy. Here it was obviously a prayer-book.

(2) *Ruffin.* The context suggests "devil." Cf. *Bussy D'Ambois,* III. ii. 24, p. 378 and note.

(3) Beggars without patents were severely punished as vagabonds.

(4) *case.* A pair. Two case are thus four.

(5) The image is of despair mixed with bitterness (gall) and

poison (stibium, antimony) and not coated with sweetness. Yet we drink it down (*carouse it off*).

(6) Lucas cites Florio's Montaigne, III. iv : "When such like repetitions pinch me, and that I looke more nearely to them, I finde them but grammaticall laments, the word and the tune wound me. Even as Preachers exclamations do often move their auditory more then their reasons."

(7) Cf. Florio's Montaigne, II. xiii : "[Killing one's self] is a meate a man must swallow without chewing." Cited by Lucas.

(8) Two pistols are aimed at Flamineo and he aims one at each of them.

(9) *cupping glasses*. Used to draw blood in blood-letting.

(10) Lucian's comic Purgatory is in the *Menippos*. Pompey's occupation is that of fixing metal ends to the tags (*points*) used to tie the Elizabethan upper garment (doublet) to the lower (hose). Charlemagne is selling strips of cloth (*lists*). King *Pippin* is a play on King Pepin the Short of the Franks, and a variety of apple.

(11) *Engine*. Contrivance.

(12) Suicides were buried at cross-roads with stakes driven through them to restrain their spirits.

(13) *doubled all your reaches*. Matched all of your trickery. Lucas suggests "eluded" for *doubled*.

(14) *Kindnesse*. Natural feeling.

(15) Henry VIII granted a charter to the Fraternity of Artillery with an exercise field called Tasel (Teazle) Close, outside Bishopsgate. The artillery—used by citizens—included cross-bows and small arms. Ordnance of the Tower was also tested there. After the crisis of 1588 the ground fell into disuse, but a revival occurred about 1610. The present Artillery Lane and Artillery St. indicate the site. Compare *Every Man in His Humour*.

(16) *Hypermnestra*. One of the fifty daughters of Danaus forced to marry the fifty sons of their father's brother Aegyptus. Danaus ordered his daughters to slay their husbands, being warned by an oracle that he would be killed by a nephew. All obeyed except Hypermnestra, who spared her husband Lynceus.

(17) *two other Instruments*. Flamineo threatens with his two pistols but is overpowered by the entering group. Probably due to their disguises Lodovico and Gasparo can get close to him and seize the weapons.

(18) *Maske*. Perhaps an indication of seizing hold of Flamineo

and the women, since in a masque the disguised masquers danced with their visitants. A *matachine* included fantastic costume.

(19) Lucas cited Nashe's *Lenten Stuff* (1599) for Fate as a spaniel "you cannot beate from you."

(20) *pillar.* Probably one of the permanent pillars which supported the projection or "heavens" over the stage. But special pillars were sometimes used on stage.

(21) This characteristic of the black-bird is in Nicholas de Montreux, *Honour's Academy.* Cited by Brown.

(22) *Conceit.* Imagination and vanity, female traits.

(23) Pliny recommended this cure for epilepsy. Cited by Lucas.

(24) A *Fox* was a kind of sword blade.

(25) *woeman.* The spelling illustrates a popular etymology of "woman," man's woe.

(26) *thou . . . thou.* Zanche and Vittoria.

(27) There were lions and leopards in the Tower from the time of Henry I. Candlemas is the 2nd of February. Brown cites Tilley C 52 : "If Candelmas day be fair and bright, winter will have another flight."

(28) Cf. William Alexander, *Julius Caesar*, II. ii. 1013–1014. "Ease comes with ease, where all by paine buy paine, / Rest we in peace, by warre let others raigne." Cited by Lucas and Brown.

(29) *Epilogue; nature a monster.* Compare *Hamlet*, III. ii. 20–39; and this from "An Excellent Actor," *Characters* (1615) : "He doth not strive to make nature monstrous, she is often seen in the same Scaene with him, but neither on Stilts nor Crutches." Cited by Lucas and Brown. Cf. also Ben Jonson's Prologue to *Every Man in His Humour.*

BUSSY D'AMBOIS

For the historical background see the general introduction. The Prologue is in neither of the quartos, and it is probably not by Chapman. It may have been written for a revival of the play at Whitehall, 7 April 1634, which reestablished the claim of the King's Men to the book after it had been performed by another company. According to Parrott, whose argument seems soundest, the play was probably written for the Children of the Chapel about 1604 and was taken over by the Children of Paul's. It was probably revised for a new production by the Queen's Revels at Whitefriars about 1610, with Nathan Field in the lead. The play must have come to the King's Men about 1616 through Field's joining that group as a sharer. Field died about 1620. The second Bussy mentioned in the Prologue is perhaps the aging Joseph Taylor, who was succeeded in the part by Eliard Swanston. The "Richard" played by Swanston was probably Richard III, whose play was performed at court about five months before the 1634 revival of *Bussy D'Ambois*. Chapman died in the same year.

DRAMATIS PERSONAE :

HENRY III. He was the third son of Henry II and Catherine de Medici, succeeding to the throne of France in 1574 on the death of his brother Charles IX. He apparently shared with his mother the planning of the Massacre of St. Bartholomew, 24 August 1572. After he had brought about the death of the Duke of Guise, he was himself assassinated by Jacques Clement, a Dominican friar, in August 1589. On his death bed he named Henry of Navarre his successor.

MONSIEUR. Title of the next younger brother of the King of France. He was François, youngest son of Catherine de Medici, Duke of Alençon and later of Anjou. He died in June 1584.

DUKE OF GUISE. He was Henri of Lorraine, third duke of Guise. He led the French Catholics in the religious wars. After temporarily seizing control of Paris by raising the mob, he was killed by the king's bodyguard at Blois in 1588.

FRIAR. In the quartos of 1607–1608 the Friar is called Comolet. A Father Comolet was a member of the conspiracy for the assassination of Henry III.

ACT I. SCENE I.

(1) In Geoffrey Whitney's *Choice of Emblems* (1586) there are emblems of a lofty pine beaten by the winds and of a girdle around the globe symbolizing Drake's voyage 1577–1580.

(2) These examples and arguments are largely drawn from Plutarch's essay on the secluded life in his *Moralia*.

(3) *t'unfold.* The sense of *unfold* here is that of revealing in order to make avoidance possible. But the Courtier perverts the instruction to the destruction of the innocent.

(4) This emblem is from Vincenzo Cartari, *Le Imagini de i Dei degli Antichi.* See Allan H. Gilbert, *The Symbolic Persons in the Masques of Ben Jonson* (Durham, 1948), pp. 10, 11, and notes.

(5) *unsweating thrift.* Cold calculation.

(6) Bussy shifts the application of command to that of ordering a dinner or going hungry.

(7) Bussy was a poet. Some of his verses are printed in Joubert (pp. 205–209).

(8) Due to small pox, the Monsieur appeared to have two noses, a phenomenon satirized in contemporary rime, according to Pierre de L'Estoile, *Journal de Henri III*.

(9) *dagger.* The court fool inherited the wooden dagger of the Morality Vice and often carried it on stage.

ACT I. SCENE II.

(1) These lines could be spoken only after the death of the old Queen in 1603.

(2) Chapman is really attacking the court of James I by contrast with Elizabeth's. Cf. also the court in *Monsieur D'Olive.*

(3) *leape yeare.* The most logical one is 1604.

(4) *Accius Noevius.* An augurer whose feat of cutting a whetstone with a razor is described in the first book of Livy's *History*.

(5) The great number of knights created by James I was the subject of much satire, as in *Eastward Ho!* and *Monsieur D'Olive.*

(6) An allusion to the Massacre of St. Bartholomew, 24 August 1572.

(7) Violence of any sort within the limits of the court was forbidden and severely punished. Cf. also lines 13–14, p. 356.

(8) Rushes were the common floor covering.

(9) Parrott thinks that *frames* must refer to the conformation of the ocean bed. But the ocean bed does not cause the surges and

Chapman is more likely to have thought of the sea as a living being.

(10) One of the many contemporary allusions to the new knights created in large numbers by James I.

(11) A fable from Aesop. Jacobs II, 219.

ACT II. SCENE I.

(1) Envy spreads (*bruits*) filth through the world yet remains *sound and healthfull*. The primary meaning of *bruits* is "proclaims." There is a mixed metaphor of evil words and matter.

(2) The duel described here probably suggested by one fought between three partisans of the Guise and three of Henry III in 1578.

(3) *Pyrrho's Opinion.* That we should be indifferent to all things since we can know nothing of reality. Pyrrho lived c. 365–275 B.C.

(4) From *Iliad*, III. 76 ff.

(5) *he.* Barrisor.

(6) *him . . . himselfe.* Bussy.

(7) *Who.* Bussy. *he.* Barrisor.

(8) *He.* Barrisor.

(9) *Foe.* Barrisor. I read the pronouns opposite to the sense Parrott makes of them.

(10) *Navarre.* Henry of Navarre, who became Henry IV of France 1589–1610. He fought many battles for the Protestant cause 1576–1589, then for his throne. He was converted to Catholicism in July 1593, and assassinated by Ravaillac on 14 May 1610.

(11) The jeweller's object was to make the unicorn drive his horn into a tree, but the unicorn in this instance impales the jeweller. The horn was greatly prized as an antidote of poisons.

(12) A metaphor of hounds chasing prey in sight.

(13) Monsieur here invokes his blood relation to the king (*Nature*) and uses *vertue* in the sense of "power." The *greatness* would be the act of pardoning Bussy, which, as king, Henry ought not do. Thus *Nature* should overrule kingship. He then argues for the necessity of maintaining reputation by a fair duel. Had Barrisor survived he should have been executed for double murder, a reputation as well as a man.

(14) Parrott cites parallels to Bussy's philosophy of the virtuous man free and above the law : *The Gentleman Usher*, V. iv. 56–60; *Byron's Conspiracy*, III. iii. 140–145; *Caesar and Pompey*, V. ii. 8–10.

Act II. Scene ii.

(1) *maritorious.* The NED lists only this use, defining it as "fond of one's husband."

(2) Female attendants might carry a book to peruse when their ladies became amorous. Parrott cites parallels in *All Fools,* II. i. 282–285 and *Monsieur D'Olive,* V. i. 190–200.

(3) An allusion to the contemporary struggle between Parliament and King James as to the limit of the king's *prerogative.* The leader of the forces who considered the king under the law was Sir Edward Coke.

(4) *Center.* The earth itself, at the center of the universe.

(5) Bradley is correct in reading this line as a declaration of abandoning one's self. Tamyra must destroy her present self in order to become Bussy's mistress.

(6) *first Orbe.* The outer sphere (*Primum Mobile*) of the Ptolemaic system, whose power emanates through and moves the others.

(7) Bussy is to tell Tamyra that he came not as her lover but to assure her (*resolve her*) that she was not guilty of Barrisor's blood. There had been rumors that the duel grew out of Barrisor's suspicion of Bussy's secret attentions to Tamyra.

(8) *any love.* That is, any love for Bussy.

(9) *perplex.* An adjective obsolete. See NED. Chapman seems to combine the senses of "puzzled" and "intricate." The use of reason cannot change women.

Act III. Scene i.

(1) *valour.* Since the primary meaning is "worth," it is interchangeable with *value* (line 15, p. 373).

(2) *oppos'd.* Set in relation to : The stone should be set to the architect's line, not vice versa. In Tamyra's metaphor Nature is the architect of her passion to which her will (*stone*) must submit.

(3) *mushrome.* Upstart. Cf. *The White Devil,* III. iii. 4, p. 269 and note.

(4) *but must consume.* That is, the *lightnings fume* will consume the embracer.

Act III. Scene ii.

(1) Plaited hay was used to protect the rider who had no boots. Cf. *Every Man in His Humour,* I. iii. Flattery now goes riding in boots made of kings' guts softened by his art.

(2) Because of Judas, red-haired men were not trusted and their bodies thought poisonous.

(3) *trusse.* The verb has several connotations. "To seize," (as a bird of prey), "to hang," "to bind," "to send packing."

(4) *suffering.* Allowing, permitting.

(5) *graduate.* Rise by degrees.

(6) *liver.* Cf. note (17) below. Tityus, a giant son of Earth and Jove was slain by Apollo for attacking Leto. In Hades his liver is gnawed by two vultures.

(7) *Ruffin.* The context suggests "ruffian," with which the word was confused. Strictly, *Ruffin* was a fiend or the Devil. Cf. *The White Devil,* V. vi. 34, p. 321.

(8) This line suggests that lines 17–18, p. 377 are ironic. The Guise actually got control of Paris on 12 May 1588, the Day of Barricades, by raising the mob.

(9) Georges D'Amboise, Cardinal and Archbishop of Rouen, chief minister of Louis XII, lived 1460–1510. Bussy was born in 1549.

(10) a pun on *ducere,* "to lead."

(11) *ingenious.* Interchangeable with "ingenuous."

(12) The monster Typhon of a hundred heads was slain by Jove's thunderbolt (*ordinance*) and buried under Aetna. See Douglas Bush, *Mythology and the Renaissance Tradition in English Poetry* (Minneapolis and London, 1932), pp. 104, 241, 277.

(13) *women that woorst may.* A proverb (Tilley C 40), usually of the weaker member in an affair or enterprise.

(14) Parrott notes *say* as a hunting term for cutting into the animal to judge its fatness.

(15) Guise was the uncle of Mme. de Beaupré, Charlotte's mistress.

(16) *apprehensions.* Mind and heart together; intelligent consciousness.

(17) *liver.* The liver was the source of the passions, especially lust.

ACT III. SCENE III.

(1) Although Monsieur has not left the stage the scene has shifted from the court to Monsieur's dwelling. This is a striking instance of the freedom of Elizabethan staging and the unimportance of "placing" scenes except to comprehend the immediate action.

(2) *Scylla and Caribdis.* Ovid, *Metamorphoses,* XIV, 70 ff.

(3) *Cerberus.* Ovid, *Metamorphoses,* IV. 450; VII, 409 ff.

(4) *fell.* The conventional epithet of the tiger, "fierce."

(5) *without a circle.* "Outside a circle." A spirit could be controlled if raised inside a drawn circle.

(6) *man of bloud.* Parrott suggests that the phrase was suggested by Edward Grimeston's translation of Jean de Serres, *A General Inventory of the History of France* (1611), in which Bussy is called a "bloody, wicked, and a furious man."

(7) *Titan.* The sun god, son of Hyperion.

(8) The cuckoo's song is always embarrassing because it suggests adultery. The association grew from the fact that the cuckoo always lays its eggs in the nests of other birds. It usually sings in the spring.

(9) Ajax ran mad when the arms of Achilles were awarded to Ulysses rather than himself. He attacked a flock of sheep, thinking it the army of the Greeks.

(10) *Jupiter Hammon.* Explained by Boas as an allusion to the adoration of Alexander the Great as the son of Jupiter Hammon.

(11) *murthering peece.* A small cannon firing chain-shot. Cf. *Hamlet,* IV. v. 95.

(12) *Lernean fenne.* The fen near Argos in which the Hydra lived.

(13) *Clotho . . . soule.* For a picture of the three fates at work see Allan Gilbert, *Symbolic Persons,* plate 55.

Act IV. Scene i.

(1) *Moon-calves.* Monstrosities of birth caused by the baleful influence of the moon.

(2) *liver.* Parrott suggests an allusion to the myth of Prometheus.

(3) The Monsieur interprets *all men else* ("all other men") as "all others but one."

(4) *box tree.* An emblem of humility.

(5) *Armenian dragons.* Parrott suggests Chapman is alluding to the "gold-guarding griffins of Scythia" (Herodotus, IV. 27).

(6) Parrott compares Vergil, *Georgics,* II. 325–326 : "tum pater omnipotens fecundis imbribus Aether coniugis in gremium laetae descendit. . . ." "Then the father almighty, Aether, descends into the lap of his joyous mate, with fruitful showers."

(7) *Cynthia.* Another name of Diana, goddess of the moon, combining the associations of child-birth and horns.

(8) *something.* Monsieur is offering a love letter by Bussy or

504

Tamyra and procured by Pero. The historical letter of Bussy, boasting of his conquest, is not relevant.

(9) *plague of Herod. Acts*, XII. 23 : "And immediately the angel of the Lord smote him, because he gave not God the glory : and he was eaten of worms, and gave up the ghost.

(10) *string*. Carrying on the musical image of *discords* in the previous line.

(11) The allusion is not in the first quarto. Parrott argues that these Irish Wars must be those of 1607 and 1608, since the next outbreak was in 1641. He concludes that the revision of *Bussy* must have been shortly thereafter. See also the note on III. iii. 9, p. 389.

(12) *inform'd*. In form or under control of reason.

(13) *him*. Monsieur.

(14) Bellerophon slew Chimera the firebreathing monster. He was an innocent, having repelled a lustful Queen.

Peleus refused the love of the wife of Acastus. She falsely accused him and he was exposed to the beasts on Mount Pelion. Chiron the centaur rescued him, knowing his innocence.

The *Athenian Prince* is Hippolytus, who refused his step-mother Phaedra. Having been killed when his own horses were frightened by a bull sent by Neptune, he was raised from the dead by Aesculapius.

(15) Cleansing the Augean stable was a labor of Hercules.

(16) An allusion to the dragon's teeth sown by Jason and Cadmus, which produced armed men.

(17) *sunne or Cerberus*. The guardian of the lower world as well as the eye of the upper half.

(18) *touch*. "Blot" or "disgrace," as well as "stroke."

(19) Alexander the Great cut the Gordian knot, after failing to unravel it. An oracle had said whoever untied it would rule Asia.

ACT IV. SCENE II.

(1) Epimetheus, brother of Prometheus, opened Pandora's box.

(2) *wreak the skie . . . artillerie*. In vengeance of Uranus, deposed by Saturn and the Titans. The Cyclops forged thunderbolts for Jove in his war with the Titans.

(3) *Behemoth*. Parrott notes that Behemoth occurs in the pronouncement of the University of Paris on the visions of Joan of Arc, and in the trial of Urbain Grandier, burnt in 1634. Reginald Scott has a note on Astaroth in his "Discourse on Devils," appended to his *Discovery of Witchcraft*, ch. XX.

(4) *Cartophylax.* Literally, guardian of papers.

(5) *great in our command.* Great among our order.

(6) The action of Monsieur and his group probably took place on the balcony.

ACT V. SCENE I.

(1) *no lawrell.* Geoffrey Whitney, *Choice of Emblems,* has a man clinging to a laurel for protection from lightning (*wild seed of vapour*). Parrott cites Pierre Matthieu, *Histoire de France* (1605), II. 145 verso, for the marginal note on a speech of the Duke de Biron : "Les hommes en dormant ne sont jamais frappez du foudre."

(2) Cf. *Aeneid,* IV. 173–175 : "Fama, malum qua non aliud velocius ullum. / mobilitate viget virisque adquirit eundo." "Fame (rumor), of evils none swifter, grows with speed and gets strength in going."

(3) *ruffin Gally.* Ruffian (pirate) galley. Cf. III. ii. (7).

(4) To "dance in a net" was a metaphor for believing oneself unseen when in full view of others. Parrott cites parallels in *Spanish Tragedy,* IV. iv. 118; *Henry V,* I. ii. 93; *All Fools,* II. i. 252; *Tragedy of Chabot,* IV. i. 136.

(5) *Pelion.* A mountain in Thessaly where Bellerophon was exposed. Cf. IV. i. (14). *Cythaeron.* Mountain in Greece noted for wild beasts.

(6) *chaine-shot.* Cf. *murthering peece,* III. iii. (11).

(7) *rape.* Cf. *The White Devil,* III. ii. line 32, p. 264.

(8) *frame.* Cf. *frames,* I. ii. (9).

ACT V. SCENE II.

(1) Cf. Seneca's *Agamemnon,* 64–72 : "non sic Libycis syrtibus aequor / furit alternos volvere fluctus, / non Euxini turget ab imis / commota vadis unda nivali / vicina polo, / ubi caeruleis immunis aquis / lucida versat plaustra Boötes, / ut praecipites regum casus / Fortuna rotat. / metui cupiunt / metuique timent, ..." "Not so on Libyan sands the sea rages with rolling wave on wave, not so the Euxine water surges, stirred to its deepest depths, near the snowy pole, where, untouched by the cerulean waves, Boötes turns his shining chariot, as the headlong fates of kings Fortune rolls. They desire to be feared and to be feared they dread, ..."

Act V. Scene iv.

(1) *revenged.* Become the prey of revenge.

(2) *Breath thee.* Take a breath in anticipation of the second attack.

(3) *speeding sleight.* A successful trick and a well-executed disguise.

(4) *enforce the spot.* Make an issue of the dishonor.

(5) According to Suetonius, Vespasian died standing.

(6) Compare Seneca, *Hercules Oetaeus,* 1518 ff. : O decus mundi, radiate Titan, / cuius ad primos Hecate vapores / lassa nocturnae levat ora bigae, / dic sub Aurora positis Sabaeis, / die sub occasu positis Hiberis, / quique sub plaustro patiuntur ursae / quique ferventi quatiuntur axe, / dic sub aeternos properare manes / Herculem et regnum canis inquieti, / unde non umquam remeabit ille. / sume quos nubes radios sequantur, / pallidus maestas speculare terras / et caput turpes nebulae pererrent." "O glory of the world, radiant Sun, at whose first emanations Hecate eases the wearied reins of her nocturnal steeds, tell the Sabaeans in the place of dawn, tell the Iberians in the place of your fall, those who suffer under the Wagon of the Bear, those who tremble for your burning axel-tree, tell them that Hercules is hastening to the eternal shades and the realm of the restless dog, from which he will never return. Let clouds cover your rays, stare the gloomy earth into pallor and let dark clouds move round your head." Bussy identifies himself with Hercules and his *frailties* with those of the dead heroes.

(7) The sight of Tamyra, sun of his life, heats his heart and liver so that they melt snowy *Pindus* (on his heart) and *Ossa* (on his liver), which flow with his bitter blood into the *Ocean of all humane life,* making it bitter.

(8) In the chorus of *Hercules Oeteus* noted above, the *virtue* of Hercules is given a place among the stars (lines 1564 ff.). The Umbra Friar's words are not much like Seneca's.

(9) *Manlesly.* Inhumanely, monstrously.

(10) Parrott notes that the image of torches held upside down and extinguished by their own power is applied in Edward Grimeston and Pierre Mathieu to Biron and the Count D'Auvergne. The sweetness of the bees (*his first parents*) passes from taste into perfume (*savour*), an image of metamorphosis from physical to spiritual.

(11) *axeltree.* The pole. Montsurry and Tamyra are as divided as the antipodes.

SELECTED BIBLIOGRAPHY

This list of works includes those given earlier in short form. The additional titles are limited to those of major scope, either for the study of the period or the individual authors.

I. BASIC GUIDES

Bentley, G. E. *The Jacobean and Caroline Stage.* 5 vols. Oxford, 1941–1956.

Chambers, E. K. *The Elizabethan Stage.* 4 vols. Oxford, 1923.

Greg, W. W. *A Bibliography of the English Printed Drama to the Restoration.* 4 vols. London, 1939–1959.

Harbage, A. *Annals of English Drama 975–1700.* Philadelphia and London, 1940.

Murray, J. A. H., *et al. The Oxford English Dictionary, Being a Corrected Re-Issue . . . of A New English Dictionary.* 13 vols. Oxford, 1933.

Nungezer, Edwin. *A Dictionary of Actors and of Other Persons Associated with the Public Representation of Plays in England Before 1642.* New Haven, 1929.

Tilley, M. P. *A Dictionary of the Proverbs in England in the Sixteenth and Seventeenth Centuries.* Ann Arbor, 1950.

II. COLLECTIONS

Baskervill, C. R., V. B. Heltzel, and A. H. Nethercot, edd. *Elizabethan and Stuart Plays.* New York, 1949.

Brooke, C. F. T., and N. B. Paradise, edd. *English Drama 1580–1642.* New York, 1933.

Jacobs, J., ed. *The Fables of Aesop as First Printed by William Caxton in 1484 with Those of Avian, Alfonso and Poggio.* 2 vols. London, 1889.

Rimbault, E. F., ed. *The Miscellaneous Works in Prose and Verse of Sir Thomas Overbury, Knt.* London, 1856.

Spencer, H., ed. *Elizabethan Plays.* Boston, 1933.

III. THEATRE

Campbell, L. B. *Scenes and Machines on the English Stage during the Renaissance.* Cambridge, 1923.

Hodges, C. W. *The Globe Restored, A Study of the Elizabethan Theatre.* London, 1953.

Linthicum, M. C. *Costume in the Drama of Shakespeare and His Contemporaries.* Oxford, 1936.

Reynolds, G. F. *The Staging of Elizabethan Plays at the Red Bull Theater 1605–1625.* New York and London, 1940.

Small, R. A. *The Stage-Quarrel between Ben Jonson and the So-Called Poetasters.* Breslau, 1899.

Sharpe, R. B. *The Real War of the Theaters: Shakespeare's Fellows in Rivalry with the Admiral's Men, 1594–1603: Repertories, Devices, and Types.* Boston and London, 1935.

Wallace, C. W. *The Children of the Chapel at Blackfriars 1597–1603.* Lincoln, 1908.

IV. STUDIES AND CRITICISM

Bennett, J. W., O. Cargill, and V. Hall, Jr., edd. *Studies in the English Renaissance Drama.* New York, 1959.

Boas, F. S. *An Introduction to Stuart Drama.* Oxford, 1946.

Bowers, F. T. *Elizabethan Revenge Tragedy 1587–1642.* Princeton, 1940.

Bradbrook, M. C. *Themes and Conventions of Elizabethan Tragedy.* Cambridge, 1935.

—— *The Growth and Structure of Elizabethan Comedy.* London, 1955.

Brown, J. R., and B. Harris, edd. *Jacobean Theatre.* London and New York, 1960.

Bush, D. *Mythology and the Renaissance Tradition in English Poetry.* Minneapolis and London, 1932.

—— *English Literature in the Earlier Seventeenth Century 1600–1660.* Oxford, 1945.

Campbell, O. J. *Comicall Satyre and Shakespeare's Troilus and Cressida*. San Marino, 1938.

Cunliffe, J. W. *The Influence of Seneca on Elizabethan Tragedy, An Essay*. London, 1893.

Doran, M. *Endeavors of Art : A Study of Form in Elizabethan Drama*. Madison, 1954.

Eliot, T. S. *Elizabethan Essays*. London, 1934.

Ellis-Fermor, U. M. *The Jacobean Drama, An Interpretation*. London, 1936.

Farnham, W. *The Medieval Heritage of Elizabethan Tragedy*. Berkeley, 1936.

Harbage, A. *Shakespeare and the Rival Traditions*. New York, 1952.

Herrick, M. T. *Tragicomedy : Its Origin and Development in Italy, France, and England*. Urbana, 1955.

Jewkes, W. T. *Act Division in Elizabethan and Jacobean Plays 1583–1616*. Hamden, 1958.

Lewis, C. S. *English Literature in the Sixteenth Century Excluding Drama*. Oxford, 1954.

Lucas, F. L. *Seneca and Elizabethan Tragedy*. Cambridge, 1922.

Ornstein, R. *The Moral Vision of Jacobean Tragedy*. Madison, 1960.

Prior, M. E. *The Language of Tragedy*. New York, 1947.

Spencer, T. *Death and Elizabethan Tragedy, A Study of Convention and Opinion in the Elizabethan Drama*. Cambridge, Mass., 1936.

Swinburne, A. C. *The Age of Shakespeare*. New York and London, 1908.

Symons, A. *Studies in the Elizabethan Drama*. New York, 1919.

Wells, H. W. *Elizabethan and Jacobean Playwrights*. New York, 1939.

Wilson, F. P. *Elizabethan and Jacobean*. Oxford, 1945.

V. BEN JONSON

Tannenbaum, S. A., and D. R. *Ben Jonson : A Concise Bibliography* [and] *Supplement*. New York, 1938, 1947.

EDITIONS

Carter, H. H., ed. *Every Man in His Humour*. New Haven, 1921.

Herford, C. H., and P. and E. Simpson, edd. *Ben Jonson*. 11 vols. Oxford, 1925–1952.

Johnston, G. B., ed. *Poems of Ben Jonson*. London, 1954.

Levin, Harry, ed. *Ben Jonson : Selected Works*. New York, 1938.

Nicholson, B., and C. H. Herford, edd. *Ben Jonson*. New York, 1957.

Simpson, P., ed. *Ben Jonson's Every Man in His Humour*. Oxford, 1921.

Walker, R. S., ed. *Ben Jonson's Timber or Discoveries*. Syracuse, 1953.

STUDIES

Bamborough, J. B. *Ben Jonson*. London and New York, 1959.

Barish, J. A. *Ben Jonson and the Language of Prose Comedy*. Cambridge, Mass., 1960.

Baum, H. W. *The Satiric and the Didactic in Ben Jonson's Comedy*. Chapel Hill, 1947.

Enck, J. J. *Jonson and the Comic Truth*. Madison, 1957.

Gilbert, A. H. *The Symbolic Persons in the Masques of Ben Jonson*. Durham, 1948.

Knights, L. C. *Drama and Society in the Age of Jonson*. London, 1937.

Musgrove, S. *Shakespeare and Jonson*. Auckland, 1957.

Noyes, R. G. *Ben Jonson on the English Stage 1660–1776*. Cambridge, Mass., 1935.

Partridge, A. C. *Studies in the Syntax of Ben Jonson's Plays*. Cambridge, 1953.

—— *The Accidence of Ben Jonson's Plays, Masques, and Entertainments, With an Appendix of Comparable Uses in Shakespeare*. Cambridge, 1953.

Partridge, E. B. *The Broken Compass, A Study of the Major Comedies of Ben Jonson*. New York, 1958.

Sackton, A. H. *Rhetoric as a Dramatic Language in Ben Jonson*. New York, 1948.

Smith, G. G. *Ben Jonson*. London, 1919.

Swinburne, A. C. *A Study of Ben Jonson*. London, 1889.

Wheeler, C. F. *Classical Mythology in the Plays, Masques, and Poems of Ben Jonson*. Princeton, 1938.

VI. JOHN MARSTON

Tannenbaum, S. A. *John Marston: A Concise Bibliography*. New York, 1940.

EDITIONS

Bullen, A. H., ed. *The Works of John Marston*. 3 vols. London, 1887.
Davenport, A., ed. *The Poems of John Marston*. Liverpool, 1961.
Harrison, G. B., ed. *The Malcontent*. London, 1933.
Wood, H. H., ed. *The Plays of John Marston*. 3 vols. Edinburgh and London, 1934–1939.

STUDIES

Allen, M. S. *The Satire of John Marston*. Columbus, 1920.
Axelrad, A. J. *Un Malcontent Elizabethain: John Marston 1576–1634*. Paris, 1955.
Deighton, K. *Marston's Works: Conjectural Readings*. London, 1893.
Pellegrini, G. *Il Teatro di John Marston*. Pisa, 1952.

VII. JOHN WEBSTER

Tannenbaum, S. A. *John Webster: A Concise Bibliography*. New York, 1941.

EDITIONS

Bentley, E., and J. A. Symonds, edd. *John Webster and Cyril Tourneur: Four Plays*. New York, 1956.
Brown, J. R., ed. *The White Devil*. London and Cambridge, Mass., 1960.
Dyce, A., ed. *The Works of John Webster*. 4 vols. London, 1830.
—— *The Works of John Webster: with Some Account of the Author and Notes*. London, 1859.
Harrison, G. B., ed. *The White Devil*. London, 1933.
Hazlitt, W., ed. *The Dramatic Works of John Webster*. 4 vols. London, 1857.
Lucas, F. L., ed. *The Complete Works of John Webster*. 4 vols. London, 1927.
—— *The White Devil*. London, 1958.

STUDIES

Bax, Clifford. *The Life of the White Devil*. London, 1940.

Bogard, T. *The Tragic Satire of John Webster*. Berkeley and Los Angeles, 1955.

Boklund, G. *The Sources of "The White Devil."* Uppsala and Cambridge, Mass., 1957.

Brooke, R. *John Webster and the Elizabethan Drama*. London, 1916.

Dent, R. W. *John Webster's Borrowing*. Berkeley and Los Angeles, 1960.

Leech, C. *John Webster, A Critical Study*. London, 1951.

Stoll, E. E. *John Webster : The Periods of his Work as Determined by his Relations to the Drama of his Day*. Boston, 1905.

VIII. GEORGE CHAPMAN

Tannenbaum, S. A., and D. R. *George Chapman : A Concise Bibliography* [and] *Supplement*. New York, 1938, 1946.

EDITIONS

Bartlett, P. B., ed. *The Poems of George Chapman*. New York and London, 1941.

Boas, F. S., ed. *Bussy D'Ambois and The Revenge of Bussy D'Ambois*. Boston, 1905.

Jacquot, J., ed. *George Chapman : Bussy D'Amboise*. Paris, 1960.

Nicoll, A., ed. *Chapman's Homer*. 2 vols. New York, 1956.

Pagnini, M., ed. *George Chapman : Bussy D'Ambois*. Bari, 1959.

Parrott, T. M., ed. *The Plays and Poems of George Chapman : The Tragedies*. London, 1910.

—— *The Plays and Poems of George Chapman : The Comedies*. London, 1914.

Phelps, W. L., ed. *George Chapman*. London and New York, 1895.

[Shepherd, R. H., ed.] *The Comedies and Tragedies of George Chapman*. 3 vols. London, 1873.

Shepherd, R. H., ed. *The Works of George Chapman*. 3 vols. London, 1874–1875.

STUDIES

Jacquot, J. *George Chapman 1559–1634: Sa Vie, Sa Poésie, Son Théâtre, Sa Pensée*. Paris, 1951.

Joubert, A. *Louis de Clermont, Sieur de Bussy d'Amboise.* Angers and Paris, 1885.

Lord, G. de F. *Homeric Renaissance: The Odyssey of George Chapman.* London, 1956.

Pagnini, M. *Forme e Motivi nella Poesie e nelle Tragedie di George Chapman.* Firenze, 1957.

Rees, E. *The Tragedies of George Chapman, Renaissance Ethics in Action.* Cambridge, Mass., 1954.

Solve, N. D. *Stuart Politics in Chapman's Tragedy of Chabot.* Ann Arbor, 1928.

Ure, P. "Chapman's 'Tragedy of Bussy D'Ambois': Problems of the Revised Quarto." *Modern Language Review,* XLVIII (July, 1953), 257–269.

THE NORTON LIBRARY
SEVENTEENTH-CENTURY SERIES

J. MAX PATRICK, *General Editor*